Geometric Greece

Geometric

Greece

J. N. COLDSTREAM

ST. MARTIN'S PRESS/NEW YORK

© J. N. Coldstream 1977

Book designed by Kenneth Day
Maps by Kenneth Clarke

All rights reserved. For information, write:
St. Martin's Press, Inc., 175 Fifth Avenue, New York, N.Y. 10010
Printed in Great Britain
Library of Congress Catalog Card Number: 77-78085
ISBN: 0-312-32365-4
First published in the United States of America in 1977

Preface

This book is the fruit of numerous pleasant visits to Greece in pursuit of things Geometric. Through the kindness of the Greek Archaeological Service and the Directors of the foreign Schools and Institutes of Archaeology in Athens, I have been privileged to see many important reserve collections. For facilities of study I record my deep gratitude to the Managing Committees of the British School at Athens, and of the Institute of Classical Studies in the University of London.

I have benefited greatly from the expert advice of many colleagues, although the responsibility for all statements and opinions in this book remains mine alone. In particular I thank Mr Vincent Desborough, Dr Reynold Higgins, Dr Vassos Karageorghis, Mr David Ridgway, and Dr John Salmon for their helpful comments on various parts of this book. I am especially grateful to Professor George Huxley for reading the entire work in typescript and in proof, and for saving me from many errors and inaccuracies.

My warmest thanks are also due to former and present members of Ernest Benn Limited: to Mr Stuart Rossiter who suggested the writing of this work, and to Mr John Collis for his skill, patience, and understanding in seeing the manuscript through the press.

I dedicate this book to my wife, who has appraised each chapter as it was written, and has given me constant encouragement at every stage.

Bedford College,   J.N.C.
London

To Nicky

Contents

CONTENTS

Charts

Maps and Plans

Acknowledgements

To the Managing Committee of the British School at Athens, and to the excavators Mr M. R. Popham and Mr L. H. Sackett, I am most grateful for permission to discuss and illustrate hitherto unpublished material from Lefkandi (Figs. 9–10, 18–19) and from Knossos (Figs. 87f, 92c). I am also indebted to the Trustees of the British Museum for allowing me to publish for the first time the vase illustrated in Fig. 28e.

The following scholars and institutions have kindly supplied me with photographs, and have courteously permitted me to reproduce them:

Åkerström, Prof. Å. 62a
Alexiou, Dr S. 12
Athens
  American School of Classical Studies:
    Agora excavations 1; 13; 34e; 36e; 37a,c,d
    Corinth excavations 7a, b; 26f, h; 27c–e; 54e, f; 55d; 57a–c
  British School of Archaeology:
    Emporio (Chios) excavations 84a
    Knossos excavations 31e; 32; 86e, g, h; 87f; 92b, c
    Lefkandi excavations 9; 10; 18; 19; 61d; 62b
    Mycenae excavations 6a–e
    Smyrna excavations 84e; 96
    Sparta excavations 52g
  Deutsches archäologisches Institut:
    Kerameikos excavations 2; 4; 5b; 14–17; 22a–d, f; 23; 24a, b; 34b–d, f; 35b, c; 40a; 100
    Olympia excavations 48b; 49; 53a, b, d; 58a; 106–9; 115a, b
    Samos excavations 30d; 83a
    Tiryns excavations 26b, c; 27b
    misc. 8f; 22e; 25b; 38a, b; 39a, b; 40b–d; 41a, c; 42b–d; 53c; 115c–d
  Ecole Française:
    Argos excavations 6f; 26a, d; 45a, b; 46a, c, d, f; 47
    Delphi excavations 40e; 58b–f
Baghdad, Iraq Museum 36d
Boardman, Mr J. 32; 50; 68
Buchner, Dr G. 73; 74; 75a–d, f; 95c
Cambitoglou, Prof. A., and Coulton, Dr J. J. (Zagora excavations) 97; 98
Copenhagen, Nationalmuseet 30c; 38d; 65a
Ede, Mr C. 84b, c

11

Eretria, Swiss excavations directed by Prof. K. Schefold 62d (Dr J-P. Descoeudres); 63, 104a (Prof. C. Berard); 104b (Dr P. Auberson)
Hanover, Kestner-Museum 65e
Istanbul, Deutsches Archäologisches Institut 84d
Jerusalem, Israel Department of Antiquities and Museums 20a
Karageorghis, Dr V. 111
Leiden, Rijksmuseum van Oudheden 36a; 55b; 67a; 70b
London, British Museum 28e; 55e; 56b–e; 65b; 66b; 78c; 79g
Morricone, Prof. L. 20c; 30a; 82a
New York, Metropolitan Museum 61c; 114
Nicholls, Dr R. V. 96
Oxford, Ashmolean Museum 7d; 57c, d; 90
Paris, Musée du Louvre 24d–f; 33a; 38c; 41b; 65f; 67b
Quilici, Prof. L. 76b
Rome, Villa Giulia Museum 113
Themelis, Dr P. G. 59d; 61d

For obtaining prints of Figs. 20a, 36b, and 38d I thank Miss J. du Plat Taylor, Mrs H. Hughes Brock, and the Rev. Mr J. Matthers respectively; and for the loan of photographs I am grateful to Mr J. Boardman (Figs. 32, 50, 68), Dr R. A. Higgins (Figs. 56d, c, e, 79f), Mrs K. R. Maxwell-Hyslop (Fig. 113), and Mr D. Ridgway (Fig. 76b).

In addition, I am indebted to the following scholars and institutions for allowing me to reproduce published illustrations:

Åkerström, Prof. Å. 77 (*GSI*)
Athens:
American School of Classical Studies 3 (*Hesperia* 21); 112a (*Hesperia* Suppl. II)
British School of Archaeology 88 (*Fortetsa*); 99 (*Greek Emporio*); 103 (*Perachora* I)
Deutsches archäologisches Institut 5a, 5c, 14b (*JdI* 77); 82b (*Samos* V); 82c, 105a (*AM* 58); 83b (*AM* 68); 105b (*JdI* 49)
Ecole Française 102 (*BCH* 60)
Benson, Prof. J. L. 24c (*JNES* 20)
Boardman, Mr J. 42a (*Greek Gems and Finger Rings*)
Buchner, Dr G. 54b, 62b (*Metropoli e Colonie . . .*, Taranto, 1963)
Copenhagen, Nationalmuseet 78d, 81 (*Exochi*); 79h, j, 80 (*Lindos* I)
Photos Hassia, Paris 91
Hampe, Prof. R. 112c (*Gleichnisse*, pl. 11)
Kunze, Prof. E. 93b (*KB*)
Munich, Antikensammlung 67c (*CVA* I)
Ohly, Prof. D. 64 (*Griechische Goldbleche*)

Note on the illustrations
All measurements are given in centimetres. Abbreviations: D. = Diameter, H. = Height, L. = Length, W. = Width.

Abbreviations

AA   *Archäologischer Anzeiger*
AAA   *Athens Annals of Archaeology* ('Αρχαιολογικὰ 'Ανάλεκτα 'Αθηνῶν)
ActaArch   Acta Archaeologica, Copenhagen
AD   'Αρχαιολογικὸν Δελτίον
AE   'Αρχαιολογικὴ 'Εφημερίς ('Εφημερὶς 'Αρχαιολογική until 1900)
AG   Archaic Greece: the City-States c. 700-500 B.C. By L. H. Jeffery (London, 1976)
Agora   The Athenian Agora (Princeton, vols. I–)
AGW   Attic Geometric Workshops: Yale Classical Studies vol. 16. By J. M. Davison
AH   The Argive Heraeum. By C. Waldstein (Cambridge, Mass., vol. I, 1902; vol. II, 1905)
AJA   American Journal of Archaeology
AM   Mitteilungen des deutschen archäologischen Instituts, Athenische Abteilung
Annales   Annales, Economies, Sociétés, Civilisations (Paris)
Ann   Annuario della Scuola Archaeologica di Atene
AntClass   Antiquité Classique
AntK   Antike Kunst
AO   The Sanctuary of Artemis Orthia at Sparta. By R. Dawkins and others (London, 1929)
AR   Archaeological Reports
ArchClass   Archeologia Classica
ArchHom   Archaeologia Homerica, vols. A–X. Ed. F. Matz and H.-G. Buchholz, Göttingen
AS   Anatolian Studies
Ay.   Ayios (Saint)
BASOR   Bulletin of the American Schools of Oriental Research
BCH   Bulletin de Correspondance Hellénique
BdA   Bolletino d'Arte
Beil.   Beilage
BICS   Bulletin of the Institute of Classical Studies, University of London
Blinkenberg   C. Blinkenberg, *Fibules grecques et orientales* (Copenhagen, 1926)
BMCat   British Museum Catalogue
BOOC   Bronzi Orientali ed Orientalizzanti a Creta nell' VIII e VII sec. A.C. By F. Canciani (Rome, 1970)
BostMusBull   Boston Museum Bulletin
BSA   Annual of the British School at Athens

13

CCO The Cretan Collection in Oxford: the Dictaean Cave and Iron Age Crete. By J. Boardman (Oxford, 1961)

CGA La Céramique géométrique de l'Argolide. By P. Courbin (Paris, 1966)

ch. chapter

ClassPhil Classical Philology

ClRh Clara Rhodos

cm. centimetre(s)

CQ Classical Quarterly

CR Classical Review

CVA Corpus Vasorum Antiquorum

DAG The Dark Age of Greece. By A. M. Snodgrass (Edinburgh, 1971)

DdA Dialoghi di Archeologia

EA see *AE*

EG Early Geometric

EGAW Early Greek Armour and Weapons. By A. M. Snodgrass (Edinburgh, 1964)

EPC Early Protocorinthian

Ergon Τὸ Ἔργον τῆς Ἀρχαιολογικῆς Ἑταιρείας

FD V Fouilles de Delphes vol. V: monuments figurés: petits bronzes, terre-cuites, antiquités diverses. By P. Perdrizet (Paris, 1908)

FD V.2 Fouilles de Delphes vol. V: monuments figurés: les statuettes de bronze. By C. Rolley, (Paris, 1969)

FGH Die Fragmente der griechischen Historiker. By F. Jacoby (ed.)

FGS see Hampe, Schefold

Fittschen K. Fittschen, Untersuchungen zum Beginn der Sagendarstellungen bei den Griechen (Berlin, 1969)

FLS Fighting on Land and Sea in Greek Geometric Art. By G. Ahlberg (Stockholm, 1971)

GDA The Greek Dark Ages. By V. R. Desborough (London, 1972)

GEN The Greeks and their Eastern Neighbours. By T. J. Dunbabin (London, 1957)

GGP Greek Geometric Pottery. By J. N. Coldstream (London, 1968)

GKG Die geometrische Kunst Griechenlands. By B. Schweitzer (Köln, 1969)

gr. grave

GRBS Greek, Roman, and Byzantine Studies

GSI Der geometrische Stil in Italien. By Å. Åkerström (Lund, 1943)

Hampe, *FGS* R. Hampe, Frühe griechischer Sagenbilder in Böotien (Athens, 1936)

Hdt. Herodotus

Higgins, *Greek TCs* R. A. Higgins, Greek Terracottas (London, 1967)

Higgins, *GRJ* R. A. Higgins, Greek and Roman Jewellery (London, 1961)

HM Homer and the Monuments. By H. L. Lorimer (London, 1950)

IGems Island Gems. By J. Boardman (London, 1963)

IM Mitteilungen des deutschen archäologischen Instituts, Abteilung Istanbul

InscrCret Inscriptiones Creticae. By M. Guarducci

JdI Jahrbuch des deutschen archäologischen Instituts

JHS Journal of Hellenic Studies

JOAI *Jahreshefte des österreichischen archäologischen Instituts*
JRS *Journal of Roman Studies*
K   *Kerameikos* vol. V. By K. Kubler (Berlin, 1954)
KB   *Kretische Bronzereliefs.* By E. Kunze (Stuttgart, 1931)
KCh   Κρητικὰ Χρονικά
km.   kilometre(s)
Lefkandi   *Excavations at Lefkandi: 1964-66.* Preliminary report, edd. M. R. Popham and L. H. Sackett (London, 1968)
LG   Late Geometric
LSAG   *The Local Scripts of Archaic Greece.* By L. H. Jeffery (Oxford, 1961)
m.   metre(s)
MA   *Monumenti Antichi*
MDOG   *Mitteilungen der deutschen Orient-gesellschaft zu Berlin*
MEFR   *Mélanges d'Archéologie et d'Histoire publiés par l'Ecole française de Rome*
MG   Middle Geometric
MusHelv   Museum Helveticum
NI   *The Nimrud Ivories in the British Museum.* By R. D. Barnett (London, 1957)
NSc   *Notizie degli Scavi*
Ohly   D. Ohly, *Griechische Goldbleche des 8 Jahrhunderts vor Christ* (Berlin, 1953)
OlB   *Bericht über die Ausgrabungen in Olympia*
OlF   *Olympische Forschungen*
OpAth   *Opuscula Atheniensia*
OpRom   *Opuscula Romana*
PAE   Πρακτικὰ τῆς Ἀρχαιολογικῆς Ἐταιρείας
PE   *Prothesis and Ekphora in Greek Geometric Art.* By G. Ahlberg (Göteborg, 1971)
PG   Protogeometric
PGP   *Protogeometric Pottery.* By V. R. Desborough (Oxford, 1952)
PGRT   Ὁ Πρωτογεωμετρικὸς Ῥυθμὸς τῆς Θεσσαλίας (Athens, 1958) Verdelis
pl.   plate
RA   *Revue archéologique*
RDAC   *Report of the Department of Antiquities, Cyprus*
RM   *Mitteilungen des deutschen archäologischen Instituts, Romische Abteilung*
SCE   *The Swedish Cyprus Expedition*
Schefold, *FGS*   K. Schefold, *Frügriechische Sagenbilder*, (Munich, 1964)
Sicilia SO   *Archeologia nella Sicilia Sud-Orientale.* Ed. G. Voza (Napoli, 1973)
StEtr   *Studi Etruschi*
TAPA   *Transactions of the American Philological Association*
TGA I   *Tombes géométriques d'Argos* vol. I. By P. Courbin (Paris, 1974)
Thuc.   Thucydides
WG   *The Western Greeks.* By T. J. Dunbabin (Oxford, 1948)

Introduction

This book deals with Greek civilization from *c.* 900 to *c.* 700 B.C., and is named after the Geometric style of pottery which flourished in Greek lands during these two centuries. The preceding and following periods are covered by two recent volumes in this series, V. R. d'A. Desborough's *The Greek Dark Ages* (1972) and L. H. Jeffery's *Archaic Greece* (1976). Within our period, darkness gives way to dawn: useful figurative terms, drawing attention to the changing nature of the evidence.

The Dark Ages in Greece had been a time of poverty, isolation, and illiteracy, when representational art was virtually unknown. Many memories were handed down orally, to be preserved in later literature; but these refer to the heroic splendours and downfall of the Mycenaean civilization, and tell us virtually nothing about the impoverished life of the eleventh and tenth centuries. Until the rise of archaeological research, very little could be known about this long and obscure period; Mr Desborough's recent analysis is based almost wholly on the material remains recovered from excavation, which offer the only evidence at first hand.

By contrast, Miss Jeffery's account of the Archaic period draws upon a rich variety of literary sources, supplemented by contemporary inscriptions; in reconstructing the history of those times, archaeology performs only an ancillary function. Although no systematic records were kept before the fifth century, the main course of events in Archaic Greece has been saved from oblivion in the central narrative and long digressions of Herodotus, and in the more disjointed memories recorded by other ancient historians.

The Geometric period began in darkness, but the eighth century witnessed remarkable advances. With the renewal of eastward commerce and the foundation of colonies in the west, Greece emerged from her isolation. Exchanges with the Near East brought the beginning of prosperity, the mastery of some skilled techniques, and knowledge of alphabetic writing; thus the darkness of illiteracy was finally dispelled. Figured art, almost forgotten during the Dark Ages, flourished once again; and an Ionic school of epic poetry reached its culmination with the composition of the Homeric poems. As communications improved, so the prestige of the great sanctuaries attracted visitors from all quarters of he Greek world. A fifth-century scholar, Hippias of Elis, calculated that the quadrennial Games at Olympia were first celebrated in 776 B.C. This date was to become the fixed point for the measurement of time; it also marks the approximate limit of later memory – apart from the memory of the heroic age. The intervening epoch, which we know as the Dark Ages, was largely forgotten; but from the later eighth century some record survives of early wars in the homeland, and of colonial foundations in Italy and Sicily.

Although the evidence for our period is predominantly archaeological, literary sources for the eighth century must not be ignored. Homer we cannot use: his epics, set in the heroic past, are coloured by an amalgam of anachronistic details, accumulated over several centuries of oral transmission; thus Homeric society cannot be assigned to any single period.[1] On the other hand, Hesiod's *Works and Days* offers an authentic picture of a farmer's life in Boeotia at the close of the eighth century. Herodotus, seeking to explain the political alignments of a later age, makes several helpful allusions to ancient alliances and enmities which originated in our period. Thucydides describes the foundation of Greek colonies in Sicily; his dates, when correlated with the earliest finds from the colonies, form one of the chief sources for the dating of Late Geometric material. Many more references to eighth-century Greece are scattered through the pages of Graeco-Roman authors, especially Strabo, Plutarch, and Pausanias.

If we consider them in isolation from the material record, these literary sources do not form a very coherent picture; and they tell us practically nothing about Greek affairs before 750 B.C. There seems little point, then, in treating them in a separate chapter; on the contrary, much is to be gained by confronting the two sources of evidence wherever the occasion arises. They are often complementary to one another; thus the literary record concerning colonization in the west, and the material evidence of eastward trade, combine to make the Euboeans the pioneers in both fields. Furthermore, the primary evidence of archaeology may sometimes supply a touchstone for testing the reliability of local traditions preserved in late literary sources: good examples of the latter are the memory of an Old Eretria (Strabo) and the alleged destruction of Asine in the Argolid (Pausanias).

The purpose of this book, then, is to provide an archaeological survey of the Geometric period, amplified where possible by information from literary sources.

Pottery is by far the most abundant category of archaeological material, and has a special importance for the historian of early Greece. First, it offers the best means of measuring time in an age without contemporary written records; the evidence for the absolute dating of Geometric pottery, which combines the foundation dates of the Sicilian colonies with the contexts datable from non-Greek historical sources, has been fully set out elsewhere and need not be repeated here.[2] Secondly, because local Geometric styles are easily distinguishable, one can detect commercial and other contacts between various regions of Greece, either through exported pots, or through the 'invisible exports' implied by influences passing from one local style to another. Thirdly, Geometric pots are almost the only non-perishable Greek objects of their time which were exported to non-Greek lands; in themselves they may not have been important articles of commerce, but their style and fabric will at least help us to recognize those parts of Greece which showed most commercial initiative. In general, the distribution of Geometric pottery is commensurate with Greek settlement and commerce; the only apparent exceptions to this rule are on the eastern confines of the Aegean homeland, where Geometric pottery was made by non-Greek Carians, but not by the Greeks of Lesbos and Aeolis. Cyprus, largely peopled by Greeks, produced her own Geometric style; but since her cultural affinities are now more with the Levant than with the Aegean, our references to that island will be confined to the rare occasions when there is contact with Greece. Various handmade fabrics, all quite distinct from any Greek Geometric, were made in the semi-Hellenic lands of Macedonia and Epirus; our concern with those northern parts is limited to their southward exchanges. Greek influence in Italy and Sicily, emanating from the colonies, can be gauged by the impact of various Greek Geometric styles upon the pottery of native neighbours.

Metalwork is often a good index of prosperity, which may be the fruit of inherited wealth, or of successful commerce. Apart from silver, the Greek homeland is not rich in ores; copper, tin, and gold had to be imported, whereas the local supply of iron could not fully meet the needs of a rapidly rising population in the eighth century. While Greece had been almost totally isolated from the outside world (c. 1025–950 B.C.), bronze and gold almost vanished;[3] their reappearance thereafter was due to the renewal of contact with the eastern Mediterranean, and in the eighth century the discovery of the Etruscan market secured for the Greeks another plentiful source of needful metals. By the late eighth century the majority of Greek metal objects are votive offerings to the gods; the huge bronze tripod cauldrons, in particular, attest the growing prestige of the great sanctuaries. In earlier Geometric times, however, most of the metalwork is found in graves, often suggesting the status of the deceased; at the top of the social scale, iron weapons and gold diadems may be buried with men, and other gold jewellery with women. The jewellery has a special interest, in that it betrays the quickening influence of oriental notions and techniques sooner than any other class of Greek material.

Two recent works, to which I am much indebted, offer comprehensive surveys of Greek Geometric art and archaeology. B. Schweitzer's *Die geometrische Kunst Griechenlands* (1969) is especially concerned with aesthetic analysis, and sets out to establish clear stylistic sequences in each form of Geometric art. A. M. Snodgrass' *The Dark Age of Greece* (1971), as its name implies, covers a wider period; the approach is historical rather than art-historical, and there are particularly helpful chapters on the non-artistic topics of metalworking techniques and burial customs. In both books, each category of material is considered in a separate chapter; but in the following pages a different arrangement will be attempted, wherein the evidence for each region is gathered together as far as possible: the local pottery style, the local burial customs, the jewellery, bronzes,[4] ivories, and seals. The aim of this treatment is to bring out the individual character of each centre during the formative period of the Greek city-state (*polis*). For the historian of early Greece one of the most pressing tasks is the study in depth of specific areas; the main body of this book is organized as a contribution towards that end.

The regional chapters fall into two unequal parts, of which the shorter covers the longer period, and vice versa. Part I surveys the years of near-darkness (c. 900–c. 770 B.C.), almost entirely ignored by literary sources; the archaeological material, too, is relatively scarce, and very unevenly distributed over the Greek homeland. This unevenness may be partly due to the hazards of excavation; but in large measure it mirrors the vastly different rates of progress in different regions. One important source of progress, as we have seen, is the recovery of contact with the eastern Mediterranean, especially with the coastal area extending from Cilicia to Palestine known as the Levant; it can be no accident, after over a century of scientific excavation, that the areas of Greece which show the most signs of this contact are those for which we have the fullest record. Outstanding in both respects are Attica and Euboea, the two regions of Greece which played the most active parts in initiating eastward commerce; indeed, recent discoveries at Lefkandi and Eretria have established the Euboeans as the leaders in this field, and have done much to dispel the obscurity of the period. Copious material has also been accumulated from Crete and the Dodecanese, islands which lay within easy reach of Levantine shipping, and (perhaps for that reason) played a more passive part in commercial exchange. With the help of full sequences in these four areas, we may divide the period into three phases,[5] of which the second (mid-ninth century) shows the most spectacular signs of progress. Into this framework we can also fit the fairly continuous material from the Argolid, the Corinthia, Boeotia, Thessaly, and the Cyclades. Ionia remains largely unknown through much of the ninth century, but the fog has lifted by the early eighth. The deepest obscurity still prevails in Laconia and in West Greece – a generic term embracing the regions from Ithaca to Messenia, including Achaea. From the scanty finds one gets the impression that these lands were still very sparsely populated, and their local chronology relative to the more progressive regions remains extremely uncertain; in each case it is impossible to distinguish what precedes 900 B.C. from what follows. We cannot, then, include these areas in the detailed narrative of our Part I; but a full account of their Late Dark Age material has already been given in the fifteenth chapter of Desborough's volume in this series, and for each of these backward areas the thread will be taken up in the appropriate section of Part II.

With Part II (c. 770–c. 700 B.C.) we enter the full daylight. Not only are the finds now very much more abundant, but their variety, complexity, and sophistication require more detailed discussion. There is a new interest in figured imagery, which finds expression in vase-painting, metalwork, and seals. The material is still very unevenly spread, and of uneven quality, drawing attention once again to the sharp distinctions between progressive and backward areas; yet every region now has something to show. The whole Greek world – including the newly founded western colonies – is considered in seven regional chapters, some of which follow the currents of influence which flowed from the leading cities to outlying parts. The sheer quantity of material betokens a rapid increase of population, which eventually caused massive emigration to colonies overseas, and wars over land at home; on each of these topics the literary record helps to throw much light.

This period is often called 'the Greek Renaissance', and with good reason. It witnessed the recovery of a prosperity unknown since Mycenaean times; it saw the rebirth of skills forgotten during the Dark Ages; meanwhile, the diffusion of epic poetry inspired all Greeks with a pride in their heroic past. These topics are too broad to be treated region by region; they will therefore be reserved for Part III, where various other aspects of eighth-century life will also receive general consideration. Houses and temples, briefly mentioned in the regional chapters, will here be treated more fully, with some remarks on the broader social and religious questions which are posed by the architectural remains. Finally, the Near Eastern contribution is briefly summarized; we pass from the occasional orientalizing experiments of our period (chiefly in metalwork) to the great Orientalizing movement which superseded the Geometric style in every branch of Greek art.

In a general work of this kind one can illustrate only a very small (but, I hope, representative) fraction of the material. Some sources of information are contained in the footnotes; others, to avoid constant repetition, are consolidated in the detailed bibliographies for each chapter.

In conclusion, one need hardly emphasize the provisional nature of this survey. Every year important new discoveries are published, confirming some theories, undermining others; sometimes resolving old controversies, sometimes posing new problems. I have refrained from overloading my text with glosses like 'in our present state of knowledge', or 'further excavation will surely throw more light on this matter', knowing that the wise reader will constantly be supplying them in his or her own mind.

NOTES

1 See A. M. Snodgrass, *JHS* 94 (1974), 114 ff.
2 See *GGP* ch. 13, especially p. 330 (here fig. 116); Snodgrass, *DAG* ch. 3; cf. R. M. Cook, *BSA* 64 (1969), 13 ff.
3 Snodgrass, *DAG* 237 ff., 246 ff.
4 The bronze figurines and tripod cauldrons are the most difficult to localize, since such a large proportion of them were dedicated at Olympia and Delphi by visitors from other lands. Even so, thanks to the finds from local sanctuaries, and with the help of legitimate analogies from the export of pottery, specialists in Geometric bronzework have made considerable progress in defining local schools; in spite of some disagreements between them on subjective matters, the bronze figurines can be included in our regional treatment without unduly straining the evidence.
5 These do not coincide with phases in any pottery sequence – a fact which may help to reassure those who fear lest ceramic studies play too dominant a part in historical reconstruction.

I

The Passing
of the Dark Ages
c. *900–770* B.C.

1 Isolation:

The Early Ninth Century

The style of pottery after which this book is named was born in Athens around 900 B.C. In the grave groups of Athenian cemeteries, and nowhere else, we can watch the full course of the transition from the preceding Protogeometric style. The new Athenian fashion was soon followed by Attica's landward neighbours. Overseas, retarded versions of Protogeometric persisted for fifty years or more, but by the end of the ninth century every major Aegean centre was producing Geometric pottery in some way related to the Athenian archetype. The diffusion of the new style need not surprise us; for the ninth-century painted pottery of Athens is outstanding in Greece for its technical excellence, its elegance of shape, and its harmony of shape and decoration. During its Early and Middle phases it was not only the most influential and sophisticated ware of its time: because of its greater sophistication, one can also observe the development of its style more precisely than that of any other regional school. This development gives us a historical lifeline for the long and obscure period discussed in the first three chapters, on which our literary sources are virtually silent.

We must begin, then, with the Early Geometric (EG) style of Athens, which moves fairly rapidly through two distinct stages, dated approximately to the first and second quarters of the ninth century. From a few Athenian graves of outstanding interest we can get some impression of the prevailing burial rites in Attica, and of the rather narrow range of other offerings accompanying the pottery, even in the richest graves. From Attica we pass on to the neighbouring lands – the Argolid, the Corinthia, and Boeotia – where the new Athenian style had a considerable impact on the local pottery, even though the local burial customs were different. Then we travel further afield to a wide maritime area where the regional pottery remained free of Attic influence, and faithful to a local Protogeometric tradition; this area extends from Thessaly as far as the northern Cyclades, and at its centre lies the extremely important site of Lefkandi in Euboea. Thereafter, a brief glance at some of the outer fringes, especially the Dodecanese and central Crete. Finally, a few general observations on the character of this Early Geometric age: on the quality of life in Greece, on the state of maritime communications within Greek waters, and on the rare signs of any contact with the outside world.

Attica

Fig. 1 shows the first, experimental phase (EG I) of the Athenian Geometric style, on six of its most characteristic shapes. Pre-eminent among the closed vessels are the urns for male and female cremations, finely painted enlargements of storage pots used in domestic life. A man's ashes were placed in an amphora with handles from neck to shoulder (fig. 1f); a broader amphora, with sharply returning handles confined to the shoulder, housed the ashes of a woman (fig. 1e). Wine was poured from a trefoil-lipped oinochoe (fig. 1a). A baggy pouring vessel, with narrower neck (*GGP* pl. 1e), would serve for either oil or wine; for want of a better name, let it be called the lekythos-oinochoe. Two forms of pyxis, globular and pointed (fig. 1c,d), have sloping lids carefully fitted to their inset rims; they could be used for a variety of solid goods – trinkets, or ointments, or food offerings. Of the open vessels, the most impressive should be the krater or mixing-bowl, although no whole example of EG I survives; the fragments show a high conical foot (e.g., *K* pl. 16). The favourite drinking-vessel, most conveniently called a kantharos, has two vertical handles from rim to body, and a low conical foot (fig. 1b); small flat-based cups, with single vertical handle and fully glazed body, are also common (*GGP* pl. 1n).

In this EG I repertoire there is not much novelty of shape. The krater is the sole survivor of a whole family of Protogeometric open vessels with high conical feet, comprising skyphoi, kantharoi, and one-handled cups (*GDA* fig. 9, pls. 26 and 30); yet some flat-based cups had been made long before the end of Proto-geometric, and some late Protogeometric kantharoi (*PGP* pl. 12) already have the low conical feet customary in EG I. Both forms of pyxis in fig. 1 are new, yet the Protogeometric variety – globular with everted lip – persists into EG I (*GGP* pl. 1g). The lekythos-oinochoe, also new, seems to replace the Protogeo-metric lekythos, now out of fashion. But amphorae and oinochoai follow on from Protogeometric in an unbroken sequence, the older tradition being per-petuated in their graceful ovoid bodies whose convexity is always carefully answered by the concave curve of the neck. Another happy legacy from Proto-geometric is the superbly lustrous quality of the black glaze, which still covers most of the surface.

The decoration of EG I vases shows a more sudden break with the past. Con-tinuity from Protogeometric is apparent only in the minor motifs: the single zigzag, the small units of check pattern, the row of solid triangle or dogtooth (fig. 1e), and the groups of opposed diagonals (fig. 1f). But there has been a revolution in the major motifs; in the Protogeometric style these had consisted mainly of circles and semicircles, drawn in concentric sets by means of a compass fitted with a multiple brush. Circular ornament is now largely rejected, and replaced by two new rectilinear motifs, the battlement and the meander. During

FIG. 1 ATHENIAN EG I POTTERY FROM THE AREOPAGUS
(a)–(e), gr. D 16:2; (f) gr. D 16:4. HS: (a) 24.7; (b) 9.9; (c) 11; (d) 14.4; (e) 40; (f) 52

this experimental phase they appear in many different guises. Thus the battle-ment, at this time the commoner of the two, is sometimes given three or more outlines (fig. 1b,e); otherwise a double outline is normal for both motifs, but at first a variety of fillings is tried out (zigzag, fig. 1d; chevron, fig. 1f; occasionally, dots) until diagonal hatching eventually proves to be the solution most congenial to Athenian taste (fig. 1a,c).

The shift from circular to rectilinear ornament was in part dictated by an even more fundamental change in the system of decoration, best seen in the neck-handled amphora and the oinochoe. On their Protogeometric precursors it had been usual to place the only decoration on the shoulder, the natural centre of the vase; there, on a spherical surface, the favourite concentric semicircles had been especially at home. But well before the beginning of Geometric an alternative scheme had been tried out, where decoration was confined to a narrow zone round the belly, the rest of the surface being covered with the shiny black glaze which had such a fascination for the potters of that time (e.g., *GDA* pl. 28a). In EG I it was felt that neck and body required separate emphasis; hence the birth of the rectilinear panel between the handles – also applied to some open vessels such as the kantharos; hence, too, the disappearance of circular motifs, no longer thought suitable for the areas which now received the ornament. On the whole, EG I decoration has an austere look, being usually limited to small panels at handle level, and single narrow zones elsewhere; but the pyxides, which have no handles to inhibit the painter, often present a cheerful exception to this austerity.

In the next phase, EG II, the Athenian Geometric style settles down to a more tranquil state; the initial ferment is over, and the range of shapes and motifs is narrower than before. New among the shapes are the broad-based oinochoe (fig. 2b) and the shallow skyphos (fig. 2c), both destined to be among the most long-lived and influential of all Athenian forms. The profile of the skyphos has an immediate effect on the kantharos (fig. 2d) and a large decorated version of the one-handled cup with two warts opposite the handle (*GGP* pl. 2c): all three shapes share a short offset lip leaning outwards, a shallow body, and a ring foot which supplants the low conical bases of EG I drinking-vessels. The globular and pointed pyxides introduced in EG I remain in the repertoire; likewise, of course, the two types of cremation amphora, which now tend to have a slightly more attenuated form, with taller neck. Once again, no krater has been recovered with profile complete; a large fragment (*K* pl. 17) preserves a high foot with at least two ribs near the junction with the body.

The new system of decoration, adumbrated in EG I, is now rigidly applied: enclosed panels between handles, continuous zones elsewhere. Furthermore, there is a much firmer distinction between large and small motifs, the latter often serving as ancillaries to the former, whether in zones or panels (fig. 2a). The meander now predominates among the large motifs, though the battlement is still found; the multiple zigzag is added to the repertoire. Ancillary motifs are virtually confined to the dogtooth, and a variety of dotted zigzag with filled apices (fig. 2a) introduced in EG I. The pointed pyxis, as before, attracts a rich accumulation of zones; otherwise, austerity still holds the field.

Alongside the wheelmade painted pottery, a fine but rather enigmatic hand-

FIG. 2 ATHENIAN EG II POTTERY FROM THE KERAMEIKOS
(a), (d), gr. 74; (b) gr. 43; (c) gr.14. HS: (a) 72.2; (b) 23.7;
(c) 6; (d) 8

made ware, decorated with incised and impressed patterns, continues from the
tenth century and appears in several EG graves of women and children. The
vase forms are now limited to hemispherical bowls, pointed pyxides, and (more
rarely) small tripod jars; there are also globular beads, spindle whorls, and hollow
balls. The decoration is more varied than in the Protogeometric stage (cf. *GDA*
142–4 fig. 15); new to the repertoire are lozenges, wavy lines, and pendent
triangles. The motifs themselves, and their liberal application all over the
surface, bear practically no relation to the ornament of the wheelmade pottery;

yet that is no reason to assume that the ware was made under foreign influence. The introduction in EG II of the pointed pyxis, in succession to a lugged globular variety, shows that their makers occasionally took some notice of the current wheelmade shapes (e.g. fig. 13c).

This handmade fabric dies out in Athens at the end of EG; elsewhere, its final appearance is in a rich MG I grave at Eleusis (p. 78).

It is now time to consider the graves themselves, and their contents other than pottery. These offerings, as we shall see, tell us rather more than the pottery about the social status of the deceased. A few of the richer grave groups deserve special mention; but we shall leave till the next chapter a number of exceptionally well-furnished burials belonging to the years of transition between Early and Middle Geometric.

Within the *floruit* of EG pottery upwards of twenty-eight Athenian graves have been recorded: eight on the north slope of the Areopagus, twelve in the Kerameikos area (all but one on the south bank of the Eridanos), and at least eight dotted about elsewhere. No one cemetery at this time can claim to be more aristocratic than another, since fairly rich EG graves are found in each area. Cremation, fashionable in Athens since the middle of the eleventh century, was still the prevailing rite, the only exceptions being in three EG I graves of children, all inhumed. One of these, recently found to the south of the Kerameikos (Odos Poulopoulou), contained a necklace of 183 faience beads, an exotic luxury for the time. In another, north of the Agora (Odos Ay. Dimitriou), a small girl was buried with two bronze bracelets, a few faience beads, and two pairs of miniature clay boots, perhaps to ease her journey into the next world; the smaller pair is cheerfully decorated with jazzy EG I ornament. In the third, on the Areopagus, nothing was found except the bones of a boy four to six years old, two sea shells, the skeleton of a piglet, and six miniature pots; yet before the end of the ninth century this grave – together with others near by, now destroyed – had been surrounded by an oval enclosure[1] built in reverence for the dead, and the precinct accumulated a considerable array of votives over the next two hundred years.

For the cremation of adults a small oblong trench was dug with a deep hole at one end for the urn-amphora, usually sunk to half its height. Of the actual ceremony the most circumstantial account is of a young woman's cremation on the Areopagus (D 16:2; *GDA* 271 fig. 29). While her body was burning on the pyre near by, her relatives and friends held a funeral feast in her honour. Oinochoai, drinking-vessels, and pyxides were thrown on to the flames and smashed.[2] After the cremation, her charred bones were gathered up and placed in the urn (fig. 1e) together with her small personal possessions: two spiral rings of electrum, pairs of bronze pins and fibulae, a small kitchen knife of iron, a clay spindle whorl, and three cylindrical bone beads. The urn was then lowered into its hole, and closed by an unburnt pyxis (fig. 1c). Two pairs of miniature clay boots, like those in the small girl's inhumation, were among the pyre debris swept into the shallow part of the trench. When the grave was finally filled in, the position of the urn was marked by a flat stone slab, supported on two small revetments to keep its weight off the vessel.

Only 3m. away was the cremation of an adult man (D 16:4), some thirty-four

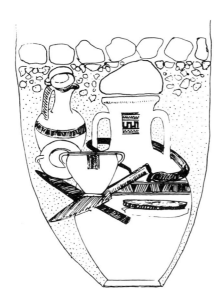

FIG. 3 AREOPAGUS, WARRIOR'S GRAVE (D 16:4). *Hesperia* 21, 280 fig. 2

years old. His possessions mark him out as a warrior, and a knight. Round the neck of the urn-amphora (fig. 1f) his iron sword had been deliberately curled and 'killed' (fig. 3): too personal a possession, perhaps, to be bequeathed to other hands, or possibly needed in the next world. His other iron equipment included a pair of socketed spearheads, a broad axe-head, a javelin point, a pair of snaffle-bits for his horses, and two knives; also a whetstone, suggesting that he was his own armourer. All these objects had been gathered into a bundle (cloth impressions still being visible), and inserted into the cavity beside his urn; and by its shoulder rested an oinochoe and three kantharoi, for his posthumous refreshment.

The cremation of another warrior, with his sword similarly 'killed' round his urn-amphora, has been recently found in a double grave north-east of the Agora (Odos Ay. Markou). The other urn-amphora is that of a woman, presumably his wife; still Protogeometric in style, this vessel might well have been used in their house for a generation, since the latest pot in the grave is an intact EG II oinochoe, and both the occupants seem to have been cremated at the same time. Here we see an extremely rare departure from the usual custom in Geometric Athens, whereby graves have one tenant only.

A similarly martial impression is made by three EG II graves of men in the Kerameikos, nos. 2, 38, and 74. Although none was as well furnished as the Areopagus warrior's grave, all three contained some offensive weapons; but since

FIG. 4 ATHENIAN EG METALWORK FROM THE KERAMEIKOS
(a) bronze bowl, gr. 74; (b) iron knife, gr. 38, L. 23.4;
(c) iron spearhead, gr. 38, L. 49.5

these had in each case been burnt on the pyre, their state of preservation is poor.
The best provided is no. 38, where the sword (fig. 5), spearhead, and curved
knife (both fig. 4) are all characteristic of the time. The sword is a fine long
specimen (0·80m.) of the flanged cut-and-thrust type, 'Naue II', which flourished throughout the Dark Ages and the Geometric period. No less orthodox is
the elegant leaf shape of the spearhead, with its continuous midrib; the unusually
long socket, a feature not found in later periods, would make the spear more
suitable for thrusting than for throwing, whereas the two lighter spearheads of
the Areopagus warrior were clearly meant to be thrown. The only other metal
offerings in these graves are the plain hemispherical bowls of bronze, used as
stoppers for all three urn-amphorae (e.g., fig. 4 with fig. 2a, gr. 74); the type was
introduced from Cyprus during the late tenth century, and in Athens enjoys its
greatest vogue in the EG and MG I periods.

Some typical personal ornaments of the time were found with an EG I woman's
cremation, Kerameikos no. 7 (fig. 5). A pair of long dress pins reflects fashions
both old and new. The combination of bronze globe with iron shank harks back
to a type made throughout the tenth century, when bronze may have been in
short supply.[3] Yet, in contrast to the flat disc head of the older type, these pins
are crowned with little finials which first appeared at the end of the Protogeo-

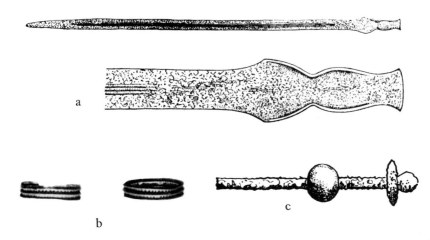

FIG. 5 ATHENIAN EG METALWORK FROM THE KERAMEIKOS
(a) iron sword, gr. 38, L. 80; (b) gold rings, gr. 7, D. 2;
(c) iron pin with bronze globe, gr. 7, detail. *JdI* 77, 100ff. figs. 18, 23

metric period, and were to become increasingly elaborate in Geometric times.
In the same context are two finger-rings, the first gold objects found in Athens
since the beginning of the Protogeometric age; their decoration of repoussé dots
suggests that they may be Cypriot imports.[4]

However restricted the range of grave goods may seem, they do at least reveal
some concern for the needs of each person after death, according to sex, age, and
station. Some offerings were evidently the personal possessions of the deceased –
a man's weapons and tools, a woman's dress ornaments and household chattels,
a child's playthings. There were also the unburnt vessels, normally packed
round the top of an adult's urn, and presumably containing food and drink for
the journey down to the underworld. But in two graves of men, Kerameikos
nos. 1 and 2, concern for the dead went even further than this. In each case,
immediately above the urn-amphora, and beside the rough stone stele which
marked the grave, there stood a large krater, to serve as a further memorial, and
also as a receptacle for libations to the dead. The idea is not quite new, as two
women buried in the same cemetery (PG grs. 37, 38) had been similarly honoured
in the tenth century, their memorials taking the form of the belly-handled
amphorae which were then the normal receptacles for female cremations. But
the EG II krater of gr. 2 is the earliest known monument to be deliberately
pierced, so that libations could seep down to the urn-amphora below. It is also
the earliest known krater to be especially designed as a memorial, being too
large[5] either to have been used in domestic life, or inserted inside the grave;
furthermore, even in its shattered state, it is nevertheless the most elaborate
artifact to have survived from this period. In a plot crowded out by later burials
one could not expect such monuments to survive intact; in these circumstances

FIG. 6 ARGIVE EG POTTERY
(a)–(c) Mycenae gr. G 603, HS. 28, 9.7, 12; (d) Mycenae gr. G 607,
H. 24; (e) Mycenae gr. G 607, H. 40; (f) Argos C 204, H. 38.2

it is a remarkable sign of respect that even the bases of both kraters were found *in situ*, and that the burials below them were among the few of this time to escape the encroachment of later graves.[6] So, in Early Geometric Athens, one can not only observe differences of wealth and status among the grave goods; in two exceptional cases, respect for distinction in this world led to posthumous honours.

Outside Athens, the record of Early Geometric Attica is meagre in the extreme; indeed, there seems to be no marked change in the pattern of settlement from Protogeometric times, when there was a large concentration of people living in and around Athens, while the Attic countryside – especially southern Attica – was very sparsely settled.[7] Marathon and Merenda have produced one EG cremation each (in the former case the urn was a hydria); and three cremation graves are reported from Eleusis, one of which[8] is said to have had its position marked by two stelai and the base of a vase. In the extreme south, there is evidence of a short-lived settlement at Thorikos; but since most of the published pottery belongs to the mid-ninth century, this site will be discussed in the next chapter.

The Argolid, the Corinthia, Boeotia

A comparison of fig. 6 with fig. 1 will show how close was the relation between Argive and Attic EG pottery. In the Argolid, as nowhere else, there are clear echoes of the experimental EG I style of Attica (fig. 6a–b); and in the local EG II phase, enclosed panels of meander or multiple zigzag are placed at handle level as in Attic, and on several of the same shapes (e.g., fig. 6d–e). The fine krater, fig. 6f, is the earliest Geometric example to survive complete; it, too, was probably based on an Attic model, to judge from fragments found in the Athenian Kerameikos. The only really individual shape is the local pointed pyxis (fig. 6c), which differs from the Attic version in having two little suspension lugs which may be pierced either horizontally or vertically. Argive EG decoration tends to be even more austere than Attic: even on the large vessels it is rare to find ornament on more than one part of the vase, and most of the drinking-vessels (i.e., skyphoi and small one-handled cups) are fully covered in glaze, without any decoration at all.

The Argolid also has its own characteristic handmade ware, manufactured in a tradition going well back into the Protogeometric period. Forms current in EG include small amphorae (neck-handled and shoulder-handled), pyxides, oinochoai with rising handle, aryballoi, and shallow hemispherical bowls. The fabric is heavy-walled and gritty, and the bodies of the closed vessels are plump, often globular. In EG we see the first sign of a new fashion for simple incised decoration applied mainly to rims and handles; the patterns, limited to short parallel strokes and single zigzag, have earned for this fabric the apt nickname of Pie Ware.[9] It has no obvious connection with the incised handmade ware of Attica, but we shall meet a related fabric in the Corinthia.

In contrast to Attic practice, inhumation had remained the prevailing rite in the Argolid ever since Mycenaean times. Most EG burials were in cist graves, lined and covered with rough stone slabs; pithoi, too, were already being employed for this purpose (Tiryns, grs. 19 and III/1), although this type of burial became much more common in the eighth century. Such vessels, in other regions, are normally reserved for children; the use of vast coarse pithoi to contain adult inhumations is typically Argive. Another local peculiarity is the habit of re-using earlier graves for later burials, in pithoi as well as in cists. Indeed, many have been used at least three times, and in these cases the offerings from earlier burials have usually been disturbed, so that the offerings from the successive burials are often hard to distinguish with any confidence.

The body of the deceased was most often placed in the grave with knees drawn up, or slightly flexed. Ornaments of bronze – finger-rings, earrings, and dress-pins – have been found *in situ* in several graves, worn by men as well as by women. The pins are outstanding for their high quality and sophistication. One of the finest,[10] found at Mycenae with the EG I pots fig. 6a–c, is more advanced than its Attic counterparts in three respects: the globe is marked off by careful mouldings on either side, the globe itself is becoming biconical, and the finial takes the form of a miniature vase.

Work in more precious materials is known so far only from Argos and Tiryns. In several EG II graves at Argos, gold ornaments have been reported: a bead in gr. 16, two hair spirals in gr. 106/1, and two earrings in a grave found near the modern telegraph office. Tiryns gr. 2 (EG I) yielded a spiral of gold wire, and the remains of a large iron pin with ivory head and sheathing. Probably also EG is the first burial of gr. XXIII; no pots survive, but it contained a necklace of faience and bone beads, three iron spearheads, and part of an iron dagger, as well as nine bronze finger-rings and another fine bronze pin.

At Argos our evidence is not confined to graves; for part of an apsidal building has been found, its destruction dated by a good deposit of EG II pottery which includes the krater fig. 6f.[11] By this time Argos was already a well-established *polis*, for the building stands above five successive levels of Protogeometric occupation; but we do not yet know when it was built, or what was its purpose.

The potters of Corinth, so it seems, did not take so readily to the new Geometric style. The florid decoration of the pointed pyxis fig. 7a may perhaps betray some awareness of Attic EG I (cf. fig. 1d); yet the shape, with its miniscule lugs, is Argive rather than Attic, and the other pots in the same grave are still in the Protogeometric tradition. A little later, however, there are clearer signs of influence from Attic EG II, seen once again in the enclosed rectangular panels at handle level (fig. 7b,d), and in the use of the hatched meander and – more commonly – the multiple zigzag. A favourite Corinthian variant of the latter has short vertical bars joining the apices to the horizontal frame. Attic EG II shapes – especially the shallow skyphos (fig. 7d) and the broad-based oinochoe – are sometimes followed; but on the whole the local preference is for a hemispherical skyphos (fig. 7c) and an oinochoe with globular body (fig. 7b); there are also a few globular lekythoi, aryballoi, and pyxides.

This liking for full, rounded forms is seen also in the plain handmade ware. The range of shapes is similar to that of the corresponding Argive fabric, with the addition of the hydria; but there is no attempt at decoration.

Corinth shares with the Argolid the practice of inhumation, the body being laid in the grave with the legs drawn up. The graves themselves are carefully

FIG. 7 CORINTHIAN AND BOEOTIAN EG POTTERY
(a) Corinth gr. *Hesperia* 39 pl. 8, 24, H. 14; (b), (c) Corinth,
gr. N. of Peirene, HS, 32.2, 11; (d) Oxford 1932.678 from Corinth,
H. 6.3; (e) Orchomenos, gr., *GGP* pl. 42c, H. 13.5

constructed: cists tend to be lined and covered with squared stone slabs, or
(more rarely) a sarcophagus[12] may be hewn out of a single poros block; or, when
the ground is hard enough, masonry may be confined to a single cover slab.[13]

FIG. 8 THESSALIAN AND CYCLADIC SUBPROTOGEOMETRIC POTTERY
(a) Marmariani 119, H. 11.5; (b) Tenos, *GGP* pl. 32e, H. 9.3;
(c) Tenos, *GGP* pl. 32c, H. 9.7; (d) Marmariani 92, H. 10;
(e) Marmariani 42, H. 20; (f) Vlasto collection, from Marmariani

Personal belongings, other than pottery, include bronze dress-pins and finger-rings; the pins which accompany fig. 7a are still of the Protogeometric type, with no finial above the disc head. Under the West Shops of the later agora a warrior was buried with a spearhead (now disintegrated), an arrowhead, and a knife, all of iron.[14]

Unlike Argos, Corinth has so far shown no evidence of settled habitation, and no steady sequence of burials, before the Early Geometric period; but from now on the record is continuous.

A sequence of Boeotian pottery, extending from the tenth century into the early eighth, can be reconstructed from the cist graves of Orchomenos, and the tumulus of Vranesi 5km. to the south-west. A grave group from Orchomenos[15] tells us that the Attic EG II style was closely imitated at this time (N.B. two shallow skyphoi and an oinochoe, all with enclosed panels containing meander or multiple zigzag); but there were other sources of inspiration, too. A link with Euboea is indicated by two skyphoi, one from each site,[16] decorated with pendent concentric semicircles; northward affinities, too, can be seen in, for example, a cup from Orchomenos with a trigger handle of Thessalian type.[17] A peculiarly

FIG. 9 EUBOEAN SUBPROTOGEOMETRIC POTTERY: SKOUBRIS GR. 33
HS: (a) 22; (b) 21; (c) 14.9; (d) 4.4; (e) 20; (f) 9.6; (g) 13; (h) 12.4;
(j) 12; (k) 12.8

Boeotian variant of the pointed pyxis, with collar and toe, appears in the grave group from Orchomenos (fig. 7e).

Detailed information about the two cemeteries is not yet available. From one of the Orchomenos cists an assorted collection of glass beads has been published,[18] but their precise context has not been stated. The Vranesi burials, also in cists, included cremations as well as inhumations, and were all covered by a low tumulus 7m. in diameter, and rising to 2m. above a central cairn. The offerings included bronze swords, gold bands, and two gold spiral earrings. Here, too, the composition of the individual grave groups has not been revealed, so that we cannot even tell whether the two sites followed one another in time, or were concurrent.

Another site where both rites occur is Medeon (or Antikyra), just over the border into Phocis, and on the north shore of the Corinthian Gulf; from here the available information is, fortunately, more precise. The tenth-century burials had all been cremations in elliptical rock-cut graves; the pottery is partly Atticizing, and partly in a West Greek Protogeometric style also found in Achaea and Ithaca.[19] During the ninth century, the graves are elliptical cists, and inhumation appears concurrently with cremation; and the pottery begins to assume a decidedly Corinthian appearance, comprising handmade aryballoi as well as painted wheelmade ware. These innovations could well be due to the arrival of some settlers from across the Gulf in the course of the early ninth century.

Euboea, Thessaly, Skyros, the Northern Cyclades

The local pottery styles within this vast area had already shown some degree of cohesion well before the first wave of Attic influence in the mid-tenth century.[20] Now, in the early ninth, Attic fashions were no longer followed in these parts, but the internal cohesion remains. The result is what we must call a Sub-Protogeometric style, based largely on Attic Protogeometric ideas, but developing them in a direction which Attic pottery never took. There are, to be sure, many local mannerisms peculiar to one region; but let us first see what is common to the whole area.

The chief common denominator is the skyphos with pendent concentric semi-circles (often intersecting), glazed offset lip, and ring foot (fig. 9f,g; fig. 8a,b). It is descended from the usual Attic Protogeometric type with full circles and high conical foot. On present evidence it was most probably evolved in Euboea about or shortly before 900 B.C.[21] and very soon spread to Thessaly and the northern Cyclades. As we shall see, the pendent-semicircle skyphos was to have a long life, extending far into the Geometric period; during the early and mid-ninth century it always has a tallish lip, slightly overhanging the body. An equally wide distribution is enjoyed by a flat-based cup, deeper than the Attic EG type and having a flaring, offset lip; most examples are glazed all over, but some from Euboea[22] are decorated with a thin scribble on the lip, recalling the Attic Proto-geometric cups from which they are ultimately derived. A third widespread shape, but with more local variation, is an amphoriskos with vertical handles on the shoulder, known from Tenos (fig. 8c), Halos gr. 6, and Lefkandi[23]; a Euboean tenth-century prototype is seen in two examples from Chalcis.[24] In addition to the pendent concentric semicircles, two rectilinear motifs are also found through-out this wide area; opposed groups of diagonals with the intervening triangles left unglazed (fig. 8d); and a tall panel containing a solid hourglass pattern, applied to the necks of closed vessels (fig. 9e).[25]

At the same time, a number of forms are peculiar to Thessaly, where the pottery has a mixed ancestry. These forms are best seen at Marmariani, in the north. By the beginning of the tenth century, or perhaps earlier still, an intrusive handmade ware had been introduced there, probably by immigrants from Macedonia; the three leading shapes are the beaked jug (with sloping or cutaway neck), the high-handled kantharos, and the cup with trigger handle. A little later, perhaps c. 950 B.C., these handmade shapes were joined by a full set of wheel-made forms imitating Attic Protogeometric, including a fine series of kraters lasting throughout the ninth century. It was from these Attic-inspired shapes that the Sub-Protogeometric style was evolved, in collusion with Euboea. Under this strong southern influence the handmade shapes, too, were soon reproduced on the wheel, and decorated in a hybrid Protogeometric manner (fig. 8d,e).[26] Perhaps in sympathy with the decoration of its handmade prototype[27] the neck of the beaked jug is often covered with a wild profusion of rectilinear ornament, which also spreads to the necks of other closed vessels during the ninth century. On the globular pyxis fig. 8f we see an unusually elegant specimen of this rectilinear Thessalian style, which is especially common among the tomb offerings at Marmariani. Plainer versions of the cutaway jug – both handmade and wheel-made – are found all over Thessaly, and also in Skyros; and in its wheelmade form this shape makes an occasional appearance at Lefkandi in Euboea, and so does one of its characteristic motifs at Marmariani, the panel of diminishing rectangles.

When we turn to the evidence other than pottery, it becomes clear that the most prosperous town in the whole area lay at its very centre – at Lefkandi in Euboea. One source of its prosperity is revealed in a number of terracotta mould fragments, rubbish from a bronze and iron foundry on the settlement (Xero-polis) swept into a pit with pottery of c. 900 B.C.[28] The date and the context are equally significant; for bronze had been in short supply during the tenth century, and the settlement had apparently been deserted for at least a hundred years before being reoccupied in the late tenth century. Now, at the turn of that century, there are signs of a renascent metal industry fostered by renewed con-tacts with Cyprus, always the most prolific supplier of copper. Of these eastward contacts there is plenty of evidence. A rich grave group of this time, Palaia Perivolia no. 22, contains a Cypriot Bichrome flask in addition to thirteen Attic and seventeen local vases.[29] Two other graves, Toumba nos. 1 and 3, yielded the head and body respectively of a locally made terracotta centaur,[30] for which Cyprus remains the most likely source of inspiration. In the opposite direction, Lefkandi has produced the closest parallels for a late Protogeometric skyphos and cup found at Amathous in Cyprus,[31] the earliest known post-Mycenaean exports to the eastern Mediterranean. Finally, the moulds themselves imply that Cyprus provided more than just the raw material; some fragments bear im-pressions of a false-spiral design often seen on a widely exported class of Cypriot rod tripod (p. 335) which may have supplied a model for the bronzeworkers of Lefkandi.

The ninth-century material from this productive site comes from a large pit deposit on the settlement, stratified above the foundry rubbish; and from about thirty graves in the three cemeteries (Skoubris, Palaia Perivolia, and Toumba), with their related pyres. The local pottery gives one the impression of an extremely conservative society; here we see the Sub-Protogeometric style at its most persistent and uncompromising. There is a full range of shapes inherited from the period of Athenian influence in the tenth century, on which cross-hatched triangles, concentric circles, and semicircles still play a major part in the decoration. In view of the wide foreign contacts around 900 B.C., this con-servatism may seem rather surprising; but thereafter it may be partly explained by a sudden decline in communications with Attica, as evidenced by the almost complete absence of Attic EG imports.[32] Yet this lapse in exchanges with Attica had no adverse effect on the prosperity of Lefkandi, or on the continuation of its eastward commerce. Out of a total of about thirty, no less than ten graves of this period contain gold; and in four cases the gold is accompanied by numerous disc-beads of faience, a material which at this early date can only have been

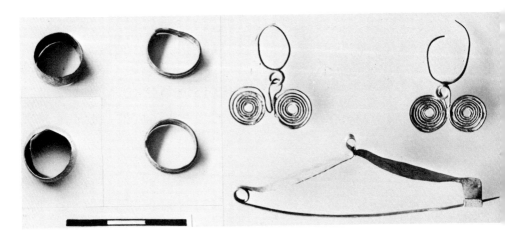

FIG. 10 METALWORK FROM LEFKANDI, TOUMBA GR. 13

worked in the eastern Mediterranean world. In another rich grave, Skoubris no. 33, the pilgrim flask (fig. 9h) is an import of oriental character, though possibly made in some other part of the Aegean.[33] The other finds from this grave consist of a disc-headed iron pin and a fragmentary iron sword; a pair of arched bronze fibulae of Protogeometric type, and four ornaments of gold: part of a spiral, two thin and narrow finger-rings, and an earring ending in two solid cones.

In another rich grave, Toumba no. 13, the gold (fig. 10) is more substantial:[34] a curious fibula derived from the Mycenaean violin-bow type, but with an ornamental loop at the centre of the bow; a pair of more elaborate earrings composed of two tightly-packed spirals of wire, recalling the northern spectacle fibulae, or the double-spiral finger-rings from Macedonia; a pair of massive finger-rings convex in section; and a more delicate pair with double carination.

In brief: during this otherwise rather bleak period, nowhere else in the Greek world has such an abundance of gold been found. Some of the ornaments – e.g., most of the twenty-odd finger-rings – may have been specially made for the grave, since they do not look solid enough to have been worn in real life; and no goldwork, as yet, shows any obvious sign of Near Eastern sophistication; but it seems likely that the metal, at least, was imported from that direction.[35]

The burial customs of Lefkandi represent a curious compromise, unparalleled elsewhere. With few exceptions, cremation was the prevailing rite, from Submycenaean times until the final burials in the later ninth century. The corpse was burnt on a pyre near by, on to which some vessels, jewellery, and dress ornaments were thrown. Afterwards the cremated remains were not placed in an urn, as in Athens;[36] instead, only a token amount of burnt bones was placed in the open grave together with the unburnt pots and personal belongings, which were sometimes placed as though round an inhumed body. The graves themselves had at first been cists; but from the late tenth century onwards it was enough to dig a simple rectangular shaft in the rock, usually closed with cover slabs resting on ledges.

As one might expect, the main concentration of Early Iron Age sites in Euboea lies in the central plain, dominated at this time by Chalcis and Lefkandi. But a recent survey has shown that there was also a scatter of coastal sites at or near the north-western cape of the island.[37] These would have served as staging-posts on the busy sea route leading from central Euboea into the landlocked gulf of Pagasae and the port of Iolcos.

Thessaly is too large a region to show any uniformity of culture or burial practices. Indeed, two quite independent traditions can be distinguished during the Dark Ages, flourishing at first in different parts of the country.[38] In the south, and especially within the gulf of Pagasae, relations with Euboea had been established well back in the eleventh century. Euboean influence is seen in the entire sequence of wheelmade Protogeometric pottery at Iolcos; and probably also in the adoption there of cist graves with single burials, although the rite preferred in Thessaly was always inhumation, as opposed to cremation at Lefkandi.

In the extreme north, meanwhile, the tholos tomb was the rule, designed for multiple inhumations. The pottery, in the first instance, was all handmade, in shapes of Macedonian origin; hence it is reasonable to assume that emigrants from Macedonia were among the first incumbents, although the actual form of the tombs must have been inherited from a local Mycenaean tradition. The most informative of these northern sites is Marmariani, where the architecture and contents of six small tholoi have been published in full. A local alternative to the tholos was the rock-cut chamber tomb; at Homolion, still further north, five such tombs have been found as against only one tholos, but all contained multiple inhumations as at Marmariani.

By the middle of the tenth century we have already learned from the pottery that these two traditions had begun to mingle with one another; first the southern wheelmade shapes were copied by the northern potters, who then proceeded to make their own handmade shapes on the wheel, and – in the early ninth century – decorate them in a hybrid manner (fig. 8); meanwhile the northern shapes appear in southern Thessaly, both in handmade and wheelmade form. We must now enquire how far the contemporary burial practices show a similar fusion between north and south.

We begin with a crumb of evidence from Theotokou on the Magnesian shore, outside the gulf of Pagasae. Here only three graves have been reported, all cists, and belonging to the eleventh, tenth, and early ninth centuries respectively. The two earlier graves held single inhumations, and wheelmade pottery in the southern manner; but in gr. A, the latest, there were four skeletons, and six out of its eighteen pots were of northern character – one handmade cutaway jug, and five wheelmade kantharoi. Another hint of northern intrusion may be gleaned from a small cemetery at Halos, on the gulf's western shore. Ten out of eleven burials were in cists, mainly for children; four contained tenth-century Protogeometric pots, the rest none at all. The eleventh and latest, dated by a group of Sub-Protogeometric vessels, was not a cist but a small round enclosure (diameter 1·60m.) resembling a miniature northern tholos.[39] At Pherae, 15km. inland from the gulf, there are no signs of northern influence in the Geometric cemetery of some forty cists; but an early ninth-century skyphos combines the shape of the Euboean pendent-semicircle variety with the decoration of cross-hatched squares characteristic of the northern handmade kantharos.

We have yet to consider Iolcos, the most important site of all, and the most puzzling. A series of forty Protogeometric cists, all with child inhumations, has been excavated within the settlement, coming to an end well before 900 B.C. The latest probably overlap by a few decades the first burials in a tholos tomb at Kapakli near by – a tomb which was to accumulate seventy adult incumbents within the next four centuries. The local custom, so it seems, was to bury children inside the walls, and adults outside. Yet it is hard to accept the tholos as belonging to the local tradition, seeing that two *adult* cist-burials, of early ninth-century date, have been discovered at Nea Ionia, less than 2km away from Iolcos; furthermore, the Nea Ionia cists are lacking in the northern pottery shapes, of which there is an abundance in the Kapakli tholos.[40] In view of the other signs of intrusive northern practices in the Pagasae region, perhaps the Kapakli tholos belonged to an immigrant northern clan, who came peacefully to settle in Iolcos, attracted, perhaps, by the greater opportunities there for dealing with the outside world.

From the published evidence, then, one gets the impression of frequent exchanges between north and south Thessaly between 950 and 850 B.C. To begin with, a sophisticated repertoire of Protogeometric shapes was introduced to the north under southern influence. At a later stage some northern forms, handmade and wheelmade, spread to the south; perhaps in the wake of northern immigrants, if we are correct in thinking that the tholos tombs of the north are the oldest in Iron Age Thessaly. Unfortunately, many more of these tholoi cannot yet be precisely dated, since their allegedly 'Geometric' contents have never been published.[41]

The rich and extensive tumulus cemetery of Vergina in Macedonia lies beyond the geographical frontiers of this book, except for its exchanges with the Aegean world to the south. In a land where handmade pottery was the rule, the sudden appearance of a local wheelmade fabric, Sub-Protogeometric in its shapes and decoration, must be a sign of southern cultural influence. For most of these wheelmade shapes – low-based skyphoi with pendent semicircles, trefoil-lipped oinochoai, amphoriskoi, and a krater – one need look no further than northern Thessaly for counterparts; and the potters of Vergina, like their southern neighbours, also did wheelmade decorated versions of their own handmade kantharoi and cutaway jugs. Two drinking-vessels, however, indicate direct contact with Euboea; a fine low-based skyphos with full circles, which looks like an import from that source of *c.* 900 B.C.; and a flat-based glazed cup with a scribble round the lip, a form otherwise known only at Lefkandi.[42] Another skyphos and another cup, both with low conical foot, may perhaps go back into the late tenth century; otherwise, the ceramic influence of the south is confined to the first half of the ninth, with no sign of any subsequent contact until well after the end of the Geometric period.[43]

As for influences in the reverse direction, we have already noted that the handmade ware of northern Thessaly follows the Macedonian tradition, and was probably introduced by Macedonian immigrants not later than the early tenth century. In metalwork, the spectacle fibula is a form of Balkan origin, and its use must have spread from north to south; its adoption at Vergina[44] is dated by the excavator to the late tenth century, presumably a little earlier than the many examples from Homolion and Marmariani. Perhaps in the same northern tradition is the pair of double-spiral gold earrings at Lefkandi (p. 42). Finally, Vergina has produced a necklace of beads in an opaque brown stone thought at first to be amber, but now more correctly diagnosed as sard;[45] one wonders whether the three 'amber' beads from Tenos (below) may not be of the same material, and from the same source.

We pass now to the island of Skyros. In spite of its apparently isolated position, the local pottery indicates close association with Euboea and Thessaly, established by the tenth century, and maintained in the Sub-Protogeometric style of the early ninth. The finds of the latter period (not yet published) include the material from four well-furnished cist graves containing 150–160 pots, gold beads, a gold ring, and fibulae, rings, bracelets, and a bowl of bronze. In some cases the pots were deposited outside the grave, a practice sometimes encountered at Lefkandi.[46]

In the northern chain of the Cycladic archipelago, pottery of this period has been found in Andros, Tenos, Rheneia, and Delos; but the only organized excavation to be published is of six cist inhumations on the hill site of Kardiani in Tenos. The graves, lined with large slabs and covered with several small ones, were strung out along a single terrace; except for no. 1, all skeletons were of adults, laid with their knees slightly drawn up. The pottery includes a good range of Sub-Protogeometric forms – amphoriskoi with vertical handles, low-based skyphoi (one with full circles, one with pendent semicircles), and fully glazed cups. A pair of bronze pins in no. 2 is still of the Protogeometric type, with disc head and plain globe. The richest grave, that of a small girl (no. 1), was furnished with a fibula, a spiral (fragmentary), two finger-rings, and two beads, all of bronze; and also the three beads said to be of amber, already mentioned above.

The Dodecanese

During the tenth century there had been many local offshoots of the Attic Protogeometric style in the eastern Aegean. Imitations were closest at Smyrna, Miletus, and Dirmil near Halicarnassus, where circular motifs were preferred and the authentic high conical feet were sometimes achieved. Attic influence had also reached Cos and Rhodes, but in a more diluted form; in those islands rectilinear ornament was more popular than circles and semicircles, and high feet tended to be flaring rather than strictly conical. The nearest westward comparisons are with the Argolid rather than with Attica, and some Coan graves have also produced handmade vessels of Argive type. Links with Cyprus, too, are apparent in three exotic shapes, all made locally: the duck-vase, the pilgrim flask, and the openwork kalathos. Among the local motifs of decoration, most notable is a cross-hatched hourglass design, used in panels.

Fig. 11 shows the immediate sequel, in the early ninth century. There is not much sign of foreign influence, but a few changes are in line with contemporary developments in the western Aegean: high feet give place to low conical or ring feet (fig. 11c), and thin panels appear for the first time on the necks of closed shapes (fig. 11g). The rare hints of an Atticizing EG style – for example the enclosed zigzag panel on an oinochoe neck in Cos gr. 22[47] – could be referred to the Argolid as plausibly as to Athens, and the handled pyxis (fig. 11d) is of Argive rather than Attic type. Two pilgrim flasks and a duck-vase from Ialysos gr. 141 show that connections with Cyprus were maintained, and two barrel-jugs from Ialysos gr. 43 (one is shown, fig. 11e,f) may well be Cypriot imports. Otherwise, the local Protogeometric tradition remains strong; on closed vases the shoulder still tends to receive the main decoration, the most popular motifs being cross-hatched triangles and hourglasses, and standing concentric semicircles.

In Cos the main evidence comes from the Seraglio cemeteries, cut into the ruins of the Mycenaean town. Its ninety-nine burials, all inhumations, extend from the tenth to the late eighth century, and offer the only continuous sequence of Protogeometric and Geometric pottery known anywhere in the Dodecanese. Twelve burials were of adults, one in a pithos and eleven in earth-cut pits; the bodies were laid with knees drawn up. The others were all child burials: three pit graves for adolescents, forty-two infants in cists, and forty-two infants in pithoi. The only well-furnished graves were cists, many of the pits and pithoi having no offerings at all; we know nothing, as yet, about the burials of prosperous adults. In some cists, pots were found inside and outside the grave, as in the Argolid; and in view of the other Argive affinities,[48] the earliest tenth-century incumbents may well have been immigrants from that direction, since there is clearly no continuity here from the Mycenaean occupation through the early Dark Ages. Offerings other than pots include iron pins with bronze globes (as in Attica and the Argolid), iron knives, bronze fibulae, finger-rings, and hair spirals in bronze or gold; and faience necklaces were found in two Protogeometric graves (nos. 10 and 63)[49] and in gr. 22 at the end of EG. Fig. 11d and g come from gr. 7,[50] together with a jug, a skyphos, and a large cup.

The Rhodian evidence is more patchy, and includes nothing before the late tenth century; for the early ninth, it is limited to Ialysos. Gr. 141, in the central area of that town, is an infant pithos burial containing a clay bell-doll, wheel-made and adorned with local EG patterns; also a bird-vase, two pilgrim flasks, a triple amphoriskos, and a tall krater foot. A local tradition of inhuming children can be traced back to a group of Protogeometric infant burials at Camirus.[51] For adults, however, cremation was to be the rule throughout the Geometric period, and two urn cremations of EG have been found in outlying parts of Ialysos. For Cremasti gr. 98, a warrior's cremation, the urn was a neck-handled amphora, as in Athens;[52] it was associated with two skyphoi, an iron sword and spearhead, an arrowhead, and a bronze utensil. The other plot, Marmaro, has a close group of three graves, of which no. 43 (fig. 11a–c, e–f) is the latest. Here the urn was a belly-handled amphora of fine proportions, still very Protogeometric in its decoration. Like its Athenian counterparts (e.g., fig. 13) it may well have held the ashes of a woman, to judge from its contents. In addition to twelve small pots, these

FIG. 11 DODECANESIAN EG POTTERY
(d), (g), Cos Seraglio gr. 7; the rest from Ialysos Marmaro gr. 43.
HS: (a) 56; (b) 17.5; (c) 6; (d) 9.6; (e–f) 7; (g) 21.3

consisted of four pins of Protogeometric type, two bronze rings, remains of three bronze fibulae, and three remarkable ornaments of faience: a fragmentary amulet with stamped circles, a figurine (lower part preserved) of the Levantine god Besh, and a pyramidal seal engraved with two prowling lions, Egyptianizing both in shape and design.

Crete

At this time the only firm chronology for this island comes from the pottery of the north central plain, which had succumbed to Attic influence well back in the tenth century. Hence arose a local Protogeometric style, best represented in the Knossos area, where the early phase lasted through most of the tenth century; during the early and mid-ninth it passed rapidly through a middle and a late stage, developing on its own lines, without any further inspiration from elsewhere. And even in the tenth century, when Athenian pottery was imported, Attic influence had never been more than superficial. Concentric circles were cautiously added to the Subminoan repertoire, neck- and belly-handled amphorae were copied, conical feet might be added to some drinking-vessels; yet a whole range of local shapes persisted throughout the early, middle, and late stages. The most notable survivals are the stirrup-jar, and deep bell-krater, the kalathos, and the deep skyphos which is a miniature of the bell-krater.

During the early ninth century the favourite motifs are circles, semicircles, lozenges (cross-hatched or checked), and cross-hatched triangles. Gridded battlements, possibly derived from the multiple-outline form of Attic EG II, appear on two vases of the late phase;[53] but the only imports of this time are from the Cyclades.[54] The local shapes show little change from the early phase: the stirrup-jar, now at the end of its long career, sometimes has an open neck; the rim of the bell-krater, plain during the early phase, is now usually reinforced with a ridge. Neck-handled amphorae with diagonal slashes on the handles are typical of the middle phase; and hydriae and globular jugs are especially common in domestic contexts.[55]

The cemeteries of Knossos extend to the west and far to the north of the main settlement, the most distant being in the suburbs of modern Herakleion. For this period the most important are near Fortetsa (1km. to the west) and at Ay. Ioannis (2km. to the north-west). Knossian burial practice was a curious mixture of old and new elements. The traditional Minoan chamber tomb, originally designed for multiple inhumations, had remained the usual form all through the Dark Ages; and there is evidence that some Minoan tombs were actually re-used by Protogeometric families.[57] But, from the late eleventh century onwards, cremation had been gradually replacing inhumation, and the change was virtually complete by the early ninth.[58] The cremated remains were usually placed in a necked pithos with painted decoration, but amphorae and bell-kraters could also serve this purpose. Smaller pots were placed beside or inside the urn, one of them often serving as a stopper. Some tombs contain large numbers of drinking-vessels which, although not smashed on the pyre as in Athens, nevertheless suggest a funeral celebration; and in Ay. Ioannis tomb IV remains of a meal were found on the floor. After each interment the doorway was blocked with a rough stone wall, and the dromos filled with earth. The tombs thus served as family vaults, with enough space to house several generations without any need of rearrangement. Nevertheless, there seems to have been a fairly sharp break in continuity around the middle of the ninth century, when the Ay. Ioannis cemetery and eight of the Fortetsa tombs[59] went out of use.

FIG. 12 CRETE: THOLOS TOMB AT GORTYN (photo S. Alexiou)

The non-ceramic offerings, where they can be securely dated to this period, are poorer than those of the tenth century.[60] Pins and fibulae look rather backward for their time – plain head and globe for the former, plain arch for the latter. Several iron spears and short swords have been reported, but none illustrated. Two objects, however, look like imports from the eastern Mediterranean: a short gold diadem of Cypriot type, with repoussé dots round the edge; and a faience figurine of the Egyptian deity Sekhmet.[61]

The southern plain of Mesara, to judge from its local pottery, was now in close communication with Knossos; and that region has produced by far the most handsome tomb of its time, an almost intact tholos recently discovered at Gortyn (fig. 12). Sunk into a flat field, its corbelled chamber is built of twenty careful courses, rising to 3m. and with a floor 2·70m. in diameter. Three large slabs frame the doorway, approached by a deep and narrow dromos cut into the rock. Of the fifty-odd vases, the pithoi and amphorae were the cremation urns; the pottery answers mainly to the middle and late phases of Knossian Proto-geometric, but the occasional appearance of the millsail pattern – and also of the neckless type of pithos – puts the final interments into the later ninth century. The other offerings included iron swords, iron spits of Cypriot type (cf.p.146, n.20), an axe-head, and a saw; one is reminded of the EG I warrior-craftsman cremated on the Athenian Areopagus (p. 31).

Since the central Protogeometric style made practically no impression on the rest of the island, it is not yet possible to say what material in the eastern and western extremities falls within the early ninth century. Most of the finds from Modi in the far west may well belong to this period; and also the latest burials in the chamber tombs at Vrokastro,[62] a hill-town overlooking the gulf of Mirabello in the east. Cremation became the general rule only in the centre of the island; elsewhere, cremation and inhumation were practised concurrently at many places.

Conclusions

Several parts of the Greek world have been omitted from this survey, because of our ignorance of the local chronology; thus, during this period, we are still in the dark about the south and west Peloponnese, the Ionian islands, and the north-west – in short, about almost all of Greece outside the Aegean. The main reason for our ignorance is that the pottery and other finds from those parts show no positive connection with Aegean Greece; one assumes that the stormy capes of the southern Peloponnese still had an inhibiting effect on sea traffic, and thereby divided the Greek coast into two parts, enjoying little or no communication with one another.

Within the Aegean world there is very little evidence from settlements in this period. For information about the relative size and importance of various towns we can only fall back on the spacing of cemeteries, unlikely to be far away from the settlements which they served. If we regard as a major site any place where the burials of this time are distributed over an area larger than a square kilometre, then five towns come into this category: Athens, Argos, Iolcos, Ialysos, and Knossos. To these we must certainly add Lefkandi whose known cemeteries, although more tightly concentrated, are not likely to have been the only burial grounds for the Xeropolis settlement nearly 1km. away; they may, on the other hand, have served another inhabited area closer than Xeropolis. At none of these major sites can we assume that the area encompassed by the cemeteries was fully inhabited; more plausibly, each major city began as an agglomeration of detached villages, each village with its own burial plot, but nevertheless linked by a feeling of belonging to the same community. An early expression of this corporate feeling is the construction of the first city wall at Smyrna in the middle of the ninth century, the earliest known fortification in any Greek *polis*.[63]

In the various lands reviewed in this chapter, the extreme diversity of burial practices is remarkable. No two regions are alike in this respect; the Greek world had already been divided up into a large number of self-conscious little communities, each with its own funerary tradition. Yet these local traditions go back well into the tenth century – with only two apparent exceptions. One is at Medeon in Phocis, where the sudden appearance of cist inhumations around 900 B.C., coinciding with an influx of pottery in the Corinthian manner, may betoken the arrival of some newcomers from Corinth, where cist inhumations were the rule. Secondly, some infiltration of north Thessalians into the Pagasae area is indicated by a similar combination of intrusive pottery with intrusive burial customs. This movement had begun within the second half of the tenth century when the Kapakli tholos received its first burials; and the slight evidence from Theotokou and Halos suggests that there was more such infiltration in the early ninth. Otherwise, this was essentially a home-keeping age; nowhere was there a major shift of population, and at no site – whether settlement or cemetery – can the initial occupation be assigned to the early ninth century.

In comparison with the previous period, there is also some evidence of a decline in trade and communications within the Aegean. Around 950 B.C., Athenian Protogeometric pottery had been widely exported, and imitated in places as far distant as Marmariani, Smyrna, Miletus, and Knossos; and also in Cos and Rhodes, where the style was perhaps introduced at second hand through settlers from the Argolid. By contrast, the EG pottery of Athens was hardly exported at all, and found virtually no imitators except in the neighbouring lands – the Corinthia, the Argolid, and Boeotia. Meanwhile, Crete and the Dodecanese were left to develop their own local styles in their own ways; yet the style with the widest circulation was undoubtedly the Sub-Protogeometric of Euboea, spread abroad to Thessaly, Skyros, and the northern Cyclades, with offshoots in Macedonia and Boeotia. However little commerce there may have been elsewhere, the Euripus channel must have continued to be a busy thoroughfare for sea traffic.

Within the area which produced EG pottery, Athens and Argos were the leading cities. The excellent quality of Argive dress ornaments, and especially the rapid development of the long pins with globes and finial heads, make it likely that some workshop in the Argolid – perhaps in Argos itself – was now setting the fashions in this field. Athens, meanwhile, led the way in pottery by inventing the Geometric style, which became known in the Argolid during its EG I phase; whereas the Corinthia and Boeotia show no knowledge of Attic Geometric before EG II. Perhaps it was easier and safer to sail across the Saronic gulf than to risk a difficult land journey along the Isthmus, or over the Cithaeron pass. Further afield, the EG style failed to reach Euboea and her commercial partners, apart from a few exports to Lefkandi. One reason for this failure may lie in the apparent lack of Attic maritime enterprise, as seen in the pattern of settlement: there is an enormous concentration in and around Athens, while on the coast only Eleusis, Marathon, and possibly Thorikos (p. 70) show any sign of habitation; and of these places only Eleusis displays any knowledge of the EG I phase.[64]

Yet this polarization of pottery styles is so curious that one wonders whether there may not also have been some antipathy between the two areas, and some danger from overseas that might also explain the lack of Attic coastal settlements.[65] Another symptom of unrest and insecurity may be seen in the custom in Athens of burying offensive weapons with male cremations, more prevalent there at this time than at any earlier or later period.[66] What is more, these cremations with weapons are in other respects, too, the best furnished male burials of their day. A man of substance, so it seems, was expected to be a warrior; and perhaps this was a time when a man could easily win his substance through the exercise of his arms.

At Lefkandi, however, it is the finery rather than the weapons which first attracts our attention. More gold, during this period, has been found there than in the rest of Greece put together. To account for this wealth, a ready explanation is at hand: the bronze foundry which had been in operation on the settlement around or just before 900 B.C., when there is also some slight evidence of trade between Euboea and Cyprus; one of the obvious motives would have been the supply of Cypriot copper for the foundry. It may be that the Athenians, too, occasionally joined in these exchanges; this would explain why hemispherical bronze bowls of Cypriot type began to be offered in Athenian graves at the end of Protogeometric, and also why Athenian potters, also at this time, began to imitate Cypriot rod tripod stands.[67] The two gold rings from Kerameikos gr. 7, decorated with repoussé dots, could well be imports from Cyprus; and so could the dotted gold diadem from Fortetsa tomb L.

Otherwise, actual imports from the eastern Mediterranean are limited to faience, a showy but cheaply produced material which was ideal for making trinkets to be exchanged in casual barter. Commonest are the necklaces of small disc beads, of which four went to Knossos, one each to Cos, Tiryns, and Athens, and several more to Lefkandi; Ialysos received a pyramidal seal, an amulet, and a figurine; there is another figurine at Fortetsa, and many more at Lefkandi. It so happens that a very similar range of trinkets is contemporarily found at Cyprus, at a time when that island was already coming under strong Levantine influence (p 67). Whether the objects were made in Cyprus by oriental prospectors, or whether they were hawked to the Cypriots from the Levant coast, it is hard not to see a similar oriental initiative in the export of similar trinkets to the Aegean; and this impression is confirmed by the high proportion of these exports found in Crete and the Dodecanese, islands which played no active part in trade at any time during the early Iron Age.

The Lefkandi finds, then, are unique in this period, not so much for the obvious indications of commerce with the Levant, as for the symptoms of wealth and prosperity which this commerce brought, in far greater measure than in any other part of Greece. The faience objects found in the cemeteries, taken by themselves, could all have been hawked by a single Phoenician trader, cruising round the Aegean; but the gold, whose metal must also have been imported from the east, implies more energy and initiative on the part of the Lefkandiots themselves. In addition to their bronze industry, their merchant shipping could have been another effective source of wealth. We have seen how a fairly homogeneous Sub-Protogeometric style spread outward from Euboea to Thessaly, Skyros, and the northern Cyclades; the maritime enterprise of the Lefkandiots, plying up and down the Euripus channel and out into the open Aegean, could have played a vigorous part in the dissemination of this style.

Yet the gold of Lefkandi must not blind us to the darkness which still prevailed elsewhere. Outside Euboea, the general impression of this age is one of isolation, parochialism, and perhaps of unrest. Apart from the Attic Geometric style, hardly anything begins at this time. Internal communications had, on the whole, deteriorated since the tenth century, and links with the outside world were rare and sporadic. Against this rather bleak background, the achievements of the next generation will seem all the more remarkable.

NOTES

1 First thought to be a house, D. Burr, *Hesperia* 2 (1933), 542 ff., but see now H. A. Thompson, *Hesperia* 37 (1968), 60.
2 From the scattered fragments, some burnt and other unburnt, seventeen have been made up, including fig. 1a–b and d; carbonized figs were also found in the pyre debris.
3 Snodgrass, *DAG* 231–2, 237–9; contra, Desborough, *GDA* 316–18.
4 cf. *SCE* II pl. 155, 16 and 20.
5 The EG I krater above gr. 1 is a more modest and serviceable vessel, and its base was not pierced.
6 Also undisturbed were grs. 7, 38, and 74, the first two being marked by stone slabs; all other EG burials in the Kerameikos, grs. 3, 4, 14, 18, 19 and 39, were badly disturbed by later graves.
7 *GDA* 159.
8 Skias, *AE* 1912, 39, gr. xli; *AJA* 44 (1940), pl. 17. 1–2, pl. 18.1.
9 A. J. B. Wace, *Mycenae* (Princeton, 1949), 84; earliest recorded example, *BSA* 50 (1955), 232 pl. 47b, found with fig. 6a–c.
10 *GDA* fig. 17 centre.
11 Courbin, *CGA* 162 n. 1.
12 *Hesperia* 33 (1964), 89.
13 *Hesperia* 17 (1948), 204.
14 See previous note.
15 *GGP* pl. 42.
16 Vranesi; *PGP* pl. 17.5.
17 T. C. Skeat, *The Dorians in Archaeology* pl. 2.8; cf. our fig. 8d.
18 *Orchomenos* I, 83 pl. 30.6–26.
19 Snodgrass, *DAG* 85 figs. 42–4.
20 Desborough, *GDA* 195–6, 348.
21 Desborough, *GDA* 197. For possible intermediate stages see *JHS* 77 (1957), 214 fig. 4a (export to Amathous), and *Lefkandi* fig. 62.
22 e.g., *Lefkandi* fig. 61.
23 e.g., Palaia Perivolia gr. 22, *AR* 1971, fig. 8 row 2 no. 3.
24 *BSA* 61 (1966), pl. 21d, 1–2.
25 Also on neck-handled amphorae: Kapakli (Iolcos), *PGRT* no. 8; Tenos, Kardiani gr. 2; Lefkandi, many examples, as well as on oinochoai.
26 For the wheelmade versions of the kantharoi see Theotokou gr. A.
27 e.g., Marmariani nos. 10, 11.
28 *Lefkandi* 28–9 fig. 67.
29 *Archaeology* 25 (1972), 17, Cypriot and Attic; *AR* 1971, fig. 8, local.
30 BSA 65 (1970), 21 ff.
31 See p. 40 n. 21.
32 A few EG II scraps from the settlement, *Lefkandi* fig. 64; in the cemeteries, no imports between Palaia Perivolia gr. 22 (*c.* 900 B.C.) and Skoubris pyre 4, shortly before 850 B.C.
33 Cf. *BSA* 12 (1905–06), 54–5 fig. 22 row 3 nos. 2, 4 from Adhromyloi in eastern Crete.
34 *AR* 1970, fig. 13.
35 On the sources of gold see *GDA* 313.
36 Except for three urn cremations in the late tenth century, when Athenian influence was strongest. See *GDA* 196.
37 See the map, *BSA* 61 (1966), 106 fig. 29.
38 *GDA* 214–15.

39 The tumulus of Halos, another northern feature, contains nothing obviously earlier than MG, and will be treated in ch. 3.

40 Here I leave out of account the intramural cists, all of which probably precede the diffusion of the northern shapes.

41 i.e., in the north, Chyretiai and Gonnos; in the Magnesian peninsula, Melea, Argalasti, and Lestiani; near the gulf of Pagasae, Sesklo and Dimini; and Ano Dranitsa, in the Pindus foothills. For bibliography see Desborough, *PGP* 131–2; Snodgrass, *DAG* 205–6. Reports of cremations in these tombs were considered untrustworthy by Heurtley and Skeat, *BSA* 31 (1930–31), 12.

42 See p. 40 n. 22.

43 However, remoter Macedonian centres – e.g., Chauchitsa in the Axios valley – went on imitating the pendent-semicircle skyphos with overhanging rim until well into the eighth century: see *PGP* 190–2 pl. 24b.

44 *GDA* 219 fig. 22b.

45 *Vergina* 254 fig. 89.

46 *BSA* 65 (1970), 21, Toumba gr. 3.

47 See *GGP* 267.

48 Snodgrass, *DAG* 163; Desborough, *GDA* 177–8.

49 *GDA* pls. 34–6.

50 *GGP* pl. 58: the inventory numbers 477 and 409 should be interchanged.

51 *PGP* 227–8.

52 A. Papapostolou, *AD* 23 (1968), A 83 no. 37, pl. 38a.

53 *Fortetsa* nos. 277, 301.

54 *Fortetsa* nos. 269, 1481.

55 *BSA* 55 (1960), 159–60 pl. 42.

56 Plan: *GDA* 226.

57 Brock, *Fortetsa* 4–5; Boardman, *BSA* 55 (1960), 143.

58 Latest inhumations: see *GGP* 233 n. 1.

59 III, IV, V, XI, Theta, Pi, BLT, L.

60 *GDA* 229–30.

61 *Fortetsa* nos. 336, 364.

62 Save tomb II, which contained LG pottery.

63 *BSA* 53–4 (1958–59), 82 n. 212; 121.

64 One vase: amphora, *AJA* 44 (1950), pl. 18.1.

65 See *GGP* 342–3, where it is suggested that the Calaurian Amphictyony may have been founded at this time within the EG area, in response to an external threat. From the Calaurian Sanctuary itself, however, the oldest published material is not earlier than the eighth century.

66 Out of a total of twenty-eight graves – of men, women, and children – eight contain offensive weapons.

67 Catling, *Cypriot Bronzework in the Mycenaean World* (Oxford, 1964), 215.

2 The Awakening in the
Mid-Ninth Century

Shortly before 850 B.C. there was a rapid advance on three fronts: in sea communications within the Aegean, in exchanges with the Near East, and, consequently, in the material prosperity of those cities taking the most active part in these exchanges. The most substantial evidence of this progress comes from well over a dozen graves at Athens and Lefkandi, all of which were furnished with a richness and variety not seen anywhere in Greece since the ruin of the Mycenaean palaces. The burials coincide with a brief period of artistic ferment in Athens – perhaps *c.* 855–830 B.C. – which saw the transition from the Early to the Middle stage of Attic Geometric pottery. Contemporary with these burials, progress of a different sort can be observed in Crete and the Dodecanese; for other regions, where the relative chronology is less clear, the narrative will be resumed in the next chapter.

Athens

The earliest of these rich graves is that of a woman, cremated on the north slope of the Areopagus shortly before the end of EG II. Her urn is a magnificent amphora with double-arc handles on the belly (fig. 13b), a type which had often served for Protogeometric female cremations; in Geometric times it appears to have been reserved for ladies of high rank, to judge from the rich offerings found in the same contexts. Perhaps this particular lady's status is more precisely indicated by a truly amazing vessel in the form of a long narrow chest and a lid surmounted by five model granaries in a row (fig. 13a). Its purpose is clearly symbolic rather than practical. Smaller clay chests, with plain lids, had already acquired a connotation of wealth in Protogeometric Athens; and one of these, an Athenian export, had been offered in an exceptionally rich grave at Lefkandi[1] just before 900 B.C. Seen in this light, the Areopagus lady's chest is uniquely ostentatious. Her model granaries, and their number, may possibly be a badge of the *pentakosiomedimnoi*, the highest social class of early Athens, whose members could produce 500 measures of grain each year from their estates.[2]

The lady had been furnished with gifts suitable to her rank, in quantity as in quality. The thirty-four painted vases – all but nine smashed on her pyre – are among the most sophisticated and inventive work of their time. Also from the pyre came fragments of twenty-one handmade incised vessels, and nine other

55

objects in the same technique – beads, balls, and spindle-whorls. Nearly all the more precious goods were housed in the urn. In bronze there were three pins (and one of iron with a bronze globe), two fibulae, and a finger-ring. In gold, six finger-rings, three composed of thin, fragile strips (cf. fig. 5b), and three broader ones, chased with patterns of lozenges or zigzags, and bordered by repoussé dots. The most splendid offering of all was a pair of massive gold ear-rings (fig. 13e), adorned with elaborate designs in granulation and filigree. These two difficult techniques had been forgotten in the Aegean world for over three centuries, and cannot have been re-learned without some guidance from the Levant. Furthermore, work of this high order can hardly have been copied from imports;[3] it must be the fruit of personal tuition. And yet, apart from the pome-granate pendants with their granulated calyx leaves,[4] there is nothing obviously oriental about the style. The angular plates, with their panelled ornament, are in the Geometric tradition, and the running-dog motif (or horizontal S's) can be matched on contemporary pins and fibulae. So it appears that these magnificent but puzzling earrings were made in Athens, perhaps by a resident Phoenician jeweller working with an eye to local taste, or, more probably, by an Athenian craftsman who had just learned the skills of granulation and filigree from a Phoenician master.

Still more evidence of eastward contacts is afforded by the non-metallic finds. A necklace, with over a thousand faience discs (fig. 13f), was punctuated by seven-teen beads of glass, and one of rock-crystal; the largest bead, of variegated glass, has a close counterpart from Sidon,[5] and it is likely that the whole necklace was imported from the east Mediterranean. Finally, three objects of ivory – two seals and a fragmentary amulet – attest the first revival of another Aegean craft, dormant since Mycenaean times. The expertise, as well as the material, must have come from the Near East. One of the seals (fig. 13d) has a pyramidal form re-calling the faience import from Ialysos gr. 43 (p. 47), yet the ornament of both seals, once again, is in the local Geometric tradition. The amulet bears traces of a crude human face, with a large prophylactic eye.

Complementary to these rich finds are the contents of four slightly later graves in the Kerameikos, where the pottery is partly or wholly of the MG I phase. Three of them, nos. 41–3, are very close together at the east end of the cemetery on the south bank of the Eridanos; their immediate neighbours are two well-furnished warriors of the previous generation (nos. 2 and 38) and a lady with rich offerings of c. 900 B.C. (PG gr. 48). These people, too, were clearly among the *aristoi* of their day. One even wonders whether this corner of the cemetery may not have been reserved for one particular *genos*, or noble clan; unfortunately, one could hardly hope to detect any sign of consanguinity in the meagre skeletal remains left by cremation. At all events, the incumbents of nos. 42–3 were regarded as men of high distinction, to judge from the monumental kraters whose pedestals were found *in situ* immediately above their urn-amphorae. The fourth and latest of the rich graves, no. 13, is that of a young warrior buried with his iron sword, and is marked by a rough stone stele. Following a new fashion, it is internally divided by another upright slab into two compartments, one for the urn and unburnt offerings, the other for the pyre debris. Among the latter, the most remarkable find was a set of four iron rings, the wheel-naves of the chariot

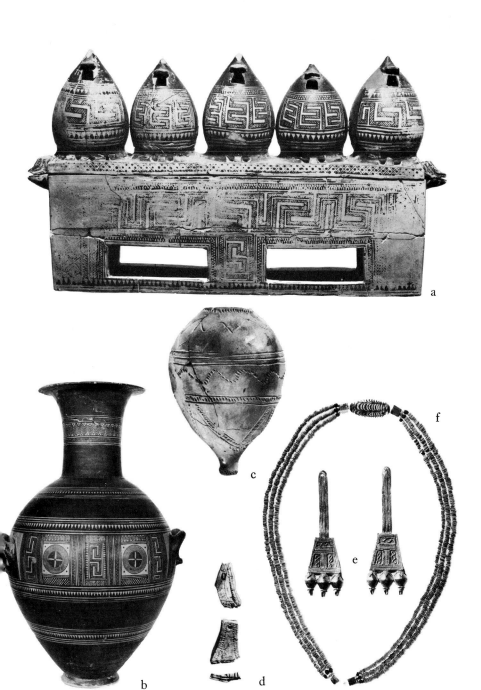

FIG. 13 AREOPAGUS, GRAVE OF A RICH ATHENIAN LADY (H 16:6)
(a) clay chest with model granaries, H. 25.3; (b) amphora, H. 71.5;
(c) handmade pyxis, H. 10.1; (d) ivory seal, H. 2.1; (e) gold earrings,
each H. 6.5; (f) necklace, D. of each faience bead 0.7

which may have carried this young aristocrat to his grave.

All four burials had been seriously damaged in post-Geometric times, and in the case of nos. 41–3 only half of each grave had survived, with hardly any of the pyre offerings; the urns, however, were all intact, and the variety of the extant finds is impressive. A lady's urn in grave 41, of the same belly-handled type as that in the Areopagus burial, contained three broad finger-rings of gold, a pair of iron pins with wooden globes, gold heads, and gold sheathing (one badly damaged), ten bronze fibulae arranged in two chains of five, and a fragmentary object of ivory. The ivory piece (fig. 14c), perhaps another seal, was in the form of two ducks' heads attached to a triangular base; like the Areopagus seals it has a border of tiny punched triangles, and probably came from the same local workshop. Of the gold rings (fig. 14a) two are plain apart from the repoussé dots on their borders; the third is of a ribbed variety also found in Lefkandi and Cyprus.[6] The pin, fig. 14b, is the first Attic specimen which will stand comparison with the finest work from the Argolid. It combines the most advanced shape (finial-and-disc head, careful mouldings above and below the globe) with a new interest in ornament – horizontal S pattern engraved round the disc, and no less than four zigzag zones round the gold sheath. There are two fairly close counterparts in bronze, decorated with crosses and zigzags, said to be from a grave group found in Attica, and now in Toronto. Quite different is the strange bronze pin from gr. 13, whose head takes the form of a man's booted foot – a curious conceit also seen on the handles of two clay cups, both from rich graves of the mid-ninth century.[7]

Even more versatile are the fibulae of this time. During the previous generation the plain Protogeometric type with stilted bow (fig. 9) had remained in vogue; the bow, swelling out in the centre, was marked off by mouldings from the catchplate and the double spring. But now, just as with the pins, there arose a desire to decorate; and decoration, on the fibulae, demanded broad, flat surfaces. On a superb gold pair now in Berlin,[8] leaf-shaped bows and long, tapering catchplates were hammered out flat, and covered with a profusion of engraver's motifs – zigzags, chevrons, crosses, and horizontal S's. This experiment, however, was still-born. A more practical solution, adopted in eight out of ten fibulae from gr. 41 (e.g., fig. 14d), was to hammer the bow into a crescent in the same plane as the catchplate. On every one, and on both sides, a swastika is flanked by two fish, all filled with pricked dots. With the two largest only the catchplate is hammered out, and more deliberately shaped into a square to receive the main decoration: in one case (fig. 14e), a very finely engraved ship (only the prow survives, but the horn, ram, and latticed balustrade can be made out), a fish swimming underneath, and a border of linked semicircles and horizontal S's. Subsidiary ornament – more horizontal S's and zigzags – appears on the long flat tongue between catchplate and bow, and a very little on the bow itself. These experimental fibulae of gr. 41 introduce the two most ambitious of all Geometric types, both of which were to have a distinguished future. The square catchplate, in particular, often received a pictorial theme, and may well have set off a similar fashion on pottery for small figured panels in square frames, first apparent in MG II.

In the next grave (no. 42) the man's urn-amphora was sealed, as usual, with a

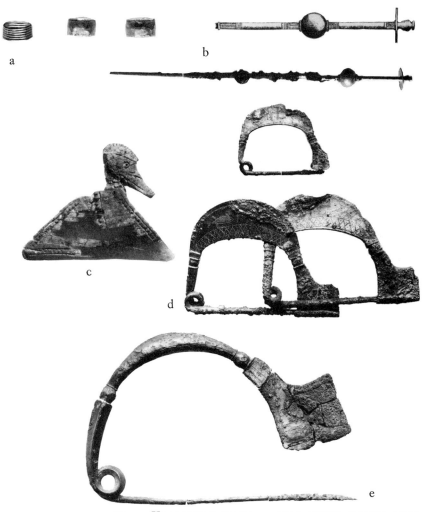

FIG. 14 KERAMEIKOS GRAVE 41: GOLD, IVORY, BRONZE, IRON
(a) gold rings, D. 1.8; (b) gilt iron pin, L. 31.2 (drawing, *JdI* 77,
106 fig. 24, 13); (c) ivory duck; (d) bronze fibulae, LS. 3.7, 7.2;
(e) bronze fibula, L. 14.6

bronze bowl; but this one, unlike the normal plain variety, bears an embossed
figured scene, and is a Levantine import (fig. 15). Six women form a procession,
each smelling a lotus flower held in the left hand, and with the right grasping the
tail of an animal; there are two goats, two bulls, and two lions. While the other
beasts go placidly on their way, one lion turns round in protest. The style has

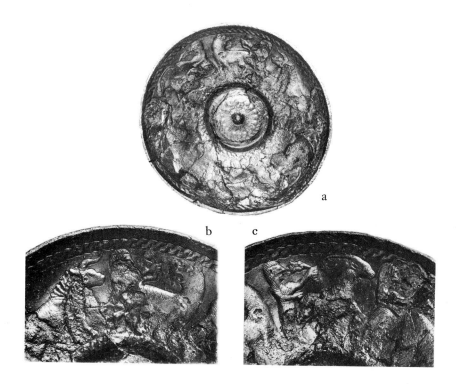

FIG. 15 KERAMEIKOS GRAVE 42: PHOENICIAN BRONZE BOWL. D. 17.5

much in common with contemporary work in the Neo-Hittite principalities of North Syria, but the cross-hatching of the ladies' wigs is an Egyptian notion. This mixture suggests the handiwork of a Phoenician craftsman, but where was his workshop? From the sanctuary of Idalion in Cyprus comes a very similar bowl, with identical subsidiary decoration (three cable zones and a central rosette) and a cult scene in a slightly more relaxed style; a later work, but in the same tradition.[9] If the cult scene was designed for the sanctuary, then Cyprus ought to be the source of the Kerameikos bowl, too; and it so happens that this is the most likely time for the founding of the main Phoenician colony on the island (p. 66).

The diadem of thin sheet gold, another form of oriental finery, makes its first appearance in Athens during this generation. There is one from gr. 42 (fig. 16a), one from gr. 43, two from gr. 13 (fig. 16b,c), and five from rich graves in other parts of the town; all except one seem to be associated with male cremations.[10] The idea almost certainly came via Cyprus, and a slightly earlier example from a Knossian tomb (p. 49) could be a Cypriot import; but the Athenian diadems all look like local work, embossed and engraved with zigzag designs in

FIG. 16 KERAMEIKOS GRAVE 42 (a) and 13 (b, c): GOLD DIADEMS LS:
(a) 31.8; (b) 9.3; (c) 38.1

the Geometric tradition. In Athens more diadems are known in this generation than at any other time before the mid-eighth century.

Athenian MG pottery will be more fully described in the next chapter; yet some tribute should here be paid to the elegance, the inventiveness, and the consumate technique of the vases offered in these rich graves. Panels of ornament, especially on the smaller vessels, are often expanded to the point where they exactly coincide with the handle attachments (fig. 17b–d), thereby achieving a happy equilibrium between shape and decoration; this was to be a hallmark of the mature MG I style. Sometimes, however, the ornament spreads all over the surface, as on the two small pots in fig. 17e,f. Of these the mug is a new form; the kantharos, with its vertical ribs or gadroons, was modelled after an elegant metallic shape. On a large scale, the same profusion of ornament is seen on the Areopagus chest (fig. 13a), a work which combines technical ingenuity with fastidious draughtsmanship. And where monumental splendour was required, the potters were equal to the challenge. Even the urns, figs. 13b and 17d, attain a size and complexity hardly seen again until the middle of the eighth century. More impressive still is the fragmentary pedestalled krater (fig. 17g,h) which stood above a nobleman's grave, no. 43; from the same workshop is a stray belly-handled amphora found also in the Kerameikos, which had probably been a lady's grave-marker (K pl. 47). These are the ancestors of the Dipylon Master's monumental vases, made nearly a century before his time. Invention here is tempered by conservatism, in that the decoration is still marshalled round concentric circles, as in Protogeometric; yet the circles are now dwarfed by a vast rectilinear design, laid out with the symmetrical precision of a formal garden. Outside, in the triangular space above the krater's handle, the painter has inserted the silhouette of a mourning woman, the first human figure in Attic art; and below the handle is a horse, perhaps to record the dead man's knightly status. The woman has a sinuous outline quite alien to later Geometric canons, and she has recently been compared to contemporary Egyptian work.[11] In this outward-looking age some knowledge of Egyptian art, if only indirect, would not be surprising. One must concede, however, that the figure could have been drawn

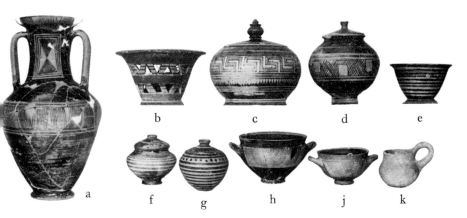

FIG 18 LEFKANDI, SKOUBRIS GRAVE 59, POTTERY
HS: (a) 37.5; (b) 10.2; (c) 10.6; (d) 13.1; (e) 7.6; (f) 7.6; (g) 8; (h) 9.3;
(j) 6.4; (k) 7.2

from life – as is suggested by the position of her arms, closer to nature than that of any subsequent Geometric mourner. At all events, these experiments in figured work are still very rare; the only other Athenian instance – apart from the Kerameikos fibulae and the Areopagus ivory disc – is a bull's head modelled in relief on a pyxis lid, where the markings on the brow have been geometricized into a set of concentric lozenges.[12]

Lefkandi

Lefkandi, in the early ninth century, had already been a prosperous place; and during this generation the grave goods are richer than ever before, and show more positive signs of contact with the eastern Mediterranean. At the same time communications with Athens, which had lapsed since the end of the tenth century, are now fully restored. The evidence for this, coming mainly from the importation of Athenian pottery, will be reviewed first, since it dates the richest, and latest, burials in the Lefkandi cemeteries which have so far been excavated,

In all, fourteen Attic Geometric vases have been found in six graves. Earliest is a cup from Skoubris pyre 4[13] near the end of EG II and very like one from the Areopagus lady's grave. There follow two pyxides, at the transition to MG; the later, from Skoubris gr. 59 (fig. 18c), is one of the earliest specimens of the flat class introduced at the beginning of MG I (p. 73), closely comparable to one

FIG. 17 KERAMEIKOS, POTTERY FROM GRAVE 42 (a–d) and 43 (e–h)
HS: (a) 23.5; (b) 6.5; (c) 6.3; (d) 77.5; (e) 7.5; (f) 10.7; (g–h) the foot
(h) is 35 high

from gr. 13 in the Kerameikos. Finally, a miscellaneous group of eleven oino-choai and feeding-cups, which take us into the middle of MG I, the date of the latest known burials; nine of these vessels are from Toumba grs. 31[14] and 33 which are among the richest graves of all. Not only do these imports fall into the same time-span as the opulent Athenian graves which we have just been considering; but five out of six graves where they occur also contain offerings in gold and other precious materials.

Elsewhere in the Aegean, especially in the Cyclades, the export of Attic MG I pottery was soon to have a marked influence on the local potters; but not so at Lefkandi, where Atticizing imitations are for the time being extremely rare, and the local Sub-Protogeometric manner persists. Among the other pots of Skou-bris gr. 59 (fig. 18) two pyxides are still of the old Protogeometric type, with everted lip; and there are also two fine specimens of the favourite pendent-semicircle skyphos.

Even more conservative is the pair of gold-plated iron pins from the same grave; the use of iron is surprising in a place with a thriving bronze industry, and the plain disc head, without even a globe, has an extremely old-fashioned look at this time. The eight bronze fibulae, on the other hand, are related to the two new Athenian types first seen in Kerameikos gr. 41. Six of them have flat crescent bows decorated with swastikas, as in Athens. This seems to be a fav-ourite type in the latest Lefkandi graves; a local adaptation, with enlarged crescent and minimal catchplate,[15] looks like the ancestor of the Boeotian figured bow fibulae which begin in LG (pp. 204–5). The two largest examples in this grave are of the square-catchplate variety and one of them (fig. 19a,b) is so like its Attic counterpart (fig. 14e) in shape and in subsidiary ornament (note espec-ially the ornament framing the panel) that it could well be an import from Athens, like the flat pyxis from the same context. The horse-taming scene is a remarkable innovation. This theme was to become popular in later Geometric art, but this is its first appearance; there are no Mycenaean precedents, but per-haps the impulse to draw such pictures may have come from the first circulation of Levantine figured art in Greece, for example the bronze bowl in fig. 15. On the other hand there is nothing oriental about the style, whereas the stiff-jointed horse is reminiscent of some LH IIIC vase-painting.[16] In brief, there is no easy explanation to account for the themes and the style of the earliest Geo-metric figured work.

Gold is even more plentiful at Lefkandi than in the previous generation. There is an abundance of broad finger-rings, solid enough to have been worn in life; those from Skoubris gr. 59 (fig. 19c) fall into two categories, ribbed and plain convex, both of which have antecedents in Cyprus. With them is a pair of gold earrings (fig. 19d) of the local type with hollow cones on the ends; a more exotic pair, each with three granulated pendants (Toumba gr. 5), suggests inspiration from the Levant. There are also four gold diadems, all of which look more oriental than those from Athens. One, with a lively frieze of assorted animals (Toumba gr. 33), could well be an import; the others, more soberly decorated with a single zigzag between repoussé dots, are more likely to be local work, although the dots recall some Cypriot originals.[17]

Other imports from the eastern Mediterranean, besides the granulated ear-

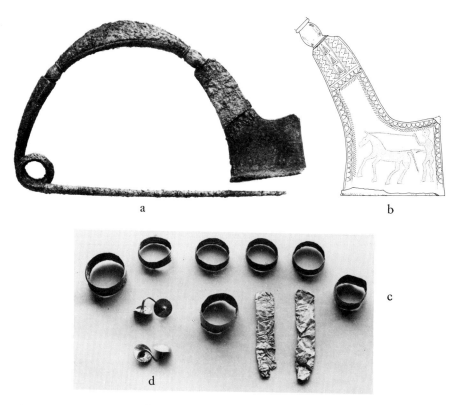

FIG. 19 LEFKANDI, SKOUBRIS GRAVE 59, BRONZE FIBULA (a–b) AND
GOLD JEWELLERY. (c–d) L. 16.2

rings and the figured diadem, include a small bronze jug of Egyptian type with
a handle in the form of a lotus flower (Toumba gr. 33); and a great deal of
faience, of which the most notable objects are three Egyptianizing seals: the first
a scarab, the second a cuboid with devices on four sides, and the third in the
form of a lion.[18] Discs of faience, for necklaces, run into several thousands.

The Levant and Cyprus

Apart from Athens and Lefkandi, no other Greek city displays any comparable
symptoms of prosperity as early as this. In view of the Levantine imports, and
the Levantine skills which were copied by local craftsmen, one assumes that this
prosperity was founded to some extent on commercial exchange with the eastern
Mediterranean; and it was probably from that direction that the materials of
gold and ivory were obtained. But what had Athens or Lefkandi to offer in
return, and which parties took the initiative in these exchanges?

For the first question the evidence is meagre. Known Greek exports of this time are limited to a very small quantity of pottery found at two sites in Palestine. From Megiddo, in the plain of Esdraelon, come two skyphos fragments of Attic MG I character, for which the nearest parallels are in Kerameikos gr. 13.[19] Tell Abu Hawam, in the bay of Haifa, has produced two pieces which are very similar to whole pots of the mid-ninth century from Lefkandi: the first is a rim sherd from a moderately deep pendent-semicircle skyphos[20] like one from Skoubris gr. 59 (fig. 18h); secondly, an almost complete cup (fig. 20a) with a line round the reserved rim, and streaky glaze on the body, just stopping short of the flat base – a type matched by several cups in a settlement deposit ('Stelio's Field') at Lefkandi. It is reassuring that these drinking-vessels appear to come from those parts of the Greek world which, at home, offer the most abundant evidence of Levantine contacts, and commercial initiative. Yet since the quantity of Aegean pottery exports is so small, one has the impression that the visits of Greek ships to the eastern Mediterranean were still very rare. By the end of the ninth century, as we shall see, some Greek merchants had begun to settle on the Syrian coast; but this movement does not seem to have begun before c. 825 B.C. (pp. 93–5). So, for the time being, we must explore the evidence for an alternative hypothesis – that Athens and Lefkandi received their Levantine imports through the initiative of Phoenician traders who were beginning to penetrate Aegean waters in search of some commodity present in Greece, but lacking in the Levant.

For the mercantile cities of Phoenicia the ninth century was a period of prosperity and expansion. To the south, the flourishing kingdom of Israel had succumbed to Phoenician cultural and artistic influence, which reached its highest point when Jezebel, princess of Tyre, was married to Ahab, king of Israel from 875 until 853 B.C. His father, king Omri, had employed Phoenician architects and craftsmen to build and furnish the new Israelite capital of Samaria in c. 880 B.C.; its fine ashlar walls are perhaps the most impressive surviving monument of Phoenician architecture of their time, since the contemporary cities of Tyre, Sidon, and Byblos have not yet been unearthed. The exports of Greek pottery to Tell Abu Hawam and Megiddo, both within the Israelite kingdom, probably belong to this period of Phoenician influence which lasted until the fall of the Omrid dynasty in 841 B.C.

In their homeland, the Phoenicians were subjected to the ravages of Assyrian armies led by king Shalmaneser III (858–825 B.C.); but it was not long before they had established their first colony overseas. This was at Kition on the southeast coast of Cyprus; the Tyrian colonists called the place Qart-hadasht, or New Town, the name which was later given to Carthage, too. This foundation must be placed well back in the ninth century since, outside the walls of the Phoenician city, a vast and handsome temple to the goddess Astarte had already been constructed of large ashlar blocks, and then destroyed by fire, before 800 B.C. The pottery from the debris of its first period includes some Attic MG I sherds from oinochoai like fig. 17a[21] and much of the red-slipped 'Samaria' ware typical of the Phoenician homeland in the late ninth century; and also about a hundred locally made unguent flasks in the Black-on-Red technique, another fabric of Phoenician origin which had been imitated in Cyprus since

FIG. 20 POTTERY WITH LEVANTINE ASSOCIATIONS
(a) Euboean cup from Tell Abu Hawam (*QDAP* 4 pl. 88 1a),
H. 9.6; (b) Black-on-Red flasks, London Institute of Archaeology.
Left: *Gerar* pl. 60, 82g, H. 8.7; centre: from Cyprus, H. 10; right:
Lachish III pl. 88, H. 9.5; (c) Coan flasks from Seraglio gr. 1,
GGP pl. 59c, b, HS. 22.8 and 13.5

well before Kition's foundation.[22] Earlier samples of this fabric and shape are
shown in fig. 20b, where only the central flask is from Cyprus, and has a dull,
slipped surface; the other two, unslipped but polished to a high orange lustre,
are Phoenician originals found in Palestinian contexts not later than the early
tenth century. This particular shape, which was widely diffused by Phoenician
commerce, is distinguished by the ridge half-way up the neck; not an elegant
idea, but an effective device for reinforcing the neck at its most vulnerable point.
The usual decoration consists of small sets of concentric circles on the shoulder,
and four thin lines round the belly.

The foundation of Kition follows a period when Phoenician influences on the
island had been steadily accumulating, and constitutes a turning-point in Cypriot
history. Three centuries had passed since the coming of Achaean refugees
escaping from the wreck of the Mycenaean civilization; as they merged with the

indigenous Cypriots, the vitality of their culture had become increasingly diluted. The arrival of the Tyrian colonists set the island moving on a new tack. Although the newcomers made no attempt, as yet, to extend their political control outside Kition, they had the effect of rousing Cyprus out of a rather torpid state, bringing it into a much closer rapport with the Levant coast.

Returning to the Aegean, we shall find some traces of Levantine influence in the Dodecanese and in Crete, the two regions which were most easily accessible to Phoenician shipping; and, unlike Athens and Lefkandi, neither of these regions shows any sign of commercial enterprise, or of any increase of wealth as a result of their Levantine contacts.

Cos

The only Dodecanesian site with material of this generation is the Seraglio cemetery of Cos, where the sequence is continuous. Here, just as the local pottery enters its MG phase, there are some remarkable innovations. The most popular offering in the graves is now a ridge-necked flask (fig. 20c), new to the local repertoire, but obviously modelled – at least in shape – on the Phoenician Black-on-Red type. Imported Phoenician originals, with a shiny orange surface, number about thirteen in the MG and LG grave groups from this cemetery. Now and again the local potters tried to emulate their fabric, substituting a darker orange slip for the polished surface of the originals, and rendering the authentic circles and lines by scoring them lightly through the slip.[23] Far more numerous are the imitations in the local Geometric style, which forsake the original decoration for rectilinear designs; motifs newly introduced from Attica (e.g., meander and battlement) are often combined with triangular patterns of local derivation.

It seems, then, that Phoenician traders were beginning to market their flasks in the Dodecanese at about the time when Kition was founded. Their colony in Cyprus would, no doubt, have served them as a forward base for any commercial ventures further west. The flasks were presumably imported for their contents of unguents, and may have answered a pressing need; in Greece, slow-pouring vessels are not at all plentiful – apart from the Coan imitations – in other EG and MG regional styles. In Cos, the Geometric imitations tend to be rather larger than the Black-on-Red originals; but if they served the same purpose, this may mean that a few Phoenician unguent manufacturers set up shop on the island, in which case they would hardly have brought their own potters with them; instead they would have been content to commission locally made containers, painted in a style congenial to their Dodecanesian customers.[24] Be that as it may, the Phoenicians were certainly marketing unguents in the Dodecanese at least a century before any Greek city had begun to organize a similar trade overseas (p. 187).

Knossos

Soon after 850 the pottery of central Crete betrays a bewildering mixture of outside influences. Some contact was established with Athens, probably through

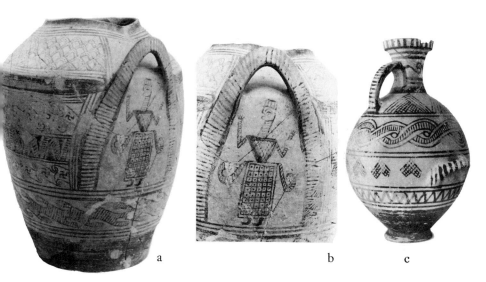

FIG. 21 KNOSSOS, PROTOGEOMETRIC B POTTERY
(a–b) *Fortetsa* 1440, H. 41; (c) *Fortetsa* 493, H. 27.7

the Cyclades; a belly-handled amphora from Fortetsa[25] is a very rough copy of the Areopagus lady's urn (fig. 13b), and on its shoulder is a curious frieze of mourning women which must be contemporary with the first Attic mourner on the krater in fig. 17g. At about this time an exotic style was evolved at Knossos, called Protogeometric B because its fabric, many of its shapes, and some of its motifs (e.g., concentric circles, concentric semicircles, and cross-hatched rectilinear motifs) are derived from the local Protogeometric tradition. It is the innovations which concern us here. A straight-sided pithos from Fortetsa (fig. 21a), itself a new shape with Cypriot affinities, is covered with freehand curvilinear ornament of a kind not seen on any other Greek pottery before the end of the eighth century, when its appearance is usually ascribed to oriental influence after the breakdown of the Geometric system; at Knossos, on the other hand, these free curvilinear patterns assert themselves before any local Geometric style had been formed. On this vase the new motifs are based on the arc and the running spiral; the cable, a third component of the style, is seen on the hydria in fig. 21c. Perhaps it takes very little to induce a Knossian potter to relapse into free curvilinear ornament, with the entire Minoan pottery sequence buried under his feet, and constantly being churned up. But the immediate source of the cable must surely be the art of the Levant, where it often serves as a border pattern on bronze bowls (e.g., fig. 15) and on ivories; indeed, it appears in a deposit of Phoenician ivories from the sanctuary of Zeus in the Idaean cave, of which some pieces may go back to the ninth century.[26] The cable is also found on a circular gold pendant from a tholos tomb near Knossos (p. 100, fig. 32b), decorated with elaborate granulation, and probably made by an oriental gold-smith who settled at Knossos at some time during the second half of the ninth century.

Oriental influence, then, must have played some part in the formation of the Protogeometric B style;[27] but there is also a strong element of native invention, combined with native conservatism. Under each handle of the pithos (fig. 21b) is a goddess, a walking illustration of the new style. Yet we have already seen how rare human figures are at this time; and we can also see, from her raised arms and her snakes attached to the waist, that her antecedents go far back into Minoan times.[28] Presumably she is the underworld protector of the person whose ashes lay in the pithos.

From Knossos and Cos we get a rather different picture of the traffic between the Aegean and the Near East. While Athenians and Euboeans took a fairly active part in these early exchanges, Cretans and Dodecanesians waited for the orientals to come to them; and there is reason to suppose that they allowed some oriental specialists to settle and practise their crafts, thereby exercising a limited influence on the local art which was not transmitted elsewhere. For this apparent contrast, the most likely explanation is geographical. As soon as trade revived, Crete and the Dodecanese offered useful staging-posts on the important routes; and their inhabitants, by staying at home, could profit from all callers, from east and west. Athens and Lefkandi look more like terminal points, and so would need to exert themselves more vigorously in the production of marketable goods. For Lefkandi a possible source of wealth is the local bronze industry which, as we have already seen, was already in operation by 900 B.C. But how can we account for the sudden florescence of Athens, as attested by the rich graves of this generation?

Thorikos

One possible answer is the demand for silver, a metal unobtainable in the eastern Mediterranean, but fairly plentiful in the Aegean. The recent excavations at Thorikos, in southern Attica, have shown that silver from the nearby mines of Laurion was already being processed in the ninth century. Here, in a large room (8 × 6m.) furnished in the usual manner with stone benches, several basins had been cut into the floor; and two of them were found to contain the substance known as litharge, i.e., the residue of lead left behind after silver had been extracted from the ore by cupellation. The room was occupied only for a short period. Most of the associated pottery is of the mid-ninth century – i.e., late EG II and early MG I; a few pieces in a rather provincial Protogeometric manner need not be much, if at all, earlier. The site was probably abandoned after an avalanche from the rocky acropolis of Velatouri; for this event a *terminus ante quem* is given by a cremation burial of *c.* 825–800[29] cut through the habitation levels in a court outside.

Here, then, a promising source of wealth was being temporarily exploited at precisely the same time as the deposition of the rich burials at Athens. One wonders if there is any connection: did the Athenian *aristoi* of the mid-ninth century grow rich by trading the silver of Thorikos with visiting Phoenician merchantmen who brought gold and other luxuries in exchange? This could only have happened if Attica had already become a political unity, if the synoecism traditionally ascribed to Theseus was already complete.[30] The possibility is well worth considering, especially since no corresponding manifestations of wealth have yet emerged from the ninth-century graves and settlement of Thorikos.[31]

Conclusions

By the end of this generation, much of the gloom of the Dark Ages had been dispelled. There had been much progress in seafaring, in the acquisition of wealth, and in commercial relations with the peoples of the Levant, especially with the Phoenicians. These exchanges brought the Greeks a supply of valuable materials, notably gold and ivory; and from oriental master-craftsmen they soon learned elaborate techniques in working them, forgotten in Greece since Mycenaean days. Another consequence was a strange ferment in the artistic sphere, which threw up some striking experiments in figured representations. Meanwhile the leading school of Geometric pottery, that of Athens, had attained maturity and self-confidence, and was beginning to set the fashion in many parts of the Greek world.

Even so, this brilliant phase did not entirely banish the spectre of the Dark Ages; this was only a false dawn. In figured art there was no further progress until the generation just before the Dipylon Master. It was a long time before there was any significant increase in eastward exchanges, even after a trading post had been set up on the Syrian shore (p. 93). And, finally, the greatest skill of the Phoenicians went unnoticed, for the time being: literacy, in the form of the Phoenician alphabet, remained unknown in the Aegean until well into the next century. This fact confirms my impression that the early exchanges with Phoenicians took place more frequently in the Aegean than in the Levant, a land which had never lost the gift of literacy, and had never known the worst deprivations of a Dark Age.

NOTES

1 Palaia Perivolia gr. 22; see p. 41.
2 E. L. Smithson, *Hesperia* 37 (1968), 96; cf. L. H. Jeffery, *AG* 88, 101 n. 6.
3 See p. 64 for a pair of gold earrings with granulation, probably Phoenician imports, found in a contemporary grave at Lefkandi.
4 In the same oriental tradition, though of Classical date, are two pendants from Marion in Cyprus: *SCE* II pl. 155.26.
5 R. A. Higgins, *BSA* 64 (1969), 145.
6 There are two more in Odos Kavalotti gr. Epsilon, another rich Athenian MG I burial: *AD* 20 (1965), B 78.
7 Berlin, *AM* 43 (1918) pls. 1, 2; Odos Kriezi gr. 7, *AAA* 1 (1968), 22 fig. 3.
8 Blinkenberg 77–8 fig. 56; A. Greifenhagen, *Berlin: Schmuckarbeiten in Edelmetall* (1970) I, 21 nos. 4–5 pl. 4.

9 K. Kübler, *Studies presented to D. M. Robinson* (Baltimore, 1953) II, 25–9.

10 Odos Kriezi gr. 7; Odos Erechtheiou gr. 6; Odos Kavalotti gr. Delta (two) and gr. Epsilon, the last in a shoulder-handled amphora, a type usually reserved for female cremations.

11 J. L. Benson, *Horse, Bird and Man* (Amherst, 1970), 92–3 pl. 32.2–4.

12 *CVA Athens* I, pl. 1.9.

13 *AAA* 2 (1969), 98 fig. 2.

14 One, *AJA* 75 (1971), 76 fig. 18.

15 *Archaeology* 25 (1972), 18 left.

16 cf. Furumark, *The Mycenaean Pottery* 241 fig. 26.8; Benson, op. cit., pl. 9.3.

17 e.g., *SCE* II pl. 156.9.

18 All three seals, and the bronze jug, are illustrated in *Archaeology* 25 (1972), 18–19.

19 *Berytus* 11 (1955), pl. 20, A 4–5; *GGP* 303–4.

20 *PGP* pl. 26.4.

21 Information kindly given me by Dr V. Karageorghis.

22 Kition: *BCH* 91 (1967), 307–9, 'Samaria' ware; *BCH* 95 (1971), 377–80, Black-on-Red. On the Phoenician origin of Black-on-Red, see F. Vandenabeele, *BCH* 92 (1968), 107–12; M. W. Prausnitz, *1st. Int. Congress of Cyprology, 1969* (Nicosia, 1972), 151–6.

23 For a later Rhodian flask in this technique see p. 249 fig. 79b.

24 I owe this suggestion to Prof. R. M. Cook.

25 *Fortetsa* pls. 24 and 144 no. 339.

26 For references see *GGP* 347 n. 6; Snodgrass (*DAG* 341) argues for a later dating.

27 See also Boardman, *BSA* 62 (1967), 64.

28 Alexiou, *KCh* 11 (1958), 287–8.

29 *Thorikos* III (1967), 38–42 figs. 44–8. For the amphora's profile cf. *PAE* 1939, 28 fig. 1, Marathon gr. 1, late MG I.

30 On the likelihood of a synoecism in Mycenaean times, see most recently R. Padgug, *GRBS* 13 (1972), 135 ff.

31 One silver fibula is said to have been found at Thorikos (Hampe, *FGS* 5–6 pls. 9, 10); but this is LG, and Boeotian work.

3 Consolidation: Late Ninth to Early Eighth Century

After this brilliant interlude, progress during the next two generations (*c.* 830–770 B.C.) was less spectacular. Although some Levantine traffic was maintained, there is less to show for it at home; the repertoire of grave goods is more restricted, and goldwork is exceptional. Athenian Middle Geometric, a settled and harmonious style of pottery, slowly worked itself out; and before long it became the common idiom of almost every Aegean centre, so that one must at least suppose some increase in maritime travel within home waters. Because the style has a marked internal development through two stages, it is a most useful yardstick for measuring time in other parts of Greece, each of which will be considered in turn. The final ferment at the end of MG II, when the first funeral and battle scenes suddenly appear on Attic pottery, will be treated with the work of the Dipylon Master in the next chapter.

Attica

We have already had a glimpse of the incipient MG style (pp. 61–3), in which complete harmony between shape and decoration had already been achieved. A fine example of this harmony is seen on a shoulder-handled amphora from Eleusis of the late ninth century (fig. 22e). The weightiest motif, a hatched meander, is placed in a panel at the point where it is most needed – i.e., exactly coinciding with the level of the handles; and ancillary zones enclose the neck and the belly. The decoration thus assumes an architectural quality; each part of the vase receives separate definition, but without any loss of overall unity. On a small scale, the skyphos in fig. 22c shows the same meticulousness in the placing of ornament. The zigzag panel is here enhanced by ancillary columns of dots, and so framed that the lower limit of the reserved area coincides with the handle roots. The spaces by the handles, instead of being glazed as in EG, are suitably filled with stars – or, in other cases, dot rosettes.

The most important new shape is the flat pyxis (fig. 22b) which takes over from the globular form at the turn from EG. In spite of its stable appearance, there are holes for suspension, just as on the pointed pyxis (which continues into MG I); table space, in a Geometric household, was evidently scarce. The underside occasionally carries an elegant leaf pattern (fig. 22d); continuous zones cover the body. The knob handles suggest some acquaintance with woodwork, and sometimes take the form of a miniature pyxis.

73

There has been a slight remodelling of the other closed shapes, which become taller and slimmer, and have a higher centre of gravity than before. Elegant vases like fig. 22f make their EG predecessors look rather ungainly by contrast. The lips of skyphoi tend to be more vertical, and sometimes tall enough to take a subsidiary zone of decoration (fig. 17c).

Once the initial ferment is over, the range of patterns settles down again to a narrow repertoire. The meander and multiple zigzag, always drawn with consummate neatness, are the only two broad motifs in common use. Among the ancillary motifs used in narrow zones, three innovations deserve notice: double axes alternating with groups of verticals; rows of dots; and gear pattern (fig. 22b).

After the static perfection of MG I, the decoration of major vases becomes richer and less restrained. After 800 B.C. the position of the handles no longer limits the extent of the main motif. On the amphora in fig. 23a, for example, the shoulder panel merges with the belly zone, thereby forming the most typical of Attic MG II compositions on a large scale: a central meander, framed on all four sides with ancillary strips, and underlined by a continuous zone running underneath the handles. A similar arrangement, but even more elaborate, is seen on the monumental krater in fig. 23d; on a small scale the same principle is applied to the kantharos in fig. 23b.

In MG II the repertoire of narrow motifs is enriched by several innovations. The dotted false spiral – or 'tangential circles' ' (fig. 23b) – and the dotted lozenge chain (K pl. 85 no. 285) are probably both adapted from metalwork. More prominent than either is the row of vertically placed chevrons, unobtrusively used as an ancillary motif in MG I, but now applied to the skyphos as its main decoration. Skyphoi like fig. 23c, with offset vertical lip, shallow body, and a panel of vertical chevrons, are copied all over the Aegean world. Of the older ancillaries, double axes with verticals, dogtooth, and steep single zigzag continue in use. Hatched meanders and multiple zigzags are still the only common broad motifs; a new and rare alternative is the panel of hatched meander hooks (K pl. 93 no. 288), the 'negative' version, as it were, of the meander.

The leading closed shapes, at this time, are the three kinds of cremation amphorae (neck-handled for men, belly- and shoulder-handled for women), the oinochoe, and the flat pyxis. Chief among the open shapes is the krater, with a ribbed and widely splaying pedestal (fig. 23d). Drinking-vessels include the skyphos, the mug, and a fine new form, the kantharos with high strap handles. We have already met an earlier version in the EG wheelmade ware of Thessaly (p. 40), and there is also a very distant ancestor in the Middle Helladic Minyan kantharos, examples of which are known to have been unearthed by eighth-century Athenians.[1] Either of these prototypes could have supplied the idea of the high strap-handles, but the body is distinctively Athenian, and modelled after the contemporary krater and skyphos. Fig. 23b, one of the earliest in the Attic

FIG. 22 ATHENIAN MG I POTTERY FROM ELEUSIS (e) AND THE KERAMEIKOS

(a) gr. 37, H. 30.5; (b/d) gr. 20, H. 9.3; (c) gr. 36, H. 6.7; (e) Eleusis 700, H. 51.5; (f) gr. 37, H. 59

FIG. 23 ATHENIAN MG II POTTERY FROM THE KERAMEIKOS
(a) gr. 86, H. 51.5; (b) gr. 69, H. 11.5; (c) gr. 22, H. 6.9;
(d) gr. 22, 52.5

sequence, comes from a man's cremation, Kerameikos gr. 69; it is unusual for this shape to be found in a woman's grave, or in a domestic context. In sixth-century vase-painting the kantharos is portrayed as the favourite vessel of Diony-sos; perhaps the association goes back to the eighth century, since an Attic kantharos of *c.* 750 B.C. was offered at the sanctuary of Dionysos at Ay. Irini on the Cycladic island of Keos.[2]

Another male preserve, also new in MG II, is a lavish version of the flat pyxis where the lid is crowned by one or more terracotta horses. Fig. 24a, with only one horse, is from the same grave as the early kantharos; in a rich burial at

FIG. 24 ATHENIAN MG II POTTERY, ANIMALS AND BIRDS
(a) *K* gr. 69, H. 10.5; (b) detail from fig. 23d; (c/e–f) details from
Paris A 514 (*GGP* pl. 4e–h); (d) detail from oinochoe London
MsC 2532 (*GGP* 26)

Anavysos (p. 80) one of the pyxides has no less than three horses. Since this class
is confined to well-furnished graves, the horses are most naturally explained as
badges of knightly status. The same may be said of the horses painted in side-
panels on the lordly krater in fig. 23d, which stood as a monument over
Kerameikos gr. 22.

These early animals, whether in three or two dimensions, show the Geometric
artist getting to grips with the rendering of natural forms, a task so rarely
attempted during the previous three centuries. To some extent he may have

been helped by chance discoveries of Mycenaean vase-painting;[3] if this is so, he was no mere copyist. The exaggerated protrusions on the horses' legs (fig. 24b), alien to Mycenaean practice, show an earnest effort to define hocks and fetlocks, based on the observation of a live animal. After this laboured start, fluency of line came quickly. Not much later, and well before the end of MG II, are the horses painted on a tall urn-pyxis in Paris (fig. 24f), drawn with grace and ease. Under the handles are a stag (fig. 24e), nearly related to the horse, but antlers and stubby tail have been substituted for mane, long tail, and fetlocks; and a row of curly-tailed but otherwise ill-defined creatures which could be pigs or lions (fig. 24c). It is typical of the time that the animals should be tucked away in inconspicuous places; but for the panels containing a single animal, early experiments on the square catchplates of fibulae (fig. 25a) might well have piloted the way. Single birds, too, make their debut in such panels; those on the shoulder of an oinochoe in London (fig. 24d), with regardant heads and fishy tails, are a favourite early type. Human beings, after the early MG I mourner (p. 61), do not seem to reappear till the closing stage of MG II, which will be treated in the next chapter.

The handmade wares of Attic MG require little comment. The fine incised fabric, seen at its most versatile in the Areopagus lady's grave, dies out in MG I; its last known appearance is in gr. Alpha at Eleusis.[4] In the same grave are two handmade aryballoi, early specimens of their kind in Attica, but based on a favourite Argive and Corinthian shape going back at least as far as 900 B.C. Further influence from that direction is implied by a fine little oinochoe in Kerameikos gr. 22 (*K* pl. 156 no. 297) whose shape and technique reflect a marked improvement in the Argive handmade fabric shortly after 800 B.C. At the same time, heavy coarse cooking-jugs continue all through the Geometric period, nearly always found in the graves of women.

The MG finds of Attica reveal a marked change in the pattern of settlement. In EG times over 90 per cent of the material came from Athens and its environs; during the MG period the cemeteries of the Attic countryside contribute an increasingly large proportion of the total corpus. Especially remarkable is the movement towards the coast. We have already observed the silver-working settlement of Thorikos, operating in the mid-ninth century. Not much later are the first graves at Palaia Kokkinia, in the Piraeus area. Many MG burials are known from Eleusis, and several from Marathon and Merenda (ancient Myrrhinous); and the earliest finds from a cemetery at Anavysos, soon after 800 B.C., indicate the presence of a flourishing settlement near by. This gradual repopulation of the coastlands, for the first time since the collapse of the Mycenaean civilization, is just what one would expect, given the ever-growing influence of the Attic MG style abroad, and the steady increase in maritime initiative which is thereby implied.

More striking is the decentralization of wealth. In contrast to the rich burials of mid-ninth-century Athens, the only outstandingly well-furnished graves of this period are two female inhumations at Eleusis on either side of 800 B.C., and two cremation burials at Anavysos, early in MG II. Both the Eleusis graves were occupied by ladies of substance, to judge from the quantity of pots, and the quality of the other offerings. The earlier one, gr. Alpha, contained thirty-five

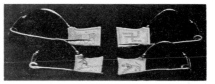

a

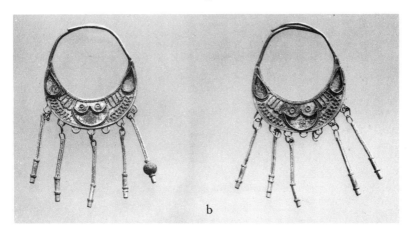

b

FIG. 25 ATHENIAN MG II GOLDWORK
(a) the Elgin fibulae: LS. 5.6 (larger pair), 4.5 (smaller pair);
(b) Eleusis, Isis, gr., earrings, W.3

pots (mainly small), a superb pair of lunate gold earrings, two finger-rings (one gold, one bronze), three square-catchplate fibulae of bronze, a necklace of gold and amber beads, an ivory hairpin, a pair of miniature clay boots, and a clay horse.

The other burial has been named the Isis grave after its most surprising find, a faience figurine of the Egyptian deity; the other offerings include three faience scarabs; two necklaces, one of faience beads, the other of faience and amber; an ivory pin; another splendid pair of lunate earrings in gold (fig. 25b); ten finger-rings in silver, bronze, and iron; two bracelets, six fibulae of bronze, and a larger fibula of silver; and about seventy small pots, including a model granary recalling the lid of the Areopagus lady's chest. The position of the grave was marked by a hydria standing above the cover slabs.

It is not difficult to believe, with the excavator,[5] that both women were the priestesses of Demeter, the goddess who presided over the local Mystery cult. He came to this conclusion partly because of the figurine of the Egyptian moon-goddess Isis, whom Herodotus (ii.59) considered to be the counterpart to Demeter. If the association with Isis really goes back as far as this, then the lunate earrings, too, might have some local relevance. At all events, even if the figurine is no more than a stray trinket acquired at random, the two graves are by far the richest ever found in the extensive Geometric cemeteries of Eleusis. Their occupants were women of high rank, who may also have earned respect as public figures – to judge from the astonishing accumulation of small pots which seem more like the last offerings of friends and admirers than the personal chattels of the ladies themselves.

The two Anavysos graves have not yet been fully published, but first reports convey the impression that they were even richer than the Eleusis burials. Gr. 51 contained two pairs of elaborate gold ornaments; lunate earrings just like the pair from Eleusis gr. Alpha, and four-spiral beads of northern character. In the other grave, no. 2, a lavishly decorated belly-handled amphora held a real treasure: a gold chain necklace with clasps in the form of snakes' heads, two gold finger-rings, part of a gold diadem with embossed animals, and four gold fibulae comparable to those from the Elgin collection (fig. 25a); also two bronze fibulae, fragments of a bronze bowl, and a faience scarab.[6]

The cemeteries of Athens, by contrast, have little to offer during this period. Another faience figurine of Egyptian character hails from a burial roughly contemporary with the Isis grave;[7] gold bands with simple zigzags or chevrons are known from four graves.[8] None of these rare luxuries comes from the Kerameikos or the Areopagus, whose burial grounds had begun to sink in the social scale. It may be that the four gold fibulae in the Elgin collection were found in Athens or its neighbourhood; but of this there can be no certainty.

Among this small but choice assembly of goldwork, the lunate earrings are worthy of special attention. Whereas the pair worn by the Areopagus lady (fig. 13e) were made to suit local taste, these are whole heartedly oriental in character (fig. 25b). The crescent form, the small cloisons for amber inlays, and the long thin pendants ending (originally) in pomegranates – all these features had for a long time been at home in the Levant. Yet no close parallels to these earrings have been found in the east, and later work of the same school admits at least one motif from the Athenian Geometric tradition (p. 126). So it has been reasonably suggested that the earrings are not imports, but rather the work of Phoenician smiths who established a school somewhere in Attica, and eventually passed on their skill to Greek pupils.[9]

The gold fibulae, on the other hand, are the finest examples of native Athenian craftsmanship. Since the experiments of Kerameikos gr. 41 the shape has pro-gressed; the bow is thicker and the square catchplate larger. At a time when fibulae were not particularly common, this seems to be the standard form of MG II; there are bronze counterparts in the Isis grave.[10] The catchplates of the Elgin fibulae (fig. 25a) carry designs on both sides, mainly figured: two swas-tikas, a ship, two grazing stags, two horses, and a lion. (In addition, birds and scorpions are reported on the Anavysos gold fibulae.) The engraving is done with a sure hand, and sometimes more fluently than contemporary work on pottery. And whereas vase-painters worked in simple silhouette until the end of the Geometric style, this engraver has already begun to embellish his figures with inner lines. The stags' bodies are zoned in a purely pictorial way recalling Mycenaean vase-painting;[11] but the horses and the lion have the thigh accurately marked as an inner line, forestalling the invention of the incised black-figure technique by Corinthian potters (p. 173) soon after 700 B.C. The lion is one of the earliest in Hellenic art; he is shown leaping into the air, shooting out his tongue, and waving his tail aloft in a typically feline fashion.

Finally, the burials themselves. Cremation is still the prevailing rite for adults, but there are also at least five adult inhumations – the first since Submycenaean times. Two of these are the richly furnished burials at Eleusis, Alpha and Isis, both laid in cists composed of rubble. The others, all in Athens, are earth-cut: Agora C 8:7, Areopagus I 18:1, and Odos Kavalotti gr. B.[12] Most, if not all, were for females. Kerameikos gr. 20, much earlier than any other inhumation there, was evidently for a small girl (the skeleton is said to measure only 1·20m.). At Eleusis a child was inhumed in a pithos closed by a low-based krater.[13]

Among the many cremations, a group of six on the Areopagus (I 18:2, 3, 5) are unusual in that the ashes are distributed over the grave, instead of being placed in a vessel. Otherwise, urn cremation is the rule. As before, the urn itself is sunk only to half its depth, leaving free space round its shoulder for placing food and drink offerings in the unburnt vessels. It was now the custom to close the urn with a skyphos, instead of a bronze bowl as in the previous two generations. Occasionally the grave is divided by a barrier into two compartments, a deep one for the urn, a shallow one for the unburnt pots;[14] this variation seems to be confined to the MG period. Five men's graves in the Kerameikos were honoured with monumental kraters, standing in the upper fill immediately above the urns; in most cases only the pedestals survive, but that from gr. 22 is nearly complete (fig. 23d). It is one of the grandest vases of its time, and preserves the earliest known horse panels at either side of the main design. Very soon afterwards, the imagery on these kraters was to become much more daring, and much more explicit.

The Argolid, the Corinthia, Boeotia

In the Argolid, the transition from EG to MG was more gradual than in Attica; once established, the local MG style is divisible into two phases according to influences continually coming from Athens. Thus, in MG I, the taut ovoid bodies of amphorae and the vertical lips of skyphoi recall their Attic contemporaries. The most individual shapes, as before, are the pyxides, which have nothing to do with Attica. The small lug-handled type continues from EG, but now usually assumes a conical foot. A globular variety with handles, which the Argolid shares with Corinth, may be provided with an inset rim (fig. 26a) or a short vertical lip. There is a passing vogue for painted aryballoi, probably introduced from Corinth (cf. fig. 26e). In general the panels of decoration have grown longer since EG, but their depth is carefully co-ordinated with the handle attachments, as in Attica. The usual motifs are meander, multiple zigzag, and cross-hatched lozenges; the small star panels on the skyphos (fig. 26b) constitute a distinctive local variant.

Argive MG II gradually parts company with the Athenian series. Foreign to Attica are the plump, rounded forms of amphorae (fig. 26d) and oinochoai. The local forms of pyxis continue on their own lines. The new type of kantharos

(e.g., fig. 23b) occasionally appears, but in the Argolid the handles are only slightly raised; on the whole the low-handled variety was preferred. Decoration is more varied and elaborate than in MG I. Dots, gear patterns, dotted lozenge chain, and false spiral are all introduced in this phase; meander hooks and hatched battlement are added to the stock of larger motifs. On closed vases, the size of panels is still limited by the handle attachments; the conjunction of neck and handle panels, level with the handles (fig. 26d), is a typically Argive arrangement. Careful scrutiny of some MG II pots will reveal the use of the multiple brush, a labour-saving tool which Argive potters began to use for rectilinear ornament around 800 B.C., closely followed by their Attic and Corinthian colleagues.[15] Finally, there are a few figured experiments: the bird-file on a lekythos-oinochoe from Tiryns (fig. 26c) is the first in Greek art, and is shortly followed by friezes of horses and stags on a kantharos from Argos (C 33). In these and other early pictures, the field is always filled with a shower of dots.

In the production of plain handmade pottery, the Argives began to set new standards of expertise around 800 B.C. Until then the coarse and heavy 'Pie Ware' had held the field; but now a fine new fabric appears, remarkable for its thin walls, its carefully levigated yellow fabric, and its smooth, shiny surface perfected by diligent paring.[16] The shapes are refined versions of 'Pie Ware' forms: small amphorae with handles on neck or shoulder, oinochoai, and shallow bowls. The new technique gradually spread to Corinth and Athens; yet even in the Argolid it did not immediately supplant the old, as one can see from a late MG II group from Mycenae[17] where a Pie Ware bowl still keeps company with several fine oinochoai.

Argive burial customs continue as before. The bodies are always inhumed, usually in cists, less often in pithoi which may be used for adults as well as for children. Either type of grave may receive two or more successive burials; and there are several cases where offerings from an earlier burial were laid out on a cist's cover when the grave received a later occupant; alternatively, the goods belonging to the first burial might be left inside, and the offerings for a second incumbent deposited on the cover.

Argive bronzeworkers still led the rest of Greece in the fashioning of long dress pins. Fig. 27a, one of four from Tiryns gr. XVI (MG I), is of a mature Geometric type which held the field throughout this period. The globe is now biconical rather than spherical; above it, and some way below it, the shank is square in section, and decorated on every side with a tremolo zigzag. Pins like this may be among the earliest dedications in the sanctuaries of the Argolid and neighbouring lands – the Argive Heraion, Athena Alea at Tegea, Aphaia on Aegina, and Hera Akraia at Perachora. In bronzework they are the counterparts

FIG. 26 ARGIVE (a–d) AND CORINTHIAN (e–h) MG POTTERY
(a) Argos gr. 176, H. 18.5; (b) Tiryns; (c) Tiryns, H. 15;
(d) Argos gr. 191, H. 28.4; (e) Clenia gr., HS. 9, 8.2; (f) Corinth,
Agora gr., Weinberg 75, H. 9; (g) Corinth, N. Cemetery gr. 18,
H. 35.5; (h) Corinth, Agora gr., Weinberg 74, H. 22.5

of the harmonious MG I style of Athenian pottery; without exaggeration they
have been said to represent 'the climax of the Greek pin'.[18]

In addition, a mid-ninth-century grave at Tiryns[19] has yielded a bronze fibula
like the Attic square-catchplate type, and there is mention of another from a
MG I grave at Berbati. There are many bronze finger-rings; three iron swords
(Argos, Makris gr. 1); an iron dagger (Tiryns gr. X); and an iron spearhead and
knife (Nauplia gr. 21).

During this period there are hints of Argive influence on lands further south.
At Tegea in Arcadia the few MG pots, as well as the pins, are Argive in style.[20]
The same applies to a MG II oinochoe from Kythera,[21] with panels on neck and
shoulder; one recalls Herodotus' statement (i.82) that Argos, before the rise of
Sparta, had once controlled Kythera and the eastern shore of the Peloponnese.
In Laconia, where most of the pottery is still in a retarded Protogeometric style,
a few pieces display Argive MG II mannerisms.[22] Perhaps this is the time when
the Spartans were beginning to break out of their early isolation, and entering
into exchanges with their northward neighbours. According to Pausanias,[23]
these exchanges were invariably warlike.

Corinth, too, produces a MG style which, in Attic terms, can be divided into
two phases. MG I is strongly influenced by Athens, and presents few local
peculiarities. The commonest shapes are oinochoai and skyphoi; alongside the
Atticizing forms, the globular oinochoe and the hemispherical skyphos survive
from the local EG. Aryballoi (fig. 26e) also continue, now more biconical than
globular. Decoration is still very restrained; the only innovations are meander
hooks – introduced here earlier than in Attica – and the row of dots, as an
ancillary. The dominant major motifs are still the meander and the multiple
zigzag, as in other Atticizing styles of this time.

At the beginning of MG II the vertical chevron enters the scene, together
with its reduplicated form, the four-limbed sigma. From their Argive colleagues
Corinthian potters soon learned to save time by drawing these motifs with the
multiple brush. Both are known in Attica, too, during this phase; but in Corinth
the chevron soon becomes the commonest of all patterns, displacing the meander
and the multiple zigzag. On very large vases, such as the pedestalled kraters
(GGP pl. 17f), meanders are still tolerated in the main panel, framed by ancillaries
in the Attic way. Otherwise, centralized compositions are deliberately avoided,
and the field is subdivided into narrow strips of chevron ornament (fig. 26h).
Typically Corinthian, too, is the placing of a narrow chevron zone below the
handle root of the oinochoe (fig. 26g). New shapes include the high-handled
kantharos, which never became popular here; more important is the low-footed
krater (fig. 26h), destined to be the standard LG form of the whole Peloponnese.
The oinochoe and the skyphos (fig. 26f) remain the commonest shapes; there are
also a few instances of the neck-handled amphora, the lekythos-oinochoe, the
aryballos, and the globular pyxis with rising handles. Every open shape displays
the usual Corinthian liking for full, hemispherical profiles; and tall ovoid oinochoai, with straight necks (fig. 26g), are characteristic of this phase.

Plain handmade ware continues from EG without much change. There are
occasional efforts to emulate the new fine-walled technique of the Argolid,[24] but
most vessels are still in the older coarse fabric. Of exceptional interest is an

amphoriskos from a MG I grave at Clenia (Cleonae), decorated like Argive 'Pie Ware'. In general, the shapes are much as before; the favourites are the hydria and the aryballos.

By the early eighth century Corinth had expanded to the size of a major Geometric city, consisting of a cluster of scattered villages. The main nucleus was in and around the site of the future Forum; but at this time two outlying areas enter the picture, both more than 1km. away from the centre. To the west, near some excellent clay beds, a small suburb grew up, with its cemetery near by; this site subsequently became the Potters' Quarter of the Archaic city. To the north, outside the later Sicyonian Gate, a prehistoric cemetery received its first burials since the Middle Bronze Age. The eleven MG II graves here (nos. 14–24), which are fairly typical of the Corinthia as a whole,[25] are all cut deep into hard ground, unlined, and covered with single blocks of sandstone. Five of them have separate compartments for the offerings, or for child burials, at the head of the grave. Above the inhumed bodies, burnt deposits contained charred animal bones – the remains of funerary banquets. For the refreshment of the deceased, a handmade hydria was sometimes left outside the grave, its mouth stopped by a skyphos.

The two best-furnished graves contained metal offerings of delicacy and distinction. The occupant of no. 16 had two rings on her fingers, of silver and electrum; and six bronze dress pins, of which two pairs conform to the standard MG type which we have met in the Argolid (e.g., fig. 27a).[26] The third pair introduces a more elaborate form (fig. 27c), considerably longer (0·50m.), and punctuated by three biconical globes, the central one being the largest; above a broad disc head, the finial consists of a long run of bead-and-reel. This baroque class of pin was to become a popular offering at sanctuaries in the later eighth century, but this is its earliest recorded context. Another pair, longer still, was among the metal objects in gr. 17, together with four shorter and more practical iron pins; also a fragmentary bronze skyphos,[27] and a bronze fibula with square catchplate and two bows side by side (fig. 27c). This, too, is the earliest recorded specimen of its kind, forestalling a Boeotian LG group by at least fifty years. Although the corpus of MG finds from Corinth is still not very large, one nevertheless gets the impression of a thriving and inventive school of bronzesmiths working there in the early eighth century.

The expansion of the Corinthian *polis* coincides with a sudden increase in Corinthian activities elsewhere. In the ninth century, exports of Corinthian pottery had been rare, and virtually confined to the immediate neighbours – Megara, Aegina, Mycenae, and Medeon across the Gulf. In MG II sporadic exports are found further afield, in Andros, Smyrna, and Knossos. A much larger quantity is conveyed down the Gulf to Delphi, Ithaca, and Vitsa in the Epirus; and for each of these places Corinth was to remain the chief source of fine painted pottery throughout the eighth century (the implications of this will be discussed in a later chapter, pp. 187–8). The same can be said of two sites nearer at hand, where the extant finds begin in *c.* 800 B.C. or shortly after: the sanctuary of Hera Akraia on the tip of the Perachora peninsula, and the cemetery of Ay. Theodoroi (ancient Crommyon) just beyond the Isthmus on the Aegean side. Strabo (380) records that Crommyon was a village in the territory of

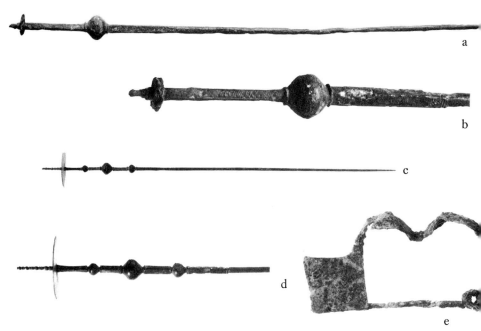

FIG. 27 PELOPONNESIAN MG PINS AND FIBULAE
(a–b) Tiryns gr. XVI, L. 25; (c–d) Corinth, N. Cemetery gr. 16,
L. 38; (e) ibid. gr. 17, L. 7.2

Corinth, but had once belonged to Megara. From the first report of the graves,
it appears that they are very similar to those of the North Cemetery at Corinth
(unlined, but with separate compartment for gifts or child burials, and covered
with single slabs); and that virtually all the pottery is Corinthian. One is thus
inclined to believe that Crommyon had already passed into Corinthian hands by
the time of these burials; but of this we cannot be certain, since the Megarians,
too, used Corinthian pottery, and nothing is known of their burial customs at
this time. In the case of Perachora, however, we are on firmer ground in thinking
that the Heraion was already owned by Corinth during the period of the earliest
finds, although its founders may well have been Megarian.[28]

Boeotia, in the MG period, is virtually unknown. Apart from two sherds from
the Kabeirion sanctuary near Thebes, all we have is about twenty-five pots from
cists at Orchomenos, and from the later burials in the Vranesi tumulus. These
are mainly in a simplified Atticizing style, without much local variation. Except
for two neck-handled amphorae, the shapes are all small: skyphoi, mugs,
lekythoi-oinochoai, small squat oinochoai, and flat pyxides (fig. 28c); also two
aryballoi, one like fig. 26e, the other handmade, both showing some connection
with Corinth.

Thessaly, Euboea, and the Cyclades

The Sub-Protogeometric style, which was shared by these three areas in the early ninth century, is now on the wane. What is new is the influence of Athenian Geometric pottery, which affects each region in different ways at different times.

In Thessaly this influence arrived late, probably not before 800 B.C. Its effect can be seen by comparing two kraters, fig. 28a and b. The first is one of the latest vases found in the tholoi of Marmariani, and shows the local rectilinear style running to seed at the end of the ninth century. Early in the eighth, contact with Athens has a refining effect on the second krater, which is from the tholos at Kapakli near Iolcos. The stem now has the ribs of the Attic pedestal, while the decoration reflects the centralized composition of Attic MG II kraters in a drastically simplified form. The meander hooks have been borrowed from the Attic stock, but the loose diagonals on each side have a Sub-Protogeometric origin (cf. p. 40 fig. 8d). This krater heads a series from the same tomb, continuing through most of the eighth century, and changing over in due course to the metopal decoration of Attic Late Geometric.

From the scanty published record it appears that inhumation was still the usual rite in Thessaly, whether in single cists as at Pherae, or in family tombs like the long-used tholos at Kapakli. A strange exception to this rule is a group of sixteen pyre cremations at Halos, covered by a tumulus; an exception all the more remarkable in that it represents a change of rite at Halos itself, following after cist inhumations in the tenth and ninth centuries. Each pyre rested on hard-baked virgin soil, making it clear that the bodies had been burnt *in situ* with the pottery and metal offerings. At the end of each ceremony the flames were extinguished by covering the pyre with large stones, heaped up into a cairn. After the final cremation, all sixteen pyres were buried under an earth tumulus about 20m. in diameter and 2m. high at the centre.

The metal offerings tell us that ten cremations were of men, and six of women. The latter were distinguished by numerous bronze fibulae, some of the Attic square-catchplate variety, the others representing a local type with a cruciform thickening on the bow (Blinkenberg Type VII4). The men were well equipped with iron weapons: eleven cut-and-thrust swords of the usual Naue II class, ten leaf-shaped spearheads, and seventeen single-edged hacking tools, perhaps for husbandry rather than war. All these objects came from the only fully excavated tumulus (A), one of ten in the neighbourhood; but more finds are reported from three other tumuli, of the same character and period.

To judge from the only datable finds, i.e., the Atticizing wheelmade pottery (mainly skyphoi, kraters, and plates), the burials extend over about two generations, in the early and mid-eighth century. Some oinochoai are still painted in a lingering Sub-Protogeometric style, but most are undecorated and almost fully glazed. Alongside these southern Geometric forms, two northern shapes are introduced – kantharoi and cutaway jugs; both are wheelmade, undecorated, and covered with glaze. Like the pyres, cairns, and tumuli, they are new to Halos at this time. The squat form of the jugs, which usually have two warts on the

shoulder, looks like a local rendering of a handmade Macedonian form. For the
burial customs, no other site offers an exact parallel; but cairns with swords are
found at Vitsa in the Epirus, cairns and tumuli at Chauchitsa in Macedonia;
while at Vergina there are tumuli with cremations – in this case in urns – and a
similar range of iron weapons. So, from this accumulation of novelties at Halos,
it appears that a further band of northerners, men and women, made their way
into the Pagasaean coastlands around 800 B.C.[29]

In Euboea, not much is known about Lefkandi during this period. After the
rich burials of the mid-ninth century, the three known cemeteries passed out of
use. Near the main settlement of Xeropolis there is mention of a destruction
deposit;[30] a homogeneous lot of pottery, datable to MG I by a few Atticizing
sherds. Perhaps the city suffered a major reverse at this time, followed by the
emigration of many of its citizens; at all events, Lefkandi seems to have become
a smaller place, since from now on the only known material is from Xeropolis
itself. The chief deposit of this period is a scrappy levelling fill, lying above the
pit of the earlier ninth century (p. 41), and preparing the ground for a Late
Geometric floor.[31] It contains about five sherds of imported Attic MG, and
about thirty local imitations, mainly MG II; yet most local pottery is still Sub-
Protogeometric, showing remarkably little development from the earlier pit fill.
The most noticeable changes are in the drinking-vessels. Cup lips now have a
single band (as fig. 20a) rather than the earlier scribble (p. 40); and the pendent-
semicircle skyphos is now made with a much shorter lip than before, quite like
fig. 28d, but still slightly overhanging the body. Large shapes continue much as
before, often with opposed diagonals round the belly, and even with concentric
semicircles on the shoulders of amphorae.

The most important event of these times is the foundation of Eretria in c. 800
B.C. The site, 10km. east of Lefkandi, has a fine harbour, and a rocky acropolis
2km. inland. Earlier finds there are limited to a Protogeometric (or Sub-Protogeometric) sherd from the sanctuary of Apollo, and a few Mycenaean pieces
from the acropolis; hardly enough to establish the existence of any older town
in situ. Soon after 800 B.C., however, the pottery begins to be plentiful; there
are some pendent-semicircle skyphoi,[32] but most of it is in an Atticizing MG II
style, skyphoi and kraters being especially common. Much of the earliest pottery
comes from the sanctuary of Apollo, where a horseshoe-shaped building had
been erected before the end of MG (p. 322 fig. 104a,H). Although nothing is
preserved above the stone foundations and the column bases of clay, the excavators have reason to believe that the walls, columns, and roof were all constructed
of bay wood, in memory of Apollo's mythical hut at Delphi.[33] The epithet
Daphnephoros, under which the god was worshipped at Eretria, would be
thereby explained.

Another source of early pottery is the West Cemetery, outside the city and by
the shore. Here the 'Geometric'[34] burials consisted of fifty child inhumations in
pithoi or amphorae, and eight adult cremations. The cremation graves were dug
into soft sand and unlined; pyres were lit in situ, offerings of pottery were
smashed on the flames, and the ashes and debris fell into the open grave. Although the grave groups were not kept separate, the only MG II pots illustrated
(Kourouniotis' figs. 2–4) are said to come from cremations.

FIG. 28 THESSALIAN, BOEOTIAN, AND CYCLADIC MG POTTERY
(a) Marmariani 135, H. 36.5; (b) Kapakli, H. 36; (c) Vranesi, H. 6.4; (d)
(d) Rheneia, H. 7.5; (e) London 55.12–20.1, Melian, H. 12;
(f) *Délos* XV, Aa 55, H. 32

It is natural to enquire whence the first Eretrians came. Strabo (403) preserves the memory of an Old Eretria, the predecessor of the historical city and distinct from it; but his directions for finding this place (60 stades from Delphinion in northern Attica) are too vague to be useful. A good case has recently been made for Lefkandi,[35] whose ancient name is otherwise unknown, and whose population declined shortly before the foundation of Eretria. The custom of open-trench cremation is common to ninth-century Lefkandi and early eighth-century Eretria, and there is also a plausible continuity in the pottery sequence. Further-more, Lefkandi lies at the eastern edge of the fertile Lelantine plain, and its position might explain why later Eretrians went to war with Chalcis (pp. 200–1) for the possession of this plain at a time when the older city would still have been held and defended by their kinsmen. One reason for the move might have been the attraction of Eretria's fine harbour, an amenity not possessed by Lefkandi; or perhaps the MG I destruction deposit at Lefkandi may betoken a serious reverse in war, causing the emigration of those inhabitants whose homes did not enjoy the security of the Xeropolis stronghold. But these matters must remain conjectural until more evidence is recovered from both cities. We have yet to learn how Lefkandiots were buried in the eighth century; as for Eretria, so vast is the area of the ancient city that we cannot yet dismiss the possibility of a sub-stantial earlier settlement, especially in the eastern quarter.[36] The only certain fact is that Eretria, from now on, becomes our chief source of information about Geometric Euboea.

In the Cycladic archipelago the influence of Attic Geometric first appears during the euphoria of the mid-ninth century, and then remains strong through-out the MG period. The islands of the northern chain – Andros, Tenos, and Rheneia – had previously favoured the Sub-Protogeometric style, following Euboea; but with the advent of Attic exports and fashions, nothing was left of the older style except for two shapes. The pendent-semicircle skyphos (fig. 28d) assumes a shallow, low-lipped form as at Lefkandi; but the lip, instead of over-hanging the rim like the Euboean skyphoi, is here swept back from the body in a concave curve. The second survivor is the shoulder-handled amphoriskos, which accepts Atticizing panel decoration in the course of MG (fig. 28e).

The other shapes are all of Attic origin: the neck- and belly-handled am-phorae, the oinochoe, the lekythos-oinochoe, the flat pyxis, the skyphos, the cup, the mug, the krater, and – in line with Attic MG II – the kantharos. The orna-ment, too, keeps in step with Athens; thus meanders and multiple zigzags predominate in MG I, and then meander hooks and vertical chevrons are intro-duced c. 800 B.C., both playing an important part in the MG II phase. Some influence, by that time, was also coming from the north-east Peloponnese; thus the Argive-Corinthian type of pyxis, globular with rising handles and conical lid (cf. fig. 26a), is known on Naxos and Kimolos; many islands make large cups with enclosed panels between warts, best paralleled in the Argolid; two oinochoai from Melos are decorated according to the Argive scheme, with panels on neck and shoulder (GGP 169 n. 3); and the slim ovoid body of several oinochoai from Delos (fig. 28f) recalls Corinth, not Athens. There is also a local preference for very large skyphoi. Nevertheless, Athens remained the chief source of new ideas all through MG, and even into the first stage of Late Geometric. The overriding influence from the Attic sequence must partly explain why Cycladic MG pottery, though found in at least ten different islands, is so homogeneous in style.

On the other hand, there is great variety in the burial customs. In the northern chain, the practice of single inhumations in cists had been known during the EG period at Kardiani on Tenos, and continues at least into MG I at Zagora on Andros, and probably on Rheneia too.[37] Five more MG inhumation graves, cut into soft rock, are reported from Naxia, the main town of Naxos; one contained fifteen pots, and a remarkable collection of thirty clay birds spreading their wings;[38] from another grave came a pair of miniature clay boots,[39] decorated with multiple zigzags like the contemporary pair from gr. Alpha at Eleusis.

In the southern islands, meanwhile, cremation had become the rule; what is more, multiple cremation wherever the evidence is preserved. On the small island of Kimolos, a cemetery by the sea contains twenty-two rectangular rock-cut graves, each said to house several cremations; the earliest pots there go back to *c.* 775–750, but most are Late Geometric. On Melos nearby, the much-plundered cemetery of Trypiti offers very little information about burials; the only systematic excavators, in 1895,[40] report hollows in the rock, traces of burning, some bones, and broken pottery of the 'Dipylon' period. These cremations surely go back into MG times, when the Melians made many large belly-handled amphorae, suitable for use as urns; some of them were exported to Thera, where their function as urns is beyond any doubt, and where they housed some of the earliest burials. The Theran custom was to place successive cremations in built chambers, laid out on terraces rising up the hill slope. The two cemeteries of ancient Thera are among the most impressive in Geometric Greece, and will be more fully treated in a later chapter; but here we should note that the oldest chambers, e.g., pp. 217–18, fig. 71, must have been constructed during this period, and offer the earliest evidence of any settled life after the great volcanic eruption in *c.* 1500 B.C. Unlike their predecessors in the Late Bronze Age, the Dorian inhabitants had the good sense to found their *polis* on the high limestone spur of Mesavouno, in the only non-volcanic part of the island. Some of the larger tombs, like the Geometric chamber tombs of Knossos, were to accumulate cremations for well over a century.

Quite different in character are the pyre cremations found recently at two remote places in the eastern part of the archipelago. On the islet of Donousa, east of Naxos, are the traces of a much-ruined apsidal house, situated above a cliff, and approached through a small square court; its purpose we do not yet know. Near by, along the top of the same cliff, are two large pyre deposits, one of which is described as 7m. long, and 60–80cm. thick. It contained piles of broken pottery, oyster shells, and animal bones, and above it is a layer of earth and a heap of stones. If the bodies, too, were burnt here (the report does not make this clear), this vast deposit would represent several cremations; in that case we might be dealing with a collapsed tumulus of roughly rectangular shape, crowned by a cairn, and retained by a rock face on the landward side, and two walls running at right angles to it and the cliff face. Much of the pyre pottery consists of large closed vases – amphorae, oinochoai, hydriai – decorated in a retarded Protogeometric style with East Greek affinities;[41] but the first pyre also contains Atticizing pottery of *c.* 800 B.C., including a small low-based krater. A similar mixture of styles is apparent among the pottery from the apsidal house. The latest report also mentions a fortification wall belonging to this site, twice rebuilt within the Geometric period; near by are traces of three houses, each with two rooms.

The other pyre site, at Tsikalario in central Naxos, is a complex of at least twenty tumuli, adjoining a small settlement which may be contemporary; both are situated on a bleak, rocky plateau, but commanding the richest inland valley on the island. A tall 'menhir', wedged in a pile of stones, stands at the entrance to the cemetery. Each tumulus is up to 10m. across; the covering layers of sand and stones were held in position by a carefully laid stone kerb, often approximating to a perfect circle. Most tumuli have one or more cremation pyres inside, usually on flat ground, but sometimes (e.g., no. 14) placed in a rectangular grave with cover slabs. The offerings were distributed between the cremations themselves, other deposits inside, and further burnt deposits outside, some of which contain animal bones. A rectangular area, no. 11, was mainly given over to offerings; the only burial here, just outside its edge, was a small cist grave for a child, with traces of a pyre and burnt bones. A puzzling feature is the frequency of large closed vessels lying outside the tumuli, and apparently containing nothing but sand; perhaps they had once held inhumed infants, whose bones might well have decomposed in these conditions.

Apart from two burials added in the sixth century (one cist, one urn cremation) the cemetery was used only during the MG period. Nearly all the painted pots are Atticizing; one of the earliest is a flat pyxis of c. 820 B.C.[42] like those from Kerameikos gr. 20 (fig. 22b), and the series continues down to c. 750 B.C. Some eastern contacts are implied by a two-handled ridge-necked flask of Cypriot type. Among the plentiful coarse ware, the most striking shape is a pithos with incised ornament, standing on tripod legs, also found in the inhumation graves at Naxia. Other finds include three clay figurines of women and three of birds, fifty-six clay loomweights, two iron swords and a dagger, a bronze fibula of East Greek type, part of a bronze spectacle fibula, a silver ring, and three gold bracelets of twisted wire.

It is not easy to accept these tumuli as a purely local phenomenon. They represent a departure from the usual practice at Naxia, where single inhumation graves go back to the eleventh century;[43] and several features suggest influence from the north Aegean. The massing of tumuli, each with its carefully laid circular kerb, is reminiscent of Vergina, as is the occasional use of two pithoi for a burial, laid mouth to mouth. In addition to the spectacle fibula, a kantharos with knobs on its high handles also has a northern look,[44] although its clay is local. It is interesting that Naxian tradition preserves a memory of intruders from Thrace, even though they are placed in a remote, legendary context.[45] Another comparable tumulus with cremations has been found at Colophon (p. 97), a city with which Naxos had other legendary connections.[46]

The Levant

In the Near East there was now a marked change in the balance of power, which proved to be beneficial to Greek commerce. The mercantile cities of the Phoenician homeland had been badly battered by the Assyrian ravages of 853–844 B.C. Thereafter the Assyrian king, Shalmaneser III, became more and more distracted by the rise of Urartu, a warlike state threatening his northern frontier. After his death in 825 B.C. Assyria suffered from internal dissensions as well as from Urartian encroachment, and for the time being ceased to harass the Levant. There the initiative was quickly seized by the Aramaean princes of the Syrian hinterland, at the expense of the sorely buffeted Phoenicians. In the south, the pro-Phoenician Omrid dynasty of Israel was overthrown by revolution in 841 B.C.; the new ruler, Jehu, became little more than a puppet of Hazael, the Aramaean king of Damascus. Further to the north, the strong Aramaean city of Hama extended its sway to the sea, and within its territory an emporium grew up at Tell Sukas on the ruins of a Phoenician town destroyed by Shalmaneser III. Further north still, another important Aramaean state had its nucleus in the inland plain of Amuq or Unqi; its only possible outlet to the coast lay along the valley of the river Orontes, which flows through a mountainous defile before reaching the sea at Al Mina.

It was here that a new trading station was founded, apparently on virgin soil, some time around 825 B.C. This is the date suggested by the earliest pottery, which indicates the origin of the first settlers. A strong Phoenician element is implied by the presence of Red Slip, Black-on-Red, and Bichrome Burnished wares. Other fabrics are typical of Cyprus, Syria, and perhaps Cilicia. There is also a handful of Greek sherds, whose frequency increases rapidly after 750 B.C.; eventually, by the seventh century, most of the pottery is from Greece. It seems, then, that there was a gradual infiltration of merchants from the Aegean; indeed, a few may have resided at Al Mina from the beginning, since the earliest datable sherds are of MG I character.[47] One might perhaps wonder why any Greeks at all were allowed by their Phoenician rivals to settle there; but we have seen that the real masters of the coast were now the Aramaean princes of the interior, who were not friendly to Phoenician interests. At all events, during the first hundred years of the emporium, Greeks can never have formed more than a small minority of the population. In the MG period (Levels X and IX, c. 825–750 B.C.) the architecture was limited to small huts on pebble foundations, laid on the natural sand; later, in Level VIII, a rambling complex of warehouses grew up, more Phoenician than Greek in character.[48]

Of the earliest Greek sherds, about one-third are Atticizing MG, the rest being from pendent-semicircle skyphoi. The two styles are represented in about the same proportions among the exports of this period to other places in the Near East (fig. 29). Taken as a whole, these vessels are mainly from the Cyclades, though probably from several different islands. A large meander skyphos from Al Mina has the deep red clay and golden mica characteristic of Naxos, an island known to have Levantine contacts at this time (p. 92). Of the pendent-semicircle skyphoi, the piece from Tell Abu Hawam looks earlier than the foundation of Al Mina, and is easily matched at Lefkandi (p. 64); but all the others are of the later, low-lipped variety, the lips being swept back in the North Cycladic manner (cf. fig. 28d). Of the other Atticizing pottery, the MG II kraters from Salamis, Amathous, and Hama are of Attic fabric, and so are the twenty skyphoi accompanying the Salamis krater; a skyphos from Amathous

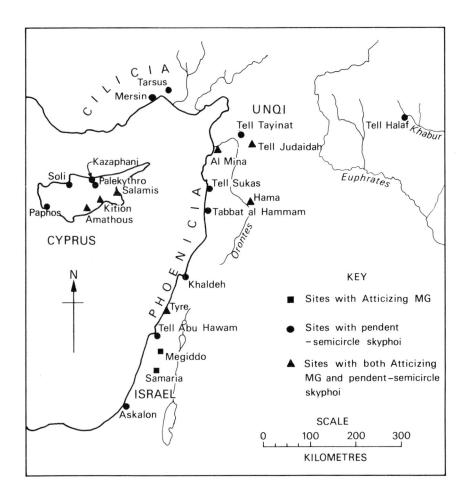

FIG. 29 GREEK MIDDLE GEOMETRIC EXPORTS TO THE NEAR EAST

looks Naxian, and the remaining sherds from Al Mina, Samaria, and Megiddo[49] could as well be Cycladic imitations as Attic originals. In this period, then, Cycladic traders were at first taking the lead, followed by a burst of Attic activity in the early eighth century. From Euboea, after the early exports to Tell Abu Hawam, there is nothing distinctive until *c.* 750 B.C.

Since most of these exports are drinking-vessels (and all are open shapes), it has been argued that they are not articles of commerce, but rather the personal chattels of Greeks living in the Near East;[50] the kind of object which later Greeks, after the return of literacy, like to inscribe with their own name (e.g.,

p. 299, fig. 95b). This may well hold good for the occasional skyphos found at other coastal emporia, e.g., Tell Sukas and Tabbat al Hammam. Others, however, have turned up in the native cremation cemetery at Hama, and there is a large consignment in a Cypriot prince's tomb at Salamis, of which the twenty Attic skyphoi might have been made to order by the same potter on the same day. Perhaps, then, the superior quality of Greek drinking ware was already appreciated in these parts, in comparison with the soft and powdery fabric of many Cypriot and Levantine cups. Even so, pottery could have formed only a small proportion of the commodities offered by Aegean visitors and residents, which must have consisted largely of perishable goods. Yet the distribution map, fig. 29, at least tells us the geographical extent of Greek trade, which was now considerably wider in the Near East than in Late Geometric times. Al Mina, so it seems, supplied not only the Aramaeans of Unqi, but, far inland, the Neo-Hittite city of Guzana, the modern Tell-Halaf.[51] In Cilicia, the exports to Tarsus and Mersin might well have radiated from an early Greek colony at Soloi, whose foundation, though remembered in later tradition,[52] we cannot yet date; the site is well known from its Roman remains, but the deeper levels have not yet been explored.

Eastern Greece

We have seen how the Dodecanesian style, from the mid-ninth century, took over a Phoenician unguent shape as one of its leading forms. A Rhodian specimen of c. 800 B.C. (fig. 30b) shows how this ridge-necked flask was adapted to local taste. In the old Dodecanesian way, the ornament is still confined to shoulder and neck; but rectilinear motifs have been borrowed from mainland Geometric and arranged in narrow, cramped zones. A happier alternative, of local inspiration, is to occupy the whole shoulder with a row of large triangles, each filled with a net of hatched lozenges.[53] A contemporary Coan skyphos (fig. 30a), in spite of its battlement, still has a Protogeometric shape, quite unaffected by western Aegean fashion. But in the early eighth century, perhaps not before the second quarter, Rhodes (yet not Cos) undergoes a brief spell of Attic influence, probably via the Cyclades; this is seen especially in a pedestalled krater from Camirus, and a set of pots from Exochi Grave V including oinochoai (fig. 30c), kantharoi, and a skyphos.

In Ionia, some Atticizing habits came to Miletus in the mid-ninth century, without entirely abolishing a lingering Protogeometric tradition. The fullest Ionian sequence is now that of Samos, which never loses touch with Athenian MG. Skyphoi and pedestalled kraters are plentiful among the early votives at the Heraion. On the kraters, the compositions are looser than in Attic; sets of circles often serve as a bulky ancillary motif (fig. 30d), and the central panel is sometimes divided between two parallel meanders.

For the burial practices of this period, the published evidence is not plentiful. Rhodes seems to have persevered with cremation for adults, and pithos inhumations for children. Fig. 30b, from Camirus gr. 80, was evidently smashed on a pyre, but the absence of any urn implies that the ashes were distributed over the grave. Very unusual are two small chamber tombs, Camirus nos. 83 and 82,

FIG. 30 EAST GREEK MG POTTERY
(a) Cos, Seraglio gr. 1, *GGP* pl. 59d, H. 7.8; (b) Camirus gr. 80,
H. 25; (c) Exochi gr. V, H. 43; (d) *Samos* V no. 22, H. 27.5

belonging to the early and mid-eighth century respectively; one wonders whether
the idea came from contemporary Crete, or from a chance discovery of a Mycenaean tomb in the neighbourhood. No bones were observed in either tomb. The
offerings in no. 82, unusually rich for their time, included two massive gold
diadems decorated with hatched meander and pricked triangles, an iron spearhead, three iron knives, and seven pots (p. 247, fig. 78a). The cemeteries of

Cos, as before, continue with inhumations in cist and earth-cut graves, and pithoi.

Across the water from the Dodecanese, several sites on the Asiatic coast are suggestive of mixed communities, Greeks living among Carians. In funerary architecture, the Carian element is usually represented by tumuli of corbelled stone, enclosing square chambers. One of these, tomb C at Asarlik (ancient Termera), contained two cremation urns, one being a neck-handled amphora of Atticizing MG II type; and also the fragments of clay sarcophagi – a Carian notion – stamped with elaborate patterns recalling East Greek Geometric of the eighth century. The same tomb included three offerings of gold: a disc-pendant with five pricked triangles, like those on the Rhodian diadems mentioned above; a short gold band with zigzag ornament; and a ring of twisted wire.

Fifty burials have been recently excavated at Iasos, reported as Protogeometric, but also containing some pottery of MG II–LG character.[54] Some are in cists, always inhumations, and mostly walled with single slabs of schist; others are in pithoi, both inhumations and cremations. So far, there is nothing obviously un-Greek about the burials; the commonest bronze objects are heavy bracelets with many spirals, and fibulae with three or more globes on the bow – a type which we shall meet again in the burials of Colophon and Crete.

The old Ionic city of Melia, adjoining the later Panionion sanctuary, also had a considerable Carian substratum. Most burials here were in simple rock clefts containing bones, fragments of pithoi suitable for cremation urns, and other sherds from Protogeometric to c. 700 B.C. Some clefts were lined with clay slabs, recalling the Carian coffins of Asarlik. Elsewhere, an oval structure resembling a Carian tumulus yielded bones and sherds, of which the earliest is an amphora neck with a zone of dogtooth, perhaps MG. According to Vitruvius (iv. 1), Melia was destroyed by the other Ionic cities owing to the arrogance of its inhabitants, and an inscription from Priene[55] places the destruction some time before the Cimmerian raids of the mid-seventh century. It is likely that all the burials precede that event.

Further north, tumuli with cremations have been reported from Colophon, of 'Geometric' but otherwise unspecified date. In the smaller tumuli, which were ringed with a stone kerb (cf. Vergina, and Tsikalario on Naxos), the burnt bones had been left on the pyres; but one large tumulus housed urn cremations. Small finds included bronze fibulae with three globes on the bow, a type also represented at Iasos, Knossos, and Vrokastro in east Crete (p. 102). Unfortunately no further details are available, since the records and the material perished in the Graeco-Turkish war of 1922–23.

Finally, mention must be made of the most impressive building so far known from this period. The first temple at the Samian Heraion (p. 327 fig. 105a) is dated to the beginning of the eighth century by a deposit of MG pottery (e.g., fig. 30d) found underneath. Its original form was a true and simple Hekatompedon, a hundred Samian feet (32·86m.) long, but only twenty (6·50m.) wide. The pitched roof rested on wooden columns, three across the front in antis, and a row of twelve down the middle of the long hall; these would have partly obscured the cult statue, whose base was placed slightly off centre at the back. Besides pottery, the votives of this time consisted mainly of clay animals made on

FIG. 31 CRETAN POTTERY: EARLY (a–b) AND MATURE (c–e) GEOMETRIC
(a, b) Teke, Platon's tomb, HS. 62, 70; (c) *Fortetsa* 530, H. 42;
(d) *Fortetsa* 611, H. 14; (e) Fortetsa, *BSA* 56 pl. 8, 2, H. 58.6

the wheel, an old technique which had survived from the end of the Bronze Age throughout the intervening dark centuries.

Crete

Cretan pottery, during this period, has a more eventful development than any other regional school. At Knossos the wild Protogeometric B style continues until shortly before 800 B.C., when there is another sudden change. The three leading shapes, necked pithos, straight-sided pithos, and bell-krater, are now succeeded by forms of non-Cretan origin. The new neckless ovoid pithos (fig. 31a) has a plump ovoid body, and a rim inset for a conical lid; with very little variation this was to remain the normal cremation urn for Knossos and central Crete for the next two centuries. Although the shape is rare in Attic, one of the earliest examples in the Fortetsa cemetery (no. 454) is an Athenian import, and may have introduced the form to the Knossians. The other major innovation, the pedestalled krater (fig. 31b), is certainly an Attic notion. Attic motifs – meander and multiple zigzag – now make their first appearance in Crete, beside curvilinear patterns surviving from Protogeometric B; here is the earliest intimation of any true Cretan Geometric style, reserved at first for grandiose funerary vases. This 'Early Geometric' phase was of brief duration; the rich mixture of ornament was too heady to last, and soon after 800 B.C. the Attic element gained the upper hand. The result was a more settled style, 'Mature Geometric', which reigned at Knossos until the mid-century. The new pithos, now equipped with four handles, is adorned in an exuberant MG II manner (fig. 31c). On an Atticizing neck-handled amphora the painter has tried his hand at a horse panel (fig. 31e); but the legs and wavy tail suggest that he was more at home in drawing bulls, like his Minoan ancestors. Pedestalled kraters, in their turn, are eventually supplanted by the low-footed type, probably introduced from Corinth, and common in domestic deposits. The other new shapes, imitated from foreign models, include the globular aryballos from Corinth, and the ridge-necked flask from the Cypro-Phoenician area. A MG cup (fig. 31d) reveals a typically Knossian compromise: a Cretan arcade pattern is enclosed in an Attic panel, painted on an Attic Geometric body shape resting on a Protogeometric conical foot. The most usual drinking-vessel is a large glazed cup with low lip and flat base.[56]

The Knossians, as before, still practised urn cremation in family tombs; yet around 850 B.C. the tombs themselves show an almost total break in continuity. In the Fortetsa groups eight old chamber tombs received no more burials after that date (p. 48), five new ones were dug in the later ninth century,[57] and only in two cases does the series of cremations span the dividing line.[58] In the northern fringes, the Ay. Ioannis cemetery also passed out of use soon after 850 B.C., while even remoter tombs at Atsalenio and Mastamba, in the suburbs of modern Herakleion, receive their first burials in Protogeometric B: remarkable evidence for the expansion of the Knossian *polis*. Two more cemeteries are much in use at this time; one is a line of chamber tombs, probably re-used Minoan, along the Kephala bank east of the Kairatos river (first burials, *c.* 900 B.C.); the other is at Teke, 1½km. north of central Knossos. One chamber tomb here produced the fine 'Early Geometric' vases, fig. 31a,b; another, a re-used Minoan tholos, yielded a surprisingly rich collection of jewellery, the most important Cretan find of this period.

From a recent study of the Teke tholos[59] it is clear that most of this treasure was buried with the first incumbent, in the late ninth century. His finery had been stored in two plain pots, found undisturbed in two cavities below the floor, to the left and right of the doorway, and just inside the chamber. For an indigenous Knossian, such ornaments would have been placed inside his urn; the idea of burying them separately, in a foundation deposit to sanctify the tomb, is as oriental as the character of the jewellery. Furthermore, the inclusion of gold and silver dumps, unworked, suggests that the owner was himself an oriental master-jeweller who came to teach and practise his craft at Knossos; at his funeral, his stock-in-trade was buried with him. Out of a total of thirty-four ornaments, three of the finest (fig. 32) display his skill to the full, and invite comparison with the equally oriental finery of Eleusis and Anavysos. Like the Eleusis earrings, the pendant no. 1 combines lunate forms, strip cloisons for inlays, and patterns in granulation and filigree; but here everything is on a more sumptuous scale, and the inlay materials – amber for the discs and rock crystal for the huge central crescent – hint more clearly at the sun-and-moon imagery of the original oriental conception. The whole thing is suspended on a magnificent gold chain ending in granulated snakes'-heads, which recall the description of the chain from Anavysos; one such finial, surely from this craftsman's hand, found its way to Ithaca.[60] An even more elaborate pendant, no. 2, has a central cable cross, a bird perched in each quarter, the whole enclosed in a cable crescent which ends in two human heads wearing flat *polos* caps, and everything defined with rows of granulated dots. The cables and headgear recall Protogeometric B vase-painting (fig. 21b), and similar longnecked birds appear later in the Knossian potter's repertoire; like the heads, they may be a concession to local taste. But the theme and style of the repeated scene on the diadem, no. 3, are wholly oriental; two heroes, perhaps Gilgamesh and Enkidu, stand back to back, each slaying a lioness.

In the second half of the ninth century, then, Knossian art was enlivened by a guild of immigrant oriental goldsmiths, who reintroduced the techniques of granulation, filigree, and inlay,[61] together with a stock of curvilinear motifs which helped to start off the Protogeometric B style in pottery. After 800 B.C. the potters soon went over to the sort of Geometric ornament which was then fashionable in most other Hellenic centres, but the metalwork was not hellenized so quickly. Fortetsa 578, a gold-leaf ornament, found inside the pithos fig. 31c, shows a pair of sparring lions, adapted from those on the Teke diadem, but now framed with Geometric zigzags and chevrons instead of the oriental running spiral. Contemporary with it are two bronze reliefs, both from the same Knossian workshop. On the quiver Fortetsa 1569 rows of similar sphinxes alternate with heraldic compositions based on the Teke diadem. The second relief, on the belt Fortetsa 1568, shows a symmetrical figured scene: in the centre, a helmeted god stands in a temple, flanked by two goddesses wearing tall *poloi*; on either side, the temple is defended by three archers against three attacking war-chariots. These works are in a semi-hellenized style, which copies oriental formulae fairly closely; but the local strain shows in the triad of deities, perhaps intended as Apollo, Artemis,

FIG. 32 CRETAN JEWELLERY FROM THE TEKE THOLOS TOMB
(a) w. 6.8; (b) w. 5.5; (c) L. 28

and Leto (cf. p. 280); and also in the uneasy compromise, in the quiver scene, between a Master of Animals flanked by two lions, and a warrior fighting a single lion. Symmetry, it seems, has been imposed at the expense of meaning.

Before we leave Knossos, some of the more mundane finds at Fortetsa deserve notice. A short bronze pin, no. 378 (Protogeometric B) introduces a typically Cretan form, with two or three ridges above and below a tall double cone; we see a more ornate variation on this type in two silver pairs from the Teke tholos (nos. 4, 21), each crowned by a gold drum-shaped head on which a bird is perched. Another novelty of Protogeometric B is a fibula with three globes on the bow,[62] found also at Vrokastro, and in the tumuli of Colophon in Asia Minor (p. 97). In an early eighth-century context, the northern spectacle fibula (Fortetsa 568) makes its earliest known appearance south of northern Thessaly. There are plenty of iron swords and spearheads; the long slender forms of the latter are characteristically Cretan. Finally, one should not forget a pleasant set of small terracotta toys for a child in Fortetsa tomb X: a boat with helmsman, a basket, and two trees on which birds have settled.

Elsewhere in Crete, urn cremation had become the rule all over the centre of the island; and there is also a report of it in the far west at Kavousi Kisamou, whence the pots bear very little resemblance to the Knossian style. Small tholoi are a rare alternative to the usual chamber tombs; one at Rhotasi in the Mesara plain (ancient Rhytion) was built in the Dark Ages, and amassed about forty cremations (c. 250 pots) of c. 900–650 B.C. It is only in the extreme east that inhumation is anywhere practised as a matter of course; a typical site there is Piskokephalo near Siteia, where ten inhumations were found in a natural cave, together with a pile of eighty pots, mainly of this period.

At Vrokastro both rites had hitherto been practised concurrently in chamber tombs, and inhumations have been found in a cave;[63] but during this period cremation is the rule for adults (and pithos inhumation for children), while the chamber tomb is supplanted by the 'bone enclosure', an irregular cluster of roughly built rooms open to the sky. The sequence of these burials shows how the local potters kept pace with Knossian Protogeometric B (enclosure 6, room 2) and 'Early Geometric' (enclosure 12, room 1), but thereafter lost touch with central Crete; any new inspiration from outside came direct from Attica, or via the Cyclades. The fibulae from the enclosures are extremely varied; alongside old-fashioned types with plain arched bow we see the new version with three globes (already noted at Knossos), a small iron specimen of the square-catchplate type, and an insular variety with tall narrow catchplate;[64] unfortunately the more developed fibulae do not occur in datable contexts. Near the bone enclosures a rectangular room served as a shrine; it contained a clay offering table adorned with a large rosette (cf. fig. 31a), fragments of human and animal figurines, and an Atticizing MG II pedestalled krater.

Conclusions

One of the clearest developments of this long period is the expansion of influence from Athenian Geometric pottery. In the EG phase it was felt only in the Argolid, the Corinthia, and Boeotia; all these regions continue to make Atticizing pottery throughout the MG period. During the brilliant interlude of the mid-ninth century the Attic style spreads to the Cyclades, and across the Aegean to Samos and Miletus, but it failed to oust the Sub-Protogeometric of Lefkandi. Around 800 B.C. Attic fashions arrive in central Crete and, rather belatedly, in Euboea and Thessaly; and eventually in Rhodes around 780 B.C., by which time some aspects of the MG II style had been accepted as a *koinē* by almost every major centre in the Aegean.[65] The Athenians themselves must be given much of the credit for propagating their style, especially in the mid-ninth century when their commerce was extremely lively; the gradual repopulation of the Attic coast is further evidence of their maritime vigour. Later on, workshops in the outlying regions could well have acquired some of their Atticizing habits at second hand, Thessalian potters from Euboea, for example, and Rhodian potters from the Cyclades; at Knossos, however, direct relations with Athens are implied by an abundance of Attic MG II imports, including a neckless cremation pithos which might have been made to order. But without making too definite pronouncements about local trade patterns, one gets the impression of a steady improvement in Aegean sea communications. And during the period of the MG II *koinē* a similar improvement is seen in the Greek lands outside the Aegean, which begin to be lured out of their former isolation; thus the Argives establish a land route through Arcadia to Laconia, while Corinthian shipping opens up the sea route to Ithaca and the Epirus. All these conclusions are based on pottery, but the occasional export of metal objects tells the same story; a northern spectacle fibula found in a Knossian tomb, for example, and the Cretan gold finial which found its way to Ithaca.

These exchanges may have had the effect of consolidating the unity of the Greek world; in communication with non-Greeks, however, there is not much sign of any corresponding progress. Here the most striking achievement is that of the Euboeans, who were making their first moves towards the west coast of Italy soon after 800 B.C. (p. 223 ff.); yet, nearer home, they seem to have lost interest in Macedonia.[66] And, in spite of the foundation of Al Mina, there is a curious stagnation in dealings with the Levant. Considerably fewer Levantine imports come to Greece than in the mid-ninth century, and the overt symptoms of wealth in this period are largely confined to four Attic graves, and one tholos tomb at Knossos. This recession may be partly due to reverses suffered by the most active trading powers. The merchants of Phoenicia were no doubt hampered by Assyrian depredations, followed by the hostility of the Aramaean states – although their colonial kinsmen at Kition would hardly have been affected. In Euboea there are hints of internal discord in the MG I destruction at Lefkandi, followed by the diminution of the settlement and the foundation of Eretria; and across the water, the migration of well-armed northerners to Halos may not have been propitious for Euboean trade with Thessaly. At all events, the few Greek sherds of this period from Al Mina seem to be Cycladic rather than Euboean, as are most of the other exports to the Near East. Attic pottery does not reappear there until well into MG II, and it is then that Levantine trinkets begin to reappear in Greece, probably conveyed as before in Phoenician boats. The impression that very few Greeks settled at Al Mina before 750 B.C. is confirmed by complete silence about the place in Greek tradition, which usually records the name of an *oikistes*, or at least the home of the founders, for any overseas settlement that could be claimed as a colony.[67]

More fruitful, at least for the future of Greek art, were the contacts established by immigrant oriental goldsmiths in Attica and Crete. In both places, the lessons they taught were mainly technical; but the Teke jeweller has a special importance in that he gave his Cretan hosts an early glimpse of Near Eastern narrative art (fig. 32c). The scenes on the Fortetsa belt and quiver are probably work of his local pupils, and are among the first figured compositions attempted by Greeks; but they do not show any of the later Greek genius for remoulding and re-creating oriental ideas to form an authentically Hellenic style.

In general, the period shows a certain stagnation in its art as well as in commerce. In the Near East, it saw no notable artistic developments, either in monumental or in small-scale work. In the Aegean, the stagnation is illustrated by the slow and repetitive course of the Attic MG style, which had already attained a limited perfection at its outset, and thereafter relied on the manipulation of infallible linear formulae. Towards the end, the only real vitality lies in the occasional experiments with small figured panels, inspired perhaps by similar work on the square plates of fibulae.

But soon after 770 B.C. there was to be a sudden quickening of tempo. In Athenian figured drawing, we pass rapidly from the tentative little panels to vast scenes of human activity, painted on monumental kraters and amphorae. Other Aegean cities, meanwhile, quickly break away from the Atticizing *koinē*, not this time through failure of communication, but through an increasingly self-conscious pride in their own way of doing things. As the divergences of style become wider than ever before, so the evidence multiplies for all aspects of life. In the next period, then, we can no longer deal with the whole Greek world in a single chapter; each region must be taken in turn, in an attempt to follow its history through the remainder of the Geometric age.

NOTES

1 *Agora* VIII 51.
2 Keos K4365: meander flanked by quatrefoils. I thank Prof. J. L. Caskey for allowing me to mention this piece.
3 J. L. Benson, *Horse, Bird and Man* 37 ff.
4 *EA* 1898, pl. 2.14–15.
5 Skias, *EA* 1898, 109–10.
6 It looks as if this grave (*AD* 21 (1966), B pl. 94a,b) may have held two cremations. At one end is the belly-handled urn-amphora containing the gold, and suggesting a female cremation; at the other, the shapes visible in the photograph (neck-handled urn-amphora, high-handled kantharos, pyxis with three terracotta horses) are all usually reserved for men.
7 *AD* 20 (1965), B 78 pl. 46, Odos Kavalotti.
8 Odos Kriezi nos. 2, 14, 40; Kynosarges, *GGP* 21.
9 R. A. Higgins, *BSA* 64 (1969), 145–6.
10 Blinkenberg 169 fig. 199.
11 cf. Furumark, *The Mycenaean Pottery* 248 fig. 5.3.
12 *AD* 20 (1965), B 78.
13 *PAE* 1954, 58 ff.
14 Kerameikos grs. 22, 30; Eleusis grs. Gamma 16, Theta 52.
15 Courbin, *CGA* 84 ff. The multiple brush was also used on a few earlier Thessalian pots, e.g. *PGP* pl. 22, 48–9.
16 Courbin, *CGA* 70 ff.
17 *BSA* 49 (1954), 261–2 pl. 46.

18 Jacobsthal, *Greek Pins* 5.
19 *AAA* 7 (1974), 24 figs. 18, 19.
20 *GGP* 352 n. 1.
21 *Kythera* Q 4 pl. 86.
22 *GGP* 214 n. 6.
23 iii.2, 2–3, 7; 7, 3–4.
24 e.g., kantharos, *Corinth* VII. 1 no. 81.
25 There are also some cists, e.g., Clenia (MG I) and Potters' Quarter gr. 5 (MG II).
26 There are also ten of these in a MG I grave at Athikia.
27 Another, *Corinth* XII no. 516, is from the same context as fig. 26f,h.
28 J. Salmon, *BSA* 67 (1972), 159 ff., has convincingly shown that the Geometric Deposit of Hera Akraia consists almost exclusively of Corinthian offerings; further, he concludes that the Corinthians wrested the peninsula from Megara at the time when their own city was founded. This event must be placed at least as early as 900 B.C., in the light of the continuous Geometric sequence found by the excavators. The discussion turns round the Megarian tribal names Heraeis and Piraeis (Plutarch, *Quaestiones Graecae* 17) which bear no relation to Megarian territory in historical times. According to Salmon's reconstruction, the Heraeis originally held the Perachora peninsula, taking the name from the deity whose sanctuary they founded; while the Piraeis, as their name implies, once dwelt in 'the land opposite' from a Megarian viewpoint – i.e., in the Corinthia itself, before the foundation of Corinth.
29 N. G. L. Hammond, *A History of Macedonia* i.403–4.
30 *Archaeology* 25 (1972), 18: 'Stelio's Field'.
31 *Lefkandi* 27–8 figs. 65–6.
32 P. G. Themelis, *AAA* 3.3 (1970), 314 fig. 1.
33 Pausanias x.5.9; J. Bérard, *AntK* 14 (1971), 59 ff.
34 Kourouniotis, *AE* 1903, 1 ff. Under this term the excavator includes Subgeometric amphorae going well down into the seventh century.
35 L. H. Sackett and M. R. Popham, *Archaeology* 25 (1972), 18–19; K. Schefold, *Führer durch Eretria* (Bern, 1972), 18–21.
36 There, in the view of P. G. Themelis, lay Old Eretria, adjacent to the later town; *AE* 1969, 157–61.
37 *PGP* 128–9.
38 *PAE* 1937–38, 117.
39 *AE* 1949, 45–7.
40 *BSA* 2 (1895–96), 70.
41 cf. also an early urn-amphora in Thera, Pfuhl E 4.
42 *AD* 20 (1965), pl. 6.
43 *GDA* 222.
44 cf. *Vergina* pl. 32.
45 *FGH* IIIb 500 F2 (Andriskos); 501 F5 (Diodorus v.50).
46 Pausanias vii.3.3.
47 *GGP* 312.
48 P. J. Riis, *Sukas* I, 162–3.
49 ibid., 144 ff. I have not seen these pieces.
50 ibid., 129.
51 Another skyphos has been reported, though not illustrated, from Nineveh, the Assyrian capital.
52 Polybius xxi.24, 10; Strabo 671.
53 *GGP* pl. 59c,g.
54 e.g., high-handled kantharoi, skyphoi with vertical offset lip, oinochoai with multiple-zigzag panel.
55 *Inschriften von Priene* no. 37.
56 *Fortetsa* 166, B (ii).
57 Tombs OD, LST, X, TFT, F.
58 *Fortetsa* tomb P; *BSA* 56 (1961), 69 ff., tomb A. *Fortetsa* II, VII, and VIII have some Protogeometric burials, but none thereafter until 'Mature Geometric'.

59 J. Boardman, *BSA* 62 (1967), 57 ff.

60 M. Robertson, *BSA* 50 (1955), 37.

61 It may be that these techniques, already known to the Minoans, were remembered in east Crete throughout the Dark Ages; see R. A. Higgins, *BSA* 64 (1969), 150.

62 *Fortetsa* no. 1106, Blinkenberg III.10.

63 *Vrokastro* 174.

64 Blinkenberg IV.1.

65 Cos appears to be an exception.

66 A pendent-semicircle skyphos occurs in an eighth-century context at Chauchitsa in the Axios valley (*BSA* 26 (1925–26), 10 fig. 3c); but its heavy overhanging lip suggests a local derivation from ninth-century Vergina, and not from the contemporary low-lipped form of Euboea.

67 Herodotus (iii.91) mentions a colony on the Syrian coast at Poseideion, founded by Amphilochos of Argos on his return from the Trojan War. Poseideion was once identified with Al Mina (Dunbabin, *GEN* 25–6); but is now more reasonably associated with Tell Basit, an emporium near by which preserves the ancient name, and where recent excavations have produced Greek pottery going back to the eighth century.

II

The Greek Renaissance,
c. 770–700 B.C.
Regional Survey

4 Athens and Attica

Around 770 B.C. Athens enters a new phase of prosperity and artistic ferment, which also saw the final passing of the Dark Ages. After the obscurity and stagnation of the previous period, there are several signs that the emergence came quite suddenly. In the Levant, we have already noted (p. 93) a burst of Athenian activity towards the end of MG II, and that is also the time when the circulation of Athenian pottery within the Aegean reaches its highest point before the sixth century.[1] Commercial energy abroad was matched by expansion and affluence at home. Like most other regions, Attica affords evidence of a rapidly rising population. In the countryside, there are many sites on the coast and in the Mesogeia plain where the earliest post-Mycenaean finds are Late Geometric (p. 133, fig. 43). In Athens itself, it appears from a count of wells within the Agora area[2] that the population increased threefold in the course of the eighth century, and a similar impression is conveyed by a sharp rise in the aggregate of graves. The further expansion of the *polis* is indicated by the first use of three new cemeteries, all in outlying areas (fig. 44): one in the modern suburb of Kallithea, the second near the later Kynosarges Gymnasium, and the third well outside the later Dipylon Gate, by the present Odos Peiraios. The Kynosarges graves offer a wealth of gold jewellery, not seen in Athens since the mid-ninth century. From the Odos Peiraios cemetery the finds appear to have been no less rich; yet its chief distinction lies in a superb group of monumental vases which stood over the burials. Current fashion required that these monuments should forsake the large linear compositions of earlier times, and in their stead carry ambitious scenes of mourning, seafaring, and battle. To meet this new challenge, a first-rate artist was at hand; after the name often given to the cemetery since its discovery in 1871, he is known as the Dipylon Master. To him belongs the credit of inventing the rich Late Geometric style of Athens; and, in the long history of Attic figured vase-painting, his is the first hand which can be recognized by a consistent and personal manner of drawing.

As before, we shall begin with the pottery: first, the output of the Dipylon Master and his contemporaries (LG I), and then the work of the later eighth century (LG II) where the best figured drawing becomes increasingly fluent and dynamic, but the quality of Geometric ornament deteriorates to the point of collapse. From the scenes on the funerary vases, coupled with the evidence from the graves themselves, we can form some impression of the current burial practices in an age when inhumation was rapidly replacing cremation as the prevailing rite. Next we shall survey contemporary Attic work in more costly media – gold diadems and other jewellery, bronze, ivory – in which the new urge towards figured imagery also found expression. Finally, some general remarks will be hazarded about the nature of Attic society in the eighth century, and the changing fortunes of Athens in relation to the rest of Greece.

Pottery: the Dipylon Master and his Successors

Earlier essays in figured drawing (pp. 77–8) had been virtually limited to single men or women, single animals, single birds; inert, and usually tucked away in small, inconspicuous panels. Quite suddenly, around 770 B.C., more ambitious themes begin to appear. A monumental krater in New York,[3] with supporting decoration still in the MG II manner, bears in its main panel a funerary *prothesis* where the dead man is laid out on the bier and surrounded by mourners, and in a lower zone an extended naval battle in which warriors fight in single combat on board ship. Similar duellists, in isolation, figure on the legs of a fragmentary tripod stand;[4] and a miniature seafight is compressed, astonishingly, on to the two sides of a small skyphos from a late MG II grave at Eleusis.[5]

These pioneer works were shortly followed by the emergence of the Dipylon Master, inventor of the Late Geometric style. His main efforts were devoted to the fashioning and embellishment of monumental vessels for his aristocratic patrons, to stand over their graves. The demand, during his career, seems to have been phenomenally high; at least thirty-five LG I grave monuments are known – if only from small fragments – and twenty-one are from the Dipylon Master's hand or workshop. These gigantic vases, well over 1m. high, are the last representatives of two time-honoured Attic forms: belly-handled amphorae for women, tall-pedestalled kraters for men. All bear scenes of mourning around the bier; the kraters, in addition, show chariot processions, a retinue of fully-armed warriors, and – during the workshop's prime (LG Ia, *c.* 760–750) – scenes of fighting on land and sea. This sudden eruption of figured painting is all the more astounding, coming as it does after four centuries when any form of representational art had been extremely rare. To judge from surviving fragments, a complete battle-krater from the Dipylon Workshop would have borne well over a hundred figures; work on this grand scale was never again attempted by vase-painters until the black-figure scenes of the early sixth century, the time of the François Vase.

Paris A 517 (fig. 33a), one of the largest extant fragments, illustrates the Master's own style. In the main scene on the front (the back is missing) he shows us the *prothesis* of a nobleman, amidst a retinue of chariots and foot-soldiers; the procession continues in the lower zone. Under the surviving handle, a warship with its rowers may perhaps allude to the interests of the dead man. All round the bier, groups of mourners tear their hair; although drawn in elevation, their grouping in relation to the bier is seen from bird's-eye view.[6] Each individual figure, too, combines two different viewpoints, so that every limb shall be visible; chest and arms in frontal view, head and lower body in profile. In the chariot teams a similar desire for clarity, leaving nothing to the

FIG. 33 ATHENIAN LG Ia POTTERY, DIPYLON WORKSHOP
(a) Paris A 517, H. 58; (b) Paris A 519, H. 38.5; (c) Athens 811, detail

a

b

c

a

b

c

d

e

f

viewer's imagination, is displayed in the careful definition of eight legs and two wheels side by side; on the bier, the checked shroud is drawn back to reveal the corpse. While it is not always easy to see, in this impersonal style, whether the mourners are men or women,[7] this painter has at least taken trouble to distinguish the sex of his dead patron; this we can see by comparing the *prothesis* on the well-known amphora Athens 804, where the deceased lady is given a long robe.

This tense, static scene has a dynamic counterpart in Paris A 519 (fig. 33b), from a krater painted by one of the Dipylon Master's closest associates; probably from the back of a krater whose front was reserved for the *prothesis*. In the upper zone a grim land-battle is being waged: casualties on the left, then three groups in combat, culminating in the collapse of a huge warrior from his chariot, wearing the so-called Dipylon shield. His peers, below, hurry to the rescue,[8] one foot in the air; in between, baleful birds of prey look forward to the outcome; behind, another combat involves a pair of Siamese twins. The clarity, once again, is remarkable. The silhouette technique requires that there shall be no substantial overlapping of figures; so the dead bodies appear to be floating in mid-air, and at the left of the lower zone we can be reasonably sure that Siamese twins are intended,[9] not two warriors side by side. The figures themselves are distinguished from one another by simple, generic traits. Death is conveyed through bent wrists and spread fingers (top left), or by a large, staring eye (top right).[10] The surviving warriors can be sorted into their respective armies according to their equipment: square shields *versus* Dipylon shields or no shield. Above all, human arms are always clearly drawn, so that we immediately recognize the activity and function of each person. And yet the underlying anatomy of every figure painted in this workshop – be he warrior, archer, rower, charioteer, or mourner – conforms to the austere archetype established by the Master himself, quite distinct from any previous experiment: abnormally tall in stature, curves reduced to a minimum, and the frontal chest presented as a slim isosceles triangle, whose sides are produced by the upper arms of the mourners. Equally individual are the horses (fig. 33a), with their tall necks, the elegant double curve of their shoulders, and the backward thrust of their hind legs.

The figured repertoire of this workshop is completed by the narrow friezes of grazing deer (fig. 33c) and kneeling regardant goats, always purely decorative in function, each animal being repeated in a standard pose. Here we have one of the few ideas in Geometric figured painting which was surely borrowed from the Near East, perhaps directly from Levantine ivory reliefs,[11] or perhaps at second hand through contemporary Attic diadems (p. 124). By his adoption of the animal frieze, the Dipylon Master was setting a precedent, fully to be exploited by the vase-painters of the next two centuries.

In his handling of linear ornament, he was no less of an innovator than in his drawing of figures. Geometric decoration had been steadily growing in

FIG. 34 ATHENIAN LG I POTTERY
(a) Athens 990, detail (total H. 123); (b) *K* gr. 24, H. 9.2;
(c) *K* gr. 24, H. 11.6; (d) *K* gr. 72, H. 52; (e) Agora gr. 18, H.8;
(f) *K* gr. 71, H. 7.5

intricacy since 800 B.C., yet even at the end of MG II much of the surface was still habitually covered with dark glaze. The Dipylon Master now breaks new ground in decorating virtually the whole vase with a continuous web of ornament, but without thereby obscuring the underlying shape. Thus the three focal areas of a larged closed vessel – belly, shoulder, and centre of neck – are emphasized just as effectively as before, either by figured scenes, or by linear designs more massive than anything seen before: huge complex meanders, or lozenge patterns resembling elaborate tapestries (*GGP* pl. 7d,e). A third possibility was to divide a main field vertically into square panels recalling the metopes of a Doric temple, often with narrow 'triglyphs' intervening (e.g. fig. 34f). This idea, occasionally used in the Dipylon Workshop, became extremely popular elsewhere; and, like the habit of overall decoration, it forms an important ingredient of the Attic LG style.

Before leaving the subject of linear ornament, we should note that the Dipylon Master was also a pioneer in thinking out small motifs suitable for filling vacant spaces in the figured fields. These filling ornaments have the effect of binding the figures into a harmonious rapport with the surrounding Geometric designs, and reducing the contrast between bold silhouette and half-tone linear ornament.

Several new LG shapes, too, are the inventions of the Dipylon Master and his colleagues. From his own hand are a giant oinochoe with a tall straight neck, and a large, round-mouthed pitcher (*GGP* pl. 7d,e); the smaller novelties of his workshop include the high-handled tankard (*GGP* pl. 8g), and a high-rimmed bowl with lid (as fig. 34f) which was eventually to supersede the flat pyxis soon after the end of LG I.

With the rise of figured painting, we have seen how the personality of an Athenian vase-painter could emerge with much greater clarity than before. Among the other artists of this generation, none is more idiosyncratic than the Hirschfeld Painter. His career coincides with the later and less inspired products of the Dipylon Workshop (LG Ib: *c.* 750–735 B.C.), whence he borrowed some minor details of linear decoration; yet his figured style could hardly be more different. He, too, supplied monumental vessels for the nobility, at a time when scenes of war were no longer fashionable, and only funerary themes were portrayed. We know of one grave amphora[12] and six grave kraters from his hand or workshop; a good example of his style is seen on Athens 990 (fig. 34a), the almost complete krater first published by the scholar after whom he is named. His human figures are remarkable for their beaky noses, reserved and dotted eyes, and the unnatural rectangle formed by the mourners' arms; thighs are shown frontally, giving the impression of bow legs; his women are distinguished by schematic breasts marked in profile. His horses are stiff and wooden, with enormously elongated cannon-bones, puny thighs, and trumpet muzzles; the wheels of their chariots have parted company with the boxes, and float in mid-air. His filling ornament is monotonously confined to dots, chevron piles, and dot rosettes. Other vases from his workshop show equally idiosyncratic goats, kneeling or standing,[13] but always looking to their front with large, enquiring eyes.

Fig. 34b–f presents a view of the Athenian style towards the end of LG I, on five common shapes made outside the two leading workshops. The skyphos and the high-handled kantharos are still the standard drinking-vessels, frequent both in domestic and in funerary contexts. The other three shapes are found mainly in graves – although, with the change of rite, the amphora loses its earlier function as a cremation urn. Flat pyxides are large and numerous at this time, and the luxurious variety crowned with a team of horses (fig. 34e) is no longer reserved for male burials. The high-rimmed bowl (fig. 34f) is an early specimen of a shape that was to become much more common in LG II, when it displaced the pyxis.

In the decoration, several new motifs deserve attention. Narrow zones often contain a row of blobs connected by tangents (fig. 34c,d), or several rows of check pattern, or a 'wolf-tooth' design composed of interlocking rows of hatched triangles (fig. 34d,f). The metopal system now reaches the height of its popularity, and can be applied to almost any shape. For the square panels the favourite motifs are the quatrefoil, the swastika, variations on the lozenge, and long-necked marsh-birds with hatching on their bodies. In the intervening 'triglyphs', check often occupies the central position (fig. 34e,f); but, as the discipline of the system weakens, the checked area may expand to the size of the metopes. At the very end of LG I, a ripely decorated amphora (fig. 34d) already contains the seeds of decay: there is a certain staleness in the ornament, the metopes are not strong enough to accentuate the greatest diameter, and the grazing deer are feeble copies of the elegant Dipylon prototype (cf. fig. 33c).

Two trends coincide in LG II, the final and restless phase of Attic Geometric. The ablest painters followed in the wake of the Dipylon Workshop, and rapidly developed a fluent and vigorous figured style. Meanwhile the more reactionary hands gradually debased the old Geometric stock of ornament to the point of exhaustion, without adding anything new. With this process of decline we shall deal first, and briefly.

The decline is well illustrated by two pitchers, fig. 35a and f. The first, Athens 16022, was made c. 730 B.C., early in LG II. In the belly zone, its metopes are smaller and less emphatic even than on the amphora in fig. 34d, the drawing is more cursive and thicker; yet the authentic form of the metope-and-triglyph scheme can still be recognized. On the second pitcher, Stuttgart KAS 9 (c. 710–700 B.C.), the metopes are swamped in a mass of verticals, the triglyphs are quite out of control, and the overall decoration has lost all its vitality: in the narrower zones, all the ornament has been clumsily mass-produced with the multiple brush. Geometric ornament has become a drudge; the painter's heart is no longer in it. Small wonder that this is one of the last big vases to be decorated in the Geometric manner; after 700 B.C. the pitcher, and with it the metopal scheme, disappear from the potter's repertoire.

Each vase comes from a well-defined workshop. The Athens pitcher is by a leading artist of LG IIa known as the Birdseed Painter, after his favourite dotted bird-files applied to most of his other work; these files were copied and debased by his successors (e.g., fig. 35f, shoulder) until the end of Geometric. The mourning ladies, with their long hair and trailing skirts, are typical of his figured style, in which he indulged himself occasionally. Among his major vases, pitchers are more numerous than amphorae, and this is generally true of the LG IIa phase.[14] His other shapes include large and lavish high-rimmed bowls,

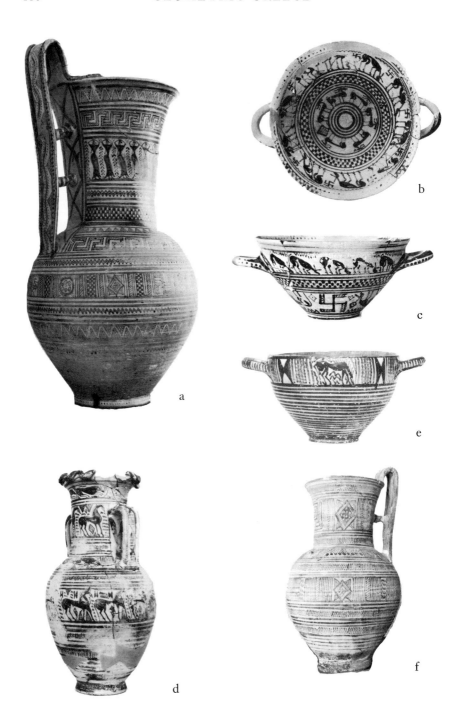

a

b

c

e

d

f

and a new, shallow kind of skyphos with ambitious decoration inside as well as on the exterior. In this class we see the first obvious signs of influence from imported Phoenician metal bowls (cf. pp. 59–60, fig. 15); inside an early LG II example by another hand (fig. 35b,c) the concentric friezes of deer are especially reminiscent of the oriental prototype.[15]

The Stuttgart pitcher (fig. 35f) exemplifies the linear decoration of a prolific and very late workshop (LG IIb), named after the amphora Athens 897.[16] By now the amphora has returned to favour as the major funerary vase, and those from this workshop are often adorned with horses and dogs, e.g., fig. 35d. The horses, of ponderous build, have a tired look; the dogs, though equally heavy and uncouth, nevertheless convey an impression of speed, and are adapted from full scenes of hunting as found on a group of LG IIa oinochoai.[17] Between these animal friezes, the linear ornament is always mass-produced with the multiple brush, as on the Stuttgart pitcher.

Among the smaller shapes of LG II, still common are the tankard, the plate, and the high-rimmed bowl, the last usually resting on a fenestrated stand. Drinking-vessels include the kantharos (now often lipless) and the kotyle (fig. 35e), newly introduced from Corinth; also the skyphos and the cup, which by LG IIb have attained a new, deep form with flaring lip, usually fully glazed; these are termed 'Phaleron ware', after the poor cemetery where they were first noted. By the end of Geometric there is a marked contrast in quality between large and small shapes, perhaps a symptom of widening social distinctions.

The heirs of the Dipylon tradition specialized in figured drawing on large shapes. Grave monuments, it seems, were going out of fashion; the huge neck-handled amphorae of the Sub-Dipylon Group (LG IIa) may have been made for this purpose, but their imagery is restricted to processions, without any *prothesis*. Their chariot teams (e.g., fig. 36a) inherit much from the Dipylon Workshop's style, but in simplified form: one horse, one wheel. Closely related is a spouted krater in London (fig. 112b), the work of a bold innovator. One side bears a procession which includes the first horseman in Geometric vase-painting, and almost the first charioteer wearing a long robe, like the well-known Classical bronze statue from Delphi. On the reverse is a scene of departure by sea, presenting the earliest ship with two rows of oarsmen, and the earliest woman to be distinguished by shoulder-length hair and a cross-hatched skirt. This may also be one of the earliest pictures of a specific myth (pp. 354–5).

In LG IIb the Dipylon tradition is represented chiefly by the workshop of the amphora Athens 894.[18] To meet the current demand for medium-sized funerary amphorae, this workshop produced a slim, tall-necked variety, often bearing a *prothesis* with mourners in the neck-panels, and always a chariot procession round the belly. Terracotta snakes, signifying the guardians of the Underworld, cling to the rim, handles, and shoulders, thus rendering the vessel quite useless

FIG. 35 ATHENIAN LG II POTTERY
(a) Athens 16022, H. 54; (b–c) K gr. 51, H. 8.7; (d) Athens 17519; (e) Athens 18496, H. 8; (f) Stuttgart KAS 9, H. 39

FIG. 36 ATHENIAN LG II POTTERY
(a) Leiden I.1909/1.1, detail; (b) Baghdad IM 52041, H. 37;
(c) Athens 17935, detail; (d) Athens, from Marathon, H. 16;
(e) Agora P 23654, H. 24

for any domestic purpose (fig. 37a). The figured drawing owes much to the
Sub-Dipylon Group, but becomes increasingly cursive and hasty. Its development within the workshop's life-span can be seen by comparing the chariot

teams on an early (fig. 36c) and a late amphora (fig. 37a). As the style loosens up, the procession seems to turn into a race; speed is certainly implied by the armed warriors who, on one amphora, jump on and off the vehicles, if these feats are to be identified with the *agon apobatikos* recorded in literary sources.[19] Sometimes a full frieze of foot-soldiers is added below the chariots, and there we see that the Dipylon shield has given place to a round type, occasionally decorated with patterns suggestive of blazonry (e.g. fig. 37b). Women, following the vogue set by the London krater, wear long hair and cross-hatched skirts; in addition to their role as mourners on the amphorae (fig. 37a), they also appear as chain-dancers on hydriai and tankards (fig. 36d), linking hands and holding branches. Deer and dogs often fill subsidiary friezes on large vases, and also the shoulders of a newly invented shape, the one-piece oinochoe; the delicate deer on fig. 36e are by the painter of the Stathatou amphora,[20] one of the most fastidious artists in the workshop. Near the end, the imagery becomes more adventurous: centaurs (fig. 36b), lions, and winged goats[21] invade the friezes, while lions, bulls, and not wholly plausible sphinxes occur in isolated scenes.[22] All these creatures, with the exception of the centaur, were introduced under the indirect influence of Near Eastern art; and with them comes the urge to imitate an oriental metallic shape, the North Syrian or Urartian cauldron on a tall conical stand (pp. 362 ff.) – although the Athenian potter has added the ring-handles of the bronze tripod cauldron traditional to Geometric Greece (fig. 37b). In the decoration of this vase, Geometric ornament has almost vanished; every available space – including even the ring-handles – is packed with figured work. The scenes depict the funeral games in honour of a dead nobleman. Successive friezes round the bowl show a foot-race (and traces of other events on fragments from the back), a four-horse chariot race, and a deer frieze; the tall panels of the stand contain armed warriors, and a rider performing an especially daring feat of dressage. Made at the very end of the Attic Geometric style, this vessel shows no lack of vigour or invention, and is full of promise for the future. It was in this workshop that the Analatos Painter, the chief exponent of the Early Protoattic style, received his early training.

Handmade ware, during LG, often rises to high technical standards. We now see less than before of the plump and heavy cooking-jug; lighter and more refined specimens can be seen in some LG grave groups.[23] The LG II well-deposits of the Agora contain new forms in thin-walled and micaceous fabric: large jugs with nipples on front, one-piece oinochoai, and two-handled jars (or kadoi);[24] with them goes a hydria from Kerameikos gr. 98. All these shapes are on the slim side, without any clear articulation in their profiles; some bear simple incised decoration, the favourite motif being the swastika.

Burial Customs

After 770 B.C. the practice of inhuming adults became much more common than before (cf. p. 81), and by 750 B.C. had supplanted cremation as the prevailing rite in Attica. This change, whatever its causes may have been,[25] is most clearly marked in the new and rich cemeteries of Odos Peiraios and Kynosarges,[26] evidently founded by leading Athenian families who had largely accepted the new rite, and appreciated the consequent need for greater burial space at a time when the older cemeteries were becoming overcrowded.

The change of rite enables us to discern family plots much more easily than before (cf. p. 56), the most positive evidence coming from the skeletons themselves. A successful analysis, proving consanguinity, has been carried out on the occupants of a terraced burial ground in the Agora area, used from just before 760 B.C. until just after 700 B.C. There are other reasons, too, for suspecting that this plot was reserved for a single family: nine adult graves, all inhumations, were carefully spaced out along the terrace, with only one instance of slight encroachment; one grave was re-used, but pains were taken not to disturb the earlier incumbent; and eight small children, inhumed in urns, were fitted in between the adult graves, instead of being consigned to a separate area according to current practice in larger cemeteries. Elsewhere, skeletal evidence is not yet available; nevertheless, by these other criteria, another family plot can be identified to the north-east of the main mass of burials south of the Eridanos. This is the so-called 'Plattenbau'[27] which, from c. 760 B.C. onwards, accumulated about three generations of burials: eight infants in urns, six older children and eleven adults in graves, all inhumed except for two adult cremations. This small plot is remarkable for its careful planning, aided by the low partitions surrounding some of the richer burials.

We now turn to the various modes of burial. In the Attic countryside, cremation remains the rule only at Anavysos and Trachones; in Athens itself, the rarity of this rite after c. 750 B.C. lends it a special interest. The rich cemetery of Odos Kriezi, where cremation was never superseded, gives us the impression of a noble clan with a conservative outlook. Yet even there, as in other cemeteries, the form of the urn has changed; no longer a clay amphora, but now quite often a cauldron of bronze (fig. 40a), usually sealed with a cover of lead, bronze, or stone, and occasionally resting on a stand of some description.[28] Whenever clay vases accompany an Attic cremation cauldron, they regularly include either a krater[29] or a neck-handled amphora,[30] shapes traditionally associated with male burials. There is thus a strong likelihood that this manner of cremation was reserved for men; and mainly for men of high standing, to judge from the elaboration and richness of the gifts found in the same contexts.[31] Soon after 700 B.C. cremation once again became the normal rite for the aristocracy, though in a different form: the body was now burnt in the grave, eventually to be covered by a grandiose tumulus, crowned with a stele.

For an adult inhumation, the body was laid in the grave on its back, both arms to the side; normally the legs were fully extended. Some of the richer Kerameikos burials, e.g., nos. 25, 26, 50, 51, have yielded traces of rectangular wooden coffins; iron fittings from the bier were found in no. 53. Offerings of pots might be placed anywhere on or around the body, most often at the feet (and sometimes

FIG. 37 ATHENIAN LG II POTTERY AND TERRACOTTA FIGURINES
(a) Agora gr. 12, H. 32.7; (b) Athens 810 (*AM* 17 pl. 10)
H. *c.* 60; (c) Agora gr. 12, H. 13.7, D. 6.8, H. 5.7, H. 8.4;
(d) Agora gr. 12, H. of left seated figure 8

a

b

c

d

even on the cover slabs). Above the burial, an ashy deposit was often swept into the grave, containing burnt sherds and animal bones. This is the debris of the funeral feast, roasted on a pyre near by; and in Agora gr. 11, where more animal bones were found inside an *unburnt* amphora by the dead man's feet, we know that he, too, received his share. With these banquets in view, the Athens 894 Workshop purveyed a wide range of miniature shapes and figurines, for smashing on the pyre; a selection is shown in fig. 37c, all found with the amphora in fig. 37a in a burnt deposit thrown over the terrace of the Agora family plot ('gr.' 12). Especially notable are the diminutive versions of the Orientalizing cauldron, fig. 37b, overladen with funerary snakes and birds; the figurines (fig. 37d), some of which were vase attachments, include birds, dogs, horses, chariot groups, mourners tearing their hair, and a fragmentary seated figure holding a pomegranate – perhaps representing Persephone, Queen of Hades.[32] In the Kerameikos, too, similar pyre offerings (though without figurines) were usually swept inside the grave (e.g., in nos. 53–6).[33] At the end of the ceremony the grave was filled with earth, and closed with stone slabs resting on the ledges prepared for them.

Children, in earlier times, had normally been given sporadic burial in inhabited areas, a custom which persists, here and there, until the end of the Geometric period;[34] but during LG it is far more usual for them to be buried in regular cemeteries, either on the edge of large cemeteries (as at Phaleron), or among their adult relations in family plots. Older children are allotted graves, like adults, and buried in the same manner. Infants, their knees drawn up, are now inhumed in urns, consisting either of coarse pithoi, or amphorae, or hydriai, or large handmade jugs; whenever necessary, the side of the urn is removed to admit them, and then carefully replaced.

Scenes on contemporary vases cannot add much to our understanding of the funeral rites, beyond what is timeless and universal in all scenes of sorrow. By far the commonest subject is the *prothesis*, portraying the dead person lying in state, and surrounded by mourners. Even within the same workshop, no two renderings are identical; thus the iconography may well reflect, in some measure, the preference and circumstances of individual families. Only three vases – all monumental – show the *ekphora* (e.g., fig. 34a), where the bier is conveyed to the grave on a four-wheeled waggon, and attended by a procession of chariots and warriors; perhaps this was a special and rare honour reserved for the highest families,[35] or perhaps the very complexity of the subject frightened off all but the most ambitious vase-painters.

After the arrival at the grave, one krater scene[36] shows the preliminaries to the funeral feast: a file of helmeted men, equipped with sword and dagger, bring a supply of fowl, fish, and meat, which they will presently dismember. On the reverse neck panel of fig. 37a three mourners offer further tokens of respect – a wreath, a dagger, and a tiny mourning figure which may represent a terracotta figurine like fig. 37d. Finally, and perhaps after the funeral, several musical sessions are seen on a group of pitchers, all from the same LG II workshop.[37] The details vary, but the underlying theme is a pair of seated figures facing each other, each rattling a pair of percussion instruments over a square structure which probably represents a grave; in the earliest scenes, the addition of Dipylon

FIG. 38 ATHENIAN LG GOLD DIADEMS
(a) Athens 15309, *K* gr. 72, L. 36; (b) Athens 813, Odos Peiraios
gr. 5, L. 36; (c) Paris 1291, L. 38.5; (d) Copenhagen 741, L. *c.* 33.5

shields implies the grave of a warrior, which the percussionists may be protecting
from evil spirits. The grave disappears in the later scenes, to be replaced by
stools and drinking-vessels, while the orchestra is augmented by lyre-players;
these revised versions may well have been influenced by similar compositions on
North Syrian stone reliefs.[38]

Gold Diadems and Other Jewellery

Earlier Attic diadems, as we have seen, had been adorned with simple Geometric
patterns (fig. 16). Now, by the end of MG, the shape is broadened to admit
animal friezes,[39] and nearly all LG examples from Attica carry figured scenes.
As several groups carry identical scenes (e.g., fig. 38a,b), it is clear that these
diadems were pressed on to a matrix – bronze is the most likely material, so
subtle is the modelling of the earlier animals. It is equally clear that the matrices

were originally made for some other purpose: they were too short for the diadems, as we can see from the repetition of the same sequences to fill the required length of gold strip; and in the middle of fig. 38b the frieze tries to turn a corner, as though forming the border of some larger rectangular object (on fig. 38a this 'corner' has been obliterated by clumsy retouching, to keep the animals in a continuous file). The primary function of the matrices is revealed by the fragments of a broader gold sheet from Eleusis, probably from the facing of a funerary jewel-box – from the same context, near a disturbed child grave, came the gold plaques of fig. 39a. This larger relief[40] allows the reconstruction of a matrix with five horizontal zones between vertical borders, and including two figured themes which recur, isolated from their original context, on LG I diadems. Similarly the original matrix for fig. 38a,b and the like may be restored as the border of a smaller box; and from these two notional matrices[41] practically all the figured work on LG I diadems can be derived.

Both matrices can now be traced back to the beginning of LG (see p. 123 n. 39 above), and their use coincides with the entire period of the figured grave monuments. It would be strange if there had been no exchange of ideas between the two media. Some animals on the diadems seem to adumbrate types adopted by the leading vase-painters: thus the stags (fig. 38a) may have been pared down to form the Dipylon Master's version (fig. 33c), while a kneeling goat from the Eleusis matrix (fig. 38c) could have influenced the Hirschfeld Painter.[42] In the other Eleusis scene, the desperate lion-fighter[43] recalls some figures in the Dipylon Workshop's battles, notably in the triangular rendering of the chest. But in other respects the diadems look more oriental both in style and in subject-matter. On LG vases, deer or goats are repeated in the same pose, forming purely decorative friezes; here, in the gold reliefs, we see these passive animals in their authentic oriental contexts, the prey of aggressive lions who pursue them, sink fangs into their rumps, and even attack men. Again, lions are seldom seen on vases before LG II, and never look even remotely feline until the end of Geometric; in fig. 38b, by contrast, the lionesses stalk their quarry like true felines, and share the same supple style as the rampant creatures on the Levantine diadem from Teke (fig. 32c). Although no comparable gold reliefs have come to light in the Near East, some oriental expertise must have gone into the making of the matrices. Like the earlier jewellery from Eleusis (p. 80), they may well be the work of a semi-hellenized guild established somewhere in Attica, catering for aristocratic patrons in Athens and Eleusis.

During the 730s B.C. new matrices came into use, showing a marked change of style and theme. The latest animal scenes, on a group of LG IIa diadems,[44] are rendered in a wooden style in which the earlier subtlety of relief has quite vanished. At the same time, purely human scenes[45] enter the repertoire: horse-men, land-battles, tumblers, dancers, girls bearing waterpots; also centaurs and sphinxes.[46] As before, the matrices were not originally designed for diadems; the careless trimming of the gold often reveals traces of a second register. In the most advanced group (Ohly's Group IV; fig. 38d) the style comes closest to the plain silhouette of vase-painting; the scenes, placed in a series of separate episodes, are now wholly Greek in character. The imagery of a kantharos from the Odos Peiraios cemetery[47] offers an interesting counterpart to these late diadems,

FIG. 39 ATHENIAN LG JEWELLERY
(a) Athens 3534-8, from Eleusis; w. of rectangular plaques 4;
(b) Athens 2604, from Spata gr. 3; L. 10

both in content and in composition. The latest recorded context is of the diadem found with the Stathatou amphora (p. 119), painted about 710 B.C.

The most elaborate jewellery of the time is seen in the five gold plaques from Eleusis (fig. 39), found in the same context as the casket relief. These form part of a large breast ornament[48] – or possibly a small girdle, if they really belonged to the rifled child's grave near by. Each plaque is made from two gold sheets, one superimposed upon the other. The lower layer is peppered with patterns in granulation, performing the function of filling ornament. The upper sheet carries the main, inlaid motifs: each cloison is reinforced by a granulated outline, and traces of the amber inlays survive in some of the triangular compartments. In a somewhat cavalier fashion, the rosette cloisons obscure some of the under-lying patterns.[49] Although the techniques are inherited from the oriental jewellers who made the MG lunate earrings (p. 80), there is some concession here to local taste: thus battlements and swastikas figure among the granulated ornament, while one of the main cloisons takes the form of a large Dipylon shield. Three more plaques from this 'Eleusis School' have been found in the sanctuary of Artemis at Brauron;[50] and it may also have been responsible for two groups of earrings with massive circular plates, all adorned with a profusion of granulated patterns combined with inlays.[51] Less ornate, but in the same tradition, is a gold necklace (fig. 39b) from gr. 3 at Spata (c. 730 B.C.) composed of five rectangular plaques with cloisons for inlays, but without granulation. The pendent gold tubes were originally threaded with beads, to give the impression of pome-granates, as on the earrings from the Isis grave (cf. fig. 25b). The same burials also contained a pair of bronze bracelets with snake-head finials.

After 750 B.C. it was no longer the fashion to place long pins in graves; but some of the latest Attic pins are also the most splendid. Three gilt iron pins from Kynosarges grs. 18 and 19 (c. 770–750 B.C.) continue the ninth-century type with finial, disc, and single globe (cf. fig. 14b); but the gold sheaths are now em-bellished with granulated triangles and zigzags, and the globe is made to look like a pomegranate.[52] In addition to an early figured diadem (p. 123 n. 39), gr. 19 also yielded three plate-fibulae in gold, similar in shape to those in the Elgin collection (fig. 25a). Five more fibulae of this class – one in gold, one in silver, three in bronze – are known to come from the aristocratic LG cemetery of Odos Peiraios,[53] although their precise contexts cannot now be determined; four small iron fibulae were found in gr. 18 (c. 740 B.C.) in the Agora family plot, and four iron and two bronze examples came from VD Ak I, a rich female burial recently found in the Kerameikos. In most LG examples the square plate tends to be proportionately larger than before; whether any carried figured decoration, as in MG, we cannot say. After LG I this class of fibula seems to die out in Attica – at any rate, it was no longer placed in graves; in Boeotia, however, it was to enjoy a distinguished future (pp. 202 ff).

Among smaller items of jewellery, two ornaments are especially noteworthy: from Kynosarges gr. 3 (LG Ia), a gilt hair-spiral with incised chevrons, indicating a link with Corinth (cf. fig. 57b); and an unusually elaborate gold finger-ring from Odoi Erysichthonos/Neleos gr. 6 (LG IIa), made of twist-braids and openwork wire.

Bronzes

Cauldrons, with their various appendages of tripod legs, ring-handles, and figurines of men and animals, form the main output of the LG bronzeworker. Some vessels of moderate size were used for male cremations (p. 120), always unadorned; most are without any attachments, and have a sharply carinated shoulder. Fig. 40a, from Kerameikos gr. 72, is an exception; there are traces of

FIG. 40 ATHENIAN LG BRONZES
(a) *K* gr. 72, cauldron, D. 44; (b–d) Acropolis 6616, H. 21;
(e) Delphi 3144, H. 19.6

iron tripod legs, and the rounded profile is also reminiscent of the tripod cauldrons currently dedicated at sanctuaries. The main difference is of scale: this vessel measures 0·44m. across, whereas the cauldrons offered to the gods (pp. 335–8) may be as much as 1·20m. in diameter, supported by bronze tripod legs anything up to 2m. high.

Since all monumental cauldrons come from sanctuaries, hardly any dating evidence is available from their contexts; and even their provenance is not easily determined, as some important sanctuaries – e.g., Delphi and Delos – are not likely to have been centres of production. In Athens, however, there is a good case for assuming the existence of a local school. The Geometric bronzes from the Acropolis include many pieces of hammered tripod legs and ring-handles, and these constitute a high proportion of the known corpus of hammered work; thus it is reasonable to see Athens as the main, though not the only, centre for hammered tripods.[54] Furthermore, on the basis of the Acropolis figurines, a distinct Athenian style can be traced throughout the development of the hammered tripods, starting somewhere in LG I, and lasting into the early seventh century. Early in the series comes the warrior Acropolis 6616 (fig. 40b–d), whose outline is similar to figures on the later kraters from the Dipylon Workshop. He originally stood on top of a large ring-handle; after the figure had been cast, his forearms were hammered out flat and pierced, so that he could brandish a spear in his right hand, and in his left hold a shield, and perhaps also the rein of his horse. Typical of the Athenian school are the oval face, the rounded chin, the flatness of the head on top; also, in the profile, the abrupt change of plane between forehead and jaw. All these traits are shared by a slightly later draped woman from Delphi (fig. 40e), which has been convincingly identified as an Attic import;[55] this diagnosis receives further support from the articulation between waist and hip, equally well-defined in both figures. But the Delphi woman does not share the upward tilt of the warrior's head; this is probably an early feature, borrowed in the first instance from North Syrian figurines, and we shall meet it again in the work of the Corinthian school (cf. fig. 58c–f).

Facial features, so far, have been rudimentary: holes for the eyes, a jagged angle for the nose, a simple slit for the mouth. In all these respects a youth from Olympia (fig. 41a), made near the end of the eighth century, shows a notable advance; and because his eyes are asymmetrical, his expression is all the more vivacious. There is also a greater fluency in his body profile; the limbs and torso, though still carefully articulated in the Geometric manner, are more roundly modelled than before. But the chief interest lies in the swinging rhythm of his pose: left foot forward, head turned sharply to the right, arms bent and held in front. He is one of the earliest figures to stand on the rim of a cauldron, his hands being riveted to the side of a hammered ring-handle. From the same workshop is a corresponding figure of a Minotaur looking to the left (fig. 41b), who must have supported the other side of a very similar (perhaps the same?) handle. If both figures are Attic, as seems likely for stylistic and technical reasons,[56] the monster would have a local relevance, and this would not be the earliest allusion to the Theseus saga by an Athenian artist (p. 355). Several later handle-holders, all from the Acropolis, are remarkable for the attenuation of their torsos, the elongation of their legs, and the increasing fluidity of their outlines;[57] they take us into a Subgeometric stage, c. 700 B.C. and soon thereafter. At the same time there was a rather painful groping after a new style, apparent in the helmeted warrior Acropolis 6613 (fig. 41c). Here the old Geometric love of articulation is being abandoned in favour of a more unified rendering of the human body, and the heavy, exaggerated facial features recall work by the

FIG. 41 ATHENIAN LG BRONZES
(a) Athens 6179, from Olympia, H. 15; (b) Paris C 7286, H. 18;
(c) Acropolis 6613, H. 20.5

Analatos painter of Early Protoattic pottery.

The latest handle figures[58] show that Athenian smiths went on making Geometric tripod cauldrons for at least two decades after *c.* 700 B.C. Eventually the
oriental type, with conical stand and protome attachments, came into fashion,
and some of its characteristic griffin heads have been found on the Acropolis.
Yet the clay copies of *c.* 700 B.C. (p. 119 fig. 37b) confuse the two types, and
suggest that the Athenians of those years had not yet acquired any first-hand
knowledge of the eastern model.

Ivories

Ivory, like gold, was supplied to Attica from the Near East, and work in both media tended to flourish when eastward contacts were most frequent. Of the earliest Athenian ivory carving we had a brief glimpse during the euphoria of the mid-ninth century (pp.56–8); thereafter, hardly anything more until a rectangular seal with a figured intaglio, and a peg handle surmounted by a bird (fig. 42a). This seal comes from a grave in Odos Kavalotti, where the precise context is not yet clear; but the theme of two men exercising a horse already appears on a MG II mug,[59] and the rubbery rendering of the figures on the seal might well be as early as this. A more angular style appears on a square seal from Kerameikos gr. VD Ak 1 (c. 740 B.C.) showing a deer on one side, and two seated figures on the other.

Of all known Geometric ivories, undoubtedly the finest are the five nude female figurines from Odos Peiraios gr. 13. Since they gradually diminish in size, all five could have been carved from a single tusk;[60] the best preserved are the largest and the smallest. The oriental prototype of these figures, representing the fertility goddess Astarte, were made by a flourishing North Syrian school which had its main centre at Hama. Original Hamathite ivories have not yet been found in Athens, but some are known to have reached all three of the Rhodian cities (p. 267) and also the Idaean cave-sanctuary in Crete. Of the nude Astarte figurines, the largest known collection is from the south-east palace at Nimrud (the Loftus Group), whither they were probably carried off by the Assyrians who destroyed the kingdom of Hama in 720 B.C.[61]

A comparison with these authentic Astartes will show how subtly the type was adapted to suit Athenian taste. Characteristic of the Syrian originals were the hard, staring eyes, with holes pierced for inlaid pupils; the flat-topped *polos* usually bearing a pattern of rosettes or leaves; the long tresses, tapering some way down the back, and with shorter locks on the cheek; and the rigid pose, arms held firmly to the sides. The Athenian master, while taking over all these traits, drastically pared down the voluptuous flesh of his plump prototypes. His smallest figure[62] has the physique of a young girl, with a gentle curve left between waist and hip; like some of the oriental versions, her head is turned slightly to one side, and her *polos* preserves the Syrian leaf pattern. Her hair, however, has been simplified into a rectangular mass confined to the back, and arranged in a pattern seen on the handles of many an Attic MG oinochoe.[63] The tresses of the largest figure (fig. 42b–d) are treated in a similar way, like a mass of Geometric chevrons; on her *polos*, a bold meander has ousted the oriental motifs. Seen from frontal view, her body has been re-created according to Geometric canons, sharply articulated at the waist, above which the triangular chest recalls the figures of LG I vase-painting. In profile she looks more oriental, at first sight; her full features are curiously like those of a much cruder face modelled on a Rhodian LG oinochoe (p. 249 fig. 79f), probably made by a Levantine settler. But the gentle curves of her body profile have a restrained loveliness never achieved by any of her Syrian prototypes; this is the first great orientalizing masterpiece, in

FIG. 42 ATHENIAN IVORIES
(a) seal from Odos Kavalotti (drawing Marion Cox); (b–d) Athens
776, from Odos Peiraios gr. 13, H. 24

which a Greek artist, by giving free rein to his creative genius, has transformed
and far surpassed his oriental model. And his technical mastery over his medium
goes far beyond any contemporary Athenian metalwork; this can be seen by
contrasting a nude female bronze figurine, Athens 6503,[64] where the modelling

is not nearly so subtle and sensitive. This ivory girl, enlivened by her graceful outline and her incipient smile, is the spiritual ancestor of the Archaic marble maidens who attended Athena by her temples on the Acropolis.

Conclusions

Between the middle and the later years of the eighth century, the fortunes of Attica underwent a marked change. The turning-point comes just before the burial with the ivory figurines (*c.* 730 B.C.), the latest grave group to contain any sign of direct contact with the eastern Mediterranean.

Before this change, Athens was still an outward-looking city. Although the export of Attic pottery seems to decline after the end of MG II, its influence is still strong in several other local schools: thus the metopal decoration of Attic LG I, and also several of its figured themes, found imitators in Boeotia, Euboea, the Cyclades, and Samos. From the Near East, actual imports to Athens are confined to a few Phoenician trinkets: a glass seal from Odos Peiraios, a glass pendant and two faience scarabs in the Agora area,[65] and the three small faience lions in the same grave as the ivories. Yet some of the more striking manifestations of Attic art in these years would have been unthinkable without the guidance of the Orient. One thinks especially of the predatory lions on the diadems, the animal friezes on diadems and grave monuments, the exquisite granulation and inlay work of the 'Eleusis School', and the nude female figurines in ivory; their very nudity is alien to Aegean tradition, and perhaps the nudity of female mourners on LG I vases – another temporary departure from normal Greek custom[66] – may owe something to oriental artistic inspiration. In composition, though not in style, Egyptian prototypes have been adduced for the Attic LG I *prothesis*,[67] and the duel scenes of MG II (p. 110) seem to have earlier counterparts in North Syrian relief orthostats.[68] The question then arises, how would these oriental ideas have been transmitted? Attic artists and craftsmen are not likely to have seen with their own eyes the monumental arts of Egypt and Syria; and although the materials of gold and ivory must have come to them from the east, such imported artifacts as have been found (in Attica, only glass and faience) seem too rare and insignificant to account for these influences by themselves. Once again we are led to suppose that the new ideas and motifs were largely introduced through eastern craftsmen settling or already settled in Attica, and passing on their crafts to Greek pupils; this is especially likely for the most elaborate Attic jewellery, which had displayed an oriental sophistication ever since the awakening of the mid-ninth century. It is a tribute to the vitality of Athenian art that the oriental models did not provoke any close imitations; on the contrary, the example of oriental figured art may have done much to stimulate the Geometric creative spirit, whose greatest outpouring is seen on the vast figured monuments of the Dipylon Workshop.

After 730 B.C. Athens rapidly loses her artistic initiative. The cursive LG II style found no imitators elsewhere, except occasionally in Boeotia. Meanwhile, even Attic potters began to borrow some ideas off imports from Corinth, the city which was now steadily rising to artistic and commercial pre-eminence. There is still a steady flow of Attic pottery to Aegina, but elsewhere only a thin scatter to Asine, Ithaca, Andros, Thera, Samos, Italy, and Sicily;[69] and these pots may well have travelled in Corinthian ships, since each site where they occur has also yielded Corinthian wares in bulk. As Athenian enterprise dwindles in Aegean waters, so the Levantine connection begins to lapse. Attica receives no more imports from that direction. The supply of granulated and inlaid jewellery seems to have dried up; and on the latest gold diadems, animal friezes of oriental character are replaced by figured themes in the Geometric tradition. Skyphoi like fig. 35b,c, with scenes painted inside, are probably based on Phoenician metal bowls, such as were now being dedicated at Olympia and Delphi; perhaps some were also on view in Athens, but the extraordinary horse-legged 'sphinx' in one of these skyphoi (p. 119 n. 22) makes one wonder whether its painter had ever seen an oriental original. The hybrid imitation of an oriental cauldron (fig. 37a) brings similar doubts to mind (p. 129). Around 700 B.C., when the 'Orientalizing' Protoattic style was just beginning, it seems that the Athenians no longer had any direct access to oriental models; new ideas could reach them only at second hand, either through the more progressive vase-painting of Corinth, or through adaptations of oriental cauldrons made by other Greeks.

These changes, around 730 B.C., coincide with a marked increase in the proportion of material coming from the Attic countryside. We have already noted some movement towards the coastlands during the MG period (p. 78), when there are many other indications of Attic commercial enterprise overseas. This process continues in LG I, when a cemetery at Vari receives its first occupants at the beginning of that phase. Between 740 and 700 B.C. a great many more sites show their first signs of habitation since Mycenaean times; but, as the map (fig. 43) shows, nearly all these places lie some way inland, either in the Mesogeia plain, or in the plain round Athens. Agriculture, rather than trade, was the main concern of these new settlers. Furthermore, as we can see from their grave goods, these years also saw a decentralization of wealth, from Athens to the countryside. From c. 770 to 740 B.C. virtually all the richest burials are in Athens itself. Hence come well over thirty figured grave monuments (not a single one from the country); at least twelve figured gold diadems; and many other gold ornaments from the new Kynosarges cemetery. Among the country burials of this time, only Eleusis can boast any comparable signs of affluence in a single find of jewellery and gold relief (p. 125). The dispersal of wealth begins in earnest during the 730s, the date of the six latest grave kraters: one, New York 14.130.15, has no known provenance, but the other five all come from country sites – two from Trachones, one fragment from Thorikos, and one fragment each (unpublished) from Merenda and Brauron. The five huge neck-handled amphorae from the Sub-Dipylon Workshop (c. 735–725 B.C.) suggest a similar story: one from Athens, one from Eleusis, one exported to Eretria, the remaining two without recorded provenance.[70] Thereafter, when grave monuments pass out of fashion, high status is probably denoted by the LG IIb amphorae and hydriae specially made for funerals and encrusted with clay snakes. Unfortunately, since so few of their provenances are known, no general conclusions can be drawn from their distribution; but here it is worth citing the Stathatou amphora from Koropi and two vases from Merenda,[71] as being among the most luxurious vases of their time. A more positive indication of wealth comes from offerings of gold: a

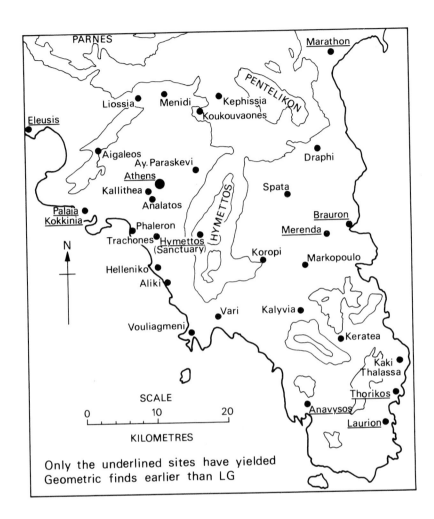

FIG. 43 ATTICA, GEOMETRIC SITES

necklace from Spata gr. 3, a late diadem from a grave at Menidi, and another found in the same grave as the Stathatou amphora at Koropi. With these three rich burials, all from inland sites, we may contrast the poverty of the later graves from the coastal site of Anavysos (where all the gold seems to come from MG II burials), and of all the graves in a new cemetery at Phaleron, beginning in *c.* 710 B.C. and lasting through most of the next century.

From all these various sources of information, a consistent picture emerges. In the middle of the eighth century, Athens was still a city with maritime and commercial interests; but by 730 B.C. many Athenians were contracting out of any enterprise abroad, and had decided to win their livelihood by agriculture. As elsewhere in the Aegean, the sheer quantity of LG material shows how rapidly the population was increasing; yet, while many Euboeans and Corinthians of these years felt impelled to leave their homelands for new colonies in the west, the Athenians had turned their backs on overseas ventures and preferred to colonize their own countryside.

This change of inclination is confirmed in an extraordinary way by the scenes on the grave kraters. On the earliest group (LG Ia) battles are often portrayed, usually involving ships; these commemorate a generation of men who had been in their prime during MG II, and perhaps won much of their wealth from the lively overseas commerce in which Athenians are then known to have been active. But on the later monumental kraters (LG Ib–IIa) the theme of ships, and of all forms of conflict, is suddenly dropped; it is as though these subjects, for some reason, were no longer considered auspicious for a man's personal monument. Did the Athenians, somewhere around 750 B.C., suffer some major reverse, severe enough to paralyse their shipping? Herodotus (v. 82–8) does indeed record the memory of an early naval war, in which Athens was worsted by Aegina with the help of Argos. Cogent reasons have been advanced for believing that Argos was then ruled by the great king Pheidon; and although the date of that monarch has been much disputed, there is a good case (pp. 154–6) for accepting the statement of Pausanias that he was active during the eighth Olympiad (748 B.C.). Finds of Geometric pottery on Aegina throw further light on this war; for, according to Herodotus, one of its economic consequences was an embargo on Attic pottery at the Aeginetan sanctuary of the local goddesses Damia and Auxesia. Although this sanctuary has not yet been located, there is plenty of material from the *polis* and the sanctuary of Aphaia to confirm Herodotus' general inference that, in happier times, Attic pottery was freely imported. In fact, the Aeginetans made no fine pottery of their own, and Attic ware forms the bulk of their Geometric imports. Yet, so far, there is a total absence of Attic LG Ib, the only imports of that time being Corinthian; later, the importation of Attic pottery was resumed in LG II, and continues through the seventh century. Thus there may well be some sub-stance in this dim memory of a conflict which sparked off the 'ancient hostility' between Athens and Aegina, and which might go far towards explaining why Athens was no longer a maritime power in the later eighth century. Such a reverse might also have hastened the rise of landed aristocrats, who established themselves securely in the most fertile land of Attica, and grew richer on its fruits: the great-great-grandfathers of the oppressive gentry against whom Solon the lawgiver was to direct the main weight of his legislation.

From the furnishing of Attic graves, one gets the impression that differences in wealth were increasing throughout the eighth century. Near the bottom of the economic scale were the occupants of the coastal cemetery at Phaleron; many were buried without any offerings at all, while the more fortunate were provided with the cheap, small, and mass-produced vessels which are pejoratively termed 'Phaleron Ware' (p. 117). In Athens itself (fig. 44), whole cemeteries may become socially stratified, as a result of the movement towards family plots. Most of the Kerameikos burials are less well provided than in earlier times, but the 'Platten-bau' group stands out as being moderately rich; three graves there, without

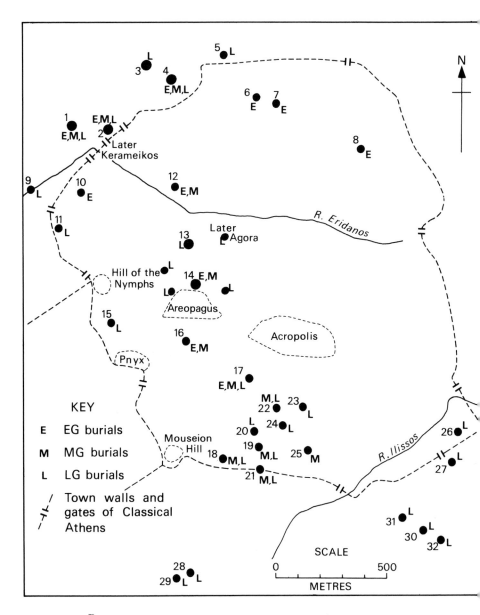

FIG. 44 PLAN OF ATHENS, SHOWING GEOMETRIC BURIALS

Key to FIG. 44

1 Kerameikos area, s. bank of R. Eridanos
2 Kerameikos area, N. bank of R. Eridanos
3 Od.(os) Peiraios
4 Od. Kriezi
5 Od. Sapphous
6 Od. Aischylou
7 Od. Ay. Dimitriou
8 Od. Ay. Markou
9 Od. Demophontos
10 Od. Poulopoulou
11 Od. Erysichthonos/Neleos
12 Od. Hadrianou
13 Agora area, family plot
14 Areopagus
15 Pnyx area
16 Acropolis, w. slope
17 Nymphaeum
18 Od. Garibaldi
19 Od. Kavalotti
20 Od. Promachou
21 Od. Erechtheiou
22 Od. Parthenonos
23 Od. Kallisperi/Karyatidon
24 Od. Robertou Galli
25 Od. Mitsaion/Zetrou
26 Olympieion area
27 Od. Ath. Diakou/Anapafseos
28 Od. Dimitrakopoulou
29 Od. Meidani
30 Od. Theophilopoulou
31 Kynosarges area, *BSA* 12
32 Kynosarges area, *AAA* 5

offerings, might perhaps have been for family slaves.[73] The Agora terrace plot creates a similar impression of medium affluence. Much higher in the social scale are the cemeteries of Kynosarges and Odos Kriezi, well supplied with gold diadems and other lordly wealth. Most aristocratic of all is the burial ground of Odos Peiraios where rich offerings are combined with the distinction of figured grave monuments – a distinction denied to all other Athenian cemeteries except for three graves in the Kerameikos area (nos. 25, 26, hS 290), where all the earlier examples have been found. Since they continue a long series going back to the tenth century, it may be that these monumental vases were reserved for the members of long-standing noble clans – the Medontidai, the Philaidai, and the Neleidai.[74]

NOTES

1 The chief recipients are the Cyclades (especially Andros and Delos), Aegina, Knossos, and – if we can believe dealers' provenances – Thebes.
2 *GGP* 360 n. 1.
3 34.11.2: *GGP* 26–8; *PE* fig. 1; *FLS* figs. 28–30, 50.
4 Toronto 957X245 + Athens 17384; G. Ahlberg, *FLS* figs. 47–8.
5 Eleusis 741; *GGP* 26–8; B. Schweitzer, *GKG* pls. 27–8; *FLS* figs. 42–3; J. Carter, *BSA* 67 (1972), 34–5 pl. 5c.
6 On the perspective see G. Ahlberg, *PE* 268 ff.
7 See Ahlberg, *PE* 42 ff., 72 ff., 114 ff.
8 For this interpretation see *Gnomon* 46 (1974), 395.
9 For their interpretation see pp. 352–4.

10 cf. a *prothesis* by the same hand, Athens 802 (*PE* fig. 7).

11 Carter, art. cit. 41.

12 *AD* 22 (1967), B pl. 89; *PE* text fig. 3.

13 *GGP* pl. 8c,e; *GKG* pl. 41.

14 Several other pitcher-painting workshops of these years have been distinguished, too numerous to mention here, and often difficult to isolate because of the thick network of mutual influences.

15 cf. Schweitzer, *GKG* 53–4.

16 J. M. Davison, *AGW* fig. 40.

17 *GGP* 76–7.

18 *AGW* fig. 33; *PE* fig. 59.

19 R. Tölle, *AA* 1963, 225; Ahlberg, *PE* 193 fig. 41e,f.

20 *GGP* pl. 11g.

21 Paris CA 1780, *CVA* Louvre XVI, pl. 39, 3–4.

22 *GKG* pls. 70, 65.

23 *K* pl. 155.

24 E. Brann, *Agora* VIII, 54–6 pls. 11, 12.

25 For some suggestions see p. 351.

26 Statistics for graves of *c.* 770–750 B.C.: Kynosarges (new excavations), 3 cremations, 6 inhumations; Odos Peiraios (1890 excavations), only 1 cremation (gr. 3), at least 4 inhumations. Contrast the older cemeteries in these years: Kerameikos, 5 cremations, 6 inhumations; Odos Kriezi, cremation apparently persists throughout the Geometric period.

27 *K* grs. 45–66, 99, 100.

28 Pnyx gr., bronze rod tripod from Cyprus; *K* gr. 72, traces of iron legs and handles attached; *K* gr. 71 and Odos Kriezi gr. 26, clay tripod stand.

29 *K* gr. 6; Odos Peiraios gr. 3 (grave monument).

30 *K* grs. 58, 71, 72; Pnyx gr.; Odos Kriezi gr. 26, also containing an iron sword.

31 e.g., fig. 34d and fig. 38a found with fig 40a.

32 For a complete example see Higgins, *Greek TCs* pl. 7f,g, New York 31.11.8.

33 Here the two 'Opferrinnen', both LG IIb, form an exception; these are narrow and shallow ditches dug *outside* the grave, each containing a homogeneous fill of pyre sweepings. It may be that these offerings were made after the funeral – perhaps on the ninth day of mourning according to later Greek custom.

34 e.g., Agora gr. N.11:1 (*c.* 700 B.C.), dug into the fill of a recently abandoned well: E. Brann, *Hesperia* 29 (1960), 413–14.

35 A more modest procession may be indicated on the pitcher London 1912.5–22.1, where the four bier scenes could represent four successive stages in the journey from house to grave, without any transport or armed retinue: see G. Ahlberg, *PE* 253–60 fig. 45a–d.

36 New York 14.130.15: J. Boardman, *JHS* 86 (1966), 1–4 pl. 2b; Ahlberg, *PE* 241–3 fig. 22e.

37 *GGP* 71–2, XIII; J. M. Cook, *BCH* 70 (1946), 97 ff.; Boardman, loc. cit. 4–5 pl. 4.

38 G. Ahlberg, *OpAth* 7 (1967), 177 ff. pls. 1–6, sees N. Syrian influence throughout the series.

39 Earliest contexts: Anavysos gr. 2 (p. 80), diadem not yet published; Kynosarges gr. 19, perhaps still MG II; Odos Kriezi gr. 26, LG Ia (electrum).

40 Ohly A 7–8 pl. 3; *GKG* pl. 229.

41 Ohly 53 ff. pls. 15, 16.

42 e.g., krater, New York 14.130.15, *GKG* pl. 41.

43 Ohly A 11 pl. 4.

44 Ohly A 15–16; add those from Odoi Erysichthonos/Neleos grs. 4 and 7, the latter found with LG IIa vases.

45 Ohly A 17–22. These now have a curious forerunner in the diadem from Odos Kriezi gr. 106, where single ships, single horses, and files of armed warriors are placed in separate panels, and seem to have been embossed *freehand*. For the best photographs see ʽΙστορία τοῦ ʽΕλληνικοῦ ῎Εθνους (Athens, 1971), 194, bottom.

46 The sphinx may have already appeared on the Eleusis matrix of LG I; see J. M. Cook, *Gnomon* 26 (1954), 109.
47 Copenhagen 727, LG IIa; *AGW* fig. 128; *GKG* pl. 69.
48 B. Segall, *Boston Bull.* 41 (1943), 44 ff., citing Levantine prototypes.
49 No less reckless is the superimposition of similar cloisons upon a frieze of horsemen on a LG IIa diadem: Ohly A 19 pls. 9, 12.
50 *Ergon* 1962, fig. 37.
51 Higgins, *BSA* 64 (1969), 148–9 pls. 39b–41d.
52 *AAA* 5 (1972), 173–4 fig. 10.
53 Blinkenberg, VIII 5f–k: Berlin 7902, gold; Copenhagen 742, silver; Copenhagen 493, 723–4, bronze.
54 cf. M. Weber, AM 86 (1971), 20 ff.
55 C. Rolley, *FD* V. 2, 28–9 no. 8.
56 See Schweitzer, *GKG* 145 ff.; M. Weber, *AM* 86 (1971), 25–6. H-V. Herrmann, however, sees them as Argive: *JdI* 79 (1964), 60–2.
57 *GKG* 147 ff. pls. 155–8.
58 *GKG* pls. 164–8.
59 *K* pl. 111 no. 2159; *GKG* pl. 26. cf. also fig. 19a,b.
60 T. J. Dunbabin, *GEN* 38–9.
61 R. D. Barnett, *NI* 44 ff. pls. 70–7; *GKG* pls. 149–50.
62 *AM* 55 (1930), pl. 8.
63 cf. *K* pl. 151.
64 *JdI* 79 (1964), 49 figs. 36–8.
65 *GGP* 349 nn. 1, 2; 361 n. 7.
66 Female mourners are always draped in Mycenaean scenes (see *PE* figs. 66d, 67a,c,d, 68a,b), and almost always in Attic LG II.
67 Benson, *Horse, Bird and Man* 88 ff. pls. 28–31; in Egyptian art, however, mourning ladies are draped.
68 Ahlberg, *FLS* 76 f. fig. 68.
69 *GGP* 361 nn. 1–5.
70 *GGP* 55 nos. 1, 2, 5, 6, 8.
71 *GGP* 57 no. 6; 59 nos. 15, 30.
72 Dunbabin, *BSA* 37 (1936–37), 83–91.
73 J. Bouzek, *Homerisches Griechenland* (Prague, 1970), 182 fig. 72.
74 cf. pp. 352–4 for a possible reference to the Neleids on three of the kraters.

5 The Argolid, Arcadia, Laconia, and Messenia

The next two chapters will be devoted to the Peloponnese, following the expanding influence of Argive and Corinthian Geometric pottery. By 750 B.C. these schools had ceased to depend on Athenian fashions, and were developing individual styles which, in their turn, soon found imitators among their Peloponnesian neighbours. Such influences will enable us to trace some main lines of communication. Thus knowledge of the Argive style spread by land through Arcadia into Laconia, and eventually as far as Messenia; these four regions will be treated together within this chapter. In the next we shall consider the diffusion of Corinthian LG ideas, which travelled by sea down the Gulf, then southward along the west coast of the Peloponnese and also northward as far as Ithaca and Acarnania.

Of the four areas included in this chapter, only the Argolid can boast a sound chronological framework within this period. This is based on a series of at least forty grave groups, illustrating the entire development of the local LG style. With the Argive pottery sequence, then, we shall begin, adding a few remarks on the current burial customs, and the scanty traces of architecture. Next we shall review the outstanding Argive achievements in metalwork – notably, a suit of bronze armour from a warrior's grave, and a fine school of bronze figurines, some made as attachments for tripod cauldrons. Then we pass to the earliest Argive seals, before considering the historical background of the Argolid as a whole during this period.

In the other three regions the material is less abundant, less well stratified, and more fragmentary. The chief Arcadian site is the sanctuary of Athena Alea at Tegea, where the local LG pottery draws on Argive inspiration, but the bronzes are more individual. Laconia, likewise, is represented chiefly by votives from Sparta and Amyclae; from their sanctuaries one can form some impression of a local LG pottery style and a local school of bronzework, both of which display local traits, yet owe something to Argive influence. Finally, after a brief glance at the very scarce material as yet available from Messenia, we shall conclude with some general observations about the rise of Sparta, and any archaeological evidence which could conceivably bear upon the First Messenian War, remembered in later tradition as the conflict after which the people of Messenia first came under Spartan rule some time in the late eighth century.

Argive LG Pottery

The local MG II phase lasts until *c.* 750 B.C. Towards its end some of the larger vases are decorated with a complexity which is characteristically Argive. Their designs, unlike those of Attic MG II, have no strong meander at the centre; instead, small metopal panels encroach on the central area, while the meander itself appears in an attenuated form.[1] Sometimes a mass of thin stripes covers the lower body in the Corinthian manner,[2] in place of the traditional dark ground. These advanced MG II vases were not made before Attic LG Ia, to judge from their use of quatrefoil metopes, hatched zigzags, and vertical wavy lines.

The Argive style reaches the limit of its complexity during a brief LG I phase, contemporary with the later figured grave monuments of Athens (LG Ib), and sometimes applied on a similarly vast scale. A giant pyxis from Argos (fig. 45a) is covered with a patchwork of metopes and panels, over which our eyes travel without coming to rest on any focal point. Horses, birds, and fish are scattered here and there, but are not given any special emphasis. In the linear decoration, three typically Argive motifs appear here for the first time: the step meander, the row of detached leaf-shaped lozenges, and the column of floating chevrons; the hatched zigzags, both horizontal and vertical, are also frequent in this local school.

Argive birds are more varied than Attic; perhaps the marshlands between Argos and the sea allowed the painters more scope for first-hand observation. Thus, on the giant pyxis, three different varieties are seen: stork-like creatures in the corners of a large circle metope; a more compact species (Great Bustards?) on the ribbon feet; and a long-legged type with sinuous neck, rather like a flamingo, often grouped in threes, either hatched or in silhouette (fig. 45c). No less various are the fish – a variety for which the local cuisine is still renowned. But the dominant part is played by the horse. The stallions on the giant pyxis are of an exclusively Argive type, characterized by the horizontal muzzle, the protruding shoulder, the bushy tail, and the backward bend of the forelegs; another local idea is the insertion of a small panel in the field above the animal's back. Man, on this vase, is confined to the spaces below the handles, which are occupied by two pairs of straining wrestlers;[3] their long, lithe bodies recall some figures from the Athenian Dipylon Workshop, and the crossing of their elongated necks binds each pair into a powerful triangular composition. Slightly earlier (*c.* 750 B.C.?), and much cruder, is a figured panel on a large krater fragment (fig. 45b), presenting a dance and a feat of horse-taming. Perhaps these activities formed part of a local festival by the sea, indicated here by two fish, a waterbird, and zigzag waves; or perhaps the various elements were not intended to form a connected scene, but are simply taken at random from the 'pattern-book' of an ambitious and inventive painter. At all events the panel combines the only three common themes of Peloponnesian Geometric figured drawing. The Corinthians were to specialize in the bird-and-wave motif. The Arcadians and Laconians showed a preference for the row of dancers, who always join hands and usually carry branches; in the Argolid, as also in Attica (p. 119), this subject was

especially popular near the end of Geometric (e.g., fig. 46e). But the favourite
Argive theme is the horse-tamer, who persists throughout LG, controlling either
one or two horses. A marshbird, or a fish, is often inserted under the horse's
belly, not merely to fill the field, but perhaps also to refer to earlier and more
detailed scenes like fig. 45b – that is, if such a scene was meant to form a coherent
unity.

Before we follow the main Argive sequence any further, the local pottery of
Asine deserves attention. Long after the other centres in the Argolid had broken
free of Athenian influence, Asinaean potters continued to show some acquaintance
with Attic LG fashions. For example, a skyphos from a house deposit of *c.* 730
B.C. (fig. 46b) is decorated with Atticizing square metopes, a system never used
on drinking-vessels made in Argos. Some larger Attic shapes, too, are imitated
here and nowhere else in the Argolid: for instance, a spouted krater,[4] and an
oinochoe related by shape and decoration to an Attic LG IIa class bearing large
sets of thick concentric circles.[5] The sequence at Asine stops abruptly in *c.* 710
B.C., when the town was destroyed and abandoned until the Hellenistic period.

We return to the more orthodox pottery of the Argolid in its LG II stage.
Figured scenes are now more frequent and prominent; the usual themes are
horse-taming and (near the end) dancing, with a few rare departures into the
realms of war, sport, and funerary ritual.[6] Linear ornament, with the aid of the
labour-saving multiple brush, becomes increasingly cursive and mechanical. The
leading shapes, which attract most of the figured drawing, are the low-footed
krater (with horizontal or vertical handles), the large kantharos with low handles,
the amphora (shoulder-handled as well as neck-handled), and a new kind of flat
pyxis with horizontal handles and vertical walls. Plainer forms include the
skyphos, the cup, and various forms of oinochoe; also the kotyle and the conical
lekythos-oinochoe, both borrowed from the Corinthian repertoire.

A high-handled krater of *c.* 725 B.C. (fig. 46a) preserves some of the grand
manner of the giant LG I pyxis, particularly in the elaborate subdivision of the
surface; but the figured drawing is now more mannered, and the filling ornament
has become a hailstorm. The horseman and his two stallions all have extremely
long legs, and each animal's neck curves round in a full semicircle. The man's
diamond-shaped chest is a typically Argive convention, also seen in bronze
figurines (fig. 49a–c). Silhouette birds are now mass-produced in continuous
files, with the multiple brush. A large kantharos of *c.* 710 B.C. (fig. 46c) is by a
less ambitious, but more accomplished, hand; his horses, placed in side-panels,
seem to gaze over a triple fence towards a meagre step-meander – a formula
which had some appeal for a Laconian imitator (fig. 52e).

Towards the end of the century much Argive work is wild and undisciplined;
but one painter's work forms a distinguished exception. He specialized in bellied
kraters with stirrup handles, on which the main motif is a neatly drawn group of
dancing women. A krater exported to Corinth (fig. 46e) shows them in a static
pose, their long girdle strings trailing on the ground.[7] In the ancillary bird files,
legs have now degenerated into mere wiggles. The Geometric pottery of Argos
ends with the splendid krater C 201;[8] its linear ornament still lies within the
scope of Geometric painting, but various details of the horse-taming panels
recall Orientalizing experiments elsewhere: for instance, the detailed rendering

a

b

c

FIG. 45 ARGIVE LG I POTTERY
(a) Argos C 209, H. 104; (b) Argos C 240, detail; (c) Mycenae
53-337, H. 24.3

FIG. 46 ARGIVE LG II POTTERY, AND HANDMADE WARE
(a) Argos C 1, H. 31; (b) Asine, from house deposit (*Asine* fig. 224
no. 6), H. 8.5; (c) Argos C 171 from gr. 45 (Panoply Grave), H. 15.2;
(d) Argos C 16, H. 22; (e) Corinth T 2545, N. cemetery gr. 47,
detail; (f) Argos C 55, H. 12.2

of the human features, the barrel-chested physique of the stallions, and the use of white paint to mark inner anatomical lines, all reminiscent of early black-figure work by the Protocorinthian school. It is likely, then, that Argive LG II lasted at least one decade into the seventh century. Thereafter, figured scenes were not often attempted; the most characteristic vase is a deep stirrup-handled krater, whose decoration is dominated increasingly by Subgeometric festoons of horizontal and vertical zigzags.

Argive handmade wares are still extremely plentiful, whether in domestic, votive, or funerary contexts; in cemeteries they are usually, though not always, associated with female burials. Although the older, coarse fabric lasts throughout the century especially for the larger shapes,[9] the new, thin-walled technique becomes increasingly common. It is seen at its best in a late MG II amphora (fig. 46d) and a LG I conical oinochoe (fig. 46f); there are also many globular and (in LG II) conical aryballoi. The clay is often more fastidiously prepared than for wheelmade pots, and always well polished with a blunt (wooden?) implement; after a relatively low firing, the surface assumes a light leather-brown hue. The smaller forms – particularly the conical aryballos – were also popular in Attica and Corinth, where they have misleadingly been classified as 'Argive Monochrome'. In fact they are local imitations, not Argive exports; and the Athenian imitators often added light rouletted patterns which are not characteristic of the Argive originals.[10] This ware continues through the seventh century.

Argive Architecture and Burial Customs

The coastal town of Asine was destroyed during the LG period, and abandoned for the next four centuries. It is thus a good place to look for Geometric domestic architecture, unencumbered by any Archaic or Classical overlay. The 'Geometric Terrace' on the acropolis preserves the foundations of several houses, including a one-roomed rectangular building ($3 \cdot 20 \times 4 \cdot 50$m.) entered through one of the long sides.[11] In the lower town, walls of this period are flimsy and scattered; but near the foot of the Barbouna hill a more substantial building, probably apsidal, is coming to light. It contains a small cobbled area which may have been used as a hearth.[12]

Eight kilometres north-east of Argos lies the Argive Heraion, the chief sanctuary of the whole region. The earliest temple there cannot be precisely dated, but the terrace on which it stands was probably prepared before 700 B.C.[13] The retaining wall is composed of long, flat, unworked boulders, laid in fairly regular courses, but without any attempt to fill the considerable crevices between them.[14] This is perhaps the most massive wall to have survived from Geometric Greece.

For the burials, inhumation remains the rule; a few cases of cremation (or part-cremation) have been suspected at Asine, Nauplia, and in the eastern quarter of Argos, but none has been proved beyond doubt.[15] As before, inhumations may be in cists or in pithoi, whether of adults or of children. Tiryns and Nauplia now show a preference for pithoi; at Asine, four children were buried in two cists below the floor of the Barbouna house, during its period of occupation.[16] Re-use of cists and pithoi is quite common, particularly at Argos, where one huge pithos (gr. 190) received three successive adult interments within the LG period. In re-used cists, earlier skeletons and offerings are often treated with such great respect that one assumes them to have been reserved for specific families.

One LG II cist, Argos gr. 45, is the grave of a warrior, outstanding both for its size (it is 3m. long) and for the variety of its contents. Although plundered in ancient times, it held the richest haul of Geometric offerings ever found in the Argolid. These will provide a good starting-point for the consideration of Argive Geometric work in various metals.

Argive Metalwork

In rich Attic graves of this time, gold ornaments were the chief indicators of prosperity; in the Argolid, wealth is more often expressed in iron. The warrior of Argos gr. 45 is now well known for his panoply of bronze armour, and his grave also contained three gold finger-rings and a piece of gold leaf with linear decoration – almost the only gold so far reported from LG burials in the Argolid; but it is the iron offerings, twelve fragmentary spits and a pair of firedogs, that mark him out as a man of substance. We are reminded of the feast of roast meat which Achilles personally cooked for the visitors of his tent at Troy: after allowing his fire to die down, he gathered together the hot embers, and duly revolved the spitted meat supported on the firedogs.[17] Just as heroic warriors did not disdain the role of cook, so our Argive warrior was furnished with the equipment for keeping a hospitable hearth and a convivial table in the next world. His pair of iron double axes, by now somewhat obsolete as offensive weapons, would enable him to hew logs for his fire.[18]

To be buried with iron spits and firedogs is a rare distinction shared by only four other men in the Greek world, all of whom were warriors: one in a tholos tomb at Kavousi in East Crete,[19] the remaining three in built tombs at three sites in Cyprus – Old Paphos, Salamis, and Patriki.[20] All ten firedogs take the form of a warship, each one resting on two stands riveted at right-angles to the ship's long body. Although there are differences of detail, the whole group is homogeneous enough for us to suppose some sharing of ideas between Argos, Crete, and Cyprus – not least because the pairs from Kavousi, Paphos, and Salamis appear to belong to the same generation as the Argos firedogs (fig. 47c), which are themselves securely dated by the accompanying pottery (e.g., fig. 46c) to *c.* 710 B.C.[21] Cyprus is the most likely place for their invention, not only because it has yielded most of the known examples, but because only there can we see a continuous tradition of offering the concomitant spits in tombs, beginning with bronze prototypes in the late eleventh century.[22]

Most of the twelve spits from the Argive warrior's grave are sadly fragmentary, but one (fig. 47a) is virtually complete; better preserved are the six from gr. 1. The usual length was *c.* 1·60m.; in section they are square or rectangular, so that the meat shall not slip when rotated over the fire. Their only unfunctional feature is the heart-shaped metallic handle, which would surely burn the cook's fingers – the Cypriots, more practical in these matters, preferred a socketed spit

FIG. 47 ARGOS, PANOPLY GRAVE, IRON AND BRONZE
(a) iron spit, L. 111; (b) bronze panoply, HS. 46 (helmet),
47.4 (corslet); (c) iron firedogs, L. 129

to which a wooden handle was attached. But it is their numbers, in this grave and in each of the warrior burials, that tell us most clearly that their significance was more than functional: six in gr. 1, twelve in gr. 45 and at Salamis (there, a neat bundle bound with two rings and a handle), eighteen at Paphos and Patriki – always a multiple of six. Already, it seems, they had become an index of wealth, a primitive currency. A century later, the memory of these spits (*oboloi* or *oboloi*) was preserved in the word for the smallest unit of the first Greek silver currency; and the handful (*drachma*) of six spits – even the doughtiest hand could grasp no more – supplied a name which has persisted as the basic unit of ancient and modern Greek money. But before the change from an iron to a silver currency could take place, it was necessary that the weight of the spits should first be standardized. This reform may possibly be ascribed to king Pheidon of Argos, although the ancient traditions relating to that monarch's monetary legislation (pp. 154–5) are somewhat confused.

Although offensive weapons are by no means uncommon in other Argive burials of this period,[23] none had eluded the eyes of the looters who ransacked this warrior's grave; but they left behind his most glorious possession, the panoply of bronze. This consists of a helmet and a corslet, both virtually complete (fig. 47b); and a few strips, perhaps from a pair of greaves.

Metallic helmets were a novel luxury in this age, hardly seen since Mycenaean times.[24] This is one of the oldest and best-preserved of the Kegelhelm class, whose component parts are hammered on to a round core, and riveted together: a conical top, separate plates for the forehead and the back of the neck, and two cheekpieces. Our helmet is crowned by a cast vertical stilt which supports a crest-holder shaped like a horseshoe, worn fore and aft. Although the cheekpieces have Mycenaean forebears,[25] the conical top and the fore-and-aft crest have their immediate precedents in an oriental type seen in Assyrian stone reliefs of the reign of Tiglath-Pileser III (745–727 B.C.), and probably native to the east Anatolian kingdom of Urartu.[26] In earlier LG vase-painting, helmets can be detected only by their backward-drooping crests (e.g., figs. 33a, b, 34a), which could well have been attached to non-metallic headgear – perhaps leather. Now, at the time of the Panoply burial, metal helmets are distinctly indicated, standing out sharply from the outline of the head; and the horseshoe crests appear on the Attic LG IIb cauldron in fig. 37b, as well as on contemporary Argive sherds.[27] The Kegelhelm seems to have been designed more for show than for safety; it left the face unguarded, it perched uneasily on top of the head, and its cone offered an easy grip for an enemy in close combat. Small wonder, then, that it was soon to be superseded by the more protective and close-fitting Corinthian helmet, which had already been evolved by 700 B.C. (p. 177).

A more useful precedent is set by the bell-shaped corslet, the earliest known body armour from Iron Age Greece. It has a remote ancestor in an early Mycenaean panoply from Dendra; but the intervening stages can be seen in a series of corslets from the Urnfield Culture of Central Europe, which offers precedents for the bell shape, and the semicircular marking of the breasts.[28] For the transmission of the idea from Central Europe back to Greece, the most likely route is through Italy, where early Greek merchants and colonists could have seen imported Urnfield body-armour. Our warrior's corslet is no beginner's piece, and can hardly be the earliest product of its local school; and, apart from its technical excellence, it also possesses a sculptural quality prophetic of another Argive masterpiece, the monumental Archaic statues of the twins Cleobis and Biton.[29] In figured art, the earliest known representation of a metal corslet is on an Attic amphora of *c.* 720 B.C.,[30] where its flaring rim projects from the hips of a warrior on horseback. This picture also tells us something about the social significance of the new bronze body armour; like the horse, the corslet is at first the preserve of the aristocratic mounted warrior, who played the leading part in early Greek wars before the rise of the hoplite soldier.[31] During the next two generations, when the notion of marshalling heavy-armed infantry in a close phalanx was gradually perfected, the bronze corslet was to become a most essential article of a hoplite soldier's panoply, and was to remain so until shortly before the Persian Wars. But this is not the place to discuss the hoplite revolution, which is a largely post-Geometric development; suffice it to say that our young Argive aristocrat was exceptionally well-armed for his day, and that his compatriots have as strong a claim as any other Greeks to be regarded as the inventors of hoplite warfare.

The other bronzes from graves – pins, fibulae, finger-rings, and bowls – require little comment. The dress pins, now longer than ever,[32] do not differ sharply from the MG type, apart from their more attenuated biconical globes, and the addition of two reels to the finial. Of the more ornate varieties from the Argive Heraion,[33] where globes and reels proliferate, it is not clear whether any precede 700 B.C. Of the square-catchplate fibulae there is one from a pithos burial at Lerna (*c.* 730 B.C.), and several fragments from the Argive Heraion;[34] all seem to be imports from Boeotia. The hemispherical bowl, now extinct in Attica, persists in Argos through the eighth century; there is also a shallower type with mobile handle from Argos gr. 6/2, which may have two counterparts in Evangelidis' grave at Mycenae.[35] Unlike its Corinthian contemporary (p. 175) it lacks the oriental omphalos; nevertheless miniature clay phialai, with conical omphaloi, have turned up in a votive *bothros* deposit on the acropolis of Tiryns,[36] which goes back to LG.

Judging from their expertise in other forms of bronzework, one would also expect Argive smiths to produce figurines of high quality. The votives dedicated at the Heraion form the starting point for distinguishing an Argive school, but its finest products have been sought out from greater sanctuaries elsewhere – especially Olympia – through affinities of style and technique.[37] It must be acknowledged that the Argive manner cannot yet be defined with the same clarity as the schools of Corinth and Sparta. Yet the Heraion horses, at least, conform fairly closely to a local type with long legs, tall neck, flattened mane, and high rump; the muzzle is usually horizontal (as in Argive LG vase-painting), hocks and fetlocks are marked on the best pieces, and the modelling throughout is rounded and truly three-dimensional. All these characteristics are combined in a superb horse from Olympia (fig. 48b), where numerous examples display this style at its finest.

The horses served two different functions. Many are attached to a solid rectangular base, separately cast, and hollowed out underneath with a design in relief or intaglio – usually a linear motif, more rarely a figured theme. The horse

a   b

FIG. 48 ARGIVE BRONZE HORSES, FROM OLYMPIA
(a) Br 5471, detail (cf. fig. 107); (b) B 1308, H. 8.5

figurines from Olympia are without bases, and this may mean that they were made locally by Argive smiths catering for compatriot votaries. The other main function of the horse was to crown the ring-handles of tripod cauldrons, for which Argos may have been an important centre of production (pp. 335–6). On the earliest class from Olympia, those with massive cast handles, the bull-protome is the favourite ornament, and we sometimes see a characteristically Argive sort of bird;[38] horses, whenever they occur at this early stage, are more summarily executed (e.g., fig. 48a; cf. p. 335). More akin to the Heraion figurines is a horse with its master, upon a later handle with openwork design.[39]

As in the local vase-painting, man's chief role is as a tamer of horses. An early and rather primitive figure from the Argive Heraion[40] probably served in this capacity, riveted on to a massive cast handle.[41] After a considerable interval, probably not before LG I, comes a stocky, powerfully-built horse-tamer from Olympia (fig. 49a–c) which has been tentatively assigned to the Argolid;[42] like his Attic contemporary (fig. 40b–d) he brandished a spear in his right hand, and with his left held the horse's rein. Very striking is the preternatural size of his head, the bold rendering of the facial features, and the incised detail of his hair. From frontal view his body is sharply articulated, and looks static and austere; but the modelling is surprisingly sensitive when seen in profile. His diamond-shaped chest, which we have already observed in the local vase-painting (cf. fig. 46a), is a typically (but not exclusively) Argive trait which we meet again in a later group of charioteers from Olympia.[43] In fig. 49d–e, one of the best pre-served, the figure is even more thick-set, and lacks the controlled co-ordination of the earlier horsetamer; but there has been progress in the shaping of the shoulder, and in the careful detail of the hands which held the reins. This proud, cheerful, and lively figure may have been dedicated by one of the first victors in the Olympic chariot race.

Argive Seals

From the Argive Heraion comes a collection of some sixty seals, all of the eighth and early seventh centuries B.C. As we have seen (pp. 56, 130), there had been a few previous experiments in ivory by Attic craftsmen; but this is the first large accumulation anywhere in Greece since the end of the Bronze Age, and these seals are all of stone. The most usual material is the soft, soapy stone conventionally called 'steatite' (more correctly, serpentine), found in several different colours; limestone and marble are rarer materials. As one would expect in an art which had been forgotten during the Dark Ages, the engraving technique is rather primitive. Many are covered with careless surface incision; even on the best (fig. 50) the designs are cut in grooves with a fairly uniform V-shaped section, so that even the figured scenes have a linear, two-dimensional look. This simple method of cutting was also practised in North Syria, where most of the earliest Greek shapes, too, have their origin; the only certain exceptions here are the rectangular seal-bases for bronze animals (p. 149), which are of local inspiration.

Because of their rudimentary style, many Geometric seals defy attribution to regional schools; but the sheer quantity from the Heraion establishes Argos as a leading centre, and the other common provenances – Mycenae, Perachora, Megara, Aegina, and Sparta – are all within reach of Argos.

The earliest class at the Argive Heraion are flat squares, bevelled on their plain sides, through which a hole is pierced – possibly for a wooden handle.[44] A clue to their date is offered by the context of one from Perachora, found with pottery not later than 720 B.C. (p. 174). Since the finest and most ambitious figured specimen was discovered and possibly made in Melos (p. 210, fig. 68a), it is possible that the inspiration for this group may have come via the Cyclades. More specifically Argive are two other classes – hemispherical and rectangular tabloid – whose figured designs sometimes remind us of the local LG pottery. Of especial interest is a tabloid now in Paris, decorated on four of its six sides; a hole passes lengthways between the two plain faces, so that the seal could have been worn as a bead or pendant. Two of the decorated sides carry abstract motifs – a chevron-filled swastika, and a stack of M-chevrons; the other two (fig. 50b) show a man with a stick or whip, and a mythical scene in which an archer threatens a centaur who waves a branch in either hand (p. 354).

Somewhat later, perhaps c. 700 B.C., is a lentoid disc from the Heraion (fig. 50a), with a typically Argive scene: two women dancing, their girdle-strings trailing down in the usual way; in the field two branches, a bird, and perhaps a snake. This is the earliest of a well-defined group[45] which takes us well into the seventh century; by this time the initiative in seal-engraving was being seized by Corinthian artists, who preferred the more tractable material of ivory (p. 177). Corinthian influence may perhaps be seen in the different size of the two faces.

One may wonder how many of these early seals were used as such. The intaglios under the bronze horses seem too big; and the majority of stone seals carry nothing more than nondescript abstract patterns, hardly distinctive enough to be easily told apart in impressions. Yet if we are right in thinking that the early squares had handles, they must have been put to some use; and it so happens that the only known impressions from a Greek Geometric seal are of square shape, showing a warrior carrying a dead comrade out of battle (p. 228 fig. 75d).

The Argolid: Conclusions

Literary references to the early history of the Argolid are more abundant than for Attica; but since they are beset with contradictions, we should begin with the archaeological evidence concerning the Argives at home, and their relations with other parts of Greece.

No site in the Argolid is more prolific than Argos itself, where fashions for the whole region were set in pottery, metalwork, and seals. From the flourishing industries in bronze and iron, and from the great terracing operation at the Argive Heraion, we get the impression of an exceptionally wealthy and powerful *polis*. The relative abundance of LG graves there implies a steep rise in population; likewise, from the siting of the cemeteries we can deduce that the town expanded considerably during LG times.[46]

Argive LG pottery is a highly individual fabric, but it resembles Attic in one respect: the best work is done on the grand scale, whereas small shapes tend to be carelessly mass-produced. As in Attica, we can assume that major vases were made for funerals of aristocrats: an aristocracy for whom horses mattered a great deal, to judge from the frequency of horse-taming scenes.[47] Apart from the size and elaboration of the clay vessels, wealth and high status can also be indicated by offerings in iron and bronze: spits, firedogs, weapons, and armour. The young nobleman buried with his bronze panoply (fig. 47) must have been one of the best-armed soldiers of his time, and gives us a vivid impression of the military might of Argos.

Communications within the Argive plain must have been close, since the LG style of Argos recurs at Mycenae, Tiryns, and Nauplia without local variation; what is more, all three sites have yielded large figured vases made in the same workshops as their counterparts from Argos.[48] About the pottery from the eastern Argolid, not much is known; at Asine, however, there are signs of an unorthodox hankering after Attic fashions, followed by destruction and abandonment in *c.* 710 B.C. As a port, Asine was more sensitive to external influence, and no other Argive site has produced a greater proportion of imported pots – Attic, Corinthian, and one Rhodian. Yet its Atticizing style, unique in the Argolid, might also suggest political separation from the main plain, from which it is isolated by low hills.

In the outside world, Argive LG pots have been found at Corinth (fig. 46e),

FIG. 49 ARGIVE BRONZE MEN, FROM OLYMPIA
(a–c) B 4600, H. 14.4; (d–e) B 1670, H. 13.6

a   b   c

d   e

Aegina, Tegea, Melos, Kythera, and Megara Hyblaea in Sicily; perhaps also at Knossos, Aetos in Ithaca, and Corcyra.[49] Yet, in spite of their wide circulation, their quantity is far too small to indicate any interest in commerce. Indeed, the pots found at sanctuaries (i.e., of Aegina, Tegea, and Ithaca) are surely personal votives left by Argive visitors, and the same applies to the Argive bronzes at Olympia and Delphi, and the Argive seals at Olympia, Aegina, and Sparta.[50] Nevertheless, the Argive LG style had a considerable influence on the local pottery of Arcadia and Laconia, and made some impression on the Messenians; and much wider contacts, however indirect, are implied by the Cretan and Cypriot counterparts for the firedogs, and the Central European and Near Eastern affinities of the bronze panoply.

The destruction of Asine is easily reconciled with the literary record. According to Pausanias (ii.36.4–5; iii.7.4; iv.14.3), the destroyer was Eratos, king of Argos; his pretext, that the Asinaeans had joined Nicander, king of Sparta in an invasion of the Argolid. Perhaps it was in one of these commotions that the warrior of the Panoply Grave lost his life, aged between twenty-five and thirty. After a long struggle the land of Asine was annexed by Argos, and the town razed except for the sanctuary of Apollo Pythaeus; this shrine has been identified at the top of the Barbouna hill, and is in fact the only source of Archaic and Classical finds anywhere on the site. The refugees from Asine were granted a new home in Messenia by their Spartan allies while the First Messenian War was still being waged (p. 163).

Before the rise of Sparta, Argos has the reputation of being the strongest state in Greece. Herodotus (i.82) recalls that she had once controlled the east Peloponnesian seaboard down to Cape Malea, together with the island of Kythera; this large domain, for a time, stood in the way of Spartan expansion.[51] These early memories must refer to the middle and later eighth century. The Malea region, rich in iron ore,[52] may have supplied Argos in a flourishing period when her iron industry was extremely productive. Now the rugged coastlands of the eastern Peloponnese are approachable only by sea, and could not have been held without a navy; nor, without warships, could the Argives have come to the rescue of the Aeginetans against an Athenian attack (Hdt. v.86). In the late eighth century, the memory of the Argive navy is preserved in the form of the iron firedogs (fig. 47c); in no subsequent period do we hear of Argos as a sea power.

The early fortunes of Argos were thought to have reached their zenith during the reign of king Pheidon, who was chiefly remembered for three achievements: his reunion of the Lot of Temenos (i.e., the whole Argolid), his standardization of *metra* (perhaps weights and measures), and his sacrilegious seizure of the Olympian sanctuary. This last event is dated by Pausanias (vi.22.2) to the eighth Olympiad, i.e., 748 B.C.; Herodotus, however (vi.127.3), implies that he was the contemporary of the tyrant Cleisthenes of Sicyon around 600 B.C., which is too late for any Argive ascendancy. Many modern historians prefer to place him in an intermediate period, seeing his hand in the Argive victory over the Spartans at Hysiai in 669 B.C., and in the usurpation of the Olympic festival by his putative allies the Pisatans in the following year; they would accordingly emend the text Pausanias to read 'twenty-eighth Olympiad'.[53] When this readjustment was

FIG. 50 ARGIVE STONE SEALS
(a) Athens 14066, *AH* II pl. 138, 22, D. 3.5; (b) Paris, Bibl. Nat.
M 5837, L. 2.2 (photographs by R. L. Wilkins)

first propounded, the archaeology of early Argos was virtually unknown, and much was made of a statement by Ephorus that Pheidon had minted the first silver coinage of Aegina – a statement now seen to be incompatible on numismatic grounds with an early seventh-century date,[54] and based on a misunderstanding of what Pheidon actually did. Herodotus, our oldest source, speaks not of coins, but more vaguely of *metra*, and it remains possible that Pheidon's reform may have governed the weight of iron spits (*oboloi*), the currency which preceded the invention of coinage. Unfortunately, the most careful scrutiny of the Argive spits[55] has not revealed any obvious consistency of weight at any time; the main difficulties for such a study are the scarcity of whole spits, the rarity of datable contexts (most are from sanctuaries, including a bundle of ninety-six from the Argive Heraion), and the inevitable hazards of corrosion and oxidization which can drastically alter the original weight. If anything can be salvaged from the confused literary tradition, it could be that Pheidon was the first ruler to recognize iron spits as an official currency, regulating the *drachma* (handful) as a fixed *metron* consisting of six *oboloi*; in which case, his legislation would have preceded the earliest known set of six in Greece (Argos gr. 1, *c.* 725 B.C.).

We return, then, to Pausanias, who places Pheidon in the mid-eighth century. A full review of the literary sources[56] has shown that there is no internal inconsistency – that is, if we exclude the impossibly low date given by Herodotus who may have confused the great Pheidon with a later namesake. It is perfectly credible that Pheidon marched an army to Olympia, seized the sanctuary and presided over the Games of 748 B.C., was later worsted by an alliance between Elis and Sparta, and eventually met his end in the 730s while interfering in the internal politics of Corinth. Archaeological evidence, because of its anonymous nature, cannot offer any decisive clue to his date;[57] but, on balance, it is reasonable to see him as the ruler of a large, strong, prosperous, and influential *polis*. As we have seen, its size was greatly increased during LG; although we know little about the settlement itself, its affluence in this period may be gauged by contrasting the rich offerings in LG graves with the poverty of burials through most of the seventh century[58] – a poverty which makes it difficult to believe in a seventh-century Pheidon. Of Argos' military might in the late eighth century, the bronze panoply is a revealing token. At this time an air of prosperity is conveyed by the flourishing local styles of pottery and bronzework, seen at their climax in monumental vases like fig. 45a, and the large cast tripods whose fragments abound at the Argive Heraion. Similar tripods are also plentiful at Olympia, whether exported from Argos, or cast *in situ* by Argive smiths. Argive LG pottery, though rarely exported, nevertheless had a profound influence in the central and southern Peloponnese: hardly surprising, if the territory of Argos in *c.* 750 B.C. had extended beyond Cape Malea. In no subsequent period can any such claims be made for the vigour and originality of Argive art, coupled with its ascendancy in other Peloponnesian lands. With good reason, the chief excavator of Geometric Argos singles out this age as 'pour l'Argolide une nouvelle et peut-être dernière époque de grandeur'.[59]

Arcadia

Almost all the Geometric finds in Arcadia are from sanctuaries. The most prolific is at Tegea, dedicated to a local goddess, Athena Alea; it offers a rich variety of bronzes, and the only substantial collection of Arcadian Geometric pottery.

Although the larger shapes are preserved only in fragments, their decoration is much indebted to Argive LG pottery.[60] The figured work includes several horses of Argive build, which may have fish under the belly, or a small enclosed panel above the back. Argive friezes of flamingo-like birds are also imitated. Dancers, too, appear, both male and female, and once together on the same vase; this, when made up,[61] proved to be a pyxis of the Argive cylindrical type, but the dancers' necks are grotesquely elongated, and the addition of a continuous string (?) across their waists is a local notion. Another sherd shows a man rowing a ship – a curious subject for a place so remote from the sea. Local taste is also reflected in an enormous drinking-horn (no. 251), and in the painting of miniature handmade pots, chiefly cups and oinochoai (nos. 232–46). Around 700 B.C., there is a hint of Laconian inspiration in the flat vertical handles of vast ritual oinochoai, adorned with painted or relief snakes.[62] Yet Argive influence continued into the first quarter of the seventh century, to judge from the fragments found on the early acropolis of Tegea's rival city, Mantinea.[63]

The Tegean bronzes are supplemented by smaller collections from two sanctuaries of Artemis, one a little further south at Mavriki, the other at Lousoi in northern Arcadia. There are a few horses, all of Argive appearance except for a yoked pair from Lousoi which have a distinctly Laconian look. More numerous, at least among the Tegean figurines, are the animals which are especially appropriate to the Arcadian landscape: the couchant bulls, for which there was plenty of rich pasture in the small upland plains; and the stags, which ranged over the surrounding mountains. There are also plenty of birds, two sheep, a dog, and – again, rather surprisingly – a dolphin. The human figures form a small but mixed group, all apparently freestanding. The most individual are the

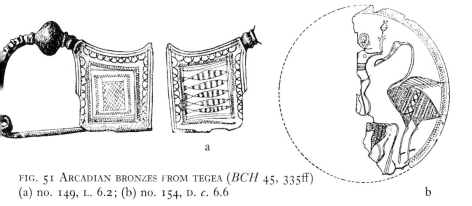

FIG. 51 ARCADIAN BRONZES FROM TEGEA (*BCH* 45, 335ff)
(a) no. 149, L. 6.2; (b) no. 154, D. *c.* 6.6   b

water-carriers and the seated men, represented at Tegea and Mavriki; two
groups of round-dancers, which have been tentatively ascribed to Arcadia;[64] and
three nude female figures riding horses side-saddle, found at Tegea, Lousoi,
and Olympia.[65] At Lousoi this last type continues in the local Archaic terracottas,
and probably represents the Arcadian Artemis (later, Artemis Soteira) who was
believed to be the daughter of Demeter and of Poseidon Hippios. On a fragmentary bronze disc from Tegea (fig. 51b) she appears again, standing precari-
ously upon an animal's back: a Mistress of Animals before whom a monstrous
bird bows in reverence, and at the same time a goddess of fertility waving a
poppy aloft.[66] The idea of showing a deity standing upon an animal could have
been borrowed from Neo-Hittite art;[67] yet, in such a conservative land as
Arcadia, the attributes of the local Artemis may well have been derived from a
Mycenaean goddess of vegetation and wild nature.

The figure style of this disc recalls the engraved plates of fibulae, especially the
Subgeometric series of Boeotia. Some fibulae of this class have been found at
Tegea and Lousoi, but the variety shown in fig. 51a seems more at home in
Arcadia; six similar examples are said to come from a grave at Andritsena.[68]
Yet there are many more of this type (Blinkenberg VII) from southern Thessaly,
and a few are known from Olympia, Delphi, the Argive Heraion, and Achaea;
they were evidently made in more than one place. The distinguishing features
are the globe on the bow, flanked by reels; and the acute angle formed by the
outer corner of the plate. Those from Arcadia all bear figured themes enclosed
in a heavy, double border. Birds and fish (as on fig. 51a) are common subjects,
and coincide on a closely related fibula from a context of *c.* 750–730 at Delphi.[69]

Laconia

Hemmed in by the mountain walls of Taÿgetus and Parnon, the Laconian plain
was more or less isolated from the rest of the Peloponnese throughout the Dark
Ages. Pottery in the local style which passes for 'Protogeometric'[70] comes
mainly from the sanctuary of Apollo at Amyclae, where it is stratified immed-

FIG. 52 LACONIAN LG POTTERY FROM AMYCLAE (d,f) AND SPARTA
(a) Chalkioikos, H. 9.5; (b) Orthia, H. 12.5; (c) Orthia, H. 6.1;
(d) Amyclae, Athens 234, H. 22; (e) Orthia, H. 7; (f) Amyclae, H. 18;
(g) Orthia

iately under a LG layer; it must, then, have persisted through the ninth into the early eighth century, and this impression is confirmed by the absence in Laconia of any settled phases corresponding to EG and MG pottery elsewhere.

Shortly before 750 B.C. this isolation was coming to an end. First there are a few imported MG sherds[71] and local imitations; and then a Laconian LG style is established, much influenced by Argive ornament. About the shapes less is known, as nearly all the material comes from sanctuaries (mainly Artemis Orthia at Sparta) where whole profiles are scarce; nevertheless, there are several hints of an abiding local tradition, inherited from the Amyclaean 'Protogeometric'. This would account for the tall, baggy shapes of many drinking-vessels, with a low centre of gravity: for instance, the authentically Laconian form of skyphos known as the lakaina (fig. 52c) and its near relations shown in fig. 52a,b.[72] Other typical shapes are the large deep tankard,[73] the tall pyxis (fig. 52d), the plate (fig. 52e), and the krater (fig. 52f). Not long before 700 B.C. the globular aryballos and the conical lekythos-oinochoe were introduced from Corinth; the latter is sometimes enlarged to a vast size for sanctuary use, and a terracotta snake may be added to its flat vertical handle.[74]

The decoration, at first, draws heavily upon the Argive stock. Especially common are the zones of leaf-shaped lozenges; hatched zigzags and step-meanders are also found, as well as the more universal meanders and meander hooks; gridded versions of the last two are a Laconian trait, and so is the close alternation of bands and stripes as on fig. 52c. As the style progresses, smaller pots tend more and more to be coated with a thin creamy slip as a ground for decoration, enhancing the contrast between light and dark. Later on, several Corinthian motifs were adopted, including thin zones of check, dotted snakes, and short rays (fig. 52g).[75] Files of small silhouette birds are occasionally found, sometimes recalling Argos, sometimes Corinth, and sometimes achieving a local compromise between the two.[76]

Figured drawing is largely confined to the two favourite themes of the Argolid: dances and horse scenes, in that order of preference. The pyxis from Amyclae (fig. 52d) shows an early LG scene of male dancing, with two lyres and a scorpion in the field. For the stiff and awkward figures the nearest Argive counterpart is on the LG I fragment, Argos C 240 (fig. 45b); but the elongated necks, the emphatic hands, and the spindly calves remind us rather of the pyxis from Tegea (p. 156 n. 61). A piece of a krater, also from Amyclae (fig. 52f, c. 720 B.C.), preserves part of a composition where horse panels flank a step-meander, clearly derived from the Argive workshop which produced fig. 46c.[77] There follow a horse scene and some female dances from the sanctuary of Artemis Orthia at Sparta,[78] on a smaller scale and in a more supple style. The Laconian LG sequence ends with the krater fragment in fig. 52g (c. 690 B.C.) where the dancing women now have their facial features marked to the point of exaggeration, like the earliest Orientalizing work from Athens and Corinth. But here no truly Orientalizing style emerges until the mid-seventh century; the interval is filled by a Subgeometric or 'Transitional' phase in which LG and Orientalizing motifs are blended in a manner which heightens yet further the contrast between light and dark.[79]

Our only information about the handmade ware comes from the Acropolis of

Sparta, where coarse sherds are reported from the 'Geometric' level, decorated with impressed circles.[80]

For Laconian bronzes the sanctuary of Artemis Orthia is the most informative site, not least because stratified layers were observed and recorded by the excavators; but more recent research[81] has shown that only the lowest 'Geometric' levels can now be dated before 700 B.C. The earliest pins are of a Subgeometric type, where beads and reels proliferate. Among the fibulae, a varied lot, the northern 'spectacle' type is surprisingly plentiful in the deepest strata.

It is only in the figurines that we find any sign of a local style, most clearly seen in the horses.[82] The Laconian type resembles the Argive in having tall legs, but the neck is lower, and the body shorter; the general effect is stiffer and more stylized. Most stand on rectangular bases, usually pierced with openwork ornament; rarely solid, as in the Argolid. The type is sufficiently idiosyncratic to be easily recognized elsewhere: there are many from Olympia (e.g., fig. 53b), a few from Delphi, a yoked pair from Lousoi, and a late one from the Spartan colony of Taras on the heel of Italy.[83] Olympia has also furnished bulls and birds in the Laconian manner (e.g., fig. 53a,d);[84] the bull, in spite of its tall equine legs, is effectively characterized by its pendulous dewlap and corkscrew tail. There are also a dog and a fawn, both from the Orthia sanctuary.

A small seated pipe-player (or drinker? fig. 53c) is one of the few human bronze figurines from Geometric Sparta. In spite of the primitive technique (the arms and legs are cylindrical rods), the general effect is bold and three-dimensional. Similar figurines are known from Mavriki in Arcadia, and from near Olympia.[85] A more substantial type of figure is seen in the famous centaur group in New York,[86] where the proportions of the equine body are characteristically Laconian. The warrior who fights the centaur has some of the stockiness of the Argive charioteer, fig. 49d,e; but his head is rounder, and the equilateral triangle of his chest recalls Laconian LG vase-painting (e.g., fig. 52d). A warrior from Olympia, Athens 6182,[87] has much the same build, and may also be Laconian. A much later and more attenuated warrior, Olympia B 5600 (c. 680 B.C.?), has been tentatively assigned to a Laconian hand,[88] on the grounds that his facial profile, with curved nose-bridge, can be matched in a contemporary terracotta from Sparta; his frontal view, however, recalls a terracotta from Argos.[89]

In addition to these freestanding figurines, a piece of a hammered tripod leg has been found at Amyclae, and part of a cast ring-handle at Sparta;[90] but these could well be imports from other Peloponnesian centres.

Messenia

If we may judge from the scattered finds of pottery, it seems that this region was almost as isolated as Laconia during the later Dark Ages. Some tenth-century links with the Aegean world have been noted, especially with the Argolid;[91] thereafter, a little-known Sub-Protogeometric fabric persists until c. 750 B.C. or soon after, when the painted pottery assumes a LG appearance.

The site with the most continuous record is Nichoria, situated on a ridge between the villages of Rizomylo and Karpophora, and overlooking the western

FIG. 53 LACONIAN BRONZES FROM SPARTA (c) AND OLYMPIA
(a) B 1760, H. 6.3; (b) B 754, H. 7; (c) *AO* pl. 77a, H. 6.6;
(d) B 880, H. 4.6

shore of the Messenian Gulf. At the settlement there is some likelihood of continuity from Mycenaean times through the Dark Ages, until a point well down in the eighth century; the post-Mycenaean architecture consists largely of houses with an apsidal plan. The neighbouring cemeteries reveal a wide variety of burial practice. During the local Protogeometric phase there are apsidal cist graves (perhaps miniatures of the prevailing house plan), pithos burials, and a small tholos tomb; inhumation seems to be the prevailing rite, although cremations, too, have been reported from the tholos. In the LG phase, two forms of burial have been reported: a chamber tomb in the Vathyrema gully to the west of the site (perhaps a Mycenaean tomb cleared out and re-used), and a pithos burial within the settlement itself. The chamber tomb contained two LG inhumations on the floor, and a sequence of pottery continuing into Classical times, which the excavator took to be evidence of a local hero cult. With the burials went a most informative group of six pots, now displayed in the Kalamata Museum. The lid of a pyxis, showing traces of four terracotta horses (no. 326), looks like an Attic import, but the others are local: an imitation of a hemispherical Corinthian kotyle (no. 311); a high-rimmed skyphos of Argive type (no. 308), bearing a panel of leaf-lozenges;[92] two much deeper skyphoi (nos. 317, 309) not unlike the Laconian lakaina, and decorated respectively with a meander panel and a leaf-lozenge panel; and, finally, a fairly deep glazed cup of local type (no. 310). The whole group, datable to *c.* 745–725 B.C., suggests a sudden widening of Messenian horizons after a long period of stagnation. The intra-mural pithos burial is that of a warrior, equipped with iron sword and spear tip, a bronze finger-ring, two bronze bowls, and three local pots of *c.* 725 B.C. – another deep glazed cup, a deep kantharos with a leaf-lozenge panel in the Argive manner, and a plate. So far, no other pottery as late as this has been found within the settlement of Nichoria, which may already have been deserted when the warrior was laid to rest.

A later pithos burial (*c.* 700 B.C.?) was found by chance just outside Kalamata, near the sanctuary of Apollo Karneios at ancient Pharai.[93] The recorded finds are all of bronze: four ornate but fragmentary Subgeometric pins, and a horse on a rectangular base which seems to be of Laconian type,[94] although the mane is hammered out in the Corinthian way. The absence of pottery is curious, and the bronzes are more what one expects to find at a sanctuary than in a grave. Yet another comparable pithos burial, this time of Archaic date, has been found at Pyla in western Messenia where, once again, the finds are all of metal, and the bronzes have affinities with Laconian votives.[95]

Other finds in western Messenia include a deposit of fully glazed pottery, LG or perhaps Subgeometric, found above the ruins of the Mycenaean Palace at Ano Englianos, and perhaps associated with an oil-press; and about twenty LG pots left as votives in the Mycenaean chamber tombs of Volimedia. Most of these are imports or imitations of Corinthian ware, and will be further discussed in the next chapter; here it is relevant to mention the only Laconian import – a deep straight-walled tankard from Angelopoulou tomb 4, in a context of *c.* 740–730 B.C.

The Southern Peloponnese: Conclusions

Broadly speaking, the archaeological evidence for the Geometric period tells much the same story for Messenia as for Laconia. Both regions were almost totally isolated until soon after 750 B.C., when communications were restored with the more progressive centres of the north-east Peloponnese. The influence of Argos is seen especially in the decoration of Laconian LG pottery throughout its development; and also perhaps in the Laconian type of bronze horse, a local variation on the Argive model. In the LG pottery of eastern Messenia the Argive leaf-lozenge motif seems to have been popular, and the adult pithos-burial at Nichoria recalls an Argive practice not often found outside the Argolid.[96]

Corinthian influence comes first to western Messenia, as evidenced by the pottery of *c.* 740–730 B.C. offered in the hero-cults at Volimedia. Somewhat later, but well before 700 B.C., the Laconian LG style also begins to adopt several Corinthian ideas. To explain the spreading of Corinthian ceramic fashions, there is plenty of evidence of Corinthian commercial enterprise by sea. Argos, on the other hand, was never much interested in trade, and the diffusion of her artistic influence must rather be connected with her political ascendancy, which extended along the whole eastern shore of the Peloponnese (pp. 154, 156).

Nevertheless, Argos was unable to stem the early expansion of the Spartan state. According to the literary record, the Spartans had already captured Amyclae by 750 B.C., and shortly afterwards annexed the southern plain of Helos, which gave them access to the sea.[97] Neither of these events, unfortunately, has any sure reflection in the material record. It could be that the seizure of Amyclae coincides with the end of the 'Protogeometric' stratum at the sanctuary of Apollo; yet there is nothing specifically Amyclaean about this 'Protogeometric' style, which is also found at Sparta and throughout Laconia. As for Helos, the site has not yet been securely located.

Concerning the wider foreign relations of Sparta, the archaeological evidence is a little more helpful. The prevalence of Laconian bronzes at Olympia lends some colour to the tradition of an early alliance between Sparta and Elis, an alliance which eventually curbed the power of king Pheidon of Argos. In Messenia, Spartan aggression is said[98] to have begun in the reign of king Teleclos (*c.* 750 B.C.), who made some conquests in the plain of Makaria around the head of the Messenian Gulf. Later, in the conflict known as the First Messenian War, the Spartans carried their attack into the hinterland; after a struggle of twenty years,[99] they finally stormed the main Messenian stronghold of Ithome, and took over the rich Stenyclaros plain. During its later stages, the war had involved most of the Peloponnese: Sparta received aid from Corinth, while the Messenian ranks were swelled by the entire force of the Arcadians, and some contingents from Argos and Sicyon.[100] This widening of the conflict led to the destruction of Asine by the men of Argos, on the grounds that her citizens had abetted a Spartan invasion of the Argolid (p. 154). In return, the Asinaean refugees were settled by their Spartan allies in a new Asine, in conquered Messenian territory. Soon after the war had ended, the Spartan authorities had to cope with a civil disturbance in their homeland, caused by a generation of disaffected youths; these youths were dispatched forthwith to found a colony at Taras, on the heel of Italy.[101]

For the end of the war, then, a *terminus ante quem* is given by the foundation of Taras; Eusebius' date of 706 B.C. is in harmony with the earliest Greek pottery found on the colonial site (p. 239). The war was still raging when old Asine was destroyed; as we have seen, this destruction can be dated to *c.* 710 B.C. by the latest deposits on the settlement. New Asine can be identified with modern Koroni, 25km. south of Nichoria on the Messenian Gulf; although the site has not yet been excavated, surface finds go back to the seventh century B.C., but no further.[102]

We cannot be far wrong, then, in dating the duration of the First Messenian War from 730 to 710 B.C.; this being so, the warrior buried in the Nichoria pithos will have lost his life in one of the earlier campaigns. The excavators, after preliminary study, felt that none of the settlement pottery is demonstrably as late as the burial; it may be that the town of Nichoria[103] had already been abandoned during the earlier Spartan invasion led by king Teleclos in *c.* 750 B.C. At all events, the general picture is one of stress and conflict – an impression intensified by the widespread growth of hero-cults in Mycenaean tombs, more numerous in Messenia than anywhere else in Greece (p. 346, fig. 110). When threatened by Spartan invaders – and, later, when reduced to helotage by Spartan oppressors – the people of Messenia had every reason to visit the tombs of their local heroes and ancestors, appealing for their help and protection.

NOTES

1 *GGP* pl. 25b.
2 e.g. *GGP* pl. 25a; cf. pl. 18c.
3 *CGA* pl. 102.
4 *Asine* 321 fig. 219, 1.
5 *OpAth* 6 (1965), 121 pl. 2: cf. *GGP* 75.
6 *GGP* 143.
7 For a contemporary Attic rendering cf. Villa Giulia 1212, *AGW* fig. 126.
8 *CGA* pls. 43–5; *GGP* pl. 30e.
9 Courbin, *CGA* 71 n. 4.
10 See Courbin, *CGA* 29 ff., 70 f., 467 f.
11 O. Frödin, *Asine* 39 ff.
12 R. Hägg, *Boreas* 4.1 (1973), 31 ff.
13 C. Blegen, *Prosymna* 18 ff.; T. Kelly, *Historia* 16 (1967), 428–9.
14 *AH* I fig. 49; *Prosymna* figs. 20, 22.
15 See N. Verdelis, *AM* 78 (1963), 55 n. 110; Courbin, *TGA* I 115 ff.
16 Hägg, loc. cit. 34–7.
17 *Iliad* ix.212 ff.; Courbin, *BCH* 81 (1957), 378–9, 384.
18 Boardman, *KCh* 23 (1971), 8.
19 Boardman, loc. cit. 5 ff.
20 Paphos: Karageorghis, *BCH* 87 (1963), 265 ff.; id., *Salamis* III 89 ff. (tomb 79); id., *RDAC* 1972, 161 ff. (Patriki tomb 1). The spits from Salamis and Paphos were at first identified as Cypriot pikes or *sigynnae*, until Karageorghis found good reason (*BCH* 94 (1970), 35 ff.) to revise his earlier diagnosis.
21 The Paphos pair might well be the earliest of all, being associated with two imported skyphoi, one LG, the other with pendent semicircles: *BCH* 87 (1963), 267 figs. 2, 3. The Patriki burial is considerably later, not before Cypro-Archaic II. From the seventh century onwards, firedogs of different design are found in Etruria and Celtic Europe: see S. Piggott, *The European Community in Later Prehistory* (*Studies in honour of C. F. C. Hawkes*), London (1971), 243 ff.
22 Kition, three bronze spits, *Liverpool Annals of Archaeology and Anthropology* 3 (1910), 107 f. pl. 29, 1–3; Lapithos, iron spits in the eleventh to ninth centuries, *SCE* I pl. 48 (tombs 409, 411), pl. 54 (tombs 422, 417). In Crete, iron spits occur first in Fortetsa tombs VI and XI, both of the tenth century; thereafter, not until *Fortetsa* tomb P (seventh century?), and in the Kavousi tholos.
23 e.g., in Argos, a short sword from gr. 6/2, three spearheads and a dagger from gr. 176/2, one spearhead from gr. 179 (*TGA* I pls. 23, 48–9), and a dagger from Kymbouropoulos gr. 6; a dagger from Mycenae gr. G II; and three spearheads from Tiryns gr. XXIII.

24 For a Submycenaean bronze helmet-attachment from Tiryns, made to fit on to a leather cap, see Snodgrass, *DAG* 317 fig. 104. A second LG helmet, very like that from gr. 45, has recently been found in another warrior's grave at Argos: *AD* 26 (1971), B 81 f. pl. 68, Odos Stavropoulou.

25 e.g., *HM* pl. 13, 1, from Ialysos.

26 Snodgrass, *EGAW*, 14 and *JHS* 83 (1963), 201. Contemporary with Tiglath-Pileser III is an Attic LG Ib burial, Odos Peiraios gr. 5, containing a small bronze tube which may be a similar vertical stilt.

27 *CGA* pl. 142, C 3944; *AH* II pl. 60, 19; cf. also the left-hand figure on the Olympia tripod leg, p. 336 fig. 108b; the forward-curving unstilted crest of the other figure typifies another Argive version of the Kegelhelm, on which see Snodgrass, *EGAW* 15 f.

28 Snodgrass, *EGAW* 79 ff.; id., op. cit. (p. 164 n. 21 ll. 5–6) 33 ff.

29 Courbin, *BCH* 81 (1957), 353; cf. especially the incision on the midriff.

30 Snodgrass, op. cit. (p. 164 n. 21 ll. 5–6) 45–6 pl. 5.

31 Aristotle, *Politics* 1289b, 36 f.

32 Longest of all are a pair from Tiryns gr. XXV, 0·42m. *BSA* 51 (1956), pl. 35 shows the relative lengths of EG and LG pins from Mycenae.

33 *AH* II pl. 137; Jacobsthal, *Greek Pins* nos. 30, 35, 44.

34 Hampe, *FGS* nos. 33, 34, 34a.

35 Courbin, *TGA* I, 130 pl. 23, B2.

36 H. Luschey, *Phiale* (Bleicherode, 1939), fig. 8.

37 See Herrmann, *JdI* 79 (1964), 24–8, 33–4, 36–9, 44–6.

38 Bouzek, *Eirene* 6 (1967), 121 fig. 3.

39 *GKG* pls. 191–2.

40 *GKG* pl. 125.

41 See Willemsen, *OlF* III 61, where cf. pl. 40, Br 7157.

42 Herrmann, art. cit. 46; Schweitzer, *GKG* 138 f.; *contra*, Rolley, *FD* V.2, 30; Weber, *AM* 86 (1971), 17 ff.

43 Schweitzer, *GKG* 147.

44 *AH* II pl. 139 nos. 43–51.

45 Boardman, *IGems* 129–30, G 12–15.

46 R. Hägg, *Boreas* 7.1; id., *Die Gräber der Argolis* I (Uppsala, 1974), 46.

47 The extreme rarity of funerary scenes is perhaps to be explained by the absence of grave monuments.

48 *GGP* 130 n. 7, 137 (Mycenae); 133–4, 137, 139 (Tiryns); 134 (Nauplia).

49 *GGP* 363–4.

50 *IGems* 117 ff., B 15, 17, 21; C 9, 17.

51 G. L. Huxley, *Early Sparta* 26.

52 Courbin, *Annales* 14 (1959), 227.

53 See, most recently, R. A. Tomlinson, *Argos and the Argolid* (1972), 81–4.

54 W. L. Brown, *Numismatic Chronicle* 10 (1950), 181 ff.

55 Courbin, art. cit. 209–31.

56 Huxley, *BCH* 82 (1958), 588–601; *Early Sparta* 28–30.

57 Except for the *negative* evidence from the latest LG pottery of Asine prior to its destruction, which implies that Eratos ruled Argos in *c.* 710 B.C.

58 Courbin *TGA* I, 150.

59 Courbin, *CGA* 566.

60 Courbin, *CGA* 500–02.

61 R. Tölle, *Frühgriechische Reigentänze* (1964), pl. 25.

62 Nos. 249, 250; cf. Sparta Museum tray 2956, *GGP* 216.

63 *BCH* 87 (1963), 766 fig. 10.

64 Schweitzer, *GKG* 164 f. fig. 98 (Olympia), pl. 193 (Petrovouni in N. Arcadia).

65 Tegea no. 49; Schweitzer, op. cit. 166 figs. 195–6 (Olympia and Lousoi).

66 V. Müller, *AA* 1922, 14–18.

67 cf. below, p. 336 fig. 108a.

68 Jacobsthal, *Greek Pins* 7–9 figs. 17–22; Schweitzer, *GKG* 217.

69 *BCH* 68–9 (1946), 42 fig. 6.
70 For the fullest treatment see Desborough, *PGP* 283–90 pl. 38, and *GDA* 240–3 pl. 55; cf. also *GGP* 212–14 pl. 46a–d.
71 Attic: *GGP* 214 n. 4; Argive, perhaps *GGP* pl. 46e.
72 The 'Protogeometric' ancestor is shown in *GGP* pl. 46a.
73 *GGP* pl. 46j.
74 *GGP* 216.
75 All three motifs appear on *AO* fig. 36.
76 e.g., *AO* fig. 39s; *BSA* 34 (1933–34), 102 fig. 1.
77 *GGP* 134f.
78 *AO* fig. 37D,E,H and fig. 38z,α; *GGP* pl. 46j.
79 E. A. Lane, *BSA* 34 (1933–34), 107–15.
80 *BSA* 28 (1927–28), 78 fig. 19.
81 Boardman, *BSA* 58 (1963), 1–7.
82 Herrmann, *JdI* 79 (1964), 20–4.
83 Benton, *JHS* 70 (1950), 21 pl. 4d: found with a Corinthian aryballos of *c.* 690–680 B.C.
84 Kunze, *100 Jahre deutsche Ausgrabungen in Olympia* (1972), nos. 6, 7. On Laconian birds see Bouzek, *Eirene* 6 (1967), 117–18 fig. 1.
85 *GKG* pl. 199, in Baltimore.
86 *GKG* pl. 185.
87 Herrmann, loc. cit. 43 figs. 22–4.
88 Kunze, *OlB* VIII, 224–31 pls. 108–9.
89 Weber, *AM* 89 (1974), 30 pl. 12.
90 Benton, *BSA* 35 (1934–35), 129–30 fig. 17d.
91 Desborough, *GDA* 250–4.
92 cf. Argos C 2464, *CGA* pl. 59.
93 *AD* 20 (1965), 207 pl. 213b.
94 cf. *AO* pl. 77b.
95 loc. cit. 208 pl. 221b; for the bronze bird and miniature vessels cf. *AO* pls. 76p, 80e.
96 If the Protogeometric pithos burials reported from Nichoria contained adults, then this practice may have come to Messenia from the Argolid during an earlier period of contact, in the tenth century.
97 Huxley, *Early Sparta* 24, 30.
98 Strabo 360.
99 Tyrtaeus *apud* Strabo 279.
100 Pausanias iv.11.1.
101 Huxley, op. cit. 37–8.
102 Valmin, *Études topographiques sur la Messénie ancienne* (Lund, 1930), 166–7; R. Hope Simpson, *BSA* 52 (1957), 249.
103 Its ancient name was perhaps Aipeia; see Hope Simpson, *BSA* 61 (1966), 131.

6 Corinth and West Greece

Corinth, at the beginning of this period, had already grown to the size of a major city; and by 700 B.C. she had become the foremost commercial power in Greece. Her fine-walled painted pottery, outstanding for its technical skill, was then being exported overseas to all the chief centres of the Greek homeland, and had begun to influence many other local Geometric styles. A few Corinthian pots were reaching the Levantine shores; but a far greater quantity was being shipped to the new Greek colonies in southern Italy and eastern Sicily, while some were purchased by Phoenician colonists as far afield as Carthage, western Sicily, and the Mediterranean coast of Spain.

It is clear, then, that Corinth already had a special interest in westward trade. With her part in the colonial movement we shall deal in due course (pp. 234–7, 242–3); the later sections of this chapter will be concerned with several regions overlooking the Corinthian Gulf, or the western seaboard of the Greek homeland, where the links with Corinth seem to have been exceptionally strong. In some areas – e.g., Achaea, Elis, western Messenia – the development of a local Geometric style was virtually stifled by Corinthian influence; while in Phocis, Ithaca, Corcyra, and the Epirus, Corinth became the main source of fine painted pottery. The significance of these close links with Corinth will be explored in a concluding section. For Corcyra there is secure literary evidence for the establishment of a Corinthian colony; were there perhaps any other places in these western regions where the ties with Corinth amounted to anything more than casual trade?

The success of Corinthian commerce must owe something to the high artistic and technical qualities of Corinthian artifacts, of which we must first take account. Corinthian pottery, at last free of Attic influence, is now the most accomplished fabric of its time; although lacking any great pretensions to figured drawing, its decoration is tastefully compounded of simple linear motifs, fine lines, and birds – until, from c. 720 B.C. onwards, a few bold pioneers suddenly abandoned Geometric principles altogether in favour of exotic plant ornament derived from the Near East, and outline drawing, thereby inaugurating the first phase of Corinth's Orientalizing style (Early Protocorinthian); nevertheless the great majority of fine pottery, until well into the seventh century, is still geometrically adorned, and yet still of consummate quality. In metalwork, Corinth possesses a distinctive school of human and animal bronze figurines, suitable for attachment to tripod cauldrons; our understanding of this school depends largely on exports to the sanctuaries of Delphi and Ithaca. Finally, shortly before 700 B.C., Corinthian ivory workers had begun to excel in the production of circular seals, whose figured decoration runs parallel to that of Protocorinthian pottery.

Corinthian LG and EPC (Early Protocorinthian) Pottery

Well before the close of MG II a typically Corinthian style was in the making. In contrast to the increasing complexity of Attic and Argive designs, the ornament here remains simple and restrained: heavy motifs are avoided, narrow zones (or panels) of vertical chevrons continue in favour, and the ground may be lightened by allowing a mass of thin lines to encroach on areas which had hitherto been glazed. Still within MG II, this last process is already carried to extremes on the lekythos-oinochoe, fig. 54e; but for most LG and EPC vases the lines usually extend no further than two-thirds of the way down the surface, leaving a glazed area below.

Our first task is to sketch the main line of development after c. 750 B.C., taking the LG and EPC phases together. For the time being we shall leave on one side the unorthodox LG style of the Thapsos Workshop, named after the Sicilian source of the first published examples; likewise, our account of EPC will in the first instance be confined to the linear vases, before dealing with the earliest Orientalizing experiments.

The LG phase begins with the invention of the kotyle, the lipless drinking-vessel which immediately assumed a leading role in the Corinthian repertoire. This new form was locally evolved from the MG II skyphos, whose offset lip has almost vanished in several Corinthian examples shortly before 750 B.C. (e.g., fig. 54a). The true kotyle, in its LG stage, has the full, hemispherical shape traditional to Corinth, but its fabric is already finer and thinner than that of earlier drinking ware; at first, the chevron panel (fig. 54b) is retained from the preceding phase, but a little later the field may be occupied by herons facing over zigzag waves (fig. 54c). Soon after 720 B.C. the shape is greatly deepened, so that the height of the EPC kotyle is nearly as great as its diameter; the standard decoration now consists of mass-produced bird-files (fig. 55d) or floating sigmas (fig. 55c). In this form the kotyle lasts into the early seventh century, when the profile often becomes straighter, and the foot narrower. A less common innovation of LG is the kyathos,[1] a lipless variant of the low-handled kantharos; it is decorated in much the same way as the kotyle, but is rarely seen after the end of LG. The krater, unlike these new drinking-vessels, retains its offset lip, but otherwise follows the kotyle towards a deeper form; the handles are usually stirrups in LG, simple straps in EPC.[2]

Pyxides are plentiful and varied. Beside the old globular type, a tall version first appears in LG; fig. 55b shows a slim and elegant EPC example with a domed conical lid. At the transition to EPC, when the globular pyxis disappears, two new varieties come into fashion: the kotyle-pyxis,[3] and the flat pyxis, of which fig. 55a is a fine early specimen. As before, Corinthian pyxides differ from Attic in possessing handles, always horizontally placed.

The standard LG oinochoe has a broad, straight neck and an ovoid body (fig. 54f) – a form which persists into EPC (fig. 56a). The lekythos-oinochoe, apparently out of fashion in LG, returns in EPC in a larger size (fig. 55c),

FIG. 54 CORINTHIAN LG POTTERY
(a) Thera, H. 6.6; (b) Pithecusae, H. 11; (c) Anavysos, Athens 14476,
H. 10.5; (d) Ithaca, Aetos R 4, H. 18; (e) Corinth, Potters' Quarter
gr. 5, H. 11.2; (f) Corinth, S. Basilica well, H. 31.6; (g) Ithaca,
Aetos R 1, H. 13.5

lavishly decorated, with tall neck and conical body. Yet the most important of EPC closed shapes is the globular aryballos, which also returns to favour after a lapse in LG, and carries a high proportion of the best Orientalizing drawing (e.g., fig. 56b,c). In its new form the body is rounder than in MG, and the neck smaller; around 700 B.C. the centre of gravity rises, and the shape begins to move towards the plump ovoid variety of the early seventh century.

In the decoration, the bird is the only living creature to find a secure place within the orthodox repertoire. Its earliest Corinthian appearance, around 750 B.C., is in Atticizing square metopes;[4] the body is hatched, and the long crest suggests the heron. From c. 740 B.C. onwards, herons are usually seen in silhouette, with drooping tail (fig. 54c), and in pairs, facing across an expanse of zigzag waves – an idea perhaps borrowed from the Argolid (p. 141). Later the waves may be omitted so that the herons can greet one another; thus they appear on one of the oldest Corinthian sherds from the colony of Syracuse, which must therefore date from c. 730 B.C.[5] Then, in EPC, crest and long tail are forgotten; the birds are reduced to a file, first with two stiff legs (fig. 55b), then only one (fig. 55c); finally, around 700 B.C., the legs are rendered as summary wiggles (fig. 55d).

Among the abstract ornament, chevrons and sigmas are frequent throughout LG, often appearing in groups separated by gaps; floating sigmas continue into EPC (fig. 55e). On larger LG vases, tall and narrow side-panels are occupied by various motifs based on the diagonal cross; half-tone patterns are at first preferred,[6] but in EPC the solid double axe is the rule.[7] New motifs in EPC include the dotted lozenge net and the dotted snake (both on fig. 55c); other patterns, such as solid rays, solid tongues, and spiral hooks, are borrowed from the minor ornament of the Orientalizing vases, and are especially common on the shoulders of globular aryballoi. As an alternative to the usual colour scheme, some LG and EPC vases are decorated with sparse ornament in white paint on a ground of dark glaze.[8]

The Thapsos Workshop departs in several respects from the orthodox LG style of Corinth. The most usual shapes are drinking-vessels; instead of the new lipless forms (kotylai and kyathoi) they are all skyphoi (fig. 54g) and kantharoi, direct descendants of their MG II prototypes. The other well-established shapes are kraters (fig. 54d), globular oinochoai, and large round-mouthed jugs. The main panel of decoration is always surrounded on all four sides by horizontal lines, which often extend to the base. The favourite motifs are the meander and meander hooks, inherited from MG; also the true running spiral, and widely-spaced vertical wavy lines. Birds, rarer than in orthodox LG, usually have projecting feathers, and look like geese; an oinochoe from Thebes portrays a ship; and part of a chariot scene can be made out on krater fragments from Delphi.[9] Most pottery from this workshop is LG; but one class of skyphoi, bearing nothing but lines and glaze,[10] occurs mainly in EPC contexts.

Although the clay is very close to that of orthodox Corinthian LG, different treatment in the kiln produces a powdery green-grey fabric recalling Archaic Corinthian pottery, but unlike the hard pink-buff of other LG fine ware. This technical disparity, in addition to the differences of style and the rare occurrences in the Corinthia, has induced some scholars to seek another home for the work-

FIG. 55 EARLY PROTOCORINTHIAN POTTERY, LINEAR DECORATION
(a) Thera K 67, H. 7; (b) Leiden VZVN 4, H. 15; (c) Naples, from
Cumae gr. 37 (*MA* 22 pl. 37, 1), H. 16.5; (d) Corinth well C,
H. 11.8; (e) London 1950.1.24.2 from Cumae, H. 9

FIG. 56 EARLY PROTOCORINTHIAN POTTERY, ORIENTALIZING
(a) Naples, from Cumae gr. 22 (*MA* 22 pl. 30, 1a), H. 31;
(b–c) London 1969.12-15.1, H. 6.8; (d) London 1950.1-24.1, H. 7.5;
(e) London 1966.4-6.1, H. 8.5

shop: Aegina has been suggested[11] and, more recently and more plausibly, Megara.[12] The Megarian theory has been tested by a chemical analysis of clay, with somewhat indecisive results;[13] but the scanty Geometric finds from Megara include no Thapsos-style pieces, only orthodox Corinthian ware. For the time being, then, it seems preferable to leave the workshop in Corinth, making an unusually conservative class of pottery chiefly for the export trade.

The Orientalizing style of EPC makes a sudden break with Geometric restraint, and is first seen in a pair of oinochoai from Cumae. Their necks are still decorated with Geometric formulae; but all the painstaking linear work has been swept away from their bodies, leaving the field free for swinging coils of plant ornament, and an experimental lotus drawn with a remarkably sure hand (fig. 56a). On the globular aryballoi a new figured style is born, all the more spontaneous because Corinth had known no earlier figured drawing. From the first, some thought was given to marking inner anatomical details. A compromise between outline and silhouette was tried out for cocks and other birds; stags and

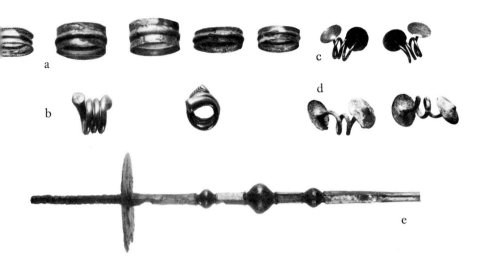

FIG. 57 CORINTHIAN JEWELLERY AND BRONZE ORNAMENTS
(a,b) Corinth, Agora gr. F; (c-d) Oxford, earrings from Corinth,
LS. 3.1, 4.4; (e) Corinth, Agora gr. F, pin, detail

bird protomes appear soon after, and the field is punctuated with trees, solid
rosettes, and cables, all of Oriental derivation.[14] Exceptionally bold is an aryballos
of c. 700 B.C. (fig. 56b,c) showing a bright-faced lion chasing a dappled deer, and
a fully-armed warrior attended by his youthful mounted squire. The outlining
technique was not destined to enjoy more than a passing fashion on these
miniature vessels, where even the thinnest line will be too heavy for the inner
markings; and perhaps it was felt that there was something unconvincing in a
system where a living creature's body is left in the same colour as his surroundings. Soon a more satisfactory solution was found by incising inner details upon
silhouette – a device cautiously used on the lotus of fig. 56a, and for the dappling
of the deer. A little later, incision was applied more confidently for a horse's
muzzle (fig. 114) or for the spine of a fish (fig. 56e). Thus, slowly but surely, the
foundations of the black-figure technique were laid by a few enterprising Corinthian hands around the turn of the seventh century.

While their delicate painted pottery was being widely exported, Corinthian
potters were also manufacturing plain handmade ware for home use, and continued to do so throughout the next century. The usual shapes are hydriae,
amphorae, and oinochoai; new forms include the lekythos-oinochoe, and a deep
krater with vertical ring-handles.[15] The clay is of a pale ivory hue. Some vases[16]
rival the technique of the finest Argive handmade wares, but in most cases the
fabric is still heavy and gritty. Of especial interest is the 'koulouri', a ring-
shaped votive cake offered to Hera Akraia in her sanctuaries at Perachora, and
(later) Solygeia near Corinth, and the colony of Corcyra.[17]

Corinthian Burial Customs and Architecture

Compared with Athens or Argos, the eighth-century evidence from Corinth is somewhat meagre; but it seems that the Corinthian *polis* was still a cluster of scattered villages, each inhuming their dead in the immediate vicinity, sometimes within the inhabited area. The only planned burial ground is the North Cemetery, no doubt serving a nearby settlement which has not yet been found. Here a number of small family plots (groups C–G, grs. 25–46) branch outwards from the MG II nucleus (p. 85). The graves of adults progress from being earth-cut pits to (in LG) cists lined with monolithic slabs; all are closed with single sandstone blocks, as before. Older children may have small cists or sarcophagi; for infants the krater (painted or handmade) is the usual receptacle. For adults, too, the krater replaced the hydria for offerings left outside the grave. The actual contents of the grave are so scanty that we cannot be sure whether the sequence continues without break into the next century; as it is, the only datable offering of the EPC period (from an outlying child burial, gr. 47) is fig. 46e, a krater of *c.* 710 B.C. imported from Argos.

In central Corinth, the area later occupied by the Roman Forum, burial plots and domestic well-deposits are interspersed.[18] One plot contained two interesting pairs of burials, the graves of each pair being occupied by a man and a woman, carefully sited at right-angles to one another. The richest burial, that of a woman (F), contained a small collection of jewellery (fig. 57a,b), while a splendid pair of long bronze pins (one, fig. 57e) had rested along a ledge dividing this grave from its neighbour – perhaps a symbol of wealth shared between husband and wife.[19] A skyphos from the other man's grave (A) dates the group to *c.* 750 B.C. Very few graves in the central region are later than this;[20] here the rapid growth of the settlement left no more room for the dead, and it appears that the wealthier burial grounds of LG and EPC still await discovery.

Around or soon after 700 B.C. the hillock to the north of the Forum area was already crowned by a monumental temple of Apollo, a precursor of the sixth-century building whose monolithic columns still stand there today.[21] Another monumental temple, the first dedicated to Poseidon at the Isthmian sanctuary, may have been built not much later than this, and was decorated – perhaps not in its earliest form – with geometric patterns painted on stucco.[22] At Perachora a much more primitive apsidal temple to Hera Akraia had stood since *c.* 800 B.C., and a clay model found there (p. 322 fig. 103) may give some impression of its appearance.

Corinthian Metalwork

Gold jewellery, of a simple sort, has been found in the graves of central Corinth, and in two votive dumps at the sanctuary of Perachora: the Geometric deposit of Hera Akraia (*c.* 800–720 B.C.), and the Limenia deposit which begins in *c.* 740 B.C. and continues into Archaic times. Broad finger-rings with a central rib are at home in the Corinthia, occurring in the Akraia deposit as well as in

Corinth gr. F (fig. 57a). Two massive hair-spirals from the same grave (fig. 57b) can be matched by a fragmentary one from the Limenia deposit, and another in an Athenian grave of c. 760–750 B.C. (p. 126, gilt bronze); like much Corinthian pottery of this time, their spiral wire is partly decorated with chevrons. The cross engraved on each end is another local trait, also appearing on a type of spiral earring pendant, to which thin hammered discs are attached. Fig. 57c, said to be from another grave in Corinth, also bears some chevrons on the wire, and similar ornaments come from Perachora; some there have been converted into pins by docking one disc and unrolling the spiral wire.[23] We have already observed some ninth-century precursors of this class from Lefkandi (fig. 19d), but the Corinthian pendants are larger and have more spirals; largest of all is a pair in Paris with massive conical plates,[24] which have a fragmentary counterpart in silver from the Limenia deposit. The plates also tend to be conical on the small bronze versions (fig. 57d), which are cast in one piece.

The enormous bronze pins from gr. F. (fig. 57e) are the finest examples of the new Corinthian type invented in MG II (p. 85), distinguished by three biconical bulbs and a long bead-and-reel finial above the disc head; the upper shank, square in section, is decorated with punched zigzag lines with dots on either side. Similar pins occur in the Akraia Deposit at Perachora, where the most elaborate example has no fewer than nine bulbs. Corinth may have led the way in manu-facturing this baroque class, which appears in many Peloponnesian sanctuaries, but nowhere else in a clear eighth-century context. Such monstrous pins cannot have been worn in real life, and rarely appear even in graves; the most intricate specimens are reserved for the gods.[25] For mortals, the older single-bulb type may well have continued in use, as it did in LG Argos (p. 149). The Perachora fibulae are a mixed lot, lacking in any obviously local characteristics; the most frequent LG types are East Greek, and Boeotian with square catchplate.

The only recorded shape of bronze vessel is the mesomphalic phiale, an oriental form; one was found between grs. A and B, another in the Limenia Deposit,[26] the omphalos in both cases being conical, as opposed to the rounded omphaloi of Archaic times.[27]

Although very few bronze figurines have been found in Corinth, a distinctive Corinthian style can be observed in the common features shared by votives at Perachora, Delphi, and Ithaca; at Olympia, too, the Corinthian style is well represented.

From Olympia comes a good specimen of the Corinthian bird pendant, fig. 58a.[28] The elegant curve of its body ends in a duck's bill, and in an upturned tail horizontally hammered out; legs are omitted, the body being joined by a short bulbous stem to a disc (as here) or to a small pyramidal stand. A later and more exotic variant resembles the farmyard cock;[29] its huge tail and crest, hammered out flat in a vertical plane, are covered with incised double circles. The body is hollow-cast, a technique not generally known to the Geometric smith; although a LG context has been claimed for a primitive imitation at Delphi,[30] it may be that none of these cocks precede 700 B.C. The type was subsequently taken up in Argos, Sparta, Thessaly, and Macedonia.

A distinct Corinthian style in free-standing horses[31] is well represented at Perachora, Delphi (fig. 58b), and Ithaca. The rectangular bases are usually

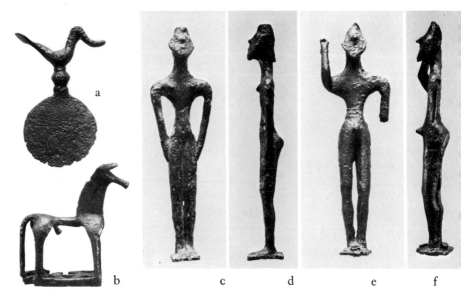

FIG. 58 CORINTHIAN BRONZE FIGURINES
(a) Olympia B 1388; (b) Delphi 4021, H. 6.9; (c–d) Delphi 7730,
H. 16.5; (e–f) Delphi 2947, H. 15.8

pierced with neat cut-out triangles. As with the birds, much use is made of the hammer, so that the horses have a two-dimensional look. The only parts with any volume are the cylindrical body and head; the legs are hammered out flat, and so is the high and broad curved neck, from which the ears project forward, continuing the curve. Incised ornament may be added here and there – for example, chevrons on the tail of fig. 58b; the necks of some later horses bear double circles (as on the cocks) or dotted zigzags (as on the long pins). Eventually, perhaps c. 700 B.C., the horses reach a more mannered stage[32] where the muzzle becomes trumpet-shaped, the head is marked off by a semicircular ridge running from cheek to ear-tip, and the legs are articulated by sharp protrusions. A free local adaptation of this type comes from the Corinthian colony of Syracuse.[33]

The human figurines were all made as attachments to the handles of tripod cauldrons, and the progress of a Corinthian style can be reconstructed from among the finds at Ithaca and Delphi. One of the earliest of all handle figures, well back in MG II, is a nude goddess from Ithaca, standing with arms to her her sides.[34] In contrast to the weak and fluid outlines of her body, her head is tilted backward in a commanding manner; this tilt and the deepset eyes, in addition to her nudity, are symptoms of North Syrian influence. Greater confidence is attained in a LG goddess from Delphi, shown in the same pose and wearing a polos (fig. 58c,d).[35] With the broadening of the shoulders the outline becomes stronger and more graceful, yet the fluidity remains; unlike contemporary figures from Athens and Argos (figs. 40b–d, 49a–c), there is no articulation here between waist and hip, and the figure has a plank-like flatness when seen in profile. There follows fig. 58e,f, first of several horse-tamers in the same tradition,[36] all tilting their heads back with the same imperious gesture. For these lithe but insubstantial warriors, a counterpart in relief may be seen in the figured panel on a cast leg from Olympia (p. 336, fig. 108b), where two contestants lay claim a tripod; this leg, distinguished by its fanned grooves, belongs to a comparatively rare class which on other grounds has been reasonably assigned to Corinth.[37]

After this group of horse-tamers the development is not so clear; but, about a generation later, another warrior from Delphi[38] probably illustrates the Corinthian style around 690 B.C. Like his Attic contemporary (fig. 41c) he supported a large hammered handle; his proportions are similarly attenuated, but the style is more carefully controlled. And, in place of the older Kegelhelm (cf. p. 148), he is shown wearing a more efficient class of helmet, forged out of a single sheet of bronze to cover the whole head. This brilliant technological discovery, achieved without any guidance from the Near East, was to become an important part of a hoplite soldier's equipment. Herodotus (iv. 180) calls it Corinthian, and he is confirmed by the frequency with which the new helmet is shown in Corinthian seventh-century art.[39] In its earliest form, invented around 700 B.C., the profile fore and aft is severely and uncomfortably vertical, and thus it appears in several non-Corinthian representations well down into the seventh century; but the creator of the Delphi warrior already knew of an improved Corinthian version, where the shape is more carefully designed to fit the head more closely, with a splaying curve to guard the back of the neck.

Corinthian Ivory Seals

The sanctuary of Perachora has yielded a splendid collection of ivory disc seals, mainly of the seventh century; but the earliest one has figured designs in a purely Geometric style, not later than 700 B.C.[41] The most usual form has a stepped profile, so that one face is larger than the other; the initial inspiration probably came from the stone seals of the Argolid, where a LG lentoid class combines this peculiarity of shape with a similar figured style (p. 151 fig. 50b)[42] In the early seventh century the Corinthian ivory seals bear the finest figured designs anywhere in Greece, comparable in theme and quality to the best Protocorinthian vase-painting. They have a wide circulation, especially in the sanctuaries of the Peloponnese and Ithaca.

Phocis

Across the Gulf, the village of Medeon had been importing fine Corinthian pottery since the beginning of the Geometric period. During the eighth century the recorded burials are all cremations but, in the absence of any local Geometric style, Corinth remains almost the only source of fine pottery; the only exceptions are a West Greek tall kantharos (cf. p. 180), and an oinochoe of Thessalian type with cutaway neck.

A cemetery at Amphissa, starting in LG, seems to tell much the same story: the fine pottery, until well into the seventh century, is Corinthian, but the metal objects come from elsewhere. The bronzes include northern spectacle fibulae, a plate fibula of Blinkenberg's Type VII (with globes on the bow), and two spiral bracelets; there are also two pairs of rather outlandish hair-spirals (one bronze, one gold), ending in irregular cylindrical plates.

Eighth-century Delphi offers evidence of cemeteries, a settlement, and a sanctuary which was destined to become one of the greatest in the Greek world. The main burial ground was always to the west, by the modern museum; there are also two smaller cemeteries, one to the east near Marmaria, the other up by the stadium in the Pylaea area where the earliest offerings are EPC globular aryballoi of *c.* 700 B.C. Concerning the burial practices very little has been published. In a miniature chamber tomb near the museum, a LG child inhumation is the second of two burials (the first is Protogeometric), and contained a pair of Type VII fibulae beside a Corinthian oinochoe; spectacle fibulae have been found in other disturbed burials near by.

The settlement grew up on the ruins of a Mycenaean town,[43] but already covered a wider area. The houses extended over the northern part of the later Hieron of Apollo, and also some way to the east near the site of the Roman baths. Nothing in these humble dwellings betrays the proximity of a great sanctuary; two domestic hearths were found in a house under the ramp of the later temple of Apollo, while a room in the eastern quarter produced a set of spindle whorls and pyramidal loom-weights. Under the Sacred Way, however, a deposit of *c.* 750–730 B.C. contained a number of objects which must be votive: for example, a Cretan shield of Idaean type (p. 288), and several bronze figurines of humans and animals, including the goddess (fig. 58c,d) who had stood on the handle of a tripod cauldron. Indeed, in the sheer quantity of bronze figurines, ring-handles, tripod legs, and cauldron fragments found in various parts of the site, Delphi is second only to Olympia. Thus, even without the hindsight offered by Classical literature, we should be forced to admit the existence of a major eighth-century shrine here, since these enormous and ornate vessels were not made for secular use. True, no temple of this period has yet been discovered; yet there are many parts of the later Hieron where deep soundings cannot be made, owing to the accumulation of later structures. Pausanias (x.5.9), following Pindar's eighth *Paean*,[44] tells us that the first temple of Apollo was a simple building, whose walls were of bay wood; an early imitation has been claimed by the excavators of Eretria in the oldest building there for Apollo Daphnephoros, erected soon after 800 B.C. (p. 88). If they and Pausanias are right, Apollo's first temple at Delphi must have been founded by 800 B.C. at the latest. This date would be consistent with the earliest tripod cauldrons from Delphi, which are somewhat later than the earliest at Olympia;[45] and also with the first imports of Corinthian pottery, probably at the end of MG I [46]– although these were found in secular contexts.

The earliest history of Delphi may be thus reconstructed, very tentatively. In late Mycenaean times, worship of a female deity is suggested by an accumulation of over two hundred female terracotta figurines, mainly of the twelfth century B.C.; this deity was remembered in later tradition as the earth-goddess, Ge. Her

FIG. 59 ACHAEAN AND ELEAN LG II POTTERY
(a,b) Patras, Pharae gr. Gamma, HS. 25, 9; (c) Patras, gr. Alpha,
H. 13; (d) Olympia, from Elean Pylos, H. 17.5

cult lapsed during the Dark Age, but it is unlikely that the sanctity of the place
was ever forgotten. Then, after three centuries without votive offerings, the
worship of Apollo became firmly established when relations with Corinth were
opened around 800 B.C. For the next hundred years and more, Corinth supplied
almost all the fine painted pottery and a fair proportion of the bronzes. The
earliest cauldron fragments cannot yet be safely assigned to any particular centre
on typological grounds; but Corinth, in view of her geographical position and her
expanding commerce, is a likely source. After 750 B.C., when local schools of
bronzework became more distinct, the Corinthian style is well represented among
the figurines; there are also a few pieces from Athens (e.g., fig. 40e), Sparta,[47] and
Argos,[48] as well as the votive shield from Crete. By the later eighth century, for
reasons which will be discussed at the end of this chapter, the fame of the sanctuary was already becoming Panhellenic.

Achaea

Discoveries in this region have been limited to small groups of graves, with offerings of pottery and metal. The pottery allows us some glimpses of a local Geometric style, but there are still long gaps in the sequence. The closest affinities are with regions further to the west, Elis and Ithaca in particular; here we have the nucleus of a wider West Greek area, within which the pottery of each district shares many common features.

Through most of the ninth century Achaea had been producing a retarded Protogeometric style in which the leading shape is the kantharos, and the most typical decoration consists of hatched triangles arranged in thick, crowded compositions.[49] Thereafter, hardly anything is known of the local style until a LG II phase at the end of the eighth century, when all West Greek schools were coming under strong influence from Corinth. Apart from a deep krater of Corinthian type,[50] the shapes still have a local flavour. The most characteristic are the broad and tall kantharoi, always with low handles (fig. 59b,c); and round-mouthed jugs with angular (fig. 59a) or baggy profiles. The decoration is usually limited to small motifs, widely spaced in narrow zones; this, too, is a West Greek feature, also found in the contemporary and slightly earlier LG pottery of Ithaca (fig. 60). Yet the motifs themselves are almost all derived from the Corinthian repertoire: for example, small groups of floating sigmas, drawn with the multiple brush; thin rays, borrowed from EPC; running spirals as in the Thapsos Workshop, sometimes reduced to detached whirligigs (fig. 59b) or S's. Corinthian, too, is the practice of covering the lower surface with fine lines. Figured drawing is limited to a few long-legged birds of Corinthian type, though without the heron's crest; a few outlined fish; and a ravenous lion pursuing a deer.[51]

The area where most discoveries have been made is that of ancient Pharae, in the upland valley between Patras and Kalavryta; the graves there are scattered over a wide tract between Chalandritsa and Katarrhaktis. Other groups of graves have been excavated near the coastal town of Aigion, and at Drepanon near the narrows of the Corinthian Gulf. The burials, always inhumations, are usually in pithoi or in cists. Although little skeletal evidence is available, most pithoi are large enough to contain adults, and one (Drepanon gr. 3) certainly housed a warrior. These burials recall Argive practice, but the cists are more individual: the long sides and one end are lined with walls of small horizontal slabs, but at the other end a single, large vertical slab is suggestive of a door; the cists are covered with several irregular boulders, sometimes heaped up into a cairn. Although the graves occur in small groups rather than in large cemeteries, several family burials may be knit together in various ways: thus, near Chalandritsa, two tumuli are said to cover groups of cists, and a number of LG II pots and metal objects came from a tholos tomb with multiple burials. In the latter case, however, the tholos may well have been built in Mycenaean times and subsequently plundered, since the finds also include a Mycenaean terracotta animal. Thus it is not impossible that the burials, too, were of Mycenaean date; if so, the Geometric objects might have been offerings to a local hero.

The metal objects, unlike the pots, are somewhat lacking in local character. Bronzes include plain finger-rings, broad flat bracelets, large conical beads, one Type VII fibula (Drepanon gr. 3), and several shortish pins with disc head and single bulb below; one, from the Chalandritsa tholos, is of a type transitional between Geometric and Orientalizing, and has a counterpart at Olympia.[52] A pithos burial, Drepanon gr. 3, contained a fine set of iron weapons – sword, spearhead, and knife – all of which can be matched among the LG graves of Argos; the same can be said of the spit fragments found in Katarrhaktis gr. 1.

Elis and Western Messenia

In Elis, Geometric cemeteries have been excavated at Olympia and Kyllene, but the material has not yet been published. Meanwhile the only available information about the local Geometric sequence comes from two well deposits of *c.* 700 B.C. at Elean Pylos and Olympia, supplemented by rare and sporadic finds from within the Olympian sanctuary. All the shapes can be matched in other West Greek regions. Thus, both wells have produced tall jugs with ovoid body and straight neck, a form already known in the earlier LG of Ithaca;[53] and the open shapes from the well at Elean Pylos – skyphoi with splaying lips and broad, low kantharoi – have close counterparts in an Achaean grave at Pharae. Many Elean vases have a dark ground relieved only by a few reserved lines; kantharoi, thus treated, are also common in Ithaca and Achaea. Decoration, when it occurs, is of the same thin character as in Achaea, often encased between Corinthianizing fine lines. A krater fragment from Elean Pylos (fig. 59e) shows part of an empty ship with sail and steering oar; both the ship and the krater profile recall an EPC vase in Toronto,[55] but the curved edge of the glaze beside the ship is a West Greek trait, also found in Ithaca at an earlier date (fig. 60a).

The fame of Olympia, to judge by the splendour and the variety of the votive offerings, was well on the way to becoming Panhellenic. The earliest history of the sanctuary is hard to elucidate (p. 331) owing to the lack of datable pottery during the early Iron Age; yet, from literary sources, it is clear that the four-yearly Games go back at least as far as 776 B.C. The monumental tripod cauldrons, dedicated in such profusion, are most plausibly explained[56] as thank-offerings of the early victors – young men of noble birth, substance, and distinction in their own cities. Their homes are recorded in lists compiled in the late fifth century by Hippias of Elis;[57] with these lists, and other literary sources, the evidence from the various styles of cauldron figurines is reasonably consistent. In the eighth century, the list gives us the impression that only Peloponnesians took part in the Games, most victors coming from the western Peloponnese. Among the bronzes, Spartan, Argive, and Corinthian styles have been clearly distinguished, and no doubt there were other centres nearer the sanctuary. Several Spartan victors are mentioned, but no Argives or Corinthians; yet a strong Argive interest is indicated by the machinations of king Pheidon (pp. 154–5), while many Corinthian bronzes could well have come to Olympia through normal maritime trade. Athenian hammered tripods make their first appearance in the last quarter of the eighth century, rather earlier than the first recorded Athenian victory in 696 B.C.

In contrast to the imposing character of the bronze offerings, the setting of the sanctuary remained simple and unpretentious. Within the Altis, the sacred grove, the most conspicuous landmark would have been the mound of Pelops, the local hero in whose honour the Games were held; a small apsidal building to the west, perhaps constructed during the eighth century, may have housed some of his votive gifts.[58] There were no other permanent structures; worship was conducted in the open air, around the ash altars of Zeus, Hera, Hestia, and the Mother of the Gods.

In the coastlands of western Messenia, a small amount of LG pottery has been briefly reported from the Pylos area. About two dozen vases were deposited in four Mycenaean chamber tombs at Volimedia,[59] no doubt as offerings to local heroes. Seven of these are Corinthian imports, a homogeneous group of c. 740–730 B.C. Apart from one Laconian vase, the others are all local, combining Corinthian and West Greek features: thus three angular oinochoai, decorated with fine lines and little else, are the local counterparts of Achaean jugs like fig. 59a, having longer necks and narrower bases. It is not yet clear how far the West Greek manner spread to eastern Messenia, although we have already noted a deep kantharos at Nichoria (p. 162), decorated with leaf-lozenges like Argive drinking-vessels.

Ithaca

Lying a few hours' sail outside the entrance to the Corinthian Gulf, this island was bound to attract many callers during a period when Italy and Sicily were being opened up to Greek merchants and colonists. Our knowledge of Ithaca at this time is based on two sanctuaries, the cave of the Nymphs in Polis Bay, and the shrine of an unknown deity on the slopes of mount Aetos. It is likely that these two sites, when taken together, present a continuous sequence throughout the Dark Ages;[60] but whereas before 800 B.C. there had been very little contact with Aegean Greece, the island came under strong Corinthian influence from the early eighth century onwards.

The Aetos cult began with a number of burnt deposits containing animal and bird bones, on to which irregular cairns were heaped. It was at first suggested that these cairns might be the memorials of cremations, but no human bones were identified among the scrappy remains. In and between the cairns, many shattered fragments of local Protogeometric vessels were found, mostly unburnt. The style,[61] which probably persisted through the ninth century, shows many West Greek features, like the contemporary wares of Acarnania and Achaea; thus the leading shape is the broad kantharos with low handles, and the decoration most often consists of hatched rectilinear patterns (triangles and lozenges) packed into close compositions. Some use was also made of concentric semicircles drawn with compasses or freehand; this motif had been learned before 900 B.C. from stray Attic imports, but was subsequently exploited by Ithacan potters in a highly idiosyncratic manner. Other votives associated with the cairns include a female clay figurine, and a bronze pin of Protogeometric type; a

FIG. 60 ITHACAN LG I (a–d) AND LG II (e–f) POTTERY FROM AETOS
(a) B 760, H. 9; (b) B 778, H. 7; (c) B 802, H. 21; (d) R 473, H. 16;
(e) R 358, H. 13; (f) B 1020, H. 15

human bronze figurine of primitive style may also be from this horizon.[62]

Around 780 B.C., when pottery from Corinth began to arrive, the cult received a new impetus. It may be that a temple was built at this time;[63] from now on the votives became more plentiful and varied, and covered a wider area. Below the cairns, three successive terrace walls were built, over which the discarded votives were dumped; here two distinct strata were observed, and can be dated by Corinthian imports, the Lower Deposit to *c.* 760–730 B.C., the Upper Deposit from *c.* 730 B.C., into the seventh century. In contrast with the huge amount of pottery which now poured in from Corinth, eighth-century imports from elsewhere are limited to three LG skyphoi: two from Euboea, one from Attica.[64] Meanwhile a fully Geometric style was established in the local ware, coming increasingly under Corinthian influence, and yet never entirely losing its individual character. After a fleeting MG stage, [65] a fairly settled LG I style (fig. 60a-d) is well represented in the Lower Deposit[66] contemporary with and influenced by Corinthian LG. Apart from a few close copies of Corinthian oinochoai and kotylai, this influence is seen chiefly in the fine banding. On the other hand, some of the favourite motifs, such as pothooks (fig. 60d) and quarter-circles (fig. 60c), seem to be locally derived from Protogeometric semicircles, and are widely spaced out in the West Greek manner. Another local notion is the 'sausage' of glaze under the handle (fig. 60a), also found in Acarnania and Elis. Of the shapes, the kantharoi and cups have prototypes among the pottery from the cairns; and for a large ovoid type of jug there are several counterparts at Olympia (p. 181) and Delphi.[65] Shortly before 700 B.C. a LG II style prevails, now more heavily dependent on Corinth; even so, the West Greek kantharos is still the leading form, and the shape of a three-handled example (fig. 60e) can be closely matched in Achaea (fig. 59c). On the neck of a conical lekythos-oinochoe (fig. 60f) the local pothooks are inserted into an otherwise purely Corinthian composition. There are occasional attempts to draw men, horses, and lions; and even to emulate the Orientalizing plant ornament of EPC, on a group of small oinochoai.[68] After the early seventh century, however, the local pottery loses its individuality.

The smaller Geometric offerings at Aetos, other than pottery, were brought from all points of the compass: amber beads and other ornaments, shipped from Italy or down the Adriatic; amulets in the form of miniature bronze vessels, such as were made in Macedonia; stone scaraboid seals from Cilicia; and a granulated gold finial from Crete, in the form of a snake's head (p. 103, cf. fig. 32a). As with the pottery, however, Corinth was the chief supplier; hence come nearly all the ivory seals (most after 700 B.C.) and a handsome group of hammered bronze horses. Yet the most impressive bronzes were found in the Polis Cave sanctuary, where a fine series of tripod cauldrons was dedicated. Before the offering of the first cauldron, the cave had already accumulated some late Mycenaean and early Protogeometric pottery, but nothing obviously votive; but from the eighth century onward the cult continued without break into Roman times, becoming associated with the local Nymphs, and with Odysseus, the local hero (p. 347).

North-West Greece

On the mainland opposite Ithaca, the districts of Aetolia and Acarnania are still very little known during the Geometric period. The available evidence comes from graves; inhumation, so it seems, was the normal rite, either in pithoi or in cists. The West Greek Protogeometric style is represented in Aetolia by a tall kantharos from Calydon, and an equally tall – and very ornate – krater from Pylene; in Acarnania, by a collection of some forty vases said to have come from graves near Agrinion. Of these, the tall kantharoi on low conical feet are of a canonical West Greek shape; but Thessalian overtones are present in the biconical oinochoai, the amphoriskoi with vertical handles, and the small baggy jugs.[69] Some larger oinochoai should not be earlier than the late ninth century, since their broader bases recall the MG of southern Greece. After the usual lozenge patterns, the next commonest is the group of vertical wavy lines drawn with a multiple brush – a loose motif not often found before LG, but nevertheless employed on two other ninth-century vases at Delphi[70] and Vergina.[71] A glimpse of Acarnanian LG is offered by nine vases from a pithos burial at Palaiomanina, on the river Achelous; by now all decoration has been discarded, apart from a 'sausage' of glaze on a copy of a Corinthian LG kyathos which dates the group; it also includes two flat-based kantharoi similar to Ithacan LG I. Of many metal finds reported from this grave, a large spiral bronze bracelet with incised chevrons has been illustrated. Another burial at Palaiomanina, said to be Protogeometric, has produced a pair of gold spiral earring pendants quite similar to fig. 57c; as on the Corinthian pair, the ends of the wire are decorated with chevrons, but the terminal discs bear repoussé dots instead of incised crosses.

For the foundation of the Corinthian colony on Corcyra, two dates are given in literary sources: 733 B.C. by Strabo (269), contemporarily with the foundation of Syracuse; 708 B.C. implied by Eusebius. A rich sanctuary, perhaps the Heraion, has produced two Geometric bronzes, not closely datable: a piece of a cast tripod leg, and a late, mannered horse in the Corinthian style, adorned with stamped circles. The earliest pottery comes from deep soundings in a disturbed cemetery near by, over which houses were built from the sixth century onwards; the only intact grave, with pottery of c. 650 B.C., is a cist lined with monolithic sandstone slabs, like the graves of the mother city (p. 174). The oldest Corinthian piece, from a krater, could be LG,[72] and a pyxis sherd[73] with a hatched battlement recalls an Ithacan pyxis of c. 750 B.C.[74] Yet the Corinthian pottery does not begin in bulk until well on in EPC, and the body of a West Greek ovoid jug[75] is no earlier. Thus, on present showing, Eusebius' low date is the more likely one for the arrival of the Corinthian colonists; yet it would be wise to reserve judgement on this matter until a sample of the earliest settlement pottery has been recovered (cf. p. 200).

In the Epirus we reach the north-western limit of the Greek world. Although the inhabitants may have spoken Greek, they had become isolated from southern Greece after the commotions at the end of the Bronze Age. Southward communications were not restored until the eighth century, largely through the initiative of Corinth.

The oracle of Zeus at Dodona was destined to become one of the most renowned sanctuaries of the Hellenic world, but before 750 B.C. its history is obscure owing to the lack of datable votives; it may be, however, that some of the coarse, handmade local pottery goes back into the Dark Ages. In LG times the recovery of contact with the south[76] is seen not so much in pottery imports (limited to one Corinthian LG krater sherd) as in the bronzes. The fragments of tripod cauldrons are all of the hammered class, of the late eighth century: several legs and a handle bearing incised patterns, a horse to crown a hammered handle, and three warriors of which the finest[77] is a handle-holder, turning his head to the left and raising his right arm as though to brandish a spear. Delphi has produced another warrior from the same workshop,[78] which may have operated somewhere in the Epirus or – more plausibly – in Corinth itself, supplying both the great oracular shrines. The other two warriors from Dodona are probably local work; their style is cruder, and the sharp edges to their belts constitute a northern trait.[79] Also local to this area is a class of fibula (Blinkenberg Type V) with geometric patterns engraved on the bow, and an elongated plate tapering to the point; many exported examples have been found at Pherae in Thessaly, and one at Delphi. Another fibula, which must be an import from the south, combines the bow of the Attic and Boeotian Type VIII with the sail-plate of Type VII, on which four fish are engraved.[80]

The most informative site in the Epirus is the settlement and cemetery of Vitsa Zagoriou, situated some 1,000m. up in the Pindus range. A bronze LG horse of Corinthian appearance is the only Geometric find so far published from the settlement. Well over a hundred graves have been opened in the cemetery, ranging in date from the early eighth century into Classical times. All the burials are fully extended inhumations in earth-cut pits, or in various kinds of cist. The importation of Corinthian pottery begins well back in MG II – perhaps as far back as the earliest use of the cemetery – and continues without break into the seventh century. The only other wheelmade vases are a West Greek LG kantharos, and a cutaway beaked jug of Thessalian character with festoons of vertical zigzag on the shoulder; there is no reason to date this vase earlier than than the eighth century. The local ware is all handmade, often bearing simple rectilinear patterns in matt paint; a similar fabric is known in western Macedonia,[81] and isolated examples of it have turned up as far south as Agrinion and Calydon. Most eighth-century graves at Vitsa are rich in metal offerings; the men are exceedingly well armed with swords, spearheads, knives, and – in one case – a bronze shield boss (gr. 34). Women may be supplied with fibulae (usually of the spectacle type), pins (often with roll-tops), spiral bracelets, and necklaces of beads in various materials including rock-crystal, glass, and gilt bronze; there is also a massive bronze diadem in gr. 113 with a circle design in repoussé dots, which has a counterpart at Aetos in Ithaca.[82]

To complete this recital of far-flung Corinthian connections, two isolated exports to the Balkan hinterlands should be mentioned; a LG skyphos in the Thapsos style, found at Tren in southern Albania,[83] and a long bronze pin with with disc and three globes like fig. 57e, said to have come from Titov Veles in the upper Vardar valley.[84]

Conclusions

Concerning the LG and EPC pottery of Corinth, three general statements of historical interest can be made. First, whereas the Attic and Argive styles are seen at their best on large grave vases, in Corinth the finest work is done on small vessels. Secondly, when compared to the performance of other regions, the export of Corinthian pottery is abnormally copious. Thirdly, these exports include a very high proportion of the finest pottery, especially in EPC – one thinks, in particular, of the globular aryballoi, the ornate lekythoi-oinochoai, and the adventurous experiments in Orientalizing ornament; in LG, likewise, almost the whole output of the Thapsos Workshop and most of the heron kotylai were exported. The apparent rarity of these fine wares in the Corinthia may prove to be illusory, if ever the wealthier burial grounds of Corinth should be discovered. There remains, however, the positive evidence of exports to illustrate the rapid expansion of Corinthian trade. By 700 B.C. fine Corinthian pottery is found at almost every major centre in the Greek world, and the influence of

Corinthian shapes and decoration can be traced to some extent in every other local school. The shapes most frequently exported are fine-walled drinking-vessels (notably, kotylai and Thapsos-type skyphoi) and EPC globular aryballoi; the wide distribution of these small and attractive containers – whatever the source of their contents – shows that from *c.* 720 B.C. onwards Corinth was actively marketing unguents, in competition with Phoenician merchants who had been plying a similar trade in the south-eastern Aegean during the previous century.

The emergence of Corinth as a major commercial power coincides approximately with a change in her constitution, from a hereditary monarchy to a narrow oligarchy. Diodorus (vii. 9) places this event in 747 B.C., when the last king was forced to share his power with over two hundred members of the royal Bacchiad *genos*. These Bacchiads, as Strabo tells us (378), were fearless in reaping the fruits of commerce, exploiting Corinth's naturally advantageous position with access to two seas. For a more urgent reason, too, the impetus towards trade must have been especially strong; in contrast to the plains of Attica, Argos, and Sparta, the territory of Corinth was not sufficiently fertile and extensive to support a rapidly rising population by agriculture alone. Eventually, a more drastic solution to this problem lay in the foundation of two substantial colonies overseas, each under the leadership of a Bacchiad nobleman: Archias in Syracuse, Chersicrates in Corcyra; and when Strabo (380) goes on to mention that Archias' contingent was composed of farmers from Tenea, an inland village of the Corinthia,[85] it becomes clear that the main motive of the expedition was to relieve overpopulation at home.

The westward interests of the Bacchiads may be reflected in the great preponderance of Corinthian exports shipped down the Gulf; and it is interesting that these exports begin to be plentiful about half a century before the foundation of Syracuse, the first recorded Corinthian colony. From literary sources[86] we hear that Apollo's oracle at Delphi first rose to fame in the late eighth century, when leaders of colonial expeditions sought the god's counsel and blessing. Archias, on his departure for Syracuse, is one of the earliest recorded visitors of historical times; yet from the finds we learn that Corinth and Delphi had been in close touch since the early eighth century, and probably since the foundation of the Apolline sanctuary. Even in those early days, Apollo's encouragement might well have been sought by merchants and travellers feeling their way towards the west. By 780 B.C. some Corinthians were already frequenting Ithaca, leaving their offerings at the island's two shrines. During the second half of the eighth century the huge quantity of Corinthian votives at Aetos makes it seem likely that a Corinthian staging-post had been set up on the island, for the benefit of ships on their way to more distant lands.[87]

Nevertheless, Corinth never enjoyed a monopoly of shipping in these western parts. In spite of obvious Corinthian influence, the local pottery of Ithaca, Achaea, Elis, western Messenia, and Acarnania preserves its collective West Greek character, presumably through maritime exchanges independent of Corinth; and some West Greek pottery was even exported to Delphi and Medeon in Phocis, to Vitsa in the Epirus, and to Corcyra. On an inscribed Ithacan vase of *c.* 700 B.C. the alphabet has affinities with Achaea rather than with Corinth, and

includes a Chalcidian lambda.[88] Also from Euboea are two imported skyphoi at
Aetos, together with a highly individual bird-and-quatrefoil design on an Ithacan
kantharos which must have been copied from a Euboean original.[89] It is not
surprising that the visitors to Ithaca – Corinthians in large numbers, a few
Achaeans and Euboeans – should all come from mother-cities of colonies in
Italy and Sicily. For many voyagers about to cross the Ionian sea for the first
time, the votives at Aetos are a tangible expression of their hopes and fears.

Further north, the foundation of the colony on Corcyra (?708 B.C.) was preceded by two generations of trade before the flag: Corinthian exports go back to
c. 730 B.C. at Dodona, and at Vitsa to the early eighth century. Before their wares
could circulate in the mountainous hinterland of the Epirus, Corinthian merchants must first have found some suitable staging-post on the Epirot shore –
possibly at Elea or Glycys Limen near the mouth of the river Acheron. Although
there is no positive sign of their presence in these parts at such an early date, the
site of Ephyra (now 4km. inland) was presumably known to the eighth-century
Bacchiad poet Eumelos; he seems to have transferred the name and epic traditions of this place to his own city, so that Corinth, at the outset of her prosperity,
should also lay claim to a heroic past.[90]

In Corcyra, archaeology cannot yet throw any light on the immediate antecedents of the Corinthian colony; but two ancient sources imply that the first
colonists had to fight for their new home. Plutarch (*Quaestiones Graecae* 11)
tells us that they ejected some Eretrians already settled there; this would be but
one episode of a general conflict in which the two leading cities of Euboea were
then entangling most of the Greek world (pp. 200–1). According to Strabo (269)
the expelled people were Liburnians, a vigorous maritime people of those parts;
but his use of the word συνοικιοῦντα could be taken to mean that Chersicrates
admitted a native element into the new city.[91] At all events, the colony soon
became a powerful maritime state, and a mixed blessing to the mother-city; it
must have asserted its complete political independence before 664 B.C., when
the Corcyraeans defeated a Corinthian fleet in one of the earliest recorded sea-
battles.[92]

NOTES

1   *GGP* pl. 19f.
2   *GGP* pls. 19h, 21k.
3   *GGP* pl. 20f.
4   e.g., *BSA* 43 (1948), pl. 3, 63.
5   *MA* 25 (1919), 539 fig. 140.
6   e.g., *AJA* 45 (1941), 33 fig. 5.
7   e.g., *GGP* pl. 21b,k.
8   e.g., *GGP* pl. 19a (LG); pls. 20f, 21d (EPC).
9   *GGP* 103 nn. 3–5.
10 *GGP* pl. 20d.

11 By S. Weinberg; see *GGP* 103 n. 8.
12 J. Boardman, *Gnomon* 42 (1970), 496.
13 id., *BSA* 68 (1973), 278–9.
14 Payne, *Protokorinthische Vasenmalerei* 10–12 pls. 5–6.
15 *Corinth* XIII pl. 11, S 9–13.
16 e.g., ibid. pl. 8, 18.3–6.
17 See J. Salmon, *BSA* 67 (1972), 180–5.
18 Map: *Hesperia* 42 (1973), 3 fig. 1.
19 C. Morgan, *AJA* 41 (1937), 544–5.
20 *AJA* 37 (1933), 567, EPC; 41 (1937), 543 n. 1., late seventh century.
21 *AD* 26 (1971), B 100.
22 O. Broneer, *AJA* 73 (1969), 232; *Isthmia* I 55.
23 *Perachora* I pl. 84, 26–9; Jacobsthal, *Greek Pins* 6–7.
24 Higgins, *BSA* 64 (1969), 148 pl. 39a.
25 Jacobsthal, op. cit. 9 ff.
26 *Perachora* I pl. 55, 1.
27 G. D. Weinberg, *Corinth* XII 69–70, no. 517; cf. p. 149.
28 For its distribution see Bouzek, *Eirene* 6 (1967), 119 fig. 2.
29 ibid. 127 fig. 9.
30 Rolley, *FD* V.2 88–9 no. 146.
31 Herrmann, *JdI* 79 (1964), 28–32 figs. 12–15.
32 e.g., *BSA* 48 (1953), pl. 65, E 194 (found inside an EPC kyathos) and E 196.
33 *JHS* 70 (1950), pl. 5c.
34 *BSA* 35 (1934–35), 62–3 no. 15 pl. 16; apparently accompanied by a horse on a handle of cauldron no. 3. *GKG* 137 pls. 128–9.
35 Found with Corinthian pottery of *c.* 750–730 B.C.; *BCH* 68–9 (1944–45), 38 ff. no. 3.
36 Followed by *FD* V.2 nos. 3, 4; cf. also *GKG* pls. 124–5 (Olympia), and Athens 7729, *AM* 86 (1971), pl. 5, 4.
37 Weber, *AM* 86 (1971), 19.
38 Delphi 3232: *GKG* 145–6 pls. 174–5; Herrmann, loc. cit. 68–9 fig. 62; Rolley, *FD* V.2 no. 15.
39 For a full study see Snodgrass, *EGAW* 20–8.
40 op. cit. fig. 2a.
41 J. Stubbings, *Perachora* II 412, A 23: (a) a horseman, (b) Ajax carrying the body of Achilles. A comparable seal from Megara is mentioned ibid. 410 n. 2.
42 Boardman, *IGems* 146–7.
43 Desborough, *GDA* 279.
44 Huxley, *Pindar's Vision of the Past* (Belfast, 1975), 25 f.
45 Rolley, *FD* V.2 101–3; id., *BCH* 97 (1973), 512 no. 1.
46 e.g., *BCH* 74 (1950), pl. 39 row 2 no. 2.
47 *FD* V.2 no. 61.
48 ibid. nos. 46 (cf. *AH* II pl. 72, 8) and 119.
49 Desborough, *GDA* 248–50; *GGP* 221–3.
50 *GGP* 230 n. 3.
51 *PAE* 1952, 410 fig. 29; *PAE* 1956, 198–200 pl. 93c.
52 *PAE* 1929, 91 fig. 7; cf. Jacobsthal, *Greek Pins* no. 73 (Olympia).
53 cf. *GGP* pl. 49b.
54 *PAE* 1956, pl. 91a, 2–3.
55 *GKG* pl. 76.
56 Herrmann, *Olympia, Heiligtum und Wettkampfstätte* (Munich, 1973), 77–8.
57 Jeffery, *AG* 24 f.
58 Herrmann, op. cit. 71–2 fig. 35, 'Haus 4'.
59 *GGP* 223.
60 Desborough, *GDA* 88; Snodgrass, *DAG* 84–6.
61 Desborough, *GDA* 243–7; *GGP* 221–3 pl. 47.
62 Benton, *BSA* 48 (1953), 348, E 189 pl. 64.
63 art. cit. 257, Wall 27.

64 *GGP* 228; 227 n. 13.
65 *GGP* 225 n. 6 pl. 49a.
66 Fig. 54d and g are among the Corinthian imports in this context.
67 *GGP* pl. 49b; cf. 226 nn. 6–7.
68 Robertson, *BSA* 43 (1948), 111–13; cf. *GGP* 232.
69 For the last two shapes cf. Halos gr. 6, *BSA* 18 (1911–12), 5 fig. 3.
70 *BCH* 61 (1937), pl. 5, 6.
71 *DAG* pl. 33b.
72 *AD* 20 (1965), B pl. 442e; cf. *Hesperia* 17 (1948), pl. 72, C 1.
73 *AD* 18 (1963), pl. 211a.
74 *GGP* pl. 49a.
75 *AD* 20 (1965), B pl. 442b.
76 For Mycenaean contacts see *GDA* 97.
77 *GKG* pl. 172.
78 Rolley, *FD* V.2 no. 11.
79 Rolley, op. cit. 44 n. 6.
80 *PAE* 1931, 87 fig. 3; for the plate cf. *GKG* fig. 111, from Olympia.
81 K. Romiopoulou, *BSA* 66 (1971), 353 ff.
82 *AD* 23 (1968), B pl. 233b; cf. *BSA* 48 (1953), pl. 69, E 243a.
83 *IIème Conférence des études albanologiques, Tirana 1968* (1970) II, 335 ff. pl. 8.
84 *AE* 1937, 512 pl. 5e.
85 cf. *GGP* 365 n. 5.
86 See W. G. Forrest, *Historia* 6 (1957), 165 ff.
87 If so, only a temporary one, as no memory of it survives in written sources, and Ithaca played no part in the subsequent colonizing programme of the Cypselid tyrants in the late seventh century (Strabo 452).
88 Robertson, *BSA* 43 (1948), 81 f. on no. 490; Jeffery, *LSAG* 230 f.
89 *BSA* 43 (1948), pl. 20 no. 313; cf. below p. 234 n. 45.
90 Huxley, *Greek Epic Poetry* (London, 1969), 61–2.
91 Hammond, *Epirus* 417–18; cf. P. Calligas, *BSA* 66 (1971), 84 n. 16.
92 Thuc. i.13.

7 Euboea, Boeotia, Thessaly, and the Cyclades

We return now to the Aegean, to consider another wide area loosely held together by common features in the local pottery. Long after other local schools had broken free of Attic influence, each of these regions continued to borrow ideas from the Athenian style during its LG I phase. To begin with, much of the borrowing must have been at first hand, when Athens was still an outward-looking city; later, with the sharp decline of Attic exports, the ceramic cohesion of this group depends more and more on the influence of Euboea which travelled west-wards to Boeotia, northwards to Thessaly, and south-eastwards through the Cycladic archipelago. The situation becomes much the same as in the early ninth century, another period when Euboea succeeded Attica as the chief source of new ideas within this area. We must grant, however, that the elaboration of LG ornament allows a much greater diversity of local tastes than was possible in the Sub-Protogeometric styles of the previous century.

For the Euboeans, the second half of the eighth century marks the climax of their commercial activity, which ranged from Central Italy to the Levantine shores. Here we are specially concerned with their record at home, and their dealings with other Greeks in the Aegean. Our information comes mainly from recent excavations at Eretria, supplemented by a few casual finds from Chalcis, and by the latest material from the Xeropolis settlement at Lefkandi. Thanks to the discoveries of the past twenty-five years, a reasonably coherent account can now be given of the Euboean LG pottery sequence. In addition, Eretria offers evidence of temple architecture, burials of warriors and civilians, and an impres-sive array of gold diadems, bronze cauldrons, and offensive weapons. Before leaving Euboea, we shall try to relate these discoveries to the literary record, which preserves the memory of a great war fought between the men of Eretria and Chalcis for the possession of the rich Lelantine plain.

For Boeotia and Thessaly the evidence is far less satisfactory. From Thessaly, indeed, hardly any LG pottery has been published; but two sanctuaries are well provided with bronze votives, whose affinities are as much with Macedonia as with any southern centre. A Boeotian LG style has for long been apparent in a large corpus of pots and fibulae, mostly from clandestine excavations; happily, during the past decade, the shortage of well-documented finds is beginning to be remedied. Finally, the Cyclades provide a rich variety of styles and materials. In painted pottery alone, four distinct local LG schools can be located in different islands: Melos, Thera, Naxos, and perhaps Paros. As for other kinds of evidence almost every island has something individual to offer. Thus Tenos specialized in making coarse pithoi, decorated with ambitious figured scenes in relief; Melos is an important source of early stone seals. On Andros a complete stone-built town of the eighth century is coming to light, and some houses have been excavated on Siphnos. Thera is remarkable for its funerary architecture. On Keos a half-forgotten Bronze Age cult was revived in LG times; but by far the most important sanctuary is on Delos, which now begins to receive a wide variety of offerings from all round the Aegean.

Euboean LG Pottery

The most important and influential personality of Euboean LG I is the Cesnola Painter, named after the discoverer of his masterpiece (fig. 61c), a huge ovoid krater exported to Kourion in Cyprus.[1] While his style and linear ornament derive from Athenian work of *c.* 750 B.C., his three figured themes appear here for the first time in Geometric painting: the oriental Tree of Life flanked by heraldic animals, the frieze of grazing horses (not found in Attic before LG II), and the horse tethered to a manger with a bird and a pendent double axe in the field.[2] The shape, too, is without precedent, although the miniature vase crowning the lid is an Attic notion.

By the same hand is a small hydria from Chalcis (fig. 61b), combining the Tree of Life composition with a three-metope scheme where birds flank a central quatrefoil. These Atticizing metopes are the usual decoration for the most popular Euboean drinking-vessel, the skyphos. An early LG type, *c.* 750 B.C., carries only one metope, and lines round the lip.[3] There follows a widely exported class of *c.* 740–725 B.C. (fig. 61a) bearing three metopes as on the Chalcis hydria, and a zone of small concentric circles round the lip which is now fairly tall and vertical. As a filling ornament in the bird metopes, a single dotted lozenge becomes the most popular choice. The birds themselves are usually of the standard Attic type, found throughout the regions considered in this chapter. On larger Euboean vases, however, more interesting versions occur; thus, on the rims of large kraters, whose fragments have been found at Al Mina and Vrokastro, we see birds in flight, with feathered wings outstretched. These are from the Cesnola Workshop; and in the same spirit are the grazing birds on the Cesnola krater itself, with their wings slightly raised. On several pieces from Eretria the wings are internally hatched and sharply bent. Another Eretrian fragment[4] shows a procession of roaring lions, and a file of warriors carrying the Dipylon shield; charioteers, similarly equipped, appear on the Vrokastro krater fragments, together with a rider armed with a round shield; and on a piece from Lefkandi, a warrior and his young squire lead a horse by the rein.[5] In all these human renderings, the combination of silhouette with hatching seems to be a Euboean characteristic.

Other larger shapes of this time include jugs of Thessalian character, with cutaway neck (fig. 61d); and spouted kraters, on which the check pattern is a favourite motif. In large compositions, the ancillary zones are most often filled by circles or blobs connected by tangents (as fig. 61c), or rows of standing cross-

FIG. 61 EUBOEAN LG I POTTERY
(a) *Délos* XV, Bb 51, H. 8.9; (b) Chalcis, H. 18.5; (c) New York
74.51.965, the Cesnola krater from Kourion, H. 115; (d) Lefkandi,
H. 17.7

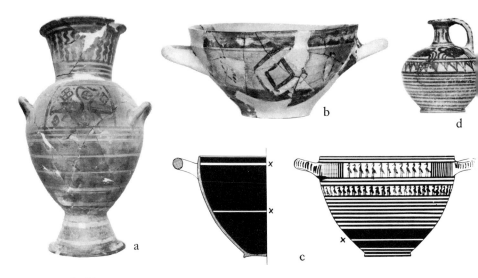

FIG. 62 EUBOEAN LG II POTTERY
(a) Athens 12856; (b) Lefkandi, H. 7.5; (c) Pithecusae, H. 9.4 (x=white paint);
(d) Eretria, H. 8.5

hatched triangles, with large dots in between (fig. 61d).

During the final, LG II phase (*c.* 725–690 B.C.) the Atticizing style is loosened to the point of collapse; and there is also a brief vogue for Corinthian shapes and ornament. These two developments are best treated separately, although they sometimes coincide on the same vase.

The deterioration of the metopal style is best seen on the skyphoi, which now begin to lose any clear articulation between lip and body. Increasing use is made of the multiple brush; thus, on the lip, the LG I circles are before long replaced by crosshatching, or dots, or careless vertical dashes. The metopal panels, now often reduced from three to two, are invaded by various forms of lozenge – either square and gridded, or with hatched frames and quartered and dotted interior. Another new motif, peculiar to Euboea, is a thick circle followed by dots inside and outside.[6] Sometimes the metopes are left empty.

A new class of skyphos, shallow and conical like those of the Attic Birdseed Painter (cf. p. 116 fig. 34b), enters the repertoire around 720 B.C. Here the metopal system has been abandoned; the decoration, floating in a free field, consists either of light, 'filling' motifs like the dot rosette, or larger patterns in double outline (e.g., hollow lozenge, swastika, or diagonal cross) filled with white slip (fig. 62b). The addition of a white wavy line to the glazed lip is another sign of the times; on larger vases, especially on kraters, glazed areas are often enlivened with a single zigzag or wavy line in white slip. Eventually, around 700 B.C., large vases begin to accept zones of vertical wavy lines in dark glaze, thick and closely set;

this becomes the usual neck decoration for Subgeometric burial amphorae, for which fig. 62a is the immediate prototype. This form, with its flaring neck, ovoid body, and conical foot, may well be descended from the Cesnola krater, although the intervening stages have yet to be found; at all events, we shall find many related versions in Boeotia and the central Cyclades. Another Subgeometric shape which Euboea shares with Boeotia is the small cup decorated with intersecting groups of near-vertical lines.[7]

To explain the arrival of Corinthian fashions, we must in this case look outside the Aegean. Corinthian imports, negligible in Euboea itself, are extremely abundant in the Euboean colony of Pithecusae, where they inspired local imitations from c. 750 B.C. onwards, and at a much earlier date than in the mother-cities. It seems likely, then, that the urge to emulate Corinthian fine pottery was communicated by the colonists to the potters of the homeland; and they, in their turn, manufactured extremely fine imitations during the period of EPC, exporting some of them to Pithecusae, Cumae, and Al Mina. A good example is fig. 62c, a kotyle which combines the stiff-legged bird-files of c. 720 B.C. with a slightly earlier, hemispherical shape (cf. p. 168 fig. 54c); the imitator departs from his original in allowing his birds two legs instead of one, in adding a second zone, and in using added white paint (shown by a cross) where the Corinthians preferred to reserve. Three closed forms in this Corinthianizing fabric also figure among the exports to Pithecusae and Cumae: the ovoid lekythos (not in itself a Corinthian shape); the globular aryballos, with a taller neck than its Corinthian prototype; and the conical lekythos-oinochoe.[8] All three shapes share the peculiarity of having a herring-bone pattern on the handle. The aryballos has also been found at home in Eretria, where one painter crowded the shoulder zone with crabs in silhouette (fig. 62d); it cannot be an accident that this creature later became an emblem on Eretrian coins, a symbol of the city's maritime aspirations. The career of this 'Painter of Crabs' lasts at least two decades into the seventh century, to judge from a menacing lion on one of his later aryballoi.[9]

Quite apart from the close imitations of Corinthian shapes, some Corinthian motifs were often lifted out of their original context to produce a thoroughly eclectic mixture: thus the EPC lozenge-net appears on the latest figured vase from the Cesnola Workshop,[10] and on the tall lips of some skyphoi from Lefkandi; on a skyphos from Al Mina and on a hydria from Eretria, three stiff-legged silhouette birds become enclosed in a metopal panel.[11]

To judge from the homogeneity of the Corinthianizing vases, and the very limited range of any genuinely Corinthian features, one would say that the vogue for first-hand imitation was very brief. Thus the potters of Euboea know the deepish hemispherical kotyle, but not the very deep EPC version which evolved soon after 720 B.C.; they know the stiff-legged bird-files, but not the later files with wiggly legs; their globular aryballoi reflect an early stage of EPC, long before the lower body began to taper in preparation for the change to the ovoid class. From these clues it seems that the Euboeans at home were open to direct influence from Corinthian originals only during the years c. 725 to c. 710 B.C.

Euboean Architecture and Burial Customs

Occupation at Lefkandi is now confined to the Xeropolis hill, where disjointed remains of the LG settlement lie immediately below the modern surface. Part of an apsidal house, 5m. wide, has a central hearth, a square stone bench up against one wall, and two successive earth floors. In the yard outside, three small circular platforms of stone may be the foundations of granaries, used in succession.[12] The town was finally abandoned around 710 B.C., in circumstances which we shall presently consider.

The most ambitious building of this time is a new temple of Apollo at Eretria, constructed soon after 750 B.C. (p. 324, fig. 104L). It is a narrow Hekatompedon, five times as long as it is wide (35 × 7–8m.), with an internal row of columns to support the pitched roof. Thus far, it resembles its earlier Samian counterpart (p. 97); but it differs in having an apsidal end in the mainland tradition, and even the long walls have a slight convex curve. This temple may already have been the second on the site: parts of an earlier front wall and anta (K) underlie its foundation, and a still earlier altar (M) in front of the temple lies on a different alignment from any existing structure. At one point the Hekatompedon almost encroaches on the venerable 'bay hut' (p. 88); two external niches were cut in the foundations, to avoid grazing the hut's outer half-columns.

Two Eretrian cemeteries afford a synoptic view of current burial practices. Infants and young children were inhumed in ornate pedestalled amphorae as fig. 62a, or in coarse pithoi with incised decoration; this we learn from the extra-mural cemetery by the sea (p. 88) where the earliest burial amphorae just precede 700 B.C.[13] Nine older children, aged from about six to sixteen years, lay in a small family cemetery just inside the later West Gate; they too were inhumed, but in small oval pits, and possibly within wooden coffins. Their grave goods include pots for food and drink, miniature pots and clay counters for play, and some jewellery. They were set slightly apart from their adult relations who were all cremated, as were the adults in the larger burial ground by the sea.

In both cemeteries the adult graves contain no unburnt offerings; nothing but the ashes, personal possessions and ornaments, and pyre debris. There is, however, a difference of ritual between the two groups, perhaps reflecting a difference in social status. The cremations by the sea, as noted above, were performed *in situ*, and fell into the open grave. But, for the seven cremations near the West Gate (c. 715–690 B.C.), the pyres were lit elsewhere, probably well outside the city; the remains were then gathered in a cloth, and deposited while still hot in a bronze cauldron, usually sealed by a lid of lead or stone. Finally, the cauldron would be laid in a pit, encased on all sides by limestone slabs, and covered with a layer of mud bricks and an earth fill. Four of the six undisturbed cremations are associated with offensive weapons, always broken or 'killed', and left in the spaces between the cauldrons and the surrounding slabs. Five of these graves form a semicircle round no. 6, the earliest, the richest, and the most carefully constructed (fig. 63a): the slab under the urn is meticulously hollowed out to take its base, and the lid here consists of a second cauldron laid upside down

b

a

FIG. 63 ERETRIA, WEST GATE, GRAVE 6 (*Eretria* III pl. 3, 10; pl. A1)
(a) burial *in situ*; (b) the cover
D. of cauldrons *c.* 48 and *c.* 54

(fig. 63b); above it, the grave was roofed by three thin slabs, superimposed. This warrior's possessions mark him out as a prince, a leader of men: four iron swords, five iron spearheads, one spearhead of bronze (a Mycenaean heirloom),[14] and a Phoenician double scarab of serpentine with a handsome gold setting.

Seen in its context, the West Gate cemetery is the preserve of a powerful and privileged *genos*. Compared with the more usual practice of open-trench cremation, the burning of the body on a separate pyre may here have been regarded as a high honour. It is interesting that the two alternative methods were already known in the cremations of ninth-century Lefkandi, the most likely site for Old Eretria; but the provision of a bronze urn is unknown before the LG period. The nearest counterparts for these burials are in Athens, where at least seven well-furnished LG cremations, all apparently male and one equipped with a sword, were housed in bronze cauldrons (pp. 120, 126). Perhaps in Athens, as in Eretria, this form of cremation was thought especially appropriate for a noble warrior, at a time when the descriptions of epic funerals were already being heard (p. 350). But whereas the Athenian cremations are dispersed in different quarters, the Eretrian warriors form a close family group: a prince surrounded by his kinsmen, and their children near by. Soon after the last burial, exceptional honours were paid to them. By the early seventh century, when the first stone fortifications of the West Gate were built, the site of the cemetery had been brought within the city – if not already before. A triangular shrine, or *heroön*, was constructed above the graves, and for the next hundred years their occupants received votive offerings of pottery and figurines, and burnt sacrifices.

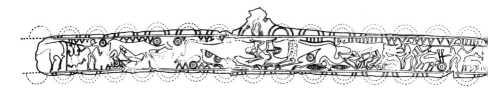

FIG. 64 ERETRIA LG GOLD DIADEM, VIENNA AM 124, Ohly fig. 25, *c.* 24

Euboean Metalwork

Three categories of metalwork are well represented in the Eretrian cemeteries: gold diadems, bronze cauldrons, and iron weapons. There is also a square-catchplate silver fibula from the sea cemetery, while the West Gate plot has yielded bracelets, pins, finger-rings, and other simple ornaments.

The diadems all conform to a local type, distinguished by a small central tongue which rested on the centre of the forehead; in Athens this feature occurs on some early MG bands,[15] but no longer in LG. The tongues and edges of the Eretrian diadems often show traces of a second frieze; the matrices, as in Athens, had originally been made for some other purpose, probably for the gold sheathing of small caskets.[16] Five out of seven diadems bear figured scenes. On the earliest (Ohly E1), the tongue shows part of a battle, including a light one-wheeled chariot of Sub-Dipylon type (*c.* 725 B.C.). There follow a single combat (E5), and two hunting scenes (E3,4) of which the former, in Vienna, is the better preserved (fig. 64). The composition is crowded, stuffed with filling ornament, but loosely co-ordinated. On the left a doe, quite unconcerned, suckles her young; meanwhile three spearmen, with their hound, have little chance of saving their small comrade from the jaws of two ravening lions. These vast, sprawling beasts have their counterparts on several Subgeometric grave-amphorae from Boeotia, and one from Euboea.[17]

The latest diadem was found in West Gate gr. 14, a rich child burial soon after 700 B.C. It is also the most wholeheartedly oriental, in style as much as in subject-matter. Two springy stags, recalling some animals on EPC aryballoi, flank a central Tree of Life; but each stag is pursued by a panther, lurking behind a lotus tree. Local taste, in this series, is seen in the choice of subject rather than in any consistent style. Thus, on the Vienna and West Gate diadems there is the same fragile compromise between a heraldic central theme, and a context of violent action; and in both these compositions, as in the other hunt scene E4, room is found for strange birds with enormous wings outstretched – a notion which had already occurred to the vase-painters of the Cesnola Workshop.

Of the cauldrons from the West Gate cremations, the pair from gr. 6 (fig. 63a,b) are the earliest.[18] Their straight, vertical walls recall some Geometric tripod cauldrons from sanctuaries;[19] perhaps the resemblance was intentional, an additional honour to the prince whose ashes they sheltered. Of the others, one is carinated (gr. 10), the rest are bellied. Two of the latest (grs. 5, 8), with their everted rims and low centre of gravity, share the shape of the oriental cauldron adorned with human and animal protomes, a type which was becoming familiar to the Greeks in the years around 700 B.C. (pp. 362ff).

The iron weapons from these cremations are all of well-known types: seven swords of the usual Naue II class, most with fine fish-tail hilts; twelve spearheads, all of a long, slender class[20] also popular in Argos and Olympia. The most striking thing about these weapons is their abundance, in a period when military equipment was not often placed in graves elsewhere. As we shall see, this was a time of conflict and danger for the Eretrians, when they had every reason to bury their fallen warriors with full military honours.

Euboea: Conclusions

After the early promise of Lefkandi, Euboea remains throughout the eighth century one of the most prosperous and progressive parts of Greece. At Eretria one is struck by the sheer size of the new Geometric city (well over one square kilometre), the corporate planning needed for the building of Apollo's Heka-tompedon, and the wealth manifest in the gold diadems and bronze cauldrons from the cemeteries; furthermore, frequent exchanges with the Levant are indicated by imports of Cypriot pottery[21] and Phoenician scarabs, and also by imitations (or imports?) of oriental cauldrons. Much less is known about Geo-metric Chalcis, most of which lies under the modern town; but sporadic finds of pottery suggest that the sequence there was similar to the Eretrian, and that Chalcis may even have been the home of the Cesnola Painter and his workshop.[22] At all events this artist, who introduced the oriental Tree of Life into Geometric art, must have lived in a city with a lively interest in the Levant, and it is no surprise that five out of the twelve vases ascribed to him and his colleagues were found in Cyprus and Al Mina.

As for the other exported vases, we are not yet in a position to suggest whether they come from Chalcis, Eretria, or Lefkandi; all we can say is that their abund-ance, and their wide distribution, serve to confirm the impression of lively com-merce given by the evidence from Euboea itself. Within the Greek homeland, a few Euboean vases reached Delos, Naxos, Samos, Ithaca, Vrokastro in east Crete, perhaps Iolcos, and perhaps Nea Anchialos in Macedonia (p. 209); but at Zagora on Andros so great is the quantity of Euboean exports that the site has been explained as an Eretrian colony, in the light of Strabo's remark (448) that Eretria had once held sway over Andros, Tenos, and Keos.[23] In the east, occa-sional exports to Cyprus show that many of the major coastal cities of that island (Salamis, Kition, Amathus, Kourion, Paphos) were being visited by Euboean merchants; but their main entrepôt was at Al Mina, where Euboean wares become especially prominent from c. 740 to c. 710 B.C., even inspiring local imitations made by resident Euboean potters.[24] In the west – to anticipate the next chapter briefly – precolonial MG II exports to Etruria and Campania are followed by imitations of Euboean (and Corinthian) LG made in the colonial entrepôt of Pithecusae, and by 730 B.C. much of the local pottery in Etruria, Calabria, and Sicily was succumbing to Euboean influence, illustrating once again the wide extent of Euboean commerce.

It is instructive, at this point, to draw a general comparison with contemporary Corinthian exports, whose aggregate must be considerably larger. The finest Corinthian wares may well have been made with export in view (pp. 186–7),[25] either for the marketing of unguents, or as surpassingly fine specimens of the potter's technique, to which the Euboeans themselves paid the compliment of trying to imitate them. The Euboean exports, on the other hand, include very few unguent containers. Open shapes form the vast majority; especially common are skyphoi, made with no greater care than those found in domestic contexts in the home cities, and not especially desirable as articles of commerce. In several places (e.g., Al Mina, Zagora, Pithecusae) these vessels are the chattels of Euboeans residing abroad, plying their trade in more profitable things. It is here that they surpass the Corinthians in adventurous initiative – in their willingness to live far from home, in pursuit of eastern and western markets.

By the end of the century, these manifold symptoms of commercial prosperity were vanishing fast. Euboean pottery exports to the Levant, to Italy and Sicily, even to the Aegean, had dwindled to almost nothing. A little earlier, c. 710 B.C., the old town of Lefkandi had been finally abandoned, probably destroyed. At Eretria, the cremations near the West Gate suggest a context of war, of which the literary record offers ample evidence.

Thucydides, in reviewing early Greek conflicts, mentions a war between Chalcis and Eretria, which embroiled the Greek world at large (i.15). He adds that each of the protagonists found allies among neighbouring pairs of states, which had their own reasons for mutual animosity. From casual allusions by other writers,[26] we learn that Corinth, Samos, and Pharsalos in Thessaly were ranged on the Chalcidian side, whereas Eretria was joined by Megara and Miletus. Other circumstantial references confirm these alignments. In Sicily, a Megarian contingent had been expelled from the Chalcidian colony of Leontini in 728 B.C.[27] Nearer home, the first Corinthian colonists of Corcyra ejected the previous Eretrian settlers, probably in 708 B.C. (p. 188); another Corinthian, Ameinocles, built four ships for Samian allies in 704 B.C.[28] Since the last two dates coincide approximately with the abandonment of Lefkandi, it is likely that the most critical period of the war was in the last decade of the eighth century, and soon after the close of the First Messenian War (p. 163); the Corinthians, who were involved in both conflicts, can hardly have fought on two fronts at once.

The immediate cause of the war[29] was a dispute over the possession of the Lelantine plain, the rich arable land which lies between Chalcis and Lefkandi, but at some distance from Eretria. The Eretrians' claim becomes easier to understand if Lefkandi were Old Eretria, whence their great-grandfathers had moved to found the new site in c. 800 B.C. (pp. 88–90). The old city, though depleted in LG times, would still have been held by their kinsmen, a potential menace and a natural target for the Chalcidian foe. It is possible that trade rivalries, in eastern and western markets, may have fanned the hostility between the opposing states; yet the implication of land hunger, as the chief *casus belli*, must be taken seriously. Chalcis had been driven by famine to found a colony at Rhegion;[30] the Eretrians, too, must have been on short commons when they drove off with slings their unfortunate compatriots who were returning home from Corcyra.[31]

Little wonder, then, that two rapidly expanding cities should have come to blows over the possession of a small but fertile plain.

About the course and outcome of the war we know very little. The Chalcidians were victorious in a land battle, in which the formidable Eretrian cavalry were routed by a contingent of Thessalian horsemen, led by Cleomachos of Pharsalos.[32] Amphidamas, a Chalcidian prince, is said to have lost his life in a sea engagement;[33] Hesiod sailed across from Boeotia to attend his funeral games, and won a tripod cauldron in the contest for song.[34] The destruction of Lefkandi – if it was their old city – must have been a severe blow to the Eretrians, who would thereby have lost any easy access to the Lelantine plain. But it is fruitless to speculate any further on the issue of a war which must have been disastrous to both sides, causing the eclipse of Chalcis and Eretria as commercial powers.

Seen in its context, the Eretrian *heroön* is an impressive war memorial, sited on a low rise just inside the West Gate which faced towards Chalcis, and doing honour to the heroes who guarded the city in death as in life.

Boeotian LG Pottery and Terracottas

Boeotian LG is a somewhat retarded style, guided by a variety of foreign influences. It begins around 740 B.C., strongly influenced by Attic LG I; later, Corinthian and Euboean ideas become recognizable, and the Athenian connection lapses. From these diverse ingredients, Boeotian potters evolved their own eclectic mixture. A Subgeometric phase lasts some way into the seventh century, probably until *c.* 670 B.C.

The local LG development is most clearly displayed in a series of large oinochoai from a single workshop;[35] a Theban workshop, if dealers' provenances are correct. Their funerary purpose is betrayed by plastic snakes attached to the handles. Fig. 65a illustrates a midway stage in the series, *c.* 720 B.C. The metopal system, the birds, and the blobs with wavy tangents are all of Attic origin; the horse panels, with their pendent axis, echo the style and iconography of the Euboean Cesnola Painter. Local taste is seen in the heavy zone of concentric circles, the use of a floating triangle as a filling ornament, the vertical zigzags (probably adapted from the Corinthian Thapsos Workshop), and a preference for filling the square panels with living creatures, rather than with linear motifs.

Fig. 65e and c represent the two favourite kinds of pyxis: the flat Attic type, more vigorously curved than the contemporary Athenian model; and the tall Corinthian variety whose lid is at first conical, then flat. Here, too, Attic and Corinthian elements are blended in the decoration: from Athens, the bird metopes, the tangential circles and blobs; from Corinth (again, the Thapsos Workshop) the vertical zigzags with bars on the apices, the single-line meander, and the eight-armed swastika. A huge enlargement of the tall pyxis is sometimes used for infant inhumations.[36]

Among the open shapes, skyphoi and kotylai are virtually unknown; small Subgeometric cups, with intersecting groups of near-vertical lines, are common to Boeotia and Euboea. The chief drinking-vessel is undoubtedly the high-handled kantharos, which often bears figured decoration (fig. 65b). Kraters **too** are quite common, and usually have pedestals (fig. 65d); the normal Geometric form is succeeded by a Subgeometric ovoid variety around 700 B.C.

Boeotian figured work is second only to Attic in the variety of its imagery; the themes include hunting, dancing, boxing (fig. 65d), horse-taming, and funerary ritual. The style of drawing was inspired, in the first instance, by the major workshops of Attic LG I; fig. 65b and d afford a glimpse of its progress – or, rather, its devolution. The warriors on the kantharos (c. 725 B.C.) still display some acquaintance with the lanky figures of the Dipylon Workshops, combined with the reserved eye favoured by the Hirschfeld Painter. By the time of the krater (c. 700 B.C.) decay has set in; note the absurdly exaggerated hands, the unsteady knees, and the general lack of co-ordination in the limbs.

During the Subgeometric phase the most remarkable shape is the large burial amphora, with a broad flaring neck, a plump ovoid body, and a tall conical or flaring foot.[37] The main panel, on the shoulder, is often figured, while the supporting decoration consists largely of vertical zigzags or wavy lines. Whereas most LG pottery from Boetia is unslipped, these vases often carry a thick white slip. The form was probably adapted from the Euboean repertoire (cf. fig. 62a); some of the motifs, too, are of Euboean character, including fierce ravening lions, birds with lozenges in the field, and very thick wavy lines. To judge from their variety of style, these amphorae may well have been made in more than one Boeotian centre.

Peculiar to Boeotia is a group of female terracotta figurines with bell-shaped skirts made on the wheel, all LG or Subgeometric. Although their provenances are not known, it is likely that they are dolls rather than idols, since the legs are separately made, and were attached below the skirt with wire or cord. Each one bears painted ornament in a Boeotian LG manner. Fig. 65f., the most ornate, combines some realistic details (locks of hair, necklace with pendants, sandals) with a decorative frieze of dancing women round the hem – perhaps indicating a textile pattern.

Boeotian Fibulae and Other Bronzes

As most of the material comes from uncontrolled excavations, not much is known about Boeotian burial customs. Inhumation appears to be the rule: there are pits for adults at Rhitsona (ancient Mycalessos), and large vases for infants at Pyri near Thebes; in an extensive cemetery by the shore of Lake Paralimni a rich female burial of LG times, covered by an earth tumulus, has been briefly reported.[38]

Among the metal finds from Boeotian cemeteries, bronze fibulae are the most frequent offerings; the local figured art is seen at its most adventurous in the engraving on their flat surfaces. The most usual type, with square catchplate and

FIG. 65 BOEOTIAN LG POTTERY AND TERRACOTTA FIGURINE
(a) Copenhagen 5371, H. 48.5; (b) London 1910.10-13.1, H. 10;
(c) Athens 11795, H. 15; (d) Athens 12896, H. 33.5; (e) Hanover
1957.84, H. 11.5; (f) Paris CA 623, H. 33

a

b

c

d

e

f

uninterrupted convex bow (Blinkenberg VIII), is of Athenian origin; it was adopted by the Boeotians at about the time when it died out in Attica (p. 126). The Boeotian examples (e.g., fig. 66a) are much larger than the Attic, the plates being anything from 4–14cm. square; to prevent the fibulae from being intolerably heavy, the bows are now hollowed out inside. A variant of this class may have three (fig. 66b) or four bows side by side, enlarging a notion which had already occurred to a Corinthian smith in MG II (p. 85). A third type, mainly Subgeometric, bears its decoration on a vast flat crescent, at least 20cm. long (fig. 66c); the catchplate is minimal, and on the stem there is a curious star-like ornament. The ancestor of this form has appeared in graves of c. 850–830 B.C. at Lefkandi (p. 64), but practically nothing is known about the intervening stages.[39]

Boeotian engravers began cautiously with a single motif on both sides of the square catchplate, taking their lead from earlier Attic fibulae (fig. 25a). The most frequent motifs, at first, were the bird and the quatrefoil, recalling Attic LG I metopal decoration. Later, birds were combined with animals and ships; later still, not much before 700 B.C., man enters the repertoire, and human scenes – often mythical – continue through the first quarter of the seventh century. Figures on square plates are usually filled with tremolo lines, giving them more substance than a mere outline.

Several artists have been distinguished. The earliest is known as the Swan Engraver,[40] after his graceful winged birds with their long, sinuous necks. An early piece from his hand or workshop appears in a grave-group of c. 730 B.C. at Lerna in the Argolid.[41] His later fibulae combine birds with horses or ships; a good example is fig. 66b, showing his characteristic filling of gentle tremolo waves, in contrast to the jagged zigzags preferred by others.

The Swan Engraver's career overlapped with the early work of two younger artists who introduced human beings into their maturer compositions. The Lion Engraver[42] is named after his favourite beast, always seen devouring the remains of his prey; his mannerisms (misplaced eye, reserved band across the animals' bellies) recur on a very late fibula showing two Labours of Heracles. A contemporary artist, the Ship Engraver,[43] specialized in fibulae with a single bow, and plates framed by intersecting semicircles. Fig. 66a shows his style in mid-career, when he was already beginning to experiment with human themes. The pair to this piece shows a man half-devoured by lions, heraldically posed; both fibulae bear identical horse-and-bird pictures on the back, the horses being rendered in a later and heavier manner than in fig. 66b. His subsequent work includes two combats between a hero and Siamese twins. The latest fibula of all[44] (c. 680 B.C.?) shows a duel and an embattled horseman – subjects borrowed from Early Orientalizing work elsewhere, but here translated into Subgeometric terms; the only concession to the times is the elimination of the narrow Geometric waist.

FIG. 66 BOEOTIAN LG AND SUBGEOMETRIC FIBULAE
(a) Athens 8199 from Thebes (EA 1892 pl. 11, 1), L. 13.5;
(b) London 94.7-19.10 from Thebes (BMCat. no. 119), L. 17.1;
(c) Berlin 31013a from Thisbe (JdI 31 pl. 17, 1), L. 21

a

b

c

These three engravers (to judge from dealers' provenances) are the leading personalities of a central Theban school. There was also a provincial school producing rougher work somewhere in eastern Boeotia,[45] whence came all the fibulae found in the Rhitsona graves; the contexts there show that these craftsmen, too, were active well into the seventh century. Their preference was for Type VIII fibulae with several bows, and the rustic character of their style is seen especially in the straight and rigid necks of the birds.

The six enormous fibulae with flat crescent bows[46] form a group by themselves, probably all made in a single Theban workshop. Fig. 66c is a good specimen of the style. As on the ninth-century Euboean prototypes, the broad centre of the bow is occupied by a circular compass-drawn emblem, elaborated in various ways. On either flank are the figured scenes, the field being filled by birds, fish, and (elsewhere) snakes. At first sight the drawing has a dry, old-fashioned look, reminiscent of the much earlier Elgin fibulae from Attica (fig. 25a). Yet the one-wheel chariots, and the running warriors on the pair to this piece,[47] are in the manner of the very latest Attic LG vase-painting; and the roaring lion on a related square-plate fibula[48] has a latticed mane betraying some acquaintance – if only indirectly – with oriental art. The most advanced crescent fibulae are the pair in London by one hand,[49] depicting the Trojan Horse and three Labours of Heracles (c. 680 B.C.?), all presented in crowded, tumultuous compositions without any consistent groundline.

For enlightenment concerning the local bronze figurines we must look to Boeotian sanctuaries. The Kabeirion, near Thebes, is said to be the provenance of a charming group in Boston: a deer suckles her fawn while a bird perches on her rump.[50] The animals have a fragile, sticklike appearance; the liberal use of the hammer, the knobbed fetlocks, and the decoration of impressed circles all indicate Corinth as the chief source of ideas. The same is true of a horse (no. 39) from the sanctuary of Apollo at Ptoion; but another horse, now in Bonn, combines the Argive type with incised decoration (including a bird) in the manner of Boeotian LG fibulae.[51] Several other groups, and also single fawns, may be attributed to this Boeotian school,[52] whose characteristics will emerge more clearly when the bronzes from the Kabeirion excavations are fully published.

Backward, clumsy, rustic, derivative: these are the derogatory epithets often applied to early (and later) Boeotian art and life, not always with justice. The Boeotians were not much concerned with artistic innovation, or with marketing their wares overseas; yet their conservatism, and their indifference to commerce, are counterbalanced in this period by a growing enthusiasm for mythical narrative, of which the poetry of Hesiod and the mature work of the Theban engravers are contemporary manifestations.

Thessaly and the North

The Thessalians favoured an Atticizing style of LG pottery, which they probably learned from Euboea. Much of the decoration is metopal: birds, quatrefoils, diagonal crosses, and gridded lozenges are common motifs. Three skyphoi from the Kapakli tholos near Volos each carry bird metopes with dotted lozenges in the field; these are either imports, or close imitations, of Euboean LG. Other open shapes are pedestalled kraters,[53] high-handled kantharoi, and cups, including one from Kapakli with the traditional trigger handle. Another local shape, the jug with cutaway neck, is still current among the later pyres of Halos, always fully glazed, and usually with groups of ridges on lip and neck;[54] decorated imitations, as we have seen, were made in Euboea (fig. 61d). The material is too sparse to allow any conclusions about the local LG development; but a few sherds from Argissa[55] afford a glimpse of a Subgeometric phase, in which the decoration consists largely of Corinthianizing panels of floating chevrons or sigmas.

The bronzes are much more plentiful, thanks to the votives from two sanctuaries, both founded in LG times. One is dedicated to Artemis Enodia at ancient Pherae, 15km. inland from the gulf of Pagasae, a place already mentioned (p. 44) for its earlier cist graves. The other, far to the west, is the sanctuary of Athena Itonia at Philia (near ancient Kierion), which has yielded a prodigious number of Geometric bronzes. Both cults, during our period, seem to have been practised in the open air.

A rather crude northern style of human figurines – mainly warriors – has long been recognized, common to western Thessaly, the Epirus (p. 185), and Thermon in Aetolia; its chief characteristics, best seen in the well-known Subgeometric warrior from Karditsa, are a long neck, short stumpy legs, and a belt with sharp edges.[56] In the Pagasaean region, however, the figures are capable of greater fluency and refinement, suggesting some southward contacts.[57] This assumption is borne out by the horses from Pherae, which are all in the Corinthian hammered style. Bird pendants from the same site include at least one Corinthian import (cf. fig. 58a), and many local pieces on horizontal bases (and many more at Philia), some of which follow the Corinthian type with upturned tail, while others are in a simpler local manner.[58] There are also a few hollow-cast cocks. In addition, both sanctuaries are rich in small bronze objects with Macedonian affinities, and mainly post-Geometric; these include birds and other animals resting on openwork cages, miniature jugs and pyxides, elaborate jug-stoppers, and biconical beads.[59]

Thessalian fibulae fall mainly into two classes. Blinkenberg's Type VII is related to the Attico-Boeotian fibula with square catchplate, from which it is probably derived; it differs in having one or more globes or swellings on the bow. The plate at first remains fairly square, but eventually acquires a sail-like form, sweeping up to an acute angle at its outer corner; it bears engraved decoration, often figured. This type has a wide distribution, and is not peculiar to Thessaly; we have often met it in the northern and central Peloponnese, where some were probably made (p. 157 fig. 51a). A good specimen of the Thessalian school, at a Subgeometric stage, has been published from Philia:[60] on the front a mare suckles her foal, and smaller animals are crammed into the field; on the back, four fish; a triple frame of small semicircles all round. The other class, Blinkenberg VI, is exclusively Thessalian; it has a long narrow plate, unengraved, and concave on its outer edge; the bow often has three globes, separated by reels. The largest ones, surely never intended for daily use, weigh 2 kilograms. It may be that all Type VI fibulae are post-Geometric; they are not found among the wholly eighth-century pyres of Halos.

The most usual kind of pin from Philia and Pherae has a small disc head, a large globe with a bead between reels above and below, and a square upper shank. This type has been called transitional between Geometric and Orientalizing.[61]

In Macedonia our main concern is with southward communications. During LG times the evidence is slender, and points mainly towards Thessaly; there are resemblances in the handmade pottery of the two regions, a few Types VI and VII fibulae came to Macedonia,[62] and we have noted the incipient vogue for Macedonian bronze ornaments among the votives at Thessalian sanctuaries. Exchanges with southern Greece are much rarer. Of Corinthian type are a bronze pin from the upper Vardar valley (p. 186 n. 84), a bronze horse at Pateli near Florina,[63] and another from Chauchitsa;[64] a Type VIII fibula is said to come from Chalcidice.[65] The only certain imports of Geometric pottery are from the mound of Nea Anchialos near Salonika, a little way inland from the Thermaic Gulf.[66] Hence came a deposit of *c.* 770–750 B.C., including a Thessalian plate and kantharos, and some Atticizing pieces of fine quality (skyphoi, kantharoi, and an amphora neck) which could well be Euboean. Perhaps they were brought by Eretrian prospectors in an area settled by their compatriots some fifty years later; for across this gulf lies Methone, the colony which, according to Plutarch, was eventually founded by those unfortunates who had already been ousted from Corcyra by the Corinthians, only to be rebuffed by the Eretrians at home (p. 200). Methone, however, remains unexcavated, as are Mende and Torone, the early Euboean colonies in the Chalcidic peninsula; so far, then, we have no archaeological confirmation of any Greek colonial settlement in the northern Aegean[67] prior to the Parian foundation of Thasos in *c.* 680 B.C.

The Western Cyclades

We begin with the site of Ay. Irini on Keos, some 40 km. from the coast of Attica. Here a prosperous town had been deserted in the twelfth century B.C.; but its temple was not entirely forgotten, and our period saw a remarkable revival of the Bronze Age cult. The object of veneration, in one of the innermost chambers, was a clay head, about half lifesize, for which a circular stand had been carefully made; the associated pottery is LG, including some Attic imports. The head joined a torso found a metre further down in the same room; this was one of many Minoan female statues of the fifteenth century B.C., whose wreckage littered the original floor. The only intervening layer contained a little Attic tenth-century pottery, but other parts of the temple showed traces of worship in Late Mycenaean times. The LG deposit, with the head, was followed by a continuous run of votives through the next four hundred years, including some Archaic sherds bearing dedications to Dionysos. Here, then, as at Delphi, a

FIG. 67 MELIAN (a,b) AND TENIAN (c) LG POTTERY
(a) Leiden RO III 84, H. 50; (b) Paris A 491. H. 20;
(c) Munich 7697, H. 25

female deity was succeeded by a male. Although the sanctity of the place may never have faded from memory, the change surely implies that the cult did not continue through the Dark Ages without break; in fact, the votives do not appear to include anything of the eleventh century, or between 900 and 750 B.C.

On Siphnos the corner of a fortified LG village has been excavated at Kastro on the east coast, in a deep pocket of earth between a cliff and the later acropolis wall. The best-preserved house, a single room some 4m. square, was furnished with a built-in cupboard, stone bases for storage pithoi, and a device for collecting precious rainwater for domestic use. The adjoining house has a central column-base. Three more one-roomed houses came to light on the steep slope below, of which one preserves a stone platform, perhaps for a bed. All the LG houses are carefully built of long schist slabs, roughly dressed outside, and laid to form irregular courses. At the inland site of Ay. Andreas, the fortifications of the Bronze Age town were repaired in LG times, and a massive new tower constructed.

The cemeteries of Melos were explored mainly during the nineteenth century, not always scientifically. From the most recently published report (1895) it appears that cremation was the prevailing rite in Geometric times (p. 91).

The LG vases from Melos conform to a distinct local style. The leading workshop[68] made kraters with pedestals (fig. 67a) or with ring feet, fenestrated stands (fig. 67b), and belly-handled amphorae; their decoration is derived, in the first instance, from Attic LG Ib. Horses, goats, and stags are often placed in metopal panels, have their eyes reserved, and owe something to the Athenian Hirschfeld Painter. Birds, fairly orthodox at first (as in our illustrations), later acquire fan tails; the latest have no tails at all. The smaller and plainer shapes are oinochoai, amphoriskoi, small hydriai, mugs, skyphoi, cups, plates, and high-rimmed bowls; their decoration is usually limited to narrow panels of dots, or vertical dashes, or vertical wavy lines, or steep single zigzag, all done with a thin brush. The simpler aspects of this style appear on the pottery with the Kimolos cremations (p. 91), and on a few skyphoi from Siphnos; a few exports reached Thera and Knossos.[69]

Melos may have played an important part in the revival of stone seal engraving. Fig. 68a, showing two men beside a tree, has already been mentioned (p. 151); made of Cycladic white limestone, it is an early and ambitious specimen of the LG flat squares, a form which became established in the Argolid. The three sides of an ogival Subgeometric seal (fig. 68b–d; c. 700–675 B.C.), unique in form and material (shell, perhaps tridacna), are occupied by heraldic centaurs holding branches, heraldic sphinxes, and a kneeling stag. About a generation later than this piece, Melos is the most likely centre for the earliest 'Island Gems', which reintroduce the lentoid and amygdaloid forms of the Late Bronze Age.

The Northern Cyclades

At Zagora, on the south-west coast of Andros, a stone-built Geometric town of 6.4 hectares has been partly explored. Since occupation is virtually limited to the eighth century, the architecture is extremely well preserved, and no other place in the Greek world offers a clearer picture of domestic life during this period. The choice of site may seem somewhat curious: a bleak and precipitous headland,

FIG. 68 MELIAN LG AND SUBGEOMETRIC SEALS
(a) Oxford 1894.5A (xxvi), H. 4.4; (b–d) Oxford 1894.5A (xxvii),
H. 1.9 (photographs R. L. Wilkins)

excellent for defence, but tormented by boisterous north winds, lacking in any natural springs within the town, and far away from the island's fertile valleys. As though to isolate themselves from the hinterland, the inhabitants fortified the saddle which gives access to the settlement; but any visitor by sea could beach his ship in either of the two little bays which flank the headland, and climb up to the houses by a winding path. Maritime trade, so it seems, was thought to be of greater moment than access to good arable land; and a lively commerce is confirmed by the proportion and variety of the imports. Attic pottery is prominent before 750 B.C.; in LG times there are many Corinthian vessels, a few 'Parian', and some ivory seals which can be matched in Chios, 110km. across the open sea. But by far the most frequent source of imported pottery is Euboea, and it has been surmised (p. 199) that Zagora was taken over by the Eretrians soon

FIG. 69 NAXIAN (a,b) AND 'PARIAN' (c–e) LG POTTERY
(a) *Delos* XV Bb 6, H. 41.7; (b) ibid. Bb41, H. 13.8; (c) ibid. Ae 74,
H. 13; (d) ibid. Ac 1, H. 31; (e) Thera J 16, H. 42

after the foundation of their own city[70] as a trading station for their merchants on their way to the east. The sudden desertion of the town, soon after 700 B.C., coincides with the recession caused by the Lelantine War, and the consequent eclipse of Euboean trade overseas.

The most conspicuous landmarks on the site are the massive fortification wall, in places 7m. thick, with its solitary gate and bastion at its south end; and the temple at the summit of the headland, which was remodelled in the sixth century, long after the town had been abandoned. But the greatest interest of Zagora attaches to the houses themselves, with their careful planning and interior furnishing; they will be treated in a later chapter (pp. 304ff), together with the evidence of domestic life from other Geometric towns.

Tenos is the chief centre for large coarse vessels bearing figured friezes in relief. Conventionally called pithoi, they take the form of huge neck-handled amphorae, whose handles were strengthened by fretwork.[71] The figures were made separately, freely modelled, and pressed on to the wall of the vase when it was still leather-hard. Almost all the relief pithoi from Tenos are known to come from the inland sanctuary of Xombourgo, where they served as storage vessels in an inner sanctum. Others, found among the LG houses of Zagora on Andros, were probably made there by a local offshoot of the Tenian school.

The earliest relief pithoi, of which only fragments survive, may not go back very far into LG; their figured themes – a row of centaurs, a male round dance, a file of striding warriors with round shields – correspond to the repertoire of Attic LG IIb amphorae, and there are also horses, regardant deer, and goats. Some early figures are surrounded by pricked dots, as though to emphasize their outline, or perhaps to ensure their adhesion to the wall of the vessel.[72]

Around 700 B.C. the relief technique reaches a more assured stage, seen on a Tenian neck fragment showing a man leading a goat (fig. 67c). The relief is shallower than before, but the outline is firmer, and more attention is paid to the modelling: especial care has been taken over the man's leg muscles, and the goat's ear and shoulder. On a body fragment which may belong to the same pithos[73] parts of two friezes can be made out: a fierce animal fight, and above it the feet and drapery of a goddess(?). It is a sign of the times that her long robe should be covered with incised and stamped patterns.[74]

A little later are a pithos from Eretria with battle scenes,[75] and another from Thebes showing a nature goddess giving birth.[76] Both conform to the Tenian school in style and choice of theme, but it is not yet clear whether they are imports or local imitations, perhaps made by travelling Tenian potters. At all events, the craft must eventually have become established in Boeotia, where the Thebes pithos is the first of a long series lasting through the seventh century. The diffusion of the Tenian relief style is yet another symptom of that *koiné* which binds together the LG and Subgeometric art of Euboea, Boeotia and the Cyclades.

The Central Cyclades

The true centre of the Cyclades is Delos, birthplace of Artemis and Apollo, round which the other islands perform their circular dance.[77] Before describing the growth of the Delian sanctuary, it will be as well to consider the chief sources of its Geometric offerings. None of the pots can be local, since Delos is a small rocky islet without clay beds. Of the two commonest fabrics one can be safely assigned to Naxos; the other, with less certainty, to Paros.

With the Naxian LG vases from Delos[78] go a number of fragments from various places in and around the main town of Naxos: the settlement itself (Grotta), the cemeteries of pit graves (Kaminia, Aplomata), and the sanctuary of Apollo on the Palati peninsula. The leading closed shapes are slim neck-handled amphorae (fig. 69a) and oinochoai, both of which have successors in the local Orientalizing style; open forms include kraters, high-handled kantharoi, and fairly large skyphoi (fig. 69b). Some of the ornament is derived from Attic LG I, as is the strict metopal system which remains in favour all through LG; hence come the usual hatched birds, and the zones of tangential blobs, motives which are also popular in Euboea and Boeotia. More individual are the hourglass panels (fig. 69b), the broad zigzag with filled apices and dotted circles (fig. 69a), and the zones of horizontal S's which span the transition to Orientalizing. In the drawing of birds, the following mannerisms are typically Naxian: the single median line instead of hatching (fig. 69b), and the marking of the wing tip in silhouette renderings.[79] Occasional essays in figured drawing include a battle scene on a piece from Kaminia, a rather static female dance on a pedestalled amphora from Delos (Bc 6), and all three of the Euboean Cesnola Painter's themes: grazing horses, horse with double axe, and heraldic goats.[80]

Soon after 700 B.C. this robust and well-ordered style passes into its Early Orientalizing stage, represented chiefly by the slim Heraldic Amphorae from Delos and Rheneia.[81]

The other common LG fabric among the finds from Delos[82] was attributed by Buschor in 1929 to Paros, because of the resemblance in fabric and style to a small amount of pottery from two Parian sites: the acropolis of the main town, and the Delion sanctuary near by. Since then, no more LG material has come from Paros, to confirm or refute Buschor's hypothesis; but a few sherds in a similar style and fabric have been found on Siphnos.[83] For the time being, then, the appellation 'Parian' must be kept within inverted commas.

Starting from close copies of Attic metopal skyphoi and kantharoi, the 'Parian' style begins to go its own way in a group of four large vessels (Ac 1–4) made in a single workshop around 730 B.C. On the spouted krater Ac 1 (fig. 69d) the painter has used a thick brush for his minor ornament (billets, wavy line, sigmas) which float loosely in the field and look somewhat overblown. On the drinking-vessels, after the Atticizing fashion has passed away, these airy and insubstantial motifs form the only decoration (fig. 69c). This typically 'Parian' manner persists into a Subgeometric phase shortly before 700 B.C., when wheels and broken cables are added to the repertoire (fig. 69e). Plump hydriai and neck-handled amphorae (Aa class) receive similarly sparse decoration, until both shapes are taken over by an Early Orientalizing painter (class Ad) who adorns them with horses, goats, griffins, and lions, but keeps the same floating motifs for his subsidiary zones. Likewise the shoulder-handled amphora in fig. 69e, a 'Parian' export to Thera, seems to have its Orientalizing successors in the early seventh-century Linear Island amphorae; but since their clay tends to be rather darker than the usual 'Parian', they may have been made in a different centre.[84]

The growing fame of Delos can be measured, in archaeological terms, by the variety of fabrics imported to the island. Before 750 B.C. the only non-Cycladic source is Athens; by 700 B.C., in addition to the copious supply of Naxian and 'Parian' vessels, there are a considerable number of Rhodian imports, and a few from Corinth, Euboea,[85] Crete,[86] and Cyprus. Here it is important to distinguish the votives left at the sanctuary from the contents of graves, which were later removed to Rheneia when the holy island was 'purified' under Athenian control.[87] It is from the Purification Trench on Rheneia, which contained the grave goods uprooted from Delos, that the great majority of pre-LG pottery comes. In the area of the later sanctuary the Protogeometric, EG and MG periods are represented by only a very thin scatter of pottery;[88] but in LG times the votive pottery becomes plentiful, especially in the neighbourhood of the Artemision. A similar story is told by the bronze offerings, of which one tripod fragment may possibly be earlier than 800 B.C., but most pieces are from hammered tripods of the late eighth century, akin to those from the Athenian acropolis.[89] In addition to the tangible offerings, a Messenian choir visited the Delian festival and sang a hymn by the Corinthian poet Eumelus (p. 342).

It is not easy to gain any clear impression of the sanctuary's architecture in Geometric times. The only certain facts are that around or shortly before 700 B.C. two temples were erected: a large Artemision (9·60 × 8·60m.) in the main Hieron, above and on the same alignment as a long and narrow Mycenaean temple; and a small, roughly square Heraion (3·40 × 2·80m.) on a virgin site halfway up mount Kynthos.[90] Both buildings were constructed in the usual Cycladic Geometric masonry, of long and thin schist slabs carefully laid; the Heraion, which is furnished with a broad bench for offerings, is not unlike the one-roomed houses of Siphnos and Andros. The history of the earlier structures is more conjectural, and it is not clear which building, if any, served as Apollo's temple during this period. One possible candidate, whose traces underlie the Archaic Oikos of the Naxians, is a long hall (20·75 × 5·20m.) with two rows of eight holes in the rock to take internal wooden columns; but its chronology remains a matter of deep obscurity, and its Archaic successor was certainly not a temple. A more plausible alternative is Temple Gamma, a narrow building (7·95 × 3·55m.) with foundations of rough granite blocks; yet this edifice is generally assigned to the Mycenaean period through its resemblance to the building under the Artemision. Nevertheless it has been suggested by the excavators that both Mycenaean temples may have remained in use all through the Dark Ages, on the grounds that Temple Gamma was never covered by later constructions, and that the Mycenaean Artemision accumulated a mass of votive offerings spanning the whole of the intervening period; these were eventually buried in what seems like a foundation deposit for the Artemision of c. 700 B.C., and include Mycenaean gold ornaments, Mycenaean ivory plaques which may have adorned a throne, many bronze arrowheads appropriate to an archer goddess, and sherds of the Mycenaean, Late Protogeometric, and LG periods. Any theory which postulates complete continuity of worship is at present weakened by the absence, anywhere on the island, of any material of the early Dark Ages;[91] we cannot even assume that there was continuity of habitation. Yet

a

b

FIG. 70 THERAN LG POTTERY
(a) Thera, Sellada tomb 64, H. 37; (b) Leiden SVL 2, H. 48

there remains the likelihood that the sanctity of the Hieron was never wholly forgotten, and that cults were practised intermittently from the tenth century onwards, until the sudden florescence in the LG period. And it may be no coincidence that, both in Mycenaean and LG times, the richest nucleus of votives is within the area consecrated to Artemis, the senior of Leto's two children according to every version of the myth (cf. p. 330).

Thera

The potters of this remote island were slow to learn a LG style, and slow to forget it. From c. 730 B.C. onwards they were chiefly concerned with the making of cremation urns, with or without necks. The neckless version (fig. 70a) is confined to the late eighth century, and resembles its Cretan counterpart (p. 271 fig. 86f) in still having a dark ground. The neckless amphora, light-ground from the start (fig. 70b), survives through a long Subgeometric phase, far into the seventh century.

The decoration of both shapes is limited to the upper half of the surface. Our two illustrations, possibly by the same hand, show most of the usual LG repertoire. The general impression is Atticizing, but the cross-hatched lozenge net implies a connection with the East Greek world. In addition there are hatched

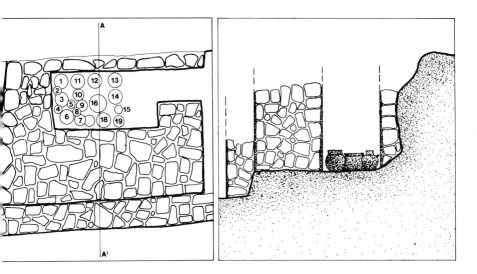

FIG. 71 THERA, MESAVOUNO TOMB 29, PLAN AND SECTION AT A'–A

birds with drooping tails, but no other living creatures. The composition of the handle zone, where a central meander is flanked by two metopes either side, comes ultimately from Athens, perhaps via Melos (cf. fig. 67a). The Subgeometric amphorae are taller and more ovoid, and their shoulder decoration becomes increasingly dominated by elaborate patterns within a circular frame.

Because the local clay is coarse and volcanic, smaller painted shapes were not often attempted. Handmade cooking-jugs and kadoi were locally made, and so were a few painted LG skyphoi, kantharoi, and plates; but in general the Therans preferred to import fine wares from Corinth, and occasionally from Crete, Rhodes, Attica, and Melos. They also imported many urns of the Linear Island class, whose adventurous Early Orientalizing decoration failed to influence the stolid Subgeometric of the local amphorae.

Geometric Thera is known to us from two cemeteries serving the main *polis*, one on the south flank of the acropolis overlooking the sea (Mesavouno), the other on the south-west side of the saddle (Sellada) which links Mesavouno with mount Prophetes Elias, the highest point on the island.[92] Both cemeteries were in continuous use from the early eighth century into the sixth. Cremation was the normal rite, the ashes being placed in urns like fig. 70, or in coarse pithoi, or (rarely) in bronze cauldrons; infants were inhumed in similar vessels. As in Crete, grave goods were put in around the urn; apart from the pottery, a few bronze fibulae of Blinkenberg's Type IV (tall narrow plates, bead(s) on the bow) may go back before 700 B.C.[93]

Some urns (e.g., Sellada gr. 18) were laid in the hillside by themselves, but during the eighth century it is more usual for the burials to be deposited in stone-built family chambers. Careful thought went into the planning of the Mesavouno cemetery, which rises up a steep slope in six terraces; special places for pyres were cut into the side of the hill, and many tombs were arranged in rows against previously constructed terrace walls. Tomb 29, one of the earliest, is built up against the rock face, and furnishes a good example of a Theran family sepulchre (fig. 71). Occupying a narrow terrace, the chamber is a rectangle measuring 2·40 × 1·30m. inside, approached through a thick sidewall by a doorway ½m. wide. The roof was of long schist slabs, four of which were found in the debris. On the floor stood twelve adult cremations, and probably one infant inhumation (no. 3). The earliest, in the two far corners (nos. 1,6), go back into MG times; the latest (no. 7) is a Linear Island amphora of the early seventh century.

In Thera one gets the impression of a conservative society, not greatly interested in the innovations in the outside world; a settled society, in which successive generations of people were laid to rest in their family tombs.

NOTES

1 On his output and workshop see *BICS* 18 (1971), 1 ff.
2 The origin and meaning of these themes are explored by P. Kahane, *AntK* 16 (1973), 114 ff.
3 *BICS* 18 (1971), 9–10 fig. 3.
4 *AntK* 11 (1968), pl. 27, 4.
5 *Lefkandi* fig. 77.
6 Boardman, *DdA* 3 (1969), 106 fig. 29b.
7 e.g., *Eretria* III pl. 16, 71.
8 e.g., *GGP* pl. 41f,g,j.
9 See J-P. Descoeudres, *BCH* 96 (1972), 269 ff.
10 Samos: *BICS* 18 (1971), 5 pl. 3d.
11 *GGP* 193.
12 *Lefkandi* 29–31 figs. 68–9.
13 A fragmentary monumental amphora of *c.* 730 B.C., imported from Athens, *EA* 1903, 15 ff. fig. 7, may also have housed an infant burial.
14 Reasonably seen as a sceptre by C. Bérard, *MusHelv* 29 (1972), 219 ff.
15 *K* gr. 43; Odos Kavalotti gr. Epsilon.
16 e.g., *AntK* 12 (1969), 73 fig. 36, 4, two gold strips of casket facing, from the sanctuary of Apollo.
17 *AR* 1971, 63 fig. 1.
18 Though not earlier than 720 B.C., for stratigraphical reasons: Bérard, *Eretria* III, 22.
19 e.g., from Olympia, *AD* 17 (1961–62), B 114 pl. 125b; less close, p. 334 fig. 106.
20 Snodgrass, *EGAW* 123 ff., Type J.
21 L. Kahil, *AntK* 10 (1967), 134–5.
22 *BICS* 18 (1971), 9.
23 J-P. Descoeudres, *AntK* 16 (1973), 87 ff.
24 Boardman, *AS* 9 (1959), 163 ff.
25 C. Roebuck, *Hesperia* 41 (1972), 116 ff.
26 Hdt. v.99; Pausanias 1.44.1; Plutarch, *Moralia* 760 E,F; cf. Forrest, *Historia* 6 (1957), 160 ff.; Boardman, *BSA* 52 (1957), 27–9; B. d'Agostino, *DdA* 1 (1967), 20 ff.
27 Thuc. vi.4.1.

28 Thuc. i.13.3.
29 Strabo 448; Plutarch, *Moralia* 153F.
30 Strabo 247.
31 Plutarch, *Quaestiones Graecae* 11.
32 Plutarch, *Moralia* 760F.
33 Plutarch, *apud Scholia, Erga* 654.
34 *Erga* 654–7.
35 *GGP* 201 nos. 4–15.
36 *AD* 21 (1966), 197–8 pl. 202a,b.
37 Boardman, *BSA* 47 (1952), 17 n. 80 nos. 1–2, 4–9; F. Canciani, *JdI* 80 (1965), 19 ff. nos. 1–6, 8–15.
38 *Teiresias* 1 (1971), 7.
39 Blinkenberg's IX 1 e–g may represent an early LG stage; cf. Schweitzer, *GKG* 226 n. 55.
40 K. De Vries, *Forschungen und Berichte* 14 (1972), 117 ff. n. 26.
41 id., *Hesperia* 43 (1974), 80 ff.
42 Schweitzer, *GKG* figs. 117–19.
43 DeVries, art. cit. 121–3, 'The Idaean Engraver'.
44 *GKG* fig. 122.
45 DeVries, art. cit. 124–7 pl. 16, 'Boeotian Group II'.
46 Schweitzer, *GKG* 226–31 figs. 123–6.
47 W. Lamb, *Greek Bronzes* 51 fig. 7b.
48 *GKG* fig. 115.
49 *GKG* figs. 125–6.
50 M. Comstock and C. Vermeule, *Greek, Roman and Etruscan Bronzes in the MFA, Boston* (1971), 5 no. 3; *GKG* pl. 189.
51 N. Himmelmann-Wildschütz, *AA* 1974, 544 ff. figs. 1–7.
52 cf. D. G. Mitten, *BostMusBull* 65 (1967), 12–15.
53 *GGP* pl. 33g.
54 *BSA* 18 (1911–12), 18 fig. 12, 3.
55 *AA* 1955, 216 fig. 15, 3–9.
56 Lamb, *Greek Bronzes* 43 pl. 17; Rolley, *FD* V.2, 44–5.
57 H. Biesantz, *Die thessalischen Grabreliefs* (Mainz, 1965), 159 pl. 51 (L 63), pl. 56 (L 80); cf. *GKG* pl. 125, Argive Heraion.
58 Bouzek, *Eirene* 6 (1967), 122 fig. 5, 10–16.
59 Bouzek, *Graeco-Macedonian Bronzes* (Prague, 1973), 192, v. sub Pherae, Philia.
60 *AD* 18 (1963), B 136 fig. 1; *AR* 1964, fig. 15.
61 Jacobsthal, *Greek Pins* 22 no. 74 (Pherae); *AD* 20 (1965), B pl. 366b (Philia).
62 Bouzek, op. cit (p. 207 n. 59) 130 ff.
63 W. A. Heurtley, *Prehistoric Macedonia* (Cambridge, 1939), 240 fig. 112m; perhaps another in Tumulus 56a at Vergina, *AD* 18 (1963), B pl. 259b.
64 *JHS* 72 (1952), 119.
65 Amandry, *Coll. H. Stathatos* I (Strasbourg, 1953), fig. 32 bottom left.
66 *AD* 20 (1965), B 421–2, pls. 471b,c (Thessalian), 472a,b (Euboean?).
67 For a helpful appraisal of the literary data see A. J. Graham, *JHS* 91 (1971), 46–7.
68 *GGP* 182–4, the Rottiers Workshop.
69 *BSA* 67 (1972), 97 nos. 124–5, 127.
70 Yet Zagora had been settled before Eretria, since the pottery associated with its first city wall goes back well into the ninth century; and early ninth-century graves have been found not far from the settlement (*Zagora* I, 1 n. 6).
71 e.g., *Zagora* I, figs. 31–2.
72 *AE* 1969, pl. 39a,b; cf. *Zagora* I, 54, fig. 29. Other early pieces: J. Schäfer, *Studien zu der griechischen Reliefpithoi* . . . (Kallmunz, 1957), 68, T 4–7.
73 *AE* 1969, pl. 42b.
74 This notion was to be fully exploited on the two masterpieces of the Tenian school showing mythical scenes: the birth of a deity (*c.* 700–675 B.C.) and the sack of Troy (*c.* 675–650 B.C.), found on Mykonos. See *AE* 1969, pls. 52–5; *AD* 18 (1963), pls. 17–28.

75 ibid. 226 pl. 46.
76 *EA* 1892, pls. 8, 9.
77 Callimachus, *Delos* 300–1.
78 *Délos* XV, classes Bb, Bc, with modifications; see *GGP* 172 n. 9, *BICS* 18 (1971), 4.
79 *GKG* fig. 31.
80 *BICS* 18 (1971), nn. 68, 71, 75.
81 *Délos* XVII, class Ba; I. Strøm, *Acta Arch* 23 (1962), 247 ff.
82 *Délos* XV, classes Aa–Af.
83 *GGP* 176.
84 Strøm, art. cit. 222 ff.
85 *Délos* XV, Bb 51–4, Bc 8.
86 *GGP* 382 n. 2.
87 Thuc. iii.104.1–2, 426 B.C. One apparent exception: *BCH* 35 (1911), 352 f. nos. 1–8, grave by Altar of Zeus Polieus.
88 *Délos* XV, 'Attique', nos. 1, 7–9; G. de Santerre, *Délos primitive et archaique* (1956), figs. 22a; 24e,h,l; 64h,j; 66d,g; 67; 73 bottom right (MG); *BCH* 35 (1911), 352 ff. figs. 4–7.
89 Rolley, *Études déliennes* (*BCH* Suppl. 1, 1973), 491 ff.
90 Its earliest votives are still LG: *Délos* X, nos. 1, 5–7, 9–10, 38, 40, 126.
91 Snodgrass, *DAG* 395–6; Desborough, *GDA* 279.
92 A third cemetery, on the north-east side of Sellada, begins *c.* 700 B.C., and continues into Classical times: *PAE* 1971, 201 ff. (description); 1970, pl. 332a, earliest pot.
93 e.g., *Thera* II, fig. 149, with the amphora fig. 148.

8 Italy and Sicily: Trade and Colonies

One of the most striking achievements of the eighth-century Greeks was the spread of their civilization to Italy and Sicily. Much of this chapter will be devoted to their first western colonies; yet some thought must also be given to their commercial exchanges with the native peoples, which began well before the arrival of the first colonists. These topics will be presented in a historical narrative covering the whole century, in which the experiences of three successive generations can be sharply distinguished.

During the first generation (c. 800–770 B.C.), and before the founding of the first colonies, Euboean merchants had already penetrated the Tyrrhenian sea, and were trading with the inhabitants of Etruria and Campania; a particular attraction of these regions was the abundance of metal ores, especially iron. These early Euboean prospectors were presumably operating from their homeland, but their successors of the second generation (c. 770–735 B.C.) established two permanent outposts in Campania, the first on the island of Pithecusae (Ischia), the second at Cumae on the mainland coast. Trade, rather than agriculture, must have been these settlers' main concern; this is the impression given by the siting of the two colonies as near as possible to the sources of metal, the lack of fertile land near by (especially on Pithecusae), and the wide variety of imports at both places, some objects coming from as far afield as the eastern Mediterranean. For this phase the term 'proto-colonial' has been coined: a phase which precedes the great wave of Greek colonial immigrants during the third generation.

Earlier Greek visitors, intent on trade, had paid little heed to the fertile coastal plains of eastern Sicily and the extreme south of Italy; but it was in these regions that every colony of the third generation was sited – ten in all, beginning with Sicilian Naxos (734 B.C.) and ending with Taras (706 B.C.). The foundation of these new states, almost all enjoying easy access to good agricultural land, helped to alleviate a pressing need of their mother-cities, at a time when their population was rapidly growing. In Athens, for example, the evidence from wells[1] suggests that the number of inhabitants increased threefold in the course of the Geometric period, and more than doubled within the eighth century. Now the Athenians, like the Argives, Boeotians, and Thessalians, possessed enough arable land to absorb this increase, and many new rural communities are known to have sprung up in the Attic countryside during this third generation (p. 133). Far less fortunate were the men of Chalcis, Corinth, Megara, and the Achaean cities, where the small amount of available land was hardly enough to feed a population rising at an analogous rate. Where land was scarce, the distress may have been accentuated by the engrossing of estates in the hands of powerful aristocratic

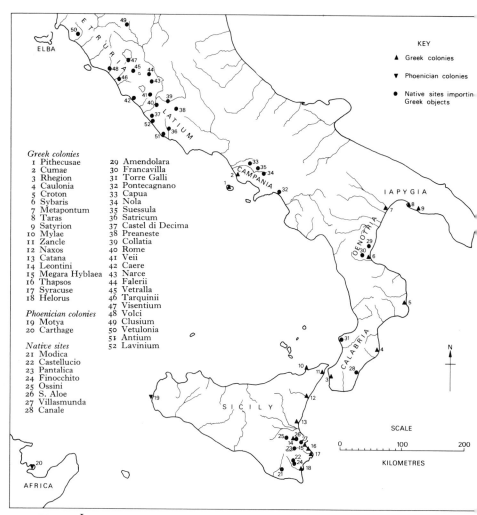

FIG. 72 ITALY AND SICILY IN THE EIGHTH CENTURY B.C.: GREEK
COLONIES, AND NATIVE SITES IMPORTING OR IMITATING GREEK POTTERY

families, like the Bacchiads of Corinth; or, for the sons of large families, by the
subdivision of plots into inconveniently small units.[2] However this may be, the
literary record offers several hints that it was chiefly land hunger that drove these
cities to send colonial expeditions overseas. We have already noted how the two
leading Euboean states went to war for the possession of a small plain, and how
a famine at Chalcis caused the foundation of Rhegion;[3] in the Corinthia, too,
there is a suggestion of hardship in 733 B.C., when many small farmers from the
inland village of Tenea joined the expedition to Syracuse.[4]

In their new homes, the colonists enjoyed complete independence from their mother-cities. After some preliminary skirmishing with the natives here and there, they settled down to a life that was largely agricultural; the eighth-century finds show little sign of the far-flung commercial connections such as are apparent at Pithecusae. Yet the colonies were not entirely blind to the advantages of maritime trade. With only one exception (Leontini) they are all situated on the coast; they seized the best harbours, and the starving Chalcidians of Rhegion chose one of the most advantageous sites of all, where they could control the commercial sea lane through the Straits. And in nearly every case there is evidence of peaceful exchanges with Sicel and Italic neighbours, seen mainly in the imports and imitations of Greek pottery found at many native sites.

First Generation: Early Exchanges with Etruria and Campania

During the Dark Ages, communications between Greece and Italy had dwindled into insignificance;[5] but from c. 800 B.C. onwards there are signs of frequent coming and going. The earliest evidence consists of over twenty MG II skyphoi found in various Italic burial grounds; the favourite pattern is a panel of vertical chevrons (cf. p. 75 fig. 23c), many are probably Euboean imports, but some may be close local imitations. In Campania the three skyphoi from the prehellenic (Osta) cemetery of Cumae have long been known, and more are now reported from the inland sites of Capua and Pontecagnano. The greatest number, however, come from Quattro Fontanili, a large cemetery of the Villanovan culture at Veii in southern Etruria; here the imported Greek drinking-vessels also include two Sub-Protogeometric skyphoi with pendent concentric semicircles.[6]

It so happens that this cemetery also offers one of the fullest and best sequences of horizontal stratigraphy anywhere in Villanovan Etruria, going back to the beginning of the Italian Iron Age. The arrangement of burials betrays an orderly turn of mind. The oldest (Veii I, ninth century) form a central kernel round which subsequent graves were placed in concentric rings; the local offerings show a steady typological development, reassuringly consistent with this horizontal stratigraphy, and also with the sequence of Greek and hellenizing pottery which helps to supply the absolute dates. The precolonial MG II skyphoi are from contexts of Veii IIA (c. 800–760 B.C.); whereas the graves of IIB, the latest period of the cemetery (c. 760–720 B.C.), contain debased local copies of these skyphoi together with the occasional LG import from Euboea.[7]

Among the local grave goods of Quattro Fontanili – and indeed of all Villanovan cemeteries in Etruria – the bronzes are more plentiful and varied than in any contemporary Greek cemetery. Especially copious are the fibulae which, as we shall see, were to find favour among the first Euboean settlers on Pithecusae; a Villanovan bronze belt, close to those from Veii IIA, was even brought home to Euboea by an early prospector.[8] In the working of iron, however, the Etruscans were a long way behind the Greeks. This metal is very rare indeed in the ninth-century graves of Veii I, where the weapons, for example, are still all of bronze; but as soon as Euboean merchants begin to call, iron is used for knives and some fibulae (Veii IIA) and, eventually, for axes, horse-bits, and swords (Veii IIB). The increasing mastery of the new metal may well have been learned from the

FIG. 73 PITHECUSAE: (a) view of site. 1. Acropolis, Monte Vico;
2. Cemetery, Valle di S. Montano; 3. Mezzavia ridge;
(b) cremation tumuli

early Greek visitors, for whom the abundance of the raw material in Etruria was
probably one of the main motives for their visits. Although the most obvious
sources of Etruscan iron[9] lie in the northern confines and on the island of Elba
(whence the colonists of Pithecusae later obtained their supplies), Veii would
have been an important market for the disposal of the ore, easily accessible to the
first Euboean prospectors.

Imports from much further afield have also turned up in the same horizon as
the MG II skyphoi at Veii and prehellenic Cumae; both sites have produced an
Egyptianizing faience figurine, as well as a number of blue paste scarabs (and
some more from Capua), all of which must have been made in the Levant,
probably by Phoenician craftsmen. Perhaps they were hawked by casual Phoenician traders; but if we recollect that these types of trinket had been imported now
and again to Euboea since the mid-ninth century (p. 65), it becomes more likely
that they were conveyed to Italy in the same ships as the skyphoi, by Euboean
merchants who also had Levantine contacts. Etruria, so it appears, already
stood at the end of a long trade route extending as far as Al Mina in the Levant,

along which the Euboeans were the most active middlemen.[10]

Second Generation: Pithecusae and Cumae

The Euboeans established their first permanent outpost on Ischia, a volcanic island near the entrance to the bay of Naples. The colony of Pithecusae (fig. 73a), at the north-west corner of the island, is easily defensible, and excellently sited for trade. A sheer acropolis (Monte Vico) is flanked by two harbours: on one side, the long beach which now serves the resort of Lacco Ameno; on the other, the deep and sheltered inlet of San Montano, leading to the valley of the ancient cemetery. Further inland, and across this valley, lies the industrial quarter on the Mezzavia ridge, where abundant evidence of metalworking has been found.

Pithecusae was evidently founded during a period of volcanic quiescence; by Classical times the town had relapsed into insignificance after repeated volcanic upheavals, and therefore attracted very little notice in the literary record. Indeed, Livy (viii. 22,5–6) is the only ancient author who remembered that its foundation was prior to that of Cumae, and hence of all other western colonies; he has been amply confirmed by the earliest pottery from the settlement and the cemetery which certainly goes back into the 750s, and it is likely that the oldest graves, and the oldest traces of habitation on the acropolis, have yet to be discovered.

According to Strabo (247), Eretrians and Chalcidians collaborated in the foundation; at first they lived together in prosperity, until a political quarrel (probably an extension of the Lelantine War) caused the Eretrians to withdraw, and the island was further depleted by earthquakes and eruptions. For the colony's earlier affluence Strabo gives two rather puzzling reasons: fertility of the soil (*eukarpia*) and gold jewellery (*chrysia*)[11]. So far, the gold ornaments from the site are few and unimpressive; yet, given the enterprise of jewellers in ninth-century Lefkandi and eighth-century Eretria, a flourishing colonial workshop on Pithecusae would not be surprising. As for the alleged *eukarpia*, the volcanic soil of the island is – and was – suitable only for the cultivation of the vine; yet the export of wine and grapes could have been an important source of wealth for the early colonists.

The most obviously gainful occupations of the Pithecusans were pursued in the metalworking quarter on the Mezzavia ridge (p. 311). Here the only domestic building is an apsidal house (I), apparently crushed by a rock fall in an earthquake of *c.* 720 B.C. and never repaired. Two other structures, built and rebuilt more than once between *c.* 750 and *c.* 675 B.C., are the workshops of blacksmiths. In one (III) the floors yielded iron ore and slag in plenty, the forge being sited in an open courtyard. The forge in the other building (IV) was protected by mud brick, and beside it were two anvils of hard blue stone. Bronze and lead, as well as iron, were worked here; of especial interest are the bow of a miscast bronze fibula, and a circular lead weight bound in a bronze ring (8·79 grams) conforming closely to the standard of the Euboean silver stater in Archaic times.[12] This last object makes one wonder whether more precious metals – perhaps including the *chrysia* of Strabo – were not also worked in the neighbourhood, since its weight is said to bear some relation to the electrum ornaments from the graves of the late eighth and early seventh centuries.

The acropolis of Monte Vico is, unfortunately, too badly eroded to yield any traces of early colonial occupation *in situ*; but more light on the iron industry is cast by an unstratified dump on its eastern slope, containing horn-shaped bellows of clay (*tuyères*), more iron slag, bases of large pots used as crucibles, and lumps of iron ore which has been analysed and confidently attributed to a particular mine on the island of Elba.[13]

The cemetery, down in the valley of San Montano, appears to be completely preserved and unplundered. The area so far excavated, probably less than 5 per cent of the whole, has already yielded over a thousand graves, of which the greater part belong to the colony's initial and most flourishing period in the eighth and early seventh centuries. From the beginning, inhumation is the usual rite for children, infants being inhumed in pithoi or other large vessels. Adults may be inhumed or cremated. For cremation, the pyre is lit some distance from the grave. The ashes are not collected into a receptacle, as at Eretria (pp. 196 f.); instead the burnt bones, pyre debris, and offerings are buried together under a circular tumulus with a diameter anything from 1·50m. to 4·50m. The pottery, in addition to the charred fragments from the pyre, often includes an unburnt oinochoe which probably quenched the embers, as in the Homeric account of Patroclus' funeral (p. 349). Fig. 73b illustrates four cremation tumuli, one of which is unopened; behind them, at a lower level, are some pit inhumations for

FIG. 74 PITHECUSAE: COLONIAL EUBOEAN LG POTTERY
(c–d) from Mezzavia ridge; remainder from cemetery.
HS: (a) 44.1; (b) 22.3; (c–d) *c.* 43; (e) 9.4; (f) 12.7

children. Their bodies usually rested in wooden coffins, whose presence has also
been suspected at Eretria; large rough stones were laid on the covers, whether to
restrain the ghosts, or to keep the burials in place. Infants were sometimes, but
not always buried in coarse jars.

No other site in the Greek world has amassed a more varied assembly of LG pottery. Fine Corinthian ware was imported in great quantity from the 750s onwards, is especially common in the cemetery, and made an immediate impression on the colonial potters; many of the earliest graves contain creditable copies of Corinthian LG oinochoai and hemispherical chevron kotylai. Pottery in a Euboean style, whether imported or local, is much less frequent among the grave offerings, but the settlement deposits now afford plenty of evidence of a vigorous colonial school deriving its inspiration from the mother-cities. At its simplest, the decoration consists of Atticizing square metopes, where the Euboean bird-and-lozenge combination is sometimes seen (fig. 74a). Figured work is often attempted, and one of the more original themes appears on a barrel-vase of oriental character (fig. 74b): three women carrying spindles, perhaps the Fates. On many other vases the painting reflects the manner of the influential Cesnola Painter (p. 192), adapting all three of his favourite subjects; hence the horse-and-axe panels on a spouted krater (fig. 74c,d), itself a Euboean shape; two goats flanking a Tree of Life (fig. 74e) under the base of a lekythos-oinochoe; and, on an otherwise Corinthianizing aryballos of c. 700 B.C., two grazing horses (fig. 74f). Towards the end of the century the Corinthian element becomes dominant, appearing at its most ambitious in the famous shipwreck krater;[14] and from Cumae there are many local versions of EPC Orientalizing closed vessels (mainly aryballoi) which were probably made in Pithecusae.

After Corinth and Euboea, Rhodes is the next most frequent source of imports: hence come many aryballoi of semi-oriental character (p. 249), and several bird-kotylai (p. 247), one of which bears the celebrated metrical inscription about Nestor's cup (p. 300). Also East Greek are two fibulae of 'Anatolian' type (Blinkenberg XII 13) from graves of c. 720–690 B.C. Attica contributed three one-piece oinochoai of LG IIb, and there are also a number of small handmade vessels conventionally called Argive Monochrome, though not necessarily of Argive origin. The tale of Greek imports is rounded off by a seal impression on the handle of a plain amphora, showing the corpse of an enormous warrior being carried out of battle by his comrade (fig. 75d); the Samian Heraion has yielded another impression[15] from the same seal, one of the flat square class made in the Argolid and the Cyclades.

Exchanges with the Italian mainland are reflected by occasional imports from three different quarters, all found in eighth-century contexts. Calabria is represented by a painted askos, Apulia by a fragmentary jar in the Daunian style, with painted geometric ornament. Etruria supplied two impasto amphorae with incised spirals (fig. 75a), of a type well known among the burials of Veii IIIA; and also many varieties of long-footed bronze fibulae (cf. Veii, end of IIB to early IIIA)[16] which were locally imitated, as we know from the miscast fibula found in the Mezzavia area.

The pottery imported from the Near East is confined to unguent containers: there are several mushroom-topped flasks of Phoenician Red Slip (fig. 75b), and several North Syrian aryballoi including one with a female head modelled in relief (fig. 75c). Far more plentiful are the oriental trinkets, most of which were found in the graves of children where they served as amulets. They fall into two classes. First, the eighty-seven stone scaraboid seals of the North Syrian Lyre-

FIG. 75 PITHECUSAE: IMPORTED POTTERY AND SEALS
(a) impasto amphora from Etruria, H. 7.6; (b) Phoenician Red Slip
flask, H. 20; (c) North Syrian face-aryballos, H. 11.7; (d) Greek
sealing, H. of impression 3.1; (e) the Bocchoris scarab, H. 1.5;
(f) North Syrian seal, Lyre-Player group, H. 2

Player group (fig. 75f), of which most come from graves of *c.* 750–720 B.C.
Secondly, over a hundred paste scarabs of Egyptian character: the earlier ones
are Levantine imitations, but many of those found with EPC aryballoi (*c.* 720–
690 B.C.) are Egyptian originals. The most celebrated of these is a scarab bearing
the cartouche of the 24th Dynasty Pharaoh Wohkerē or Bocchoris (fig. 75e),[17]
which provides the most solid evidence for the absolute dating of EPC pottery.
Bocchoris had a brief and undistinguished reign (718–712 B.C.) before being
ousted and burnt alive by his successor Shabaka the Ethiopian; the scarab can

hardly have been made later than his death, nor is it likely that such a fragile object was kept for long before being placed in the grave.

The description of the Pithecusan finds has taken us well down into the late eighth century, when the colony attained its greatest prosperity. We must now return to the other important event of our second generation, the founding of the colony at Cumae.

The acropolis of Cumae, an isolated knoll commanding the rich Campanian plain, can easily be seen from the island of Pithecusae on the mainland shore immediately opposite. Memories concerning the foundation are various, but not necessarily inconsistent. The general impression is that Chalcis took the initiative, but did not supply all the settlers. From Livy (viii.22,5–6) we gather that a contingent sailed across from Pithecusae. Eretrians, according to Dionysios of Halicarnassos (vii.3), were also among the first colonists, whether from Pithecusae or from their homeland. Strabo (243) records two founders, Megasthenes of Chalcis and Hippocles of Cyme, the Greek town which gave its name to the colony. We are not told whether this Cyme is the large Aeolian city on the Anatolian coast, or the village on the eastern shore of Euboea; the latter is the more likely, not least because East Greek finds are very scarce at Cumae. True, Pseudo-Scymnus (238–9) makes Aeolian colonists follow after the Chalcidians; but they could well be Boeotian Aeolians, whose descendants emerge from epigraphical evidence in Neapolis (Naples), a daughter-colony of Cumae.[18] Later Cumaeans were to be the first Greeks encountered by the Romans, who called them Graeci; the name is probably based on the Graioi, a group of eastern Boeotians who may have migrated to Cumae in the wake of their Euboean neighbours.

Before the establishment of the Greek city, the acropolis of Cumae was held in force by an indigenous Italic people. The thirty-six native graves excavated by Osta fall into a well-defined horizon of the early eighth century,[19] contemporary with Veii IIA, and showing similar contacts with early Euboean prospectors through the importation of MG II skyphoi. These natives were presumably overwhelmed and evicted by the first colonists.[20] The date of this event cannot yet be precisely fixed,[21] but must fall somewhere within the bracket 760–735 B.C., later than the foundation of Pithecusae, but before[22] the initial Greek settlement of Sicily. It is unfortunate that the archaeological evidence is still very incomplete, as the cemeteries (native and Greek) were carelessly dug during the nineteenth century, and the acropolis has never been explored down to its deepest level. Thus, in the light of written sources, the earliest colonial horizon has yet to be recovered, none of the extant finds being older than c. 720 B.C. To make matters worse, in the recorded sequence of graves there remains a chronological gap between the latest native and the earliest Greek. A proposal to insert into this gap a final phase of native occupation,[23] entirely reconstructed out of objects from clandestine digging, is courageous but somewhat hazardous. For the time being, then, the foundation date must float within wide limits.

As long as the earliest colonial material is missing, it is hard to fathom the motives of the first settlers: were they chiefly commercial,[24] as on Pithecusae, or chiefly agrarian,[25] as in the Sicilian colonies? Geographical evidence is equivocal: there is no natural harbour as on Pithecusae, but traces of an ancient port, now silted up, have been found about 1 km. south of the acropolis;[26] and although the soil near the acropolis is poor and sandy, the rich land of the Phlegraean Fields lies within easy reach. All we can say for certain is that the new *polis* was capable of expansion in a way that Pithecusae was not; while the volcanic island lost many of its settlers through frequent upheavals, Cumae steadily grew in size[27] and prosperity.

The late-eighth-century pottery, as we have it, includes a colonial figured fragment from the acropolis showing a file of horsemen in the Euboean tradition;[28] otherwise the early material is all from the cemetery, and recalls the contemporary grave groups of Pithecusae. Here, too, Corinth is the chief source of imports; but there are also a few Euboean unguent vessels,[29] many Pithecusan imitations of Corinthian aryballoi (Cumae itself has no claybeds), and a few semi-oriental aryballoi of Rhodian origin.

Among the metal ornaments, the frequency of silver is striking; this metal was often used for fibulae (mainly long-footed Etrurian types), beads, hair-spirals, bracelets, armlets, and finger-rings, and especially for the setting of scarabs. The scarabs, too, are extremely numerous, and bear witness to continued exchanges with the Near East. Surprisingly, only one North Syrian seal has been preserved from Cumae, but this may be due to the carelessness of the excavations.[30]

As on Pithecusae, these oriental trinkets occur only in inhumation graves, where they probably served as amulets for children; not much skeletal evidence has been preserved, but the small size of many graves, and the absence of weapons, support a reasonable assumption on the analogy of Pithecusae and Eretria, that Cumaean children were normally inhumed.[31] The similarity of custom extends to the use of wooden coffins, with large stones placed on the covers. Adults were cremated, usually in bronze cauldrons which were hedged in and covered by stone slabs; a princely burial of *c.* 700 B.C. or soon after (Artiaco gr. 104),[32] furnished with a rich store of silver ornaments, bronze vessels, and iron weapons, is an impressive counterpart to the 'prince' buried near the West Gate at Eretria (pp. 196–7). The most interesting cauldron, however, does not come from any organized excavation; it belongs to the Urartian or North Syrian type with bull's-head protomes,[33] with a profile similar to the latest cauldrons from the same Eretrian cemetery.

The foundation of these two colonies enabled the Euboeans to intensify their commercial exchanges with their Italic neighbours. The chief clue to their activity is the wide diffusion of Greek or hellenizing pottery, nearly always painted in the Euboean tradition; Corinthian exports are not at all common before 700 B.C. Among the native sites of Campania, the cemeteries of Capua and Pontecagnano are still the main sources of this pottery; of particular interest are the two chevron kotylai from Capua and San Marzano sul Sarno, Pithecusan copies of Corinthian LG;[34] and, from Pontecagnano, a local burial jar painted with metopal decoration in the Euboean LG manner.[35] There seem to have been fewer contacts with Latium, where the eighth-century evidence is confined to a LG skyphos from Collatia[36] and a few sherds from Rome.[37]

The most frequent exchanges, however, were with the Etruscans. We have already noted how Villanovan types of fibula became fashionable among the early colonists, and how iron ore from Elba was supplied to the merchants of Pithecusae; and the metal-rich areas of northern Etruria, immediately opposite

FIG. 76 ETRUSCAN LG POTTERY
(a) Tarquinii, Selciatello Sopra gr. 160, H. 41; (b) Caere, H. 34

Elba, are the most likely sources of copper and silver for the Greek settlers. In
return, imports and imitations of Greek pottery continue at Veii throughout the
final phase of the Quattro Fontanili cemetery (IIB: c. 760–720 B.C.), and similar
material of that period occurs at Tarquinii, Vetralla, Narce, Falerii, Vulci,
Visentium, and even as far north as Clusium; but not, at this early date, at Popu-
lonia, Vetulonia, or any other sites in the northern metalliferous region. It seems,
then, that the Pithecusans acquired their ores through the markets of southern
Etruria, and may not have been permitted direct access to the mines.

Nowhere, in fact, did the Greeks of our period succeed in establishing their
own outpost in Etruria, as they did in Campania. Yet there are grounds for
thinking that some of their craftsmen, at least, set up shop in the towns of
southern Etruria, where many of the local hellenizing vases reproduce the shapes
and ornament of Euboean LG fairly closely. This is especially true of many skyphoi and kraters,[38] and also a hydria of c. 750 B.C. from Tarquinii (fig. 76a) which
was put to use as a cremation urn. From these beginnings there arose a local
Geometric style, applied to Greek and non-Greek shapes alike. It persevered in a
diluted form until well after 700 B.C., and long after any first-hand knowledge of

Euboean originals. By then, the commercial initiative had passed to Corinth, whose pottery was to offer a fresh repertoire of ideas to expatriate and native craftsmen; hence the birth of the Italo-Corinthian style of the seventh century, in which most ideas are Corinthian, but some Euboean Subgeometric motifs still find a place.[39]

A third source of inspiration is illustrated by a clay stand of *c.* 710 B.C. from Caere (fig. 76b). The painting is still authentically Euboean Geometric: the cavaliers recall the colonial piece from the Cumaean acropolis, and the unusual crosshatching of the torso can be matched at Lefkandi and Eretria. But the bulbous shape is oriental, simulating the stands of the bronze protome cauldrons, such as were beginning to reach Etruria at this time; the most famous example is that from the Barberini Tomb at Praeneste (pp. 362 f. fig. 113), whose stand carries a pair of lion-sphinxes in relief. Exotic metalwork of this kind was to set off a powerful Orientalizing movement in the native art of Etruria, in which the oriental models were copied with far less discrimination than in Greece. By whom were these *orientalia* conveyed to Etruria, and by what routes? To this question there is no simple answer that is at all satisfactory. In the Levant, the most energetic middlemen were the Phoenicians; their colonial movement in the western Mediterranean was already far advanced by 700 B.C., and their part in Tyrrhenian trade will be reviewed presently. But some of the credit must also be accorded to the Euboeans, who by now had been active in Levantine markets for at least four generations, and had probably been the suppliers of small oriental trinkets to Italy since *c.* 800 B.C. Their claim is further substantiated by the protome cauldron from Cumae, by cauldrons of similar profile from Eretria, and by the five North Syrian seals from Etruria, of the same class as the vast number from Pithecusae.

Third Generation: The First Sicilian Colonies

Many Euboean traders of our first and second generations must have sailed through the Straits of Messina, in search of Italian metal; but Sicily, which lacks any mineral resources, failed to attract much attention from them. The native Sicel cemetery of Villasmunda, a little way inland from Megara Hyblaea, has yielded a MG II chevron skyphos and three Corinthianizing vessels of *c.* 750–740 B.C. (one chevron kotyle and two kyathoi);[40] this is the only clear evidence of Greek visitors before the arrival of the first colonists.

The great colonial movement to Sicily began with the foundation of Naxos in 734 B.C. [41] Theocles of Chalcis was the founder, but the colony's name implies that the Chalcidian contingent was swelled by emigrants from the Cycladic island.[42] On arrival Theocles dedicated an altar outside the town to Apollo the Guide (Archegetes), the sponsor of all colonial expeditions. The site is a promontory just south of Taormina, not far from the southern approach to the Straits. According to the fourth-century historian Ephorus,[43] the settlers were attracted there by the fertility of the soil, and the insignificance of the local natives. Soundings around the north bay – presumably the ancient harbour – have produced copious deposits from the earliest years of the colony, and some still earlier Sicel ware; but the stratification is not yet clear, and there may even be a gap in time between the two horizons.[44] Corinthian LG imports are much in evidence among the earliest Greek pottery, together with local imitations of Euboean types; one of the very oldest pieces[45] is from a colonial copy of a skyphos like fig. 61a. The early Greek cemetery and the altar of Apollo Archegetes have yet to be discovered.

In the following year, according to Thucydides (vi.3.2), a Corinthian expedition founded the colony of Syracuse. The leader was Archias, a member of the Bacchiad oligarchy; but most of his party were land-hungry farmers from the inland village of Tenea.[46] The new city, as ideally sited for agriculture as for sea communications, was destined to become one of the greatest powers in the Greek world. A vast circular harbour is partly sheltered by Ortygia, the narrow island which has always been the nucleus of the town; about 1km. long, it enjoys a perennial supply of fresh water from the fountain of Arethusa, probably named by some earlier Chalcidian prospector after the spring in his own city.

Ortygia was not won without a struggle; Archias' first exploit was to subdue and expel the former Sicel inhabitants. Traces of their presence have been found at several points, especially in the centre of the island where foundations of native oval huts underlie the sanctuary of Athena. Some pottery from here, painted with geometric patterns, has been thought to show pre-colonial Greek influence; but this view is not entirely convincing, nor is the stratification clear.[47]

Having seized the island, the colonists raised an altar to Athena, whence come some of the oldest Greek sherds (p. 170 n. 5). Square-roomed houses were built near by; their remains, with late eighth-century pottery, were found immediately above a native layer, and below a sixth-century Ionic temple. Very soon the town expanded to the adjoining part of the mainland, where eighth-century deposits occur under the later agora, and under the modern railway station.[48]

A little farther inland lies Fusco, the earliest colonial cemetery. In reviewing the burial practices we shall concentrate on the dozen-odd graves prior to c. 680 B.C. Corinthian customs are followed in many details: the usual rite is inhumation, either in sarcophagi or in rectangular rock-cut pits; kraters may house infants (gr. 394), or be left on the slabs above adult burials (gr. 216). Rare departures from these rules may betray the presence of a few non-Corinthian settlers. A youth cremated in a bronze cauldron (gr. 219) could be a Chalcidian. A pithos containing the skeletons of two young men (gr. 337) reminds us of an Argive practice; it is worth noting that the literary record preserves a dim (and probably garbled) memory of an Argive ruler Pollis,[49] and that several of the Fusco kraters are in an Argive Subgeometric style,[50] probably the work of an immigrant Argive potter. Most of the pottery, however, is imported Corinthian, aryballoi being especially common. *Orientalia* are represented here by only three scarabs, in contrast to the enormous mass from Pithecusae. Bronze offerings are absent from the earliest graves, but soon after 700 B.C. there are Orientalizing Greek pins, and long-footed fibulae of Etruscan character. A hammered horse, locally made in a Corinthian style, has already been mentioned (p.176 n.33).

The Chalcidians, meanwhile, had not been idle. Under the leadership of Theocles, expeditions set out from Naxos in 728 B.C. to found new colonies at

Leontini and Catana.[51] Thereby they gained access to the plain of the river Symaethus, the richest land in Sicily. At its northern end is the coastal town of Catana, with a good harbour; thanks to the effusions of Etna, its early colonial levels have so far eluded discovery. Leontini, guarding the southern part of the plain, lies 10km. inland and must have been a predominantly agrarian settlement. In the Thucydidean account, Sicel inhabitants were driven off the site by the first colonists; but Polyaenus, a writer of the second century A.D., records how Greeks and natives lived together for a while before the latter were finally expelled.[52] Here the archaeological evidence favours the later writer. Deposits of pottery from the early colonial acropolis (S. Mauro) go back to Corinthian and Euboean LG; but down in the valley of S. Aloe immediately below, much of the pottery from the Sicel cemetery runs into the earliest years of the colony, taking its decoration from the colonists' wares: thus the local jars are adorned sometimes with Euboean-style birds (fig. 77a), and sometimes with spare Corinthian motifs done with a multiple brush (fig. 77b). The latest pots from S. Aloe are probably well before 700 B.C.; eventually the deserted native settlement, on the Metapiccola hill near by, was absorbed within the Archaic Greek city wall.

Many hardships and frustrations were endured by the founders of Megara Hyblaea.[53] At first the Megarian emigrants settled at Trotilon, a rocky headland with a pirates' creek, but far from any good arable land. Thence they joined forces with the Chalcidians of Leontini, only to be thrown out after a short time.[54] Their next home was Thapsos, a low-lying and waterless peninsula where their Mycenaean forbears had formerly traded. Here Lamis, their leader, died; his grave may well be a solitary eighth-century burial in a re-used Bronze Age chamber tomb, accompanied by the two Corinthian LG skyphoi in the style to which Thapsos has given its name (pp. 168, 170–1). Finally a Sicel king, Hyblon, settled them in a more suitable coastal site, which they named after their mother-city and their new benefactor. Excavation of the settlement has turned up a large quantity of LG pottery, among which Corinthian imports form a high proportion; the oldest are five chevron kotylai, followed by Thapsostype skyphoi by the hundred.[55] Other imports include a few Attic, Argive, and Rhodian pieces; there are also a number of colonial imitations based mainly on Corinthian, but making some use of Euboean motifs.[56] The eighth-century cemetery still awaits discovery.

The Megarians' unhappy wanderings make them seem like tyros in western exploration; reckless amateurs, who had not sufficiently spied out the land. Perhaps the best land had already been seized by Chalcidian and Corinthian settlers; and perhaps the woes of the Megarians were increased by the hardening of political alignments at home,[57] where Corinth had become the enemy of their own mother-city, and the friend of Chalcis (p. 200). Such a theory is weakened by the initial welcome given by the Chalcidians of Leontini, before they drove the Megarians out; but it may explain the generosity of the Sicel king Hyblon. His capital, Hybla, is almost certainly at Pantalica, 20km. inland from Syracuse: a towering citadel, whose flanks are combed with five centuries of rock-cut chamber tombs, whose summit bears the foundations of a large palatial building. Hyblon's kingdom had already been buffeted by the Corinthians of Syracuse, when they thrust his subjects out of their maritime post on Ortygia; and the

FIG. 77 SICEL AND CALABRIAN GEOMETRIC POTTERY
(a,b) S. Aloe near Leontini; (c–d) Canale, Calabria

encroachment of the Chalcidians on his northern border must also have alarmed
him. Small wonder, then, that he received the Megarians kindly, having heard of
their hostility to all previous Greek interlopers, and hoping for effective Greek
allies. To no avail, however: Pantalica was finally destroyed around 700 B.C.,[59] and
at about this time the Syracusans set up a military station at Helorus,[60] to keep
watch on the Sicels of those parts. Indeed, the memory of Hyblon's kingdom
may explain why the Syracusans were to adopt an unusually repressive policy
towards their Sicel neighbours, driving their settlements out of the immediate

vicinity, either deep into the hinterland, or into the island's arid south-east corner.[61]

Against these initial disturbances we must set some evidence for peaceful exchanges. Greek pots, imported and colonial, were purveyed to the natives by Euboeans and Corinthians alike. At once there arose a Sicel Geometric style, preserving several native shapes (e.g., the plump amphorae, fig. 77a–b), but borrowing its decoration from the colonial fabric, in which the Corinthian element was usually stronger than the Euboean.

The Settlement of the Straits of Messina

Zancle, as Messina was originally called, took its name from the native word for a sickle; for that is the shape of the ancient Greek colony, enclosing an excellent harbour. It was settled in two stages,[62] first by pirates from Cumae, later by a joint expedition from Cumae and Chalcis which parcelled out the land in a not very fertile region. We are left to conjecture whether this strategic place had to be rescued by the two mother-cities from lawless freebooters, or whether 'pirates' means Cumaean merchants, seen through the suspicious eyes of the farmers who came with the second expedition. Neither event has a precise date in literary sources, but a small sanctuary deposit from the end of the 'sickle' includes several EPC vessels, and a sherd from a late LG heron kotyle of the 720s.[63]

The foundation of an outpost at Mylae[64] gave the Zanclaeans a much more fertile tract of land. The site lies across a long peninsula on the north coast of Sicily, looking out to the Aeolian islands. An early colonial cemetery has been explored, overlying a native cemetery of the indigenous Ausonian culture, not used after c. 950 B.C. As one would expect of Euboean settlers, cremation is the rule.[65] The ashes were placed in urns, either local handmade pithoi, or various types of imported wheelmade vessel; painted hydriai, with Cycladic affinities, were often used in the seventh century. The graves are sparsely furnished. Bronzes are limited to a few finger-rings, bracelets, and long-footed fibulae of Etruscan type. The oldest datable pots are Corinthian globular aryballoi, which agree well with the foundation date of 716 B.C. given by Eusebius.[66]

Chalcidian control of the Straits was assured by the founding of Rhegion on the Italian shore. From Strabo (257) we gather that the main body of settlers sailed from Chalcis after a bad harvest, and with the blessing of Delphi; but some initiative was also taken by the Zanclaeans, who supplied one of the two founders. The new city was further reinforced by a body of exiles from Messenia, perhaps soon after its foundation. Since the hinterland is arid and mountainous, there cannot have been much scope for farming; viticulture, fishing, and – above all – maritime commerce must have been the chief sources of livelihood. The only eighth-century find from Rhegion is an oinochoe in the Corinthian Thapsos style,[67] perhaps a local imitation, and not later than the 720s.

The Rhegians were soon trading with their Calabrian neighbours. In the native cemetery of Canale, under the toe of Italy, two dozen hellenizing pots occur beside indigenous impasto ware. The small amphorae (fig. 77c,d) may be modelled on the local jars, but there are also oinochoai and drinking-vessels of Greek character. The decoration is drawn exclusively from the Euboean repertoire, including quatrefoils, hollow lozenges, tangential blobs, and birds with bent wings. From their lack of finesse, one would judge that these vessels were made by native potters;[68] but the LG metopal style must have been communicated by Euboean imports or visitors at about the time when Rhegion was founded. Canale is situated in the hills immediately above the coastal site of Locri Epizephyrii; when a Greek colony was established there in 673 B.C., the people of Canale seem to have migrated further inland.[69]

The Achaean Colonies

The 'instep' of Italy had more to offer the farmer than the trader. Good harbours are rare, and the exiguous mineral resources had little attraction for the early Greek prospector. Then, soon after the initial migration to Sicily, the fertile lands by the Ionian sea began to receive a great influx of agricultural settlers, many of Peloponnesian stock. The Achaeans led the way, with the foundation of Sybaris and Croton.

The founder of Sybaris was Is[70] of Helice, a city on the Achaean coast. The settlers laid out their town between the rivers Sybaris and Crathis, names which they brought with them from their homeland. There was no natural harbour, but the site commands a land route across to the Tyrrhenian shore; Sybarite interests in that direction led to the foundation of a daughter-colony at Poseidonia (Paestum) in the seventh century. Yet it was chiefly the prodigious fertility of the surrounding plain which was to make Sybaris the most prosperous and luxurious city in all Italy,[71] until its eventual destruction by the Crotoniates in 510 B.C. The whole site now lies under 4–6m. of silt; in the early 1960s it was rediscovered with the help of a proton magnetometer. Preliminary soundings have yielded samples of the earliest pottery, consisting largely of Corinthian imports. The foundation is dated to 709 B.C. by Eusebius, and to 720 B.C. by Pseudo-Scymnus (359–60); the latter is the more plausible reckoning, since the oldest sherds are from Thapsos-type skyphoi not later than the 720s.[72]

The expedition to Croton was led by Myscellus of Rhypes, an inland city of Achaea. He had previously coveted Sybaris; but his compatriots were already settling there, and the Delphic oracle warned him to be content with Croton,[73] a site with a reasonable harbour and a small arable plain. The foundation is placed by Eusebius in the same year as Sybaris. No finds from Croton are old enough to throw any light on the matter; but its daughter-colony, Caulonia, has yielded a deposit of Corinthianizing pottery[74] not much later than 700 B.C.

The coming of the Achaean settlers had a catastrophic effect upon the native Oenotrians.[75] Many indigenous communities, living on or near the sea, were driven out by the first colonists; some moved to strongholds further inland, while others were resettled near their former homes, but in smaller numbers and in reduced circumstances. For example: a little way north of Sybaris, the native settlements of Francavilla Marittima and Amendolara had been prosperous places during the eighth century, with an abundance of metal objects; Francavilla, in addition, has produced two scarabs, a North Syrian seal, and two Corinthian LG pots, evidence of Greek precolonial trade.[76] Shortly before 700 B.C. both towns were deserted; but life in each case was resumed on a neighbouring hill, and the new settlements became hamlets in the territory of Sybaris. With the hamlet at Amendolara goes a cemetery with a steady sequence of Greek imports, beginning with a Thapsos-type skyphos, followed by Subgeometric skyphoi, and deep kantharoi of Achaean character.[77]

Taras

The Spartans of these years did not lack land, nor were they much inclined towards trade; their only westward colonial venture was dictated by a national emergency.[78] During the twenty years of the First Messenian War (pp. 163–4) a large number of illegitimate children had been born to Spartiate mothers, whose husbands were away fighting in Messenia. These children were dubbed Partheniai and deprived of citizen rights. On reaching manhood after the war, they plotted a revolution, but were foiled; they were accordingly despatched forthwith to found a colony overseas. Phalanthus, their leader, consulted the Delphic oracle and received this reply: 'I grant thee Satyrion, to dwell in the rich land of Taras, and to become a bane to the Iapygians'.

Satyrion, near the modern Leporano, lies 12km. south-east of Taras. Both places had been visited and possibly settled by Mycenaean merchants; during the Dark Ages they had passed into the hands of the local Iapygians, who made an individual style of painted Geometric pottery quite unlike any Greek school. At Satyrion the stratification is quite clear. From the Iapygian levels there are several pieces which have been claimed as Cycladic Protogeometric, but the first clear indication of precolonial Greek trade is a Corinthian LG mug of c. 730 B.C.[79] Then follows a layer of sterile sand, and above that a stratum beginning in c. 700 B.C., containing nothing but Greek material. By now the place had become an outpost in the territory of the Spartan colony of Taras.

Taras itself possessed an outstandingly fine haven for shipping: an outer and inner harbour, separated by a narrow channel.[80] The nucleus of the Greek city was on a tongue-shaped peninsula east of the channel; on the other side, in the outskirts of modern Taranto, the prehellenic settlement lay on the headland known as Scoglio del Tonno ('Tunnyfish rock'). The stratification here is confused, but with the latest Iapygian pottery are many Greek imports and colonial pieces of c. 700 B.C., including two fragments of Laconian LG plates which should be the chattels of the first colonists. The site had now been taken over by the Spartan settlers, who founded their own city across the channel – in 706 B.C. according to Eusebius. The oldest finds there are from intramural graves, usually pit inhumations; but the earliest of all is an urn cremation, with a late EPC aryballos and skyphos.

Once the colonists had become established, there were no immediate signs of any peaceful exchange with the native neighbours. Iapygian Geometric was succeeded around 700 B.C. by the Daunian style,[81] which shows no sign of any Greek influence before the late seventh century. This striking lack of rapport may be partly due to the non-commercial character of the colonists, who would have viewed the natives as a military menace rather than as a potential market. No doubt the Delphic answer was delivered to Phalanthus with a shrewd understanding of the Spartan temperament.

The Western Phoenicians

We have now reviewed the full extent of the Greek colonial migration during the eighth century; just as any further expansion towards the north of Italy was prevented by the Etruscans, so a parallel colonial movement from the Levant impeded any further progress towards the west. Harried by Assyrian aggression, and tempted by the prospect of lucrative new markets, many Phoenicians of these years left their homeland for the western Mediterranean. By 700 B.C. they had established outposts in North Africa, western Sicily, Sardinia, and southern Spain. In each region, their commercial dealings with Greeks are attested by imported Greek pottery, and by the local imitations which these imports inspired. Some reference, then, must be made to these western Phoenicians, to set the Greek colonial movement in its wider context.

Carthage, a colony of Tyre, was the chief Phoenician outpost in North Africa, and probably the most ancient – although Timaeus' date of 814 B.C.[82] is likely to prove too early by a couple of generations. The oldest known material was found on virgin soil within the precinct of Tanith, the western Phoenician counterpart of the Levantine Astarte. The deposit is dated to c. 740–710 B.C. by six local pots influenced by Corinthian LG, though perhaps not at first hand; Corinthianizing ware from Pithecusae may have supplied some of the inspiration. Shortly afterwards, EPC aryballoi and kotylai turn up in the cemeteries. No other African colony offers any eighth-century material. It has been surmised that the first Carthaginians may have thwarted several Euboean attempts to gain a foothold in these parts, where memories of place-names such as 'Euboea', 'Pithecusae', and 'the Naxian islands' were dimly preserved.[83]

In Sicily, the Phoenicians founded their first outpost on Motya, a small island in a lagoon off the west coast. Here, too, Greek and hellenizing pots are among the earliest finds, which go back to c. 720–710 B.C.: there are EPC aryballoi, kotylai, and a late Thapsos-type skyphos; a few colonial pieces from eastern Sicily; and Phoenician imitations of Subgeometric skyphoi. There is no archaeological evidence to support the surmise of Thucydides (vi.2.6), that Phoenician traders once had stations all round the Sicilian coast before the arrival of the Greeks; on the contrary, it appears that the Greeks actually forestalled them in founding colonies on the island.

Motya was a very strategic choice of site, which helped the Phoenicians to gain control of the narrows between Sicily and Africa, and also secured them a route across to Etruria without the need to run the gauntlet of Euboean piracy in the Straits. When the art of Etruria succumbed to oriental influences, some of the new ideas can be traced to Phoenician rather than Euboean contacts: for instance, the sprawling 'Phoenician' palmette,[84] a favourite motif in Etruria, but absent from the Orientalizing art of Greece. A clear indication of Phoenician-Etruscan trade around 700 B.C. is given by two faience situlae of identical design, both bearing the scarab of the Pharaoh Bocchoris, and both of Phoenician make; one was found on Motya, the other at Tarquinii.

In Sardinia the Phoenicians were well established by the end of the eighth century. The fullest sequence comes from a sanctuary at Sulcis, on an islet off the south-western corner; one vessel there, a native shape, is decorated in a Euboean LG style with bird-and-lozenge panels,[85] perhaps a sign of relations with Pithecusae. A much-discussed stone inscription from Nora near by carries Phoenician lettering typical of the late ninth century in the homeland, but the script may be provincial and therefore old-fashioned and later.

One place mentioned on the Nora stone is Tarshish, a remote port whence king Hiram of Tyre (c. 975–950 B.C.) had once obtained gold, silver, ivory, apes, and peacocks.[86] Tarshish is usually identified with Herodotus' Tartessos, where Samians and Phocaeans traded in Archaic times; and also with Gades (Cadiz), the Phoenician colony beyond the Pillars of Heracles to which the literary record assigns an implausibly high antiquity.[87] So far, the earliest Phoenician finds from Spain are of the later eighth century, and come from two coastal sites near Málaga: the cemetery of Almuñecar (or Sexi) and the commercial settlement of Toscanos. Both places have produced EPC kotylai of c. 700 B.C., and from Toscanos there is also a Cypro-Phoenician Bichrome jug of this time. The settlement there was equipped with spacious warehouses at the end of the eighth century, and some evidence of metalworking has been found; supplies of gold, silver, and copper would have come from the rich river valleys of the interior – the Guadalquivir, the Guadiana, and the Río Tinto. If the excavators are right in supposing Toscanos to be a secondary colony,[88] perhaps an earlier Phoenician outpost may yet be found in the region of Cadiz. Meanwhile it seems best to regard king Hiram's merchants as pre-colonial prospectors.

Conclusions

It remains to distinguish the achievements of the various Greeks who came to Italy and Sicily during the eighth century, whether as visitors or as permanent settlers.

To the Euboeans belongs the credit for rediscovering the western world. In return for the ores of Etruria they marketed pottery, oriental artifacts, and iron-working skills in a land where the Iron Age had barely begun. From Euboean LG pottery the Etruscans gained their first acquaintance with Greek art. Later, the Etruscan Orientalizing movement owed much of its impetus to the luxuries brought by Euboean middlemen; and the formation of the Etruscan alphabet was prompted by the Chalcidian colonial script (p. 300). The Euboean outpost of Pithecusae, sited for trade with Etruria and Campania, has the look of an international emporium such as we find in no other early Greek colony; to judge from its busy industrial quarter, the Pithecusans themselves profited greatly from this trade, yet the abundance of oriental objects gives us the impression that many merchants from the homeland also passed this way.

When overpopulation in Greece caused a mass exodus of agrarian colonists, the Chalcidians secured the best land in Sicily, and gained control of the Straits; hardly surprising, in view of the local knowledge which must have been amassed by Euboean mariners of the previous two generations.

As a general rule, the agrarian colonists were not at all tolerant in their initial dealings with indigenous peoples. Previous inhabitants were forced out, not only from the chosen sites, but from the coastal plains near by; the new colonies needed to secure enough arable land, and could not afford to turn a blind eye to any defensible native citadel within striking distance. The Chalcidians of Leontini were unusually humane in allowing a Sicel community to remain on the next hill, if only for a while; unusual, too, is the degree of commercial activity implied by the Euboean-style native pots at S. Aloe, and at Canale in Calabria. At the other extreme, the Spartans of Taras not only ejected the Iapygians from the neighbourhood, but remained aloof from them for a considerable time. The Achaeans of Sybaris, after creating much havoc among the coastal Oenotrians, permitted some resettlement on a smaller scale, and peaceful exchanges were soon resumed. The Corinthians of Syracuse were up against a wily opponent in king Hyblon, if it was through an understanding of inter-Greek feuds that he welcomed the Megarians; after the fall of his kingdom, the Sicels were driven deep into the interior, but the affinities of their pottery imply some trade with the colonists.

In addition to their one colonial enterprise, the Corinthians were also the chief exporters of fine pottery to all the western colonies from *c.* 750 B.C. onwards. As we have already seen (pp. 187 ff.), Corinth's trade has a strong westward bias, and the finest products of her potter's quarter were probably intended for export. The natural conclusion is that these exports were conveyed by the Corinthians themselves, rather than by Euboean middlemen; in fact, the proportion of Corinthian pottery at Eretria and Chalcis is far lower than in their western colonies, and we must recall that Corinthian merchants already had a useful forward station on Ithaca. They were especially active in the marketing of unguents; previously, the leading specialists in this field had been the Phoenicians, but from *c.* 720 B.C. onwards we find even their own colonists at Carthage and Motya importing Corinthian aryballoi.

Until the very end of the eighth century, very little Corinthian pottery had reached the Italic peoples of Etruria and Campania, where the commercial initiative had rested in Euboean hands. After the end of the Lelantine War, however, the energies of Chalcis and Eretria were exhausted; Corinthian wares began to flood all the Italian markets, and Corinth supplanted Euboea as the chief source of inspiration for Italian potters. Meanwhile the extent of Greek commerce increased, many notable sites receiving their first Greek imports at this time: for instance, Caere in Etruria, Castel di Decima and Marino in Latium, Nola and Suessula in Campania.

It is fitting to close this chapter with a literary tradition which reflects the commercial inclination of Corinth's rulers during the early seventh century, and also the willingness of Greek merchants and artisans (cf. p. 232) to reside in Etruria. The story cannot be traced back earlier than the time of Polybius; (*c.* 150 B.C.),[89] yet it is consistent with the archaeological facts, and unlikely to be a fictional fabrication.[90]

Demaratus, a Bacchiad nobleman of Corinth, increased his fortune greatly by trading with Etruria; he made many journeys there in his own merchant ship, sold his cargo to the Etruscans, and brought Etruscan goods back to Greece. When the Bacchiad oligarchy was overthrown by the tyrant Cypselus (*c.* 656 B.C.), he prudently left Corinth for good; sailing away with a staff of three artisans and all his possessions, he went to live among his friends in Tarquinii. There he married an Etruscan lady of high birth, who bore him two sons, Arruns and Lucumo. The younger son, a crafty and ambitious character, migrated to Rome; there he seized power, and became the fifth of the seven kings, Lucius Tarquinius Priscus.

NOTES

1 *GGP* 360 n. 1.
2 Even in bountiful Boeotia, Hesiod (*Erga* 376) advises farmers to have only one son. Engrossing at Corinth may have affected the views of a local lawgiver, Pheidon: see Aristotle, *Politics* 1265, b12.
3 Strabo 257.
4 Strabo 380.
5 One sherd from Scoglio del Tonno near Taras may possibly be Greek Protogeometric (W. Taylour, *Mycenaean Pottery in Italy* 118–19 no. 165 pl. 14, 19). See also p. 239 above.
6 *BSA* 68 (1973), 191–2 fig. 1; *NSc* 1972, 256 fig. 36, gr. AA β–γ, 1.
7 e.g., *NSc* 1963, 214 fig. 89c,d.
8 J. Close-Brooks, *BICS* 14 (1967), 22–3 pl. 1.
9 F–W. von Hase, *RM* 79 (1972), 162–4 fig. 1.
10 Some intermediate points along this route are suggested by the find-places of scarabs in pre-colonial contexts: Cumae, which supplied the interior of Campania; Torre Galli in Calabria (*MA* 31 (1926), figs. 30, 35; cf. la Genière, *MEFR* 76 (1964), 12 f.); and Francavilla near Sybaris (pp. 238–9).
11 Like Buchner (in *The Italian Iron Age*, ed. D. and F. Ridgway, London 1975), I follow the reading of most MSS, as against *chryseia* (gold mines) given in a single late MS. Geological research has shown that there never were any gold deposits on the island.
12 J. Klein, *Expedition* 14 (1972), 37 fig. 5.
13 G. Marinelli *apud* G. Buchner, *DdA* 3 (1969), 97–8.
14 S. Brunnsåker, *OpRom* 4 (1962), 165 ff. figs. 1–8; cf. *GGP* 195.
15 *AM* 66 (1941), pl. 11, 416.
16 Close-Brooks, *StEtr* 35 (1967), 327–9.
17 P. Bosticco, *La Parola del Passato* 12 (1957), 218 sub no. 102.
18 Dunbabin, *WG* 7 n. 2.
19 Müller-Karpe's Prehellenic I; for the dating see Close-Brooks, *StEtr* 35 (1967), 323 ff.
20 For valid arguments against co-existence see H. Hencken, *Tarquinia, Villanovans, and early Etruscans* (1968), 650–1.
21 The foundation date of 1051 B.C., given by Velleius Paterculus and Eusebius, must be ignored.
22 As Strabo (243) implies.
23 Müller-Karpe's Prehellenic II; cf. Hencken, ibid.
24 Dunbabin, *WG* 7.
25 G. Vallet, *Rhégion et Zancle* (1958), 57 n. 3.
26 R. F. Paget, *JRS* 58 (1968), 152 ff.
27 A clue is offered by the distance from the acropolis of the colonial cemeteries: 600m. for the earliest recorded grave (Artiaco gr. 103 *bis*), up to 2km. for the Archaic and Classical burials.
28 Buchner, *RM* 60–1 (1954–55), 51 ff. fig. 3.
29 e.g., *GGP* pl. 41f,g,j.
30 Boardman and Buchner, *JdI* 81 (1966), 23.

31 C. Bérard, *Eretria* III, 51 n. 38.
32 *MA* 13 (1903), 225 ff.
33 Copenhagen 4952; P. Amandry in *Studies presented to H. Goldman* (1956), 242–3 pl. 28,
34 W. Johannowsky, *DdA* 3 (1969), 35 figs. 8c, 13c; B. d'Agostino, *MEFR* 82 (1970). 604 fig. 14.
35 id., *DdA* 3 (1969), 56 fig. 16.
36 *StEtr* 41 (1973), 510 pl. 93d.
37 e.g., *RM* 71 (1964), 8 pl. 2, 1. E. La Rocca in *Civiltà del Lazio primitivo* (Rome, 1976), 367 ff. pl. 21B.
38 See, in particular, *StEtr* 37 (1969), pl. 38a,b, and 39 (1971), pl. 48c, both from Vulci.
39 e.g., *GSI* pl. 24, 1 and 3, oinochoai of Corinthian type, bearing heavy vertical waves in the Euboean manner (cf. fig. 62a).
40 G. Voza, *Sicilia SO* 57–9 pl. 16.
41 Thuc. vi.3.1.
42 Confirmed by Hellanicus (*FGH* 4F 82) and Ephorus (*FGH* 70F 137a,b).
43 *apud* Strabo 267.
44 *DdA* 3 (1969), 128, 144–6, 160.
45 P. Pelagatti, *BdA* 57 (1972), 219 fig. 38b.
46 Strabo 380; cf. p. 187.
47 *GGP* 374; cf. Dunbabin, *WG* 13 n. 5.
48 Map: *WG* 49 fig. E nos. 7, 8.
49 Athenaeus 31b.
50 e.g., *BCH* 60 (1936), pls. 11b, 12, 13a.
51 Thuc. vi.3.3.
52 *Strategemata* v.5.1.
53 Thuc. vi.4.1.
54 Six months, according to Polyaenus (ibid.); but not before they themselves had ejected the Sicels.
55 After comparing their copious finds with the much sparser early material from Syracuse, the excavators (G. Vallet–F. Villard, *BCH* 76 (1952), 289 ff.; *DdA* 3 (1969), 138 ff.) have argued that Megara Hyblaea, Naxos, Leontini, and Catana were all settled during the 750s, at least two decades before the Syracusan foundation. My reasons for adhering to Thucydides' dates have been given in *GGP* 324–5.
56 e.g., gridded lozenge, *Megara Hyblaea* II, pl. 135, 6.
57 Dunbabin, *WG* 16–19.
58 L. Bernabò Brea, *Sicily before the Greeks* (1957), 162–3 fig. 39 pls. 64–5.
59 One of the latest finds is a solitary EPC sherd: id., *Sicilia SO* 53. In *Parola del Passato* 23 (1968), 161 ff. Bernabò Brea offers a different reconstruction of events, based on the higher dating for Megara Hyblaea (above n. 55).
60 G. Voza, *Sicilia SO* 117–20 no. 381.
61 For the main Sicel sites after 700 B.C. see Åkerström, *GSI* 21–3 (Period IV), with map p. 10.
62 Thuc. vi.4.5–6.
63 Vallet, *Rhégion et Zancle* (1958), 140 pl. 7b top left; cf. p. 168 fig. 54c.
64 Strabo 272.
65 Except perhaps for children; three cists, too small for any but infants, held inhumations.
66 cf. *GGP* 326 n. 4.
67 Vallet, op. cit. 37 pl. 5, 1.
68 The only Greek import here is an Attic LG IIb oinochoe (*GSI* 40 fig. 12, 2) which was not found in the organized excavations.
69 J. de la Genière, *MEFR* 76 (1964), 22–3; cf. Polybius xii.6.2–5.
70 Strabo 263; the name may not be complete.
71 Diodorus xii.9.
72 *NSc* 1970, Suppl. 90 fig. 79 nos. 181–2; p. 139.
73 Strabo 262.
74 *MA* 23 (1914), 816 fig. 77.

75 La Genière, *MEFR* 82 (1970), 621 ff.
76 P. Zancani Montuoro, *Atti e Memorie* N.S. 6–7 (1965–66), 11 n. 11; *DdA* 3 (1969), 132–3 fig. B.
77 La Genière, *MEFR* 85 (1973), 7 ff. The kantharoi continue into sixth-century contexts at Sala Consilina (art. cit. 21–2 with refs.).
78 Strabo 278–9.
79 *NSc* 1964, 77 fig. 23; cf. *BSA* 48 (1953), pl. 58 no. 1029.
80 Plan, *WG* 88.
81 D. Randall-MacIver, *The Iron Age in Italy* (Oxford, 1927), 211–32.
82 Dionysios of Halicarnassos i.74.
83 H. Treidler, *Historia* 8 (1959), 257 ff.
84 R. M. Cook, *Greek Painted Pottery*[2] (1972), 147 fig. 25; Close-Brooks, *NSc* 1965, 57 fig. 5, 82.
85 G. Pesce, *Sardegna punica* (1961), 70 fig. 116.
86 *I Kings* x.22.
87 Founded in 1110 B.C., according to Velleius i.2.4.
88 H. G. Niemeyer, *MDOG* 104 (1972), 30 ff.
89 vi.11a.10.
90 A. Blakeway, *JRS* 25 (1935), 171–3; the most detailed account is Dionysios of Halicarnassos iii.46.3.

9 Eastern Greece and Anatolia

A loose unity links the sites of the East Greek world during the eighth century. Over a wide area, extending from Rhodes to Chios and from Caria to the river Hermus, the local LG pottery shares many features in common; the same is true of some bronzes, especially fibulae. Most of our evidence comes from Rhodes, Cos, Samos, and Chios, partly because many of the most flourishing centres are to be found there; but we must also remember that these large offshore islands have been more fully explored than the Greek sites of western Anatolia.

We begin with Rhodes, where the East Greek LG style was probably invented. Its full development can be followed through a sequence of some thirty grave groups from Ialysos, Camirus, and the Lindian village of Exochi. These places supply information about the local burial customs, and about small offerings in gold, silver, and bronze. Metal objects are also well represented among the votives of Athena at Lindos, as are local terracottas and oriental ivories. The Geometric cemeteries of Cos, under the modern capital town, come to an abrupt end in the middle of Rhodian LG. On Samos, as before, virtually all the material is from the Heraion; a local school of pottery combines East Greek and Atticizing ideas, and there are also plenty of terracottas and bronzes, both local and oriental. Two small sanctuaries on Chios, at Kato Phana and Emporio, afford a glimpse of the local LG pottery and bronzes.

The Greek cities of western Anatolia were by now well established. Several Carian sites, too, were producing LG pottery under Rhodian influence; some are semi-hellenized towns on the coast (e.g., Halicarnassos, Iasos), while others lie deep in the native hinterland. Our knowledge of southern Ionia is based on scattered finds from the city of Miletus, supplemented by a few pieces from Melia and Ephesus. The north Ionic town of Old Smyrna offers much evidence of domestic architecture, and a local LG style related to Chiot but also open to influence from mainland Greece. Aeolis and Lesbos imported a good deal of LG ware, mainly East Greek; but for some mysterious reason their local pottery was made in a grey monochrome fabric, in the Anatolian tradition. From *c.* 750 B.C. onwards the north-east Aegean began to receive Greek settlers; Troy, after lying desolate for over three centuries, was repeopled by a party of Aeolians.

Compared with the Corinthians and Euboeans, the eastern Greeks showed little enterprise as travellers or as traders. Yet, with the general improvement in communications, it was natural that they should become better acquainted with the peoples of the Anatolian hinterland, and especially with the powerful kingdom of Phrygia. These exchanges will be briefly considered towards the end of this chapter.

246

Rhodian LG Pottery and Terracottas

A cup from Camirus tomb 82 (fig. 78a) shows the local style at the end of MG in a state of restless ferment. Meanders and circles, after a long currency, are now subjected to bizarre variations, and confined within unequal vertical divisions. At the outset of the LG phase (c. 740 B.C.) the decoration settles down to a more regular metopal scheme, illustrated by the kotyle fig. 78b. The shape, with a nicked rim, is adapted from the earliest Corinthian version (cf. fig. 54a); but the metopal motifs are authentically Rhodian. Most striking is the local Tree of Life, here reduced to a hatched triangular base and two squared hooks; the idea had already been adumbrated on the Camirus cup. Other compartments may be occupied by hatched lozenges in double outline, by a pair of meander hooks, and especially by large birds, the only living creatures to find a regular place in the Rhodian repertoire. This vessel is one of a large number from the Bird-Kotyle Workshop, as we may call it. The same craftsmen also made oinochoai, jugs, and kraters, but it was through the export of their kotylai that their style pervaded the whole East Greek world. At first there are four metopes; then, around 700 B.C., only three; thereafter the shape becomes shallower, and turns into the well-known 'bird-bowl' which keeps its Subgeometric character all through the seventh century. To judge from the sources of the earlier kotylai, Ialysos was the original home of this workshop; later, the same manner was copied and adapted in almost all the major East Greek centres.

In another workshop, the metopes carry birds with angular necks, dense piles of zigzag, and clumps of four Rhodian Trees. The shapes are skyphoi, high-handled kantharoi, and large funerary oinochoai with openwork snakes running across the handles (fig. 78c). The output of this Bird-and-Zigzag Workshop is limited to western Rhodes (mainly Camirus and Siana), and to the earlier part of LG.

Rhodian LG ornament owes very little to other Geometric schools, but two themes were adapted from oriental ivories: the cable[1] and, more frequently, the palm-tree. The krater, fig. 78e, shows a late and debased palm, well after 700 B.C.; but earlier renderings[2] are closer to nature, and also to a favourite motif of Levantine ivory-workers,[3] whose products were reaching Rhodes in some quantity.

As a general rule, the Rhodians favoured a metopal system, even on the shoulders of closed vases where it looks rather uncomfortable. There was also a preference for cross-hatched ornament, particularly in the later stages; even the full meander is often treated in this way (fig. 78d). Dark glaze covers more of the surface than was customary in LG schools further west: thus the decoration of closed shapes rarely descends below the belly, while on open vessels the ornament is often hemmed in by the glaze, which is carried up to the rim and sometimes round the lip as well. These general remarks apply not only to Rhodes, but in large measure to all LG pottery made in eastern Greece.

Most of the commoner shapes have been mentioned already. The chief open vessels are the nicked kotyle, the skyphos, the high-handled kantharos, and the

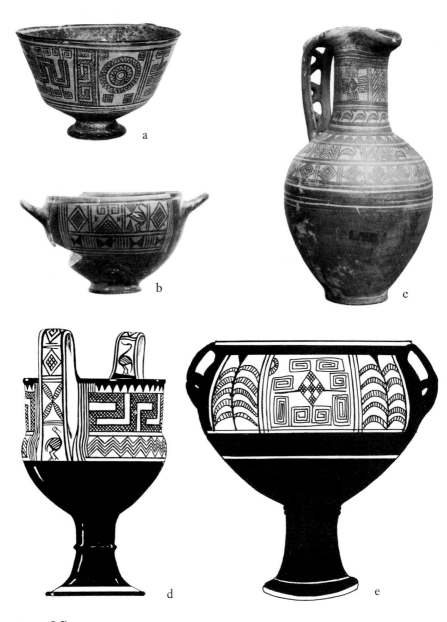

FIG. 78 RHODIAN LG POTTERY
(a) Rhodes 14737, Camirus, H. 12.5; (b) *Thera* II fig. 80, H. 10;
(c) London 85.12-13.6, Camirus, H. 39; (d) Rhodes (lost), Exochi,
H. 27; (e) Copenhagen 12432, Exochi, H. 45

krater; some kantharoi, and all kraters, have tall pedestals (fig. 78d,e). Among closed forms, amphorae were never popular; but oinochoai are plentiful, especially those with tall, narrow necks. Ridge-necked lekythoi, of oriental derivation, continue from MG; and round-mouthed jugs came into fashion around 700 B.C. From the contexts of a few Corinthian imports and imitations, we learn that Rhodian LG continued until c. 680 B.C. In spite of a few early experiments,[4] no settled Orientalizing style – in the usual sense of the word when applied to Greek vase-painting – was established before the middle of the seventh century.

We have, however, left on one side several classes of Rhodian pottery which, although made within LG times, are already orientalizing in the sense that they imitate Cypro-Levantine unguent vessels. This is by no means a new development; but whereas earlier adaptations (p. 68 fig. 20c) had usually been clothed with Geometric motifs and assimilated to the Dodecanesian MG style, now we find many close reproductions of oriental shapes, oriental fabric, and oriental linear decoration. Thus, on a close Rhodian copy of a Black-on-Red III oinochoe (fig. 79a) a slip was added to simulate the shiny orange surface of the Cypriot original. Freer adaptations of Black-on-Red shapes may have a darker slip, in which case the circle ornament is lightly scored through the slip (fig. 79b). Likewise a local mushroom-topped flask (fig. 79c) is based on the Phoenician Red Slip type (cf. fig. 75b), but with a thicker and darker slip. The usual form of aryballos, fig. 79d, is derived from a Cypriot White-Painted IV ridge-necked flask, and ultimately from a North Syrian prototype with a polished yellow surface; the Rhodian version omits the ridge and shortens the neck, yet takes on the spaghetti-like ornament from Cyprus,[5] and often tries to emulate the shiny surface of the North Syrian original. The human face in relief, as a form of ornament on the neck of a vessel (fig. 79e,f), is another North Syrian notion which Rhodes shares with Cyprus, derived ultimately from North Syrian flasks like fig. 75c. The lady on the neck of the Rhodian oinochoe wears massive earrings, and the low placing of her ears gives her a Semitic look: her profile is curiously reminiscent of the largest ivory girl from Athens (pp. 130–2 fig. 42c), a contemporary but much finer work also made under North Syrian influence.

Most of these imitations of oriental work have been found at Ialysos, the only site where their full range is to be found; here, evidently, was the main centre for their production. The aryballoi (fig. 79d) were widely exported across the Aegean, and even as far as the western colonies.

Rhodes is a prolific source of Geometric terracotta figurines; most are from sanctuaries, but some have been found in graves. The types include humans, horses, and a bird,[6] and are nearly always solid and handmade. A nude woman from Camirus (fig. 79g) displays the most typical features of the local style: head thrown back, huge nose, straight mouth, hair falling to the shoulders. Sometimes the surface is painted with LG motifs, as on a rider's torso from Lindos (no. 1860). Thence also comes an impressive male head (fig. 79h,j) with paint added for the beard, moustache, eyes, and hair.

Rhodian Burial Customs and Metalwork

The normal Rhodian practice, as before, was to inhume children in pithoi, and to cremate adults in rectangular graves.[7] The pyres were usually lit in the grave itself, and most of the offerings smashed upon them; the remains were left *in situ*, instead of being gathered into an urn. In three rich cremations at Ialysos (grs. 51, 57, 58) animal bones are the debris of a funeral feast. A curious and exclusively Rhodian habit, beginning in LG, was to dig four cavities into the tomb floor, one at each corner, usually undercutting the sides. Pottery, other offerings, and animal bones have sometimes been found in these holes;[8] but perhaps their main purpose was to secure the ends of the two horizontal stakes which kept the pyre fuel off the floor and thus provided a draught for the flames.

Conspicuous among the metal offerings are bronze fibulae, silver and gold earrings, and gold diadems. Of fibulae the Rhodians were extraordinarily prodigal; for example, Ialysos gr. 58, an adult cremation, yielded the charred fragments of nineteen. Over fifteen hundred came to light at the sanctuary of Athena at Lindos; their diversity, as well as their great abundance, inspired their excavator, C. Blinkenberg, to write what is still the standard work on all Greek fibulae. His Type IV, whose distinguishing feature is its tall and narrow plate, is at home all over eastern Greece, not least in Rhodes. Three specimens from Lindos, fig. 80a–c, represent the main classes present in Rhodian LG graves;[9] the bow may be plain, leech-shaped, or tricked out with globes and lenticular reels. The first two classes may carry one or more birds perched on the bow – an exclusively Rhodian notion, and the birds usually have the angular neck characteristic of the Bird-and-Zigzag Workshop (fig. 78c). Our fourth example (fig. 80d), distinguished by its symmetrical and semicircular bow, belongs to a type (XII) which the eastern Greeks learned from the peoples of the Anatolian hinterland (p. 266).

Spiral earrings, in silver and gold, have been found in Ialysos grs. 56–8 (*c.* 730–710 B.C.). These are simplified versions of the Corinthian type, having only one and a half coils. The spirals may either be thick, and without terminals; or thinner, and ending in flat discs. Both varieties continue in Rhodes throughout the seventh century.[10]

Several gold bands have emerged from the cemeteries of Camirus and Exochi, though only in two burials can the associated finds be traced. A pair from Camirus tomb 82 (p. 96), found with pottery of *c.* 750 B.C. (e.g., fig. 78a), are decorated with linear motifs only: a large central meander flanked by pricked triangles. In Camirus gr. 201 a very late LG krater and a Subgeometric bird-bowl (*c.* 680–670 B.C.) keep company with another pair of gold bands, clearly intended for the mouth rather than the brow;[11] their ornament is placed in metopal panels containing six-leaved rosettes within circles, and griffins which are already Orientalizing. Within this chronological bracket we must fit the sporadic finds. A diadem from Camirus in London[12] bears rich linear ornament of LG character, including motifs from both dated finds – pricked triangles, and an ornate six-leaved rosette; it was probably made near the end of the eighth

FIG. 79 RHODIAN IMITATIONS OF LEVANTINE WARES: RHODIAN
TERRACOTTA FIGURINES
(a) Rhodes 11753, Ialysos gr. 57, H. 20; (b) Rhodes 11742, Ialysos
gr. 56, H. 10; (c) Rhodes 10649, Ialysos gr. 17, H. 11;
(d) Rhodes 14079, Camirus gr. 45, H. 8.1; (e) Rhodes 11741,
Ialysos gr. 56, H. 14; (f) Rhodes 11791, Ialysos gr. 58, H. 19;
(g) London cat. no. 5, Camirus, H. 20; (h–j) *Lindos* I no. 1861, H. 4.5

century. A little later, perhaps, are the three figured bands from Exochi. Z 51,
showing two chariots converging upon a central medallion, was carelessly pressed
upon a matrix which had at least three zones, like many of the diadems from
Athens and Eretria. More fastidious is the execution of Z 52–3, two fragments
from the same matrix whose composition is restored in fig. 81. Here we see a
hunter mounted on a chariot; he pursues a motley crowd of lions, bulls, stags,
wild goats, and birds, arranged in two zones and hardly aware of their danger.

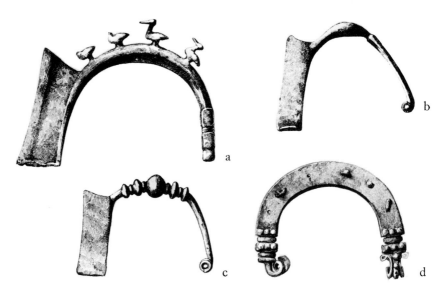

FIG. 80 RHODIAN LG BRONZE FIBULAE, FROM LINDOS
(a) no. 48, L. 12.1; (b) no. 50, L. 8.8; (c) no. 60, H. 8.1;
(d) no. 119a, L. 9.8

Although the style and treatment are still Geometric, the theme of hunting from a chariot recalls the monumental stone reliefs in oriental palaces.

Cos

Most of the LG finds from this island come from the Geometric cemeteries under the modern, Roman, and Hellenistic town. The latest graves there take us down to *c.* 710 B.C., but no further. There are also among the richest: one child's cist inhumation, Seraglio no. 14, yielded over a hundred pots, many of them placed above the slabs.

The local LG style is related to Rhodian, but less versatile and more conservative. The only common shapes are oinochoai, ridge-necked lekythoi, skyphoi, and cups. The lekythoi usually receive Geometric ornament, but some copy the fabric and motifs of the Cypro-Phoenician Black-on-Red model (cf. p. 67 fig. 20b). Most skyphoi still have a strangely Protogeometric look, with flaring lips, low conical feet, and – sometimes – small sets of concentric circles.[13] The deep glazed cups are of a class also present on Rhodes and Samos: the rim overhangs an almost vertical wall, sharply curving in towards a narrow base. Rarer and more exotic shapes include ring-vases, barrel-vases, fairly naturalistic duck-vases, and bell-dolls made on the wheel.[14] The absence of aryballoi and kotylai confirms the impression that the later stages of Coan LG have yet to be found.

FIG. 81 RHODIAN LG DIADEM (*Exochi* fig. 191)
Reconstruction, based on Exochi Z 52-3, L. *c.* 26

The decoration, as in MG, is still organized in narrow horizontal strips. On large closed vessels[15] these strips occupy the shoulder, and may be interrupted by vertical divisions; but the Rhodian system of equal metopes is virtually unknown. The favourite motifs are battlements, lozenges, triangular lozenge nets, and single zigzag. The Rhodian Tree, and its derivatives, occasionally appears; cables and palm-trees are seen only on the most advanced vases such as fig. 82a, which look contemporary with mid-LG Rhodian work.[16]

The sequence from these cemeteries had been continuous since the tenth century; why does it end so abruptly around 710 B.C.? For the next two centuries no finds have been reported from anywhere in the area of the modern town. One possible explanation of this apparent lacuna is suggested by the literary evidence, in the light of recent topographical research.[17] Strabo (657) and Diodorus (xv.76,2) refer to a migration of Coans in 366 B.C. from an older site (Cos Astypalaia) to their 'present' town, for which the pre-Dorian name Meropis was remembered in earlier allusions. Cos Meropis is reasonably seen as the town under modern Cos, occupied in Mycenaean, Geometric, Hellenistic, and Roman times; Astypalaia has been located on a steep hill near the other end of the island, where Geometric to Classical sherds have been found on the surface. Cos Astypalaia had evidently been the sovereign city for some time before 366 B.C.; perhaps it first became so at the end of the eighth century, after a general move from Cos Meropis. However, until Astypalaia has been explored by deep soundings, this can be no more than a very tentative hypothesis.

Samos

The first temple of Hera, the earliest Hekatompedon in Greece, had been erected at the beginning of the eighth century (p. 97). Not long afterwards the Samians set another precedent by surrounding the temple with a narrow colonnade (*pteron*), extending the roof to cover it. The columns were of wood, on stone bases; there were seventeen on the long sides, seven across the front, and six at the back (p. 327 fig. 105a). East of the Hekatompedon lay the altar for burnt sacrifices; it is sited on a different alignment, and had already been built and rebuilt before any temple was planned. With the growing prestige of the sanctuary, the altar was remodelled at least twice[18] more during the life of the first

Hekatompedon, each time on a larger scale. Altars III (fig. 105b) and IV (middle and later eighth century) were encased within walls of rectangular ashlar blocks, dressed on the outside: for Geometric structures, an unusual refinement.

Around 700 B.C.[19] the festal area south of the temple was flooded when a branch of the river Imbrasos burst its eastern bank. Nests of plain whole pots were found in the alluvial sand and gravel, perhaps washed away from the wreckage of hucksters' booths. A more catastrophic inundation in c. 660 B.C. destroyed the temple and altar as well; both were soon rebuilt in a more monumental manner, which need not concern us here.

A broad distinction can be made among the finds of LG pottery from the Heraion. The southern and western areas, with their wells and inundation deposits, have yielded several hundreds of small vessels, both open and closed, bearing little or no ornament. Most of the finely decorated ware comes from the votive layers in the immediate neighbourhood of the temple and altar, and is in a fragmentary state; almost all the shapes there are open. They include pedestalled kraters, high-handled kantharoi (often very large and ornate), nicked kotylai like the Rhodian ones, skyphoi, and deep glazed cups – either straight-walled or bell-shaped;[20] also handsome trays, with leaf ornament on both sides (fig. 82b). Among the deposits of plainer pottery the chief closed shapes are oinochoai, jugs, and amphorae, all three shapes often lacking any articulation between neck and body.

Samian LG decoration, in its earlier stage, was still susceptible to Attic influence, more so than any other eastern Aegean centre. Atticizing ideas were now probably transmitted through Cycladic and Euboean imports;[21] hence a metopal system using quatrefoils and hatched birds, and other Atticizing motifs like tangential blobs, hatched tongues, and the leaf pattern of fig. 82b. A large kantharos bears a simplified *prothesis* scene, one of the few Geometric representations outside Attica.[22] Horses appear several times, owing something to Naxos and Euboea; but the long mane, streaming halfway down the back (fig. 82c), is a local notion. After c. 730 B.C. a Rhodian element was introduced through the imports and local imitations of bird-kotylai; thus the Rhodian Tree, with its derivatives (e.g., fig. 82c, centre), passed into the Samian repertoire. Corinthian influence was slight and arrived late, largely confined to the panels of floating zigzags or chevrons seen on many Subgeometric drinking-vessels.

From these ingredients the Samians improvised freely and imaginatively. The most adventurous work appears on large kantharoi. Fig. 82c shows a rich design combining swimming fish of Early Protocorinthian origin, clumps of Rhodian Trees, and horses adapted from the Atticizing tradition, one being stalked by a lion. Their reserved eyes, their heavy hooves, their angular fetlocks, and the open stride of their forelegs indicate a date at the very end of the local LG, around 690 B.C.[23] Thereafter the most enterprising hands quickly evolved an Early Orientalizing style, in which lions and volute trees played important parts.[24] Yet many smaller vessels were decorated in a dry Subgeometric manner – especially skyphoi, whose lips often bear an incised or painted wavy line. Among them we may recognize the prototype of the popular 'Ionian cups' of Archaic times.[25]

Hera received a wide variety of terracotta figurines, both handmade and

FIG. 82 COAN AND SAMIAN LG POTTERY
(a) Cos 900; (b) *Samos* V no. 105, D. 26.5; (c) Samos K 805, kantharos, detail
(*AM* 58, 98, fig. 40)

wheelmade. The former are mainly horses, with a few bulls, rams, and humans;
they are not often found before LG, though a horse's head and neck came from
a context well before 750 B.C.[26] Their execution is somewhat crude, apart from
one (imported?) horse recalling those on Attic LG I pyxis lids.[27] More accomplished are the larger wheelmade animals, chiefly bulls, made in a technique
which could well have survived locally from the end of the Bronze Age.[28] Wheelmade humans first appear here in LG; their robes usually reach to the ground,
and their heads are tilted back like the Rhodian figures.[29] Samos continued to
manufacture them through most of the seventh century, even after the mould
had come into use for finer work – e.g., the human faces applied to the necks of

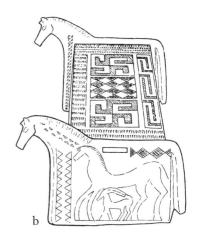

FIG. 83 SAMOS, FINDS FROM THE HERAION
(a) Bronze lion combat, B 190, H. 9; (b) wooden stand,
reconstruction (*AM* 68, 91 fig. 3), L. *c.* 53

small amphorae.[30] How are we to account for the survival of this old-fashioned
technique long after its disappearance elsewhere in Greece? One possible reason
is the example set by wheelmade figures imported from Cyprus, which were
reaching Samos from 700 B.C. onwards.[31]

Wood is normally a perishable material; but the marshy terrain of the Heraion
has allowed many wooden objects to be recovered in good condition. One of the
most spectacular finds is a piece of sacred furniture, decorated in the style of
c. 720–700 B.C. In fig. 83b the excavators have restored on paper what seems to
be a large footstool in the form of a condensed chariot team; the restoration is
reasonably certain, since the footboard and almost the whole of one sideboard
were recovered. Perhaps we are meant to visualize a team of four: the two trace-
horses incised on the outer faces, and the two yoke-horses indicated partly in
three dimensions, their heads and tails projecting from the sideboards. Among
several suggestions concerning the purpose of this object, the most plausible is
that it served as a stand, on which the primitive wooden cult-image of Hera was
carried in festival processions.[32] If this were so, the Samians would have been
adapting to the needs of their own cult the Neo-Hittite convention of mounting
a standing deity upon a base formed by two lions; a good example is the
monumental group from Zinjirli.[33]

Although a number of bronze figurines have been found at the Heraion, it is
not yet clear whether there was any local production in Geometric times. At all
events, the most remarkable pieces have strong Peloponnesian affinities. A
warrior hero is embattled with a lion, aided by his dog who is worrying the
beast's foreleg (fig. 83a); the man's stocky physique, and the fluent style of the

whole, recall the charioteer from Olympia (pp. 150–1 fig. 49d,e), probably a late work of the Argive LG school. Likewise a team of two horses[34] is stiffly stylized in the Laconian manner, while another horse[35] has much in common with the hammered Corinthian type.

From c. 700 B.C. onwards the Heraion received an abundance of oriental votives in bronze and ivory, of a diversity unmatched anywhere else in the Greek world. These will be briefly considered in the concluding section of this chapter.

Chios

This island is virtually unknown during the Dark Ages; but the LG period is well represented by votives from two places on its southern shore. The sanctuary of Apollo at ancient Phanai (Kato Phana) has produced rich deposits going back to c. 750 B.C. in the neighbourhood of a Geometric enclosure wall. The other site, Emporio, has two sanctuaries: one by the harbour, with well-stratified votives sealed by early walls; the other, dedicated to Athena, upon the acropolis of the upper town. Some houses in this town (p. 308) also go back into the eighth century; but nowhere at Emporio do the finds begin in quantity before c. 720 B.C., and at no Chiot sanctuary is there any trace of a Geometric temple.

As is the case at many sanctuaries, the pottery is fragmentary, and consists chiefly of open shapes: pedestalled kraters, skyphoi, kantharoi, nicked kotylai, and deep cups with low conical foot; also a few baggy oinochoai and jugs. Apart from the Rhodian-style ornament of the kotylai, metopal decoration is avoided. A krater design, fig. 84a, illustrates the usual Chiot way of covering a large surface: several horizontal strips in the centre, flanked by two vertical columns either side. The horizontal divisions may contain S's alternating with dots, meander hooks, crosses, or zigzags; in the vertical columns we find hatched and outlined lozenge chains, zigzags, stacked triangles, meander hooks, and a cross-hatched motif consisting of four triangles attached to a central lozenge. Figured work, though crude, is more plentiful than in any other LG school of eastern Greece; there are birds, goats, horses, riders, and a hero levelling his long spear at a lion.[36]

This local Geometric style persevered through much of the seventh century, when it reached a fussy 'Subgeometric' stage – although the use of the term is somewhat illogical in the absence of any Early Orientalizing decoration. The old stock of motifs persisted, with the addition of the check pattern, and dot-filled meander designs. One shape, the skyphos, underwent a peculiarly Chiot development: in its 'Subgeometric' form the offset lip became increasingly tall and the foot began to rise, until we can recognize the precursor of the Archaic Chiot chalice.[37]

Bronze fibulae were frequently offered at both sites. As on Rhodes, the usual type is Blinkenberg IV, with tall and narrow plate. The most popular varieties correspond to those from Lindos (e.g., fig. 80a–c), with the addition of IV 9–10 which have a single globe or swelling on the bow, and the exception of the exclusively Rhodian version adorned with birds. Also present is the Anatolian type (e.g., fig. 80d). Related to it are the handles of bronze belts, of Phrygian inspiration; as the stratification of Emporio shows, these handles were to become

increasingly elaborate through the seventh century. The belts have been reasonably interpreted by the excavator as the dedications offered by girls just before
their marriage. The other bronzes include spiral earrings ending in discs, like
those from Rhodes; and broad bracelets from Emporio, with pricked circular
decoration.

In ivory, each site has produced a rectangular seal of *c.* 700 B.C., of a characteristically East Greek type: a recumbent lion is modelled on the back, and the
devices are a man beside a sphinx (Phanai), and a sphinx approaching a tree
(Emporio). Other seals of this class have turned up at Camirus, and on Delos,
Paros, and Ithaca.[38]

Caria

The chief settlements of the Dorian Greeks were at Cnidus and Halicarnassos,
each situated on the southern shore of a long peninsula.[39] During this period
they are known to us only from surface sherds; but we are better informed about
the native Lelegians, the neighbours of Halicarnassos. Their towns are usually
on fortified hilltops; for their tombs they favoured rectangular chambers in
corbelled masonry, each approached by a dromos, and covered with a tumulus
of rubble. These tombs were designed as family vaults, and the type perseveres
from the eleventh until the fifth century. We have already remarked (p. 97) on
the tumuli of ancient Termera (Asarlik), containing urn cremations, and pieces
of clay coffins with incised designs of East Greek LG character.[40] A tumulus at
ancient Pedasa (Gökçeler) apparently contained Geometric pottery and bronze
fibulae with a globe on the bow.[41] Another group of eighth-century pots, including some large vessels with elaborate decoration, comes from a tomb at Dirmil,
possibly the ancient Termile.[42]

To the north of the Halicarnassos peninsula, the small Greek town of Iasos is
situated on a promontory in a corner of the Bargylian gulf. The settlement has
yielded a fair amount of eighth-century Geometric pottery, associated with
fragmentary house walls and floors. On the isthmus, just outside the inhabited
area, lies the cemetery of cist inhumations and pithos burials, to which allusion
has already been made (p. 97). Most of the published pottery here is of MG II
character, but a few skyphoi have loose chevron designs which must go into the
early years of LG.[43]

From Iasos it is an easy journey into the plain of Mylasa, some 20km. inland.
Here we are well beyond the limit of early Greek settlement, and it was here that
the Hecatomnid dynasty of Caria rose to power in later times. Before Mausolus
moved the town of Mylasa down to the site of modern Milas, it most probably
occupied the stronghold of Beçin (or Peçin) at the southern edge of the plain.[44]
With this site go three large cist graves containing local LG and Subgeometric
pottery, and bronze fibulae chiefly of Type IV.9. The graves were lined with
rough walling, and were designed for multiple inhumations; grs. 2 and 3 contained fifteen and nine skeletons respectively. A few kilometres further east lies
the sanctuary of the Carian god Sinuri, where the earliest offerings include
pottery in the same style as that from Beçin. Further inland still, two Sub-

FIG. 84 CHIOT, CARIAN, AND IONIC LG POTTERY
(a) Chios, *Emporio* no. 35 (reconstruction), H. *c.* 33;
(b,c) London market, Carian style; (d) Izmir, from Miletus, H. 4;
(e) Izmir, from Old Smyrna, H. 22

geometric pots (a squat oinochoe and a shallow kotyle) were recovered from the region of Hellenistic Stratoniceia, found with cremation ashes in a pithos.

Caria produced a distinct LG style, whose progress can now be followed through whole pots from graves. A local development from MG can be seen in the Iasos cemetery, where the series appears to end around 725 B.C.; the pottery from the three Beçin cists begins at the beginning of LG (*c.* 740 B.C.?), and takes us well into the seventh century, probably into the second quarter.

The most individual shape is a plump amphoriskos whose broad neck passes into the body without articulation; a larger version in coarse fabric serves as an urn at Iasos.[45] Oinochoai, after the end of MG, tend to be of squat proportions;[46] several large ones from the Dirmil tomb, carrying unruly Subgeometric ornament, have sharp carinations above and below the belly. Jugs, like amphoriskoi, lack articulation, and some plump specimens are handmade in coarse ware.

Skyphoi, of the standard LG shape, are at first the favourite drinking-vessels; they are decorated with vertical wavy lines, or floating chevrons, or small sets of concentric circles. There are also high-handled kantharoi at Iasos, and deep cups of Dodecanesian type at both sites; the latter sometimes carry rich meander and lozenge designs,[47] but most are coated with glaze. The nicked kotyle, a Rhodian invention, occurs in fragments (perhaps imports?) at the Iasos settlement, but not at all in the cemetery. On the other hand, its frequency at Beçin implies that it had ousted the skyphos in later LG, not least because all the kotylai from there are based on the tri-metopal version, which was hardly current even in Rhodes before 700 B.C. Carian LG imitations are deeper than their Rhodian counterparts; in the decoration, some keep to the original repertoire of lozenges, Trees (fig. 84b), and birds; on others the panels are taller and narrower, and local motifs creep in – for instance, thin cross-hatched leaves (fig. 84c) and one or two columns of floating dashes. The end of the LG series is marked by a kotyle combining birds, leaves, and dashes with a sketchy Orientalizing volute tree.[48] Thereafter we see a shallower Subgeometric version,[49] not unconnected with the Rhodian bird-bowl.

Ionia

Today the ruins of Miletus are 7km. inland, surrounded by two millennia of alluvial silt from the river Meander; but in early Greek times the city was gradually spreading across a large peninsula, which pointed northwards into what was then the gulf of Latmos. Many of the Geometric remains have come to light on a low headland on the western shore, above the Mycenaean settlement, and below or near the foundations of two successive temples of Athena (seventh and fifth centuries).

Much in evidence are a number of oval structures, each consisting of a stone or clay platform within an enclosing wall. The excavators explain them as shrines built by the Carians living within the Ionic city, the descendants of the Carians who had occupied the site before the arrival of the first Ionic settlers around 1050 B.C.[50] Apart from one seventh-century example, these oval buildings seem to go well back into the Geometric period. One of them, of LG date, rests upon the remains of the Mycenaean fortification wall, and below the foundations of the fifth-century Athenaion. Another underlies LG house walls in the southern quarter, and with it are associated two handmade terracotta horses of a very primitive appearance.[51]

The domestic architecture is less well preserved; but one substantial Geometric house, east of the temple, has a footing three courses deep, and a well-built drain near by.[52] This house fell victim to a fire which the excavators date to c. 700 B.C.;[53] possibly not a general conflagration, since it left no trace nearer the Athenaion.[54]

In moments of danger, a ready refuge was available on the hill now called

Kalabak Tepe ('Hat Hill'), which commands the root of the peninsula. Perhaps this was the acropolis in Geometric times; eighth-century house walls have been reported there, as well as a carefully laid terrace wall which forestalls the polygonal masonry of the Archaic period.[55]

The LG pottery from Miletus is too fragmentary to allow a clear view of the local style. A connection with Rhodes is apparent through the imports and imitations of bird-kotylai. Otherwise there is no steadfast attempt to apply the metopal system; the local preference is for small sets of circles, dots, battlements, ladders, and scribbles, often loosely composed. Rare ventures into representational drawing include scenes of swimming birds, and padded dancers with triangular stomachs (fig. 84d). A Milesian Orientalizing style begins soon after 700 B.C., but Subgeometric decoration continues in the form of horizontal S's, diagonal crosses, check pattern, and mannered elaborations of the meander.[56]

The territory of Miletus embraced the oracular shrine of Apollo at Didyma. Recent excavations there have traced two parallel walls of the earliest *temenos*, within the area covered by the open-air cella of the vast Hellenistic temple. The oldest pottery published from the site goes back to the end of the eighth century.[57]

The small town of Melia still had a considerable Carian element among its people, to judge from its burial customs (p. 97). In LG times the acropolis was fortified with an oval circuit of rough walling, enclosing an area *c.* 200 × 90m. A bastion, an inner flight of steps, and ten internal buttresses were added, perhaps a little later. Remarkably few traces survive of the contemporary buildings inside – perhaps a sign of the thoroughness with which the town was destroyed by the other Ionic cities[58] soon after 700 B.C.

The early Ionic city of Ephesus still eludes discovery. Trials on the north and west slopes of mount Pion produced a few sherds of *c.* 700 B.C., but no architecture to go with them. Among the rich votives at the sanctuary of Artemis, only a single sherd goes back as far as LG.[59]

Smyrna, on the contrary, is much better known in this period, although much important evidence – architectural and ceramic – awaits publication. Unlike Miletus and Ephesus, the site (Bayraklı) was never encumbered with large Hellenistic and Roman edifices. After its destruction by the Lydians in *c.* 600 B.C. the place became an insignificant village, and eventually Alexander the Great persuaded the Smyrnaeans to refound their city where modern Izmir now stands.

Old Smyrna, like Miletus, stood on a promontory from which the sea has subsequently receded. From *c.* 850 B.C. onwards the town was protected by a series of fortification walls, which have been fully studied; some idea of the houses can be obtained from preliminary reports. They were built on mud brick on a stone foundation, each with only one room. Within the Geometric period, two main phases have been distinguished.[60] During the ninth century, rectangular plans were in fashion; one of the larger houses (6 × 10m.) preserves carbonized traces of wooden cross-beams for a flat or lean-to roof, as well as pithoi and unbaked clay basins for storage.[61] This house almost abuts on to the first town wall, the earliest known circuit of the Greek Iron Age. It was constructed of mud brick, reinforced with a stone fill and facing in the outer foundations; especially remarkable are the fine ashlar blocks on one of its tower faces.

After a destruction, the town was rebuilt from *c.* 750 B.C. onwards. The circuit was remodelled on a more massive scale (fig. 96a), the thickness being increased from 4·75m. to 9·50m.; an interior stone fill was added to the foundations, faced with roughly fitted polygonal blocks.[62] The LG houses, however, were hardly worthy of these fortifications. Flimsy cottages are dotted chaotically over the excavated area, usually oval or apsidal (fig. 96c), rarely rectangular; one small circular structure, with a basement entirely built of stone, was probably a granary (fig. 96b). The town was in danger of becoming a slum; but another severe destruction in the early seventh century,[63] perhaps caused by Gyges of Lydia, led to a radical replanning of the town on more spacious and regular lines.

The fragmentary krater, fig. 84e, allows a glimpse of the local LG style at a fairly early stage. The quatrefoils and swastikas are drawn from the Atticizing repertoire, but the general design recalls the Chiot system, thin horizontal strips flanked either side by vertical columns. A little later, Rhodian influence appears in the metopal decoration of nicked kotylai, although some bear the chevron panel[64] characteristic of the Corinthian LG prototype. Around 700 B.C. the krater was superseded by the dinos; the only published fragment shows an early rendering of the seven-stringed lyre,[65] an improvement on the four-stringed version seen in eighth-century representations.[66] Its invention is ascribed to the Aeolic poet Terpander of Antissa, who flourished *c.* 675 B.C.

Alongside the painted Geometric pottery, the Smyrnaeans also manufactured a grey monochrome ware, which was plentiful in the earliest Greek levels, scarce during the eighth century, but popular once again in the seventh. This ware is ultimately derived from Anatolian grey pottery of the second millennium; during our period it was especially characteristic of the regions settled by Aeolic Greeks, to which we now turn.

The North-East Aegean

Herodotus (i.150) records that the first Ionians of Smyrna were Colophonian interlopers, who wrested the town from Aeolian Greeks already settled there. Previously, Smyrna had marked the southern limit of the Aeolian region, which extended as far north as Pitane, and also included the large offshore island of Lesbos. These Aeolians, according to literary sources,[67] had migrated from their former homes in Boeotia and Thessaly at least as early as the parallel movement of Ionians; yet the archaeological record casts very little light on them before the late eighth century, apart from their brief tenure of Smyrna. This gap in our knowledge is due partly to lack of excavation and research, but partly also to the comparatively unhelpful nature of the material so far recovered. Unlike all other Greeks, the eastern Aeolians of our period did not make any painted Geometric pottery; we are thus denied what is elsewhere the most effective means of constructing a sure local sequence. True, from *c.* 730 B.C. onwards, a few Geometric imports supply clues to chronology and external relations; thus East Greek LG pots of Rhodian character have been found at Antissa on Lesbos, Pitane, Myrina, Cyme, and the site of Burunjuk in the Hermus valley thought by some scholars to have been the ancient Larisa.[68] In addition, Antissa received some LG imports from Corinth and the Cyclades, and after 700 B.C. Burunjuk began to make its own

Subgeometric and Orientalizing pottery. But otherwise we are driven back upon the accomplished but somewhat featureless grey monochrome ware, the only fine ware made in the Aeolian region during the Geometric period.

The most informative Aeolian site is Antissa, a small *polis* on the north-west coast of Lesbos. Of especial interest are two apsidal buildings, one super-imposed upon the other, and facing in opposite directions; cross-walls divided the earlier structure into four rooms, the later one into two. The large dimensions (max. 17·25 × 5·50m.), and the hearth in the later building, make it seem probable that both were temples. The second building, with its sophisticated polygonal masonry, can hardly have been constructed before the beginning of the seventh century. Its predecessor, to judge from the Rhodian and Cycladic sherds associated with it, was in use until 700 B.C., and possibly a little later;[69] its con-struction may go back as far as the ninth century, but a date after 800 B.C. is also possible.[70]

Both buildings produced plenty of grey monochrome pottery fired in a reduc-ing kiln, a fabric of Anatolian character which had been at home on Lesbos since the Middle Bronze Age and was to persist as late as the sixth century. The pottery from the earlier apsidal temple, though fragmentary, illustrates the shapes current in Geometric times, many of which are related to the Geometric reper-toire elsewhere: for example, kraters, bellied kantharoi with high handles, plates or dishes with reflex handles, neck-handled amphorae, and trefoil-lipped oinochoai. Any ornament is always incised; the usual motifs are unruly meander designs of East Greek character, hatched triangles, and multiple scribbles or wavy lines done with a comb – a traditional notion inherited from the grey ware of the late second millennium. There is, indeed, a Late Bronze Age level immedi-ately under the apsidal buildings, but it remains doubtful whether occupation was continuous all through the Dark Ages. At present we have no reliable archaeological evidence concerning the coming of the first Aeolians to Lesbos. We can only surmise that they employed indigenous potters to manufacture shapes of Greek character, and it is natural to look for parallels in their original mainland homes, with which some connections were surely maintained after their migration. In fact, three of the most individual forms have counterparts in ninth-century Thessaly: a pedestalled krater with two horizontal and two vertical handles, an ovoid lekythos, and an oinochoe with ridges below the lip and between neck and shoulder;[71] also worthy of note is the frequency of the high-handled kantharos, apparently the favourite drinking-vessel in both regions.

During the later eighth century the Troad, too, began to receive Aeolic settlers, probably from Lesbos. At two sites on the west coast, Hamaxitus and Colonae, the evidence is limited to surface sherds;[72] but the fully published excavations at Troy itself are a rich source of information. Here, to judge from the earliest Geometric imports,[73] the city was refounded around 750 B.C. (Troy VIII), after lying desolate for some 350 years. From the start, most of the pottery is Aeolic grey ware, often incised with the same kind of Geometric ornament as at Antissa. There is also a fine-walled painted fabric of Subgeometric character, called G 2-3 after the *locus* where it was first noted: typical shapes are amphorae, jugs, dinoi, deep cups, and deep kantharoi with vertical walls; decoration is neat but spare, normally limited to rims and shoulders, and consisting largely of hori-

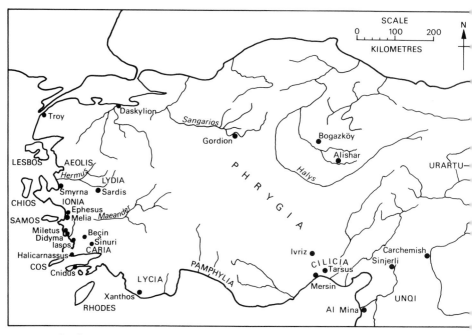

FIG. 85 ANATOLIA IN THE EARLY IRON AGE

zontal S's, vertical zigzags, and spiral hooks perhaps borrowed from Corinthian imports. The excavators of Troy believe this ware to be imported; its home should be somewhere within the Aeolic region, since it has also turned up in both of the apsidal buildings at Antissa, and in an early sanctuary on Samothrace (an island not inhabited by Greeks before 700 B.C.).[74] The deep kantharos is the prototype of the *karchesion*, a Lesbian drinking-vessel mentioned in the poetry of Sappho. Similar ornament, though on different shapes, occurs on the pottery from a cremation cemetery on the non-Greek island of Lemnos.[75]

The Anatolian Hinterland

A hundred kilometres due east of Rhodes lies the mountainous land of Lycia, inhabited by a hardy and robust Anatolian people. Xanthos, their chief town, was first settled in the late eighth century, as we learn from a handful of Rhodian and Cycladic LG sherds from the deepest levels. A local Geometric ware takes some of its ideas from the Aegean, but the techniques – Black-on-Red and Bichrome – are those of Cilicia and Cyprus. Similar painted pottery has been found over a wide area of south-west Anatolia, inland from Caria up the Meander valley, and over the upland regions into Pamphylia. Surface sherds from these inland parts betray some acquaintance with East Greek LG, seen in the nicked rims of drinking-vessels, and cross-hatched meander designs.[76]

Between the Ionians and the rising kingdom of Lydia there were intermittent exchanges; hardly surprising, since only 90km. inland from Old Smyrna stands the Lydian capital, Sardis. A deep sounding there has revealed a series of floors going back from the seventh century into the Late Bronze Age, interspersed with gravel from the river Pactolus which often burst its banks. Greek affinities have been claimed for the local painted pottery from Submycenaean onwards, perhaps lending colour to a statement by Herodotus (i.7.4) that a Heraclid dynasty had reigned here for 505 years before the throne was usurped by Gyges the Mermnad (c. 680 B.C.). The frequency of pendent semicircles might suggest some links with the Aegean between 900 and 750 B.C.; in LG times there are further local imitations of Greek Geometric, a few imported sherds from eastern Greece, and – eventually – Corinthian kotylai of c. 700 B.C.[77]

It was not until the reign of Gyges that the Lydians became strong enough to threaten the Ionian Greeks; but another power, further to the east, reached its zenith during the years around 700 B.C. Central Anatolia was then dominated by the kingdom of Phrygia, whose territory extended from the Propontis to the bend of the river Halys. In Assyrian records its people appear as the Mushki, whose ruler Mita blocked the advance of king Sargon II between 717 and 709 B.C. Here we may surely discern the resplendent monarch whom the Greeks remembered as Midas son of Gordios, whose touch turned everything to gold, who married a Greek princess from Aeolic Cyme[78] and who offered his own throne to Apollo at Delphi – the first foreign ruler to make a dedication at that sanctuary.[79] He – or a later king of that name – took his own life when his kingdom was overrun by Cimmerian nomads in 696 B.C. according to Eusebius, or in 676 B.C. if we follow Julius Africanus.

Excavations at Gordion, the capital city, have helped to bring this semi-legendary figure into historical focus. A severe destruction by fire is attributed to the Cimmerians, after which the main citadel ceased to be occupied for a considerable time. One of the latest objects from the debris is a local ivory plaque showing a cavalryman with a Corinthian helmet, perhaps a Greek mercenary soldier;[80] its style and equipment are easier to reconcile with the later destruction date given by Africanus, although neither source commands very much authority.

Before this disaster, the *floruit* of the Phrygian kingdom was brief, perhaps not more than two generations; yet the finds of this period, both from the city and from the impressive royal tumulus burials, reveal a material culture which was in several respects far in advance of the Greek world. This is true especially of the architecture and the bronzework. The buildings – whether princely halls or artisans' workshops – were spaciously designed on the *megaron* plan; the largest residence, evidently a palace, measures 32 × 19m. and had an internal gallery. Much use was made of timber, both for bedding courses and for framing the mud-brick walls; some floors were adorned with pebble mosaic, some walls with simple fresco designs. Gabled roofs, whose low incline foreshadows later Greek temples, are suggested at Gordion by sketchy 'doodles' incised on stone, and by monumental rock façades in western Phrygia, which may go back into the eighth century.[81]

It is the bronzes, however, which attracted most attention in the Aegean world. To start with the simplest form: the fibula with a symmetrical and semicircular bow (Type XII), often imitated in the East Greek area (e.g., fig. 80d), is a Phrygian invention, occurring in many varieties at Gordion. Its shape was adapted to form the handle of the Phrygian belt, a type which found many imitators in the Ionic region, especially on Chios. A Phrygian class of shallow bowl, to which ring-handles were attached through horizontal spools, reached Greek sanctuaries on both sides of the Aegean. Other bronze types made at Gordion are not Phrygian inventions, but adapted from lands further east: for instance, the mesomphalic phiale, derived from North Syrian or Phoenician models; and the cauldron with protomes in the form of bulls' heads or male sirens ('Assurattaschen'), also found in the distant kingdom of Urartu in the Armenian highlands. All these vessels were locally imitated by Greeks from c. 700 B.C. onwards; knowledge of them may have come overland via Phrygia, or (more probably) by sea from the North Syrian emporia (p. 363).

The Phrygians were especially rich in timber and wool, and by good fortune we can admire their skill in working each of these perishable materials. The burial chamber of the largest tumulus at Gordion (MMT), itself lined with cedar wood, contained a wealth of wooden furniture which had been miraculously preserved in the dry atmosphere. A wooden screen, perhaps the back of a throne such as Midas offered at Delphi, is a magnificent piece of marquetry;[82] its entire surface is covered with patterns in dark yew inlaid into light boxwood, the chief motifs being disjointed swastikas, lozenge nets, and square labyrinthine compositions. From another tumulus (Gordion III) a few scraps of cloth were recovered, adorned with brightly coloured zigzag patterns; but a fuller impression of Phrygian textiles can be obtained from the rock relief at Ivriz, just within the western limit of the Neo-Hittite region.[83] Here king Urpalla (or Warpalawas) of Tyana wears two garments: the outer mantle is fastened by a fibula of Type XII.9, while the long robe underneath carries the same kind of rectilinear ornament (including the disjointed swastikas) as the Gordion throne, organized in small square units. This monument can hardly have been carved after c. 720 B.C., since Urpalla is known to have submitted to king Tiglath-Pileser III of Assyria in 738 B.C.

The potters of Gordion worked in two fabrics: the monochrome grey found all over north-western Anatolia, and (c. 725–675 B.C.) a most accomplished painted ware, which borrowed its close rectilinear ornament from textiles and wood-work, adding metopal panels of birds and animals drawn in outline. It may be fruitless to look for any direct currents of influence on or from Greek Geometric pottery,[84] since no Greek vessels reached Phrygia until after the Cimmerian destruction, and no Phrygian pottery of any period has been reported from the Aegean. Yet it is quite likely that some of the more intricate rectilinear designs of Rhodian and Samian LG owe something to Phrygian marquetry;[85] the adoption of the disjointed swastika on the wooden stand from Samos (fig. 83b) suggests that Midas' throne at Delphi was by no means the only piece of Phrygian furniture to reach the Greek world.

Conclusions

By western Aegean standards, the LG art of eastern Greece is conservative, ill-disciplined, and somewhat unadventurous. Figured work was rarely attempted on pottery, and a loose Geometric style persevered well into the early seventh century. In working gold and bronze, or in engraving seals, no East Greek centre could vie with the finest achievements of Athens or the Peloponnese. This lack of artistic initiative goes with a rather passive attitude towards the outside world, also noticeable in earlier periods (p. 70). Not that the East Greeks suffered from parochial isolation; on the contrary, the oriental imports to Rhodes and Samos are as numerous and varied as anywhere in Greece. Nevertheless we are faced with the paradox that the Greeks who lived furthest to the east were among the last to feel the quickening influence of oriental art.

Only the Rhodians showed any positive signs of commercial energy. Within the eastern Aegean area, the circulation of their nicked kotylai was the chief cause of any overriding unity between the various East Greek LG schools. Further afield, these popular drinking-vessels reached the western colonies, mainland Greece, and – in some quantity – Al Mina, where we assume them to be the chattels of the Rhodian merchants who began to reside there from c. 725 B.C. onwards. Against this native Rhodian initiative we must set the unguent vessels made of local clay but copying Cypriot, Phoenician, and North Syrian types in shape, decoration, and fabric. Just as close copies of Euboean LG were made in Etruria by resident Euboean potters (p. 232), even so we must admit the presence in Rhodes of Phoenician unguent factories, now probably staffed by their own potters (cf. p. 68 n. 24). The chief centre for these shapes is Ialysos, a traditional outpost of Phoenicians according to later Rhodian historians;[86] there, among a Greek majority, we may visualize a small enclave of Phoenicians, engaged in an unguent trade which certainly went back to the ninth century (p. 67). One of their products, the aryballos with spaghetti ornament (fig. 79d), was widely marketed, but only in a westerly direction: often to the western colonies, sometimes to Thera, Delos, and Aegina, never to other East Greek centres, and never to the eastern Mediterranean where the Levantine originals were readily available.

Rhodes and Samos clearly lay on the route of Levantine ships entering the Aegean, to judge from the copious oriental imports found on both islands. At least six ivories of the Phoenician and North Syrian schools have been recorded from Rhodes, corresponding to groups discovered at the Assyrian palace of Nimrud in contexts not earlier than the eighth century;[87] the finest is Lindos 1582, a nude female figurine probably made in Hama,[88] of a type which provided the inspiration for the masterpiece of the Athenian school (pp. 130–2 fig. 42b-d). The Samian Heraion received Egyptian as well as Levantine ivories, terracottas from Cyprus, and bronzes from Egypt, Cyprus, Phrygia, North Syria, Luristan, and possibly Urartu. All these *orientalia* came from deposits not closed before 700 B.C.; yet some of the Levantine ivories, at least, belong to eighth-century types,[89] and would have been displayed in the sanctuary for some time before they were discarded. Also worth mentioning are the North Syrian seals of the Lyre-Player group (cf. fig. 75f), which reached Rhodes, Samos, and Chios in considerable quantity.

Levantine trade hardly touched the Greek cities of Asia Minor. For them the eighth century was a time of consolidation, punctuated by minor commotions. Of especial interest are the city walls of Smyrna and Melia, in view of the rarity of Greek fortifications during the Geometric period. Perhaps they reflect the insecurity of dwellers in a large foreign land; yet the only recorded wars of this time were between Greeks. It could be that the damage at Smyrna, prior to the rebuilding of the walls in the mid-eighth century, was caused by the seizure of the Aeolic town by the Ionians.[90] The circuit of walls at Melia, a more rough-and-ready affair, suggests a hasty attempt to defend the town against the concerted Ionian expedition which eventually destroyed it; this conflict must be placed soon after 700 B.C., before the Ionian Greeks had to face any common danger from the expansion of the Lydian kingdom.

These Greek cities were indeed fortunate, in that they were able to consolidate their power during this period without being threatened by any large and organized Anatolian state. In the south-west, the Carians lived in small communities, some within or near Greek cities on the coast (Halicarnassos, Iasos, Miletus, Melia) and others in their own inland settlements; even there they became sufficiently hellenized to manufacture their own style of LG pottery, under Dodecanesian influence. The Lydians showed little interest in their western neighbours before the rise of Gyges; he was probably the cause of early seventh-century destructions at Smyrna and Miletus,[91] but his further designs against the Ionians were foiled by the marauding expeditions of Cimmerian nomads. The Phrygians had already established a strong, centralized kingdom by the late eighth century, but most of their energies were absorbed in keeping the Assyrians at bay on their south-eastern frontier. With the Greeks their only common boundary would have been with the Aeolians, both in the upper Caïcus valley, and eventually in the north-west after the Aeolian expansion into the Troad. Perhaps it was they who, for the time being, obstructed any Greek settlement within the Propontis, for which there is no archaeological confirmation until well after 700 B.C.[92] At all events, the Greeks remembered the great Midas as a monarch well disposed towards themselves, and friendly relations are also implied by the export and imitations of useful Phrygian articles in bronze – bowls, fibulae, and belts. But, as we shall see in due course, the Phrygians played only a very minor part in bringing about the great Orientalizing movement in Greek pictorial art.

NOTES

1 *GKG* fig. 60.
2 *GKG* figs. 51–2, pls. 91–2; cf. our fig. 82a (Cos).
3 e.g., Frankfort, *The Art and Architecture of the Ancient Near East* (1963), 192 fig. 93, from Arslan Tash.
4 e.g., *GKG* figs. 54, 61.
5 cf. *Exochi* 160 fig. 224.

6 Ialysos gr. 58, *ClRh* 3 fig. 93.
7 Adult inhumation, e.g., Camirus gr. 25 (*ClRh* 6–7, 79 f.), is extremely rare.
8 e.g., Ialysos gr. 62, Exochi grs. A–C.
9 See especially Ialysos grs. 8, 56, 58, 62 (*ClRh* 3); Camirus grs. 22, 25 (*ClRh* 6–7); Exochi grs. A, B, F.
10 Higgins, *GRJ* 106–7.
11 Ohly 70 n. 11 fig. 38.
12 *BM Cat. Jewellery* no. 1158 pl. 13.
13 e.g., *Ann* 8–9 (1925–26), 267 fig. 48.
14 Higgins, *Greek TCs* 20 pl. 6e.
15 e.g., *GGP* pl. 63e.
16 e.g., *GKG* pl. 92. For more palm-and-cable vases from Cos see *Samos* V, pl. 89 nos. 496, 499.
17 G. E. Bean and J. M. Cook, *BSA* 52 (1957), 119–26.
18 Some doubt still obscures the date of Altar V: according to H. Walter, not earlier than the second Hekatompedon (*Samos* V, 47, 86, 'vor 650'); but Buschor preferred a date still within the eighth century (*AM* 58 (1933), 150, 163 fig. 15). The few pieces of pottery published from the fill (e.g., fig. 82b,c) seem not later than 690 B.C.
19 *JHS* 91 (1971), 203.
20 *GGP* pl. 64d,e.
21 e.g., *AM* 58 (1933), Beil. 18, 1 (Cycladic); ibid. Beil. 39, 1 and *Samos* V, nos. 282–8 (Euboean).
22 *PE* fig. 51a,b.
23 cf. the horses on the splendid krater Argos C 201, *GGP* pl. 30e.
24 Walter, *Samos* V, 47 ff.
25 e.g., *AM* 74 (1959), Beil. 33, 3–4.
26 *AM* 65 (1940), Beil. 82 no. 1193.
27 Ibid. Beil. 58 no. 448; cf. above p. 115 fig. 34e.
28 R. V. Nicholls, *Blaiklock Essays* (1970), 15.
29 e.g., Higgins, *Greek TCs* pl. 6e.
30 e.g., *AM* 72 (1957), Beil. 62, 2.
31 G. Schmidt, *Samos* XII, 96.
32 Ohly, *AM* 68 (1953), 93. Aethlius, a local historian of Classical times, refers to the earliest cult-image as a wooden plank (*sanis*): *FGH* 536 F3.
33 *GKG* pl. 71.
34 *AM* 74 (1959), 16 ff., Beil. 26, 1–3, from the first inundation deposit.
35 ibid. Beil. 27, 1.
36 *BSA* 35 (1934–35), pl. 35, 28–36; *Greek Emporio* fig. 64.
37 Boardman, *Greek Emporio* 119–20 fig. 74.
38 Boardman, *IGems* 154.
39 On the Archaic and earlier site of Cnidus (Burgaz) see Bean and Cook, *BSA* 47 (1952), 173 ff.
40 e.g., square hooks, rosettes within circles: *BMCat.* I.1, A 1110–16.
41 Maiuri, *Ann* 4–5 (1921–22), 427 ff.; *ClRh* I, 184.
42 C. Özgünel, *Belleten* 40 (1976), 3ff. A Protogeometric group from this site has already been published: Desborough, *GDA* 180–3 with refs.
43 e.g., *Ann* 47–8 (1969–70), 472 fig. 12c top left; 473 fig. 13a bottom right.
44 J. M. Cook, *AR* 1960, 51 fig. 23.
45 *Ann* 43–4 (1965–66), 503 ff. figs. 122–3.
46 *Belleten* 35 (1971), pl. 5, 17 (early); *AM* 12 (1887), 226 fig. 3 (very late).
47 Iasos: *Ann* 43–4 (1965–66), 417 fig. 25; 45–6 (1967–68), 557 f. fig. 23c; cf. our fig. 78a.
48 *Belleten* 35 (1971), pl. 29, 36.
49 ibid. pl. 30, 48; *AM* 12 (1887), 227 fig. 4.
50 cf. Hdt. i.146.2.
51 *IM* 19–20 (1969–70), 119 f. fig. 3, Beil. 21, 3–4 .The lines along the back recall the Mycenaean type, e.g., *BSA* 66 (1971), pl. 27a, 53–197.

52 cf. Snodgrass, *DAG* 429 fig. 136.

53 P. Hommel, *IM* 9–10 (1959–60), 38 ff. fig. 1, Beil. 19, 58–9. The three pots published from the burnt layer look no later than MG, but many LG burnt sherds were recovered from elsewhere.

54 cf. A. Mallwitz, *IM* 18 (1968), 123.

55 A. von Gerkan, *Milet* I.8, 27 ff. pl. 16, 2. The pottery which dates these walls remains unpublished.

56 e.g., *IM* 7 (1957), pl. 38.

57 *IM* 13–14 (1963–64), 42 ff.

58 G. Huxley, *The Early Ionians* (1966), 47–8, with refs.

59 *GGP* 297 nn 2, 3.

60 For the late Protogeometric oval house see Desborough, *GDA* 183–4 pl. 37.

61 Akurgal, *Die Kunst Anatoliens* (Berlin, 1951), 9–11 fig. 2.

62 R. V. Nicholls, *BSA* 53–4 (1958–59), 51 fig. 7, Wall 2; pl. 10b,c.

63 The latest sherds published from these houses include some from Corinthian imports of 700–675 B.C., with rayed bases, e.g., ibid. 140–1 no. 33; pls. 23–4 nos. 42, 58, 69.

64 *GGP* pl. 63c.

65 *JHS* 71 (1951), 248 fig. 8.

66 R. Tölle, *Frühgriechische Reigentänze* (Waldsassen, 1964), Beil. 5, 1–25.

67 See Huxley, *The Early Ionians* 26–9.

68 Pitane: Schweitzer, *GKG* 106 f.; for the other sites, *GGP* 297–8.

69 W. Lamb, *BSA* 32 (1931–32), 58, mention of Rhodian bird-bowls; also pl. 23, 9.

70 Ostensibly the earliest finds are three sherds of Protogeometric character, ibid. 56 fig. 9a–c, from 'inside *and below* the early apsidal building' (my italics); on these pieces cf. Desborough, *PGP* 217–18.

71 *BSA* 31 (1930–31), 170 fig. 3; 32 (1931–32), 53 pl. 21 nos. 12, 14, 15; cf. *BSA* 31 (1930–31), pl. 9 no. 136 and pl. 5 nos. 70, 71 (Marmariani); 18 (1911–12), 16 fig. 10, 4 (Halos); and *PGRT* pl. 4 no. 19 (Kapakli).

72 J. M. Cook, *The Troad* (Oxford, 1973), 218, 231.

73 *GGP* 376 no. 6.

74 *Troy* IV, 253–5; *Hesperia* 21 (1952), 34 ff.

75 *Ann* 15–16 (1932–33), figs. 168, 192, 222.

76 *AS* 14 (1964), 30 ff. figs. 5, 7.

77 *BASOR* 186 (1967), fig. 8; 162 (1961), fig. 5 top row; fig. 9.

78 Aristotle fr. 611.37 (ed. Rose); cf. H. T. Wade-Gery, *The Poet of the Iliad* (Cambridge, 1952), 7 n. 21; Huxley, *GRBS* 2 (1959), 94–7.

79 Hdt. i.14.2.

80 *AJA* 64 (1960), 240 pl. 60 fig. 25c.

81 E. Haspels, *The Highlands of Phrygia* (Princeton, 1971), 103–4 figs. 8, 157–8; but cf. Young, *Hesperia* 38 (1969), 273 ff.

82 *GKG* fig. 50.

83 Barnett, *JHS* 68 (1948), 8–9 fig. 6.

84 *GGP* 378–9.

85 Schweitzer, *GKG* 89, 111.

86 *BICS* 16 (1969), 1 ff.

87 Barnett, *NI* 45 (*Lindos* I, nos. 420–1, 1581–2); 51 fig. 15, 134 fig. 56 (Ialysos).

88 Riis, *Sukas* I, 170 fig. 61a.

89 Barnett, *JHS* 68 (1948), 3–4 pls. 1b, 3b.

90 E. Akurgal, *Die Kunst Anatoliens* 11–12: for other views see *BSA* 53–4 (1958–59), 13–14 (J. M. Cook) and 123 (R. V. Nicholls). A secure *terminus ante quem* is 688 B.C., when an Ionian from Smyrna was victorious at the Olympic games: Pausanias v.8.7.

91 Hdt. i.14.

92 A. J. Graham, *JHS* 91 (1971), 41–2.

10 Crete

It remains to consider the great island of Crete, at the time of her final emergence from the Dark Ages.

Owing to the local tradition of building in stone rather than in mud brick, traces of eighth-century architecture are more substantial here than in most other districts; one thinks especially of the settlements at Phaistos, Vrokastro, and Kavousi, and the sanctuary of Apollo at Dreros. The cave shrines of Ida and Dicte have yielded a rich variety of metal offerings, among which the votive bronze shields from the Idaean cave are of outstanding interest; their designs in relief form the chief corpus of Cretan figured art during this period, orientalizing in style and theme, yet beginning well back in the eighth century. Far less spectacular is the local pottery, where figured decoration is extremely rare; but with pottery we must begin, because it provides the only secure foundation for chronology, and also affords the clearest view of regional variations within the island.

LG Pottery

First, some broad geographical distinctions. A full sequence from the Knossos area illustrates the progress of the most advanced Cretan school, and the most sensitive to outside influence. This north-central style can be traced as far west as Eleutherna, and as far east as the gulf of Mirabello. A southern school, based on the Mesara plain and the surrounding foothills, is deeply influenced by Knossos, but more conservative in some respects. The eastern peninsula, from Vrokastro onwards, favoured a wild and undisciplined style showing very few links with the central schools. In the far west, practically nothing is known about the pottery of this period.

In the Knossian repertoire the most imposing shape is the ovoid cremation pithos, which illustrates the full development of the north-central style throughout this period. Until *c.* 750 B.C. these pithoi were exuberantly adorned in the Attic MG II manner (p. 99 fig. 31c). Thereafter, during the LG phase, Athenian influence wanes, but the decoration remains predominantly dark-ground; indeed, the ornament now occupies less space than before, often being confined to the shoulder. Many designs are still composed in the MG way, with a large central panel surrounded by ancillaries. On the LG pithos, fig. 86f, the panel is stopped by metopes – a typically Cretan arrangement also applied to LG kraters, oinochoai (fig. 86a,h), and the larger skyphoi and cups. Many motifs, too, survive from the previous phase: meanders, battlements, and multiple zigzags in the main panels; outlined tongues and hatched or dotted lozenges in narrower zones, where rows of thin leaves are also popular. To enliven the dark zones, painting in added white becomes increasingly common throughout LG: at first for small circles only (fig. 86f), but by the end of LG white may be used for any motif, and even to reinforce reserved lines (fig. 86g).

In general, the LG style of Knossos is not very enterprising; but one workshop forms a distinguished exception. It produced a fine series of plump, four-handled pithoi on tripod ribbon feet; related in style are some large cups (e.g., fig. 86e) and – less closely – some ovoid lekythoi with a ridge on the neck.[1] The decoration is chiefly metopal, and the metopes are often filled by a large predatory bird with fan-tail and raised, curved wing (fig. 86g). Sometimes a whole family of birds is indicated by several necks and heads emerging from the same body (fig. 86e). Of the accompanying linear motifs most are peculiar to Crete, and were probably invented within this Bird Workshop: the most characteristic are a lozenge design, interrupted either by a quatrefoil (fig. 86g) or by a diagonal cross (as fig. 86a,f); a circle, quartered and dotted; a square guilloche, also dotted;[2] and a simple lotus volute (fig. 86g). The last two motifs, together with a Tree of Life,[3] appear only on the latest pithoi from this workshop, around 710–700 B.C.; these explore the way towards the local Orientalizing style, which manifests itself in a class of polychrome pithoi on tripod feet, brilliantly adorned in red, white, and blue.[4]

Lids for the cremation pithoi are of four types, of which the first two often occur by themselves in domestic contexts. Conical lids with knob handles usually fit their urns, and conform to them in decoration. More ornate is a domed class, frequently decorated with florid curvilinear ornament,[5] and rarely fitting the pithoi with which they were found. Most striking of all are those with central omphaloi[6] or animal protomes; both varieties recall the Idaean bronze shields, and perhaps they were originally meant to be votives hung on a wall, rather than lids for cremation urns. Fortetsa no. 1414, with a calf's-head protome, bears the only known figured scene of Cretan LG, where Zeus brandishes a thunderbolt in front of a mantic tripod.[7]

The other Knossian shapes require little comment. Hydriae, globular jugs, and slim neck-handled amphorae are especially common in domestic contexts; the amphorae have counterparts in Naxian LG (fig. 69a), but the type had been known at Knossos since the early eighth century.[8] The one-piece oinochoe (fig. 86a) often appears in tombs, as do three unguent shapes of foreign derivation: first, the local copies of the Cypro-Phoenician flask (fig. 86d), which reproduce the circular decoration, as well as the shape, of their ridge-necked prototype; second, the ovoid lekythoi of 'Praisos' type,[9] combining the oriental neck-ridge with elegant decoration in the local manner; third, and commonest, the globular aryballos, first introduced to Crete from the Corinthian MG repertoire, and usually carrying cross-hatched triangles or double circles on the shoulder (fig. 86b,c). Of the open shapes, the shallow kotyle is also of Corinthian origin; towards the end of LG it becomes as common as the skyphos. Large cups, deep and bellied, are remarkable for their thin fabric; most are fully glazed. Kraters, low-footed and with a tallish offset lip (fig. 86h), come mainly from the settlement.

Finally, the plain kitchenware deserves mention, made of gritty red clay, often thrown on the wheel, and surprisingly thin-walled. The leading shape is a tripod

FIG. 86 KNOSSIAN LG POTTERY
(a) *Fortetsa* 977, H. 22.8; (b,c,d) *Fortetsa* nos. 832, 738, 829,
HS, 6.5, 7.5, 9.5; (e) *Fortetsa* 1369, H. 10; (f) *Fortetsa* 824, H. 40.5;
(g) *Fortetsa* 1441, detail; (h) Knossos, Stopford well no. 39,
BSA 55, 164 fig. 7, H. 24.5

cookpot, probably a revival from the Minoan repertoire.[10]

The Geometric of southern Crete may be treated as a provincial and retarded variant of the north-central style. Many of the smaller shapes are the same: for instance, globular aryballoi, ridge-necked flasks, skyphoi, and black cups. The differences are most clearly seen in the cremation pithoi; although the neckless ovoid type of Knossos is not unknown,[11] most southern pithoi belong to two older varieties – the straight-sided and the necked ovoid (fig. 87a,b), which in north-central Crete had passed out of fashion soon after 800 B.C. (p. 99). By LG times, as at Knossos, decoration is confined to the upper part of the surface; the curvilinear ornament of fig. 87a, compounded of Protogeometric B and LG elements, is typical of this region, where the severe rectilinear style of Attic MG had been much less influential than in the north. Shortly before 700 B.C. the southern potters caught the prevailing enthusiasm for added white circles, which are just visible on both our illustrations. The ovoid pithos, fig. 87b, is of an extremely plump southern type with vestigial neck, which persists in the cemetery of Arkades all through the seventh century.

The pottery of the extreme east bears very little resemblance to the central styles, and the shapes are even more conservative than in the south. Thus bell-kraters and high-footed skyphoi (fig. 87e) survive from the Protogeometric repertoire; and the cremation pithoi (a rare shape here, as inhumation was still the prevailing rite) are usually of the old-fashioned type with straight sides. The leading closed shapes are slim neck-handled amphorae, oinochoai, globular pyxides, and hydriai.

The decoration consists largely of free-hand curvilinear ornament and small sets of concentric circles, a repertoire which probably came to this region in the late ninth century, during a brief period of contact with Knossian Protogeometric B. Soon after 800 B.C. a few Attic MG features are occasionally seen – meander designs, vertical chevrons, and low-based skyphoi.[12] But the Atticizing element was never very strong, and was soon diluted; thus the painter of fig. 87e has done his best to transform the hatched meander into a curvilinear motif. Later on, zones of close ornament cover the whole surface, without much regard for the shape. Once again, curvilinear ornament predominates, the favourite motifs being spirals, cables, arcs, and tongues; the local practice is to add hatching to the background, rather than to the motifs themselves. A hydria and a pedestalled cup, fig. 87c and d, come from a single workshop at Kavousi, where this eastern LG style can be seen at its ripest. A later hydria from the same site[13] bears a chariot scene on the shoulder, one of the rare attempts at figured drawing; this is Subgeometric work of the early seventh century.

FIG. 87 LG POTTERY FROM SOUTH (a,b) AND EAST (c–e) CRETE; KNOSSIAN RELIEF PITHOS (f)
(a) Herakleion 8126, Arkades, H. 53.6; (b) Herakleion 8008, Arkades, H. 33.2; (c) Herakleion 697, Kavousi, H. 37; (d) Herakleion 741, Kavousi, H. 16.6; (e) Herakleion 2225, from Adhromyloi, H. 10; (f) Knossos, Unexplored Mansion, D, of roundels 5

What little pottery has been published from the far west gives a similar impression of isolation. Vases from a cremation tomb at Kavousi Kisamou include a straight-sided pithos, a plump oinochoe, several broad-necked amphoriskoi, and a deep, bellied cup. Decoration is sparse, and severely recti-linear; a characteristic motif is the check pattern, in which alternate compart-ments are cross-hatched.[14] The lack of rapport with the Knossian style makes this group difficult to date; it could well be earlier than LG.

Shortly before 700 B.C. figured relief begins to appear on Cretan storage pithoi, the oldest examples being a few fragments from the Knossos area. In contrast to the freely modelled relief of the Tenian school (p. 213), the pioneer artists of Crete used circular or rectangular stamps, repeating the same design around a horizontal zone. The earliest themes are a single horse,[15] a cavalier (fig. 87f),[16] and an armed warrior,[17] all rendered in a loose, almost Subgeometric manner.

Burial Customs

In such a large island, uniformity of burial practice is hardly to be expected. One can speak of a general rule, to which there are sporadic exceptions.

By far the commonest form of burial is the urn cremation, placed in a family tomb – usually a rock-cut chamber tomb, but not infrequently a built tholos. This custom prevails over most of the island: in the centre, the south, the extreme west, and as far east as the passes leading into the Mirabello region. A good example is provided by a re-used Minoan[18] chamber tomb at Knossos (fig. 88), less disturbed than most. The chamber, only 1·25m. in diameter, is approached by a gently sloping dromos, with a step just inside the doorway. In all, fourteen urns were deposited, representing about seven generations (c. 850–650 B.C.).[19] When the floor was filled, an upper layer was begun; after the chamber had been packed to capacity, the last two cremations were left in the dromos, and protected by a rough blocking wall. Besides the ashes, most urns contained at least one aryballos, the other vase offerings being placed near by.

The tholoi in use during this period are scattered over many parts of the island: Knossos (Teke, p. 100) and Ay. Paraskies in the north-central plain; in the south, Rhotasi, Kourtes, and Arkades tombs R and L; Papoura in the Lasithi plain; further east, Anavlokhos, Vrokastro, Kavousi, Sykia-Adhromyloi, and Praisos. Most of these tombs had been used continuously since the tenth or ninth century; some (e.g., Teke, Praisos tomb A) are re-used Minoan, while those at Sykia-Adhromyloi have the square chambers characteristic of the early Dark Age site of Karphi.[20] The tomb at Ay. Paraskies is one of the few to have been constructed in LG times, to which the earliest burials belong; partly sunk in flat ground, its miniscule chamber (height and diameter 1·40m.) was completely filled with some two dozen cremations within little more than a century. Apart from the oriental jeweller's treasure in the Teke chamber, these tholoi are no better furnished than the chamber tombs; hence there is no reason to associate them with families of high rank or status, unlike the princely tholoi of the Late Bronze Age.

Other forms of cremation burial are rare, and confined to one particular site: such are the unroofed 'bone enclosures' of Vrokastro (p. 102), the isolated pithos

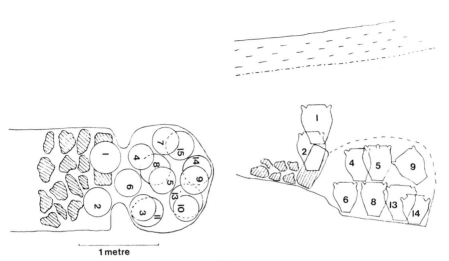

FIG. 88 FORTETSA TOMB VII, PLAN AND SECTION
After *Fortetsa* pl. 157

1 metre

burials near Episkopi Pediados, and the curious 'urnfield' of Arkades where each urn stands in a stone dish and is covered by a large domestic basin placed upside down. This large practice, for which a North Syrian origin has been suggested,[21] occurs mainly in the seventh century, but a few of the urns may go back into the eighth;[22] at all events the use of the 'urnfield' is contemporary with most of the cremations in the more conventional tholos tombs. The cemeteries of Dreros are doubly unorthodox in that they contain individual cremations in pits and cists, inhumations in pithoi, and no collective tombs at all.

In the eastern peninsula, excavation data are rather scarce; but one gets the impression that the burial customs there were altogether different. Cremation occurs only at Vrokastro (the 'bone enclosures') and Kavousi, two sites overlooking the gulf of Mirabello. Further east still, in the remote and hilly country inland from Siteia, the normal rite seems to have been inhumation; instances have been reported at Piskokephalo and Praisos. The normal family tombs were either tholoi (at the places mentioned above), or natural caves; examples of the latter, containing eighth-century offerings, have been found at Piskokephalo, Zou, Praisos, and a site near Epano Zakro known as Stou Koukou tou Kephali. Later, perhaps, are the rectangular rock-cut shafts, also intended for multiple burials; one at Praisos (tomb C) received its first incumbent – a warrior – shortly before 700 B.C., while another, at Kavousi, is probably of the seventh century.

Settlements

We begin with Vrokastro and Kavousi, two hilltop strongholds settled by refugees during the commotions at the end of the Bronze Age. It is hardly possible to unravel their architectural history; but, to judge from the latest pottery, it appears that both places were abandoned around or soon after 700 B.C. The existing remains must therefore belong in large measure to the eighth century, although the plans may go back to the eleventh.

The builders of Vrokastro were at the mercy of their terrain. Faced with a rugged peak, they took little trouble over terracing. Here and there, uneven ground was levelled with a fill of red earth; elsewhere, walls were built up against rock, separating outcrops from living space. Hence the chaotic layout,[23] with its many curved walls and narrow cubicles; it is hard to see where one house ends and the next begins. The masonry is all rubble, unworked, but with some clay bonding. Column bases were found in three out of more than thirty rooms. The only apparent amenity is a town drain, running alongside a street. The published plan represents only half of the excavated area, which extended some way down the north slope overlooking the gulf of Mirabello.

The 'castle' of Kavousi,[24] perched on the summit of Vronda ('Thunder') hill, is more carefully planned, and more solidly built. There are thirteen rooms, for the most part rectangular, and larger than those at Vrokastro. They rise up seven successive terraces, and yet preserve a fairly consistent orientation. The finest pottery is said to come from room 11 on the lowest terrace, the innermost part of a well-aligned *megaron* suite measuring 8 × 13·50m. Here, perhaps, were the chieftain's own quarters.

Of the larger towns, the most substantial remains are at Phaistos, around and above the ruins of the Minoan palace and its dependencies. Geometric houses have been explored in three quarters: Ay. Photini (north-east), Chalara (south-east), and, in greatest abundance, on the south-west slope leading up to the palace area. This quarter seems to have been abandoned after a disastrous earthquake in the early seventh century; hence the good preservation of the Geometric walls, which stand up to 2·50m. high. A close concatenation of about thirty rooms[25] lies partly over the Bronze Age town, and partly over the west court of the first palace. Some walls rest on Minoan foundations; the masonry consists largely of dressed blocks retrieved from Minoan debris, and often laid in tidy ashlar courses. The rooms are either rectangular or trapezoidal, and for the most part follow the north-south orientation of the Minoan palace. Six are provided with hearths (usually central), one has a stone bench along the wall (R_3), another (G) encloses a potter's kiln;[26] here and there, patches of stone floor-paving survive. The excavator believes that this quarter was occupied continuously from Subminoan until LG times; the complicated stratigraphy has not yet been unravelled in detail, but the earliest clear deposit so far published is a nest of ninth-century whole pots (Protogeometric B) from room P. The largest room (AA), measuring 8 × 6m., has a central oval hearth lined with slabs, a huge storage pithos in one corner, and a mass of LG and Early Orientalizing pots which date the earthquake.[27] But perhaps the most impressive feature of Geometric Phaistos is the paved road, 3m. wide (fig. 89), which forms the western limit of this quarter; starting from above the west court of the palace, it winds down the hill through the south-eastern Chalara district, where it remained in use even in Hellenistic times.

Dreros, a town in the mountains west of Mirabello, offers a rare glimpse of eighth-century public life. In a hollow between two citadels lie the remains of

FIG. 89 PHAISTOS, PAVED STREET IN GEOMETRIC TOWN

the earliest known agora in the Greek world. A flat rectangular expanse, *c.* 23 × 40m., is limited at its south-west corner by a flight of seven steps built on a natural slope, almost all that survives of an extensive stepped area which once ran all the way along the south side, and continued in short returns at both ends. This primitive theatre would have been the setting for public assemblies, both religious and political. In providing steps for large gatherings of citizens, Dreros set a precedent for all the theatres and bouleuteria of Archaic and Classical times. We need not be surprised that the idea should first have arisen in Crete, where the original inspiration must have come from the stepped theatral areas of the Minoan palaces.

The agora of Dreros is part of a carefully planned ensemble which includes a small rectangular temple built on exactly the same alignment, and approached from the place of assembly by two uphill paths. The construction of the agora may thus be dated by the earliest pottery from the temple, which goes back to *c.* 725–700 B.C.

Sanctuaries

The temple of Dreros (fig. 102) is a rectangular building, 10·90 × 7·20m. Of its elevation we know nothing, except that the walls were entirely built of stone; at the back, the south-west corner still rises 2·50m. high, composed of small rough blocks laid in fairly regular courses. For the front, where very little remains of the foundations, the excavator suggested a conjectural restoration with a shallow porch in front of the doorway, on the analogy of mainland temple models.[28] But the chief interest of this temple lies in its interior furnishing, which tells us a good deal about the cult. Sacrifices were burnt in a central rectangular hearth, lined with stone slabs; the smoke was perhaps released through a skylight or lantern resting on two columns, of which one stone base survives. Against the back wall, at the right-hand corner, a stone bench served to display the votives. Beside the bench stood an altar, supported on orthostat slabs; in its wreckage were found a large number of goats' horns, two sacrificial knives, and the three small cult-statues of hammered bronze (*sphyrelata*) which had originally stood upon the altar. Immediately in front, on the floor, was a circular stone table for offerings. The statues – one male and two female (fig. 91) – have been tentatively identified as Apollo, Artemis, and their mother Leto, on the assumption that this is the temple of Apollo Delphinios mentioned in a long Hellenistic inscription also found at Dreros.[29] As for the altar with the goats' horns, some see a connection with the horn altar (*Keraton*) within the Apolline sanctuary on Delos, round which Theseus and his fourteen young companions were supposed to have danced the Crane dance after their deliverance from the Minotaur.[30]

Several features of this temple are typically Cretan, and have a long history. The bench and the offering table, like the theatral steps outside, are legacies from the Minoan tradition; a comparison has often been drawn with the furnishing of the thirteenth-century shrine of the Double Axes at Knossos.[31] The provision of an interior hearth is a notion introduced by Mycenaean settlers, but later assimilated to Cretan custom during the Dark Ages: for example, in the large *megaron* houses of Karphi. In Geometric sanctuaries outside Crete, sacrificial hearths and altars were usually kept outside the temple.

A much larger temple on the acropolis of Gortyn (16 × 13·65m.) also has a corner bench for votives, and a central sacrificial pit (*bothros*) lined with slabs. The most curious feature here is the presence of at least three interior compartments, whose purpose is not clear. The outer foundations are remarkable for their monumental masonry, especially the large and regular blocks of alabaster at the south-west corner. The construction of this building may be considerably later than the Protogeometric date suggested by the excavators; the sherds which are cited as evidence[32] could well come from the Dark Age settlement lying immediately underneath, and objects of votive character (e.g., terracotta figurines and plaques) do not occur in quantity before the seventh century. The temple was frequently remodelled, and was still standing in Roman times.

The local tradition of interior hearths and offering benches was continued in the two seventh-century temples at Prinias. Yet it must not be forgotten that Cretan cults were conducted in several other kinds of environment, often far from any settlement, and often without any temple at all. The Minoan cave shrines of Ida and Dicte continued to receive rich offerings in Geometric and later times. Spectacular finds have recently been made in an urban sanctuary at Arkades (Afrati), and also in the remote mountain shrine of Kato Symi; at both places it appears that worship during the Geometric period was carried out in the open air. At Knossos, an open-air sanctuary of Demeter received its first votives during the eighth century, including wheelmade figurines of humans and animals similar to those from the Samian Heraion.

Jewellery

The most distinguished gold ornaments of this period have been found at three sites: the Idaean cave sanctuary, the tholos tomb of Teke near Knossos (later deposits), and the cemetery of Praisos.

A crescent pendant and a rectangular plaque, both from the Idaean cave,[33] were made in a Knossian workshop deeply influenced by the oriental manner of the Teke jeweller. Much use is still made of granulation; the cloisons on the plaque and the granulated designs on the crescent (zigzag and horizontal S's) recall the contemporary gold belt from Eleusis (p. 125 fig. 39a). On the plaque, the three frontal female figures have faces very like those on a pendant by the Teke craftsman (p. 100 fig. 32,b). Their stance and drapery set the fashion for many forms of Cretan art in the next century: holding their arms firmly to their sides, they wear *poloi*, girdles, shawls over their backs, and long robes decorated with a vertical strip down the front. Between these ladies are two curious designs, variously interpreted as bulls' heads or as busts of the Egyptian Hathor;[34] in either case the representation would be much garbled.

The Teke tholos continued to receive burials through the eighth into the early seventh century, and a deposit of jewellery found in the dromos can be dated on stratigraphical grounds to a late period of the tomb's use – though not to the very latest.[35] The most interesting pieces here are two hollow male figurines carrying rams (*kriophoroi*), of which one is well preserved. Modelled in the round, it consists of two halves beaten on to their matrices and soldered together. No granulation is used; but the facial features are now more realistically portrayed than on the Idaean plaque, and represent a later and more hellenized stage of the Knossian jeweller's art. The domed head, and the long locks of hair ending in spiral curls, are in the manner of the bronze *sphyrelaton* of Apollo from Dreros (fig. 91).

The jewellery from Praisos includes a fragmentary repoussé sphinx in the Knossian orientalizing manner,[36] and a finger-ring whose long, diamond-shaped bezel is perpendicular to the hoop. Eastern influence is apparent in the decoration of inlays, openwork zigzags, and granulation; but the shape is descended from the Minoan type of signet ring with a large elliptical bezel. Perhaps this form was remembered in eastern Crete all through the Dark Ages: a plain version occurs in a tenth- to ninth-century context at Vrokastro,[37] and two more are reported from the tholoi at Sykia-Adhromyloi.[38]

Bronzes

Before discussing the Idaean shields and other orientalizing figured reliefs, we shall begin with the more orthodox kinds of object which have counterparts elsewhere in Greece.

Pins and fibulae often occur in tombs and sanctuaries. Most pins are relatively short, and follow the local type established in the late ninth century (p. 101), with a small disc and finial, a long biconical swelling, and two or three ridges

a   b   c

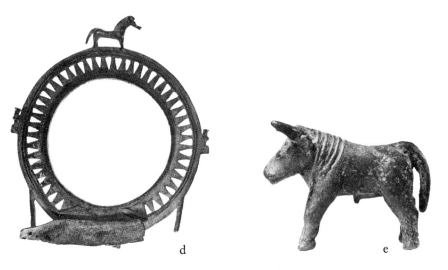

d   e

FIG. 90 CRETAN BRONZE FIGURINES AND TRIPOD HANDLE
(a–c) Oxford AE 599, Dictaean cave, H. 9; (d) Oxford AE 24,
1894.139, Patsos cave, H. 6.8; (e) Oxford G 391, Idaean cave, D. 23.2

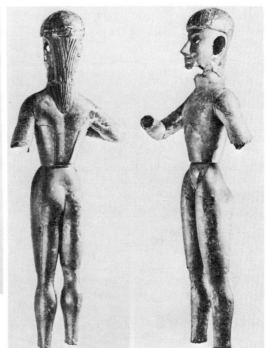

FIG. 91 CULT STATUES OF HAMMERED BRONZE (*Sphyrelata*) FROM DREROS
H. of tallest 80

above and below.[39] This variety lasts into the seventh century, when the top of the shank often tapers towards the disc, as on a fine gold pair from Fortetsa (nos. 1091–2). The fibulae are more varied, but the favourite types are Blinkenberg's III 10 and 11, with a small plate and several globes on the bow.

Two sanctuaries of Zeus, in the Idaean cave and at Palaikastro, have yielded plenty of fragments from cast tripod cauldrons, and a few more pieces have come from Praisos, Anavlokhos, and Arkades. The impulse to make such vessels probably came from the mainland during the LG phase,[40] but Cretan smiths soon evolved their own version. This has simpler moulding and ornament than most Peloponnesian varieties: the legs usually bear a Y-shaped fillet down the outer surface,[41] and the ring-handles have openwork dogtooth or zigzag between fillets. On a handle from the Idaean shrine (fig. 90d), the birds perched on each side are unparalleled; but the horse, with its flattened and notched mane, is typical of the Cretan style. No human attachments are known.

A rare form of stand, elaborately adorned with openwork figured scenes, is represented by three sets of fragments from the Idaean cave,[42] Kato Symi, and the dromos of the Teke tholos (*c.* 700 B.C.). This kind of support has its origin in twelfth-century Cyprus, where the complete examples are four-sided, crowned with an upper ring to take the vessel, and often run on wheels. Among the Cretan pieces are orientalizing double volutes, such as served as capitals for the vertical rods on the Cypriot models. The figured scenes, however, seem to be fully hellenized, in the Geometric manner: the Idaean fragments, as restored in the Herakleion Museum, portray a ship scene like that on p. 354 fig. 112b, with assorted animals filling up the rest of the field. A clay imitation from Karphi tells us that the Cretans already knew about these stands by the eleventh century. There is no further trace of them before the fragments from Ida and Teke; yet, during this long interval, three examples of the rod-tripod stand, another Cypriot type which is closely related, occur in late Dark-Age contexts at Vrokastro and in the Knossos area.[43]

The bronze figurines have not received much study, and it may be optimistic to suppose that any settled style arose on this island. The favourite animal, as always in Crete, is the bull; fig. 90e is treated with greater sympathy and understanding than its Laconian counterpart, fig. 53a. Of the horse we have already had a glimpse, on the ring-handle from the Idaean cave. Not much interest was shown in human anatomy: legs tend to be short and stumpy, trunks spool-like or plank-like, necks too long, and ears boldly protruding. When a formless body is combined with a backward tilt of the head, oriental affinities – or even imports – are usually suspected; yet two of the most oriental-looking women, from Vrokastro and Kato Symi,[44] raise their arms in the old Minoan gesture of benediction. Slightly more voluptuous – in spite of her almost cubic head – is a nude from the Dictaean cave (fig. 90a–c), who wears a flat *polos* (like most Cretan females) and an elaborate necklace; the hair streaming down her back reminds us of Levantine ivory figurines.[45] Towards the end of the century, the faces become more lifelike and expressive; among the best pieces of this stage are a standing youth,[46] and a seated minstrel singing to a four-stringed lyre.[47]

A fine youth from the Arkades sanctuary[48] echoes the style of the *kriophoros* from Teke, and also of the *sphyrelaton* cult statue of Apollo from Dreros (fig. 91). All three should be dated around 700 B.C., well before the Teke tholos passed out of use, well before the canons of Daedalic art (pp. 365–6) became established, but not earlier than the oldest votives at Dreros.[49] Common to all these figures are the domed head, the straight locks curling only at the fringe, and the bodily proportions. How are we to explain this uniformity of style in three artists working in different techniques and on different scales? We must at least suppose that they were working in the same place; and the common factor is surely the Knossian orientalizing tradition, now fully assimilated to Hellenic taste. The creator of the *sphyrelata*, hammering out his bronze plates on a wooden core, was merely applying the jeweller's repoussé technique to a monumental task and a less tractable metal. His style and iconography are influenced by earlier and semi-hellenized Knossian relief work, like the triad of deities in the central panel of the Fortetsa belt (p. 100); his two goddesses wear what is by now becoming their traditional Cretan dress (p. 281). The restrained rendering of the human facial features is unusual in Geometric art, but may be explained by the unusually large scale;[50] even so, the hollow eyes, when filled with their original inlays, would have seemed sufficiently formidable and awe-inspiring to the worshipper.

We come at last to the orientalizing figured reliefs. The Knossian school, in

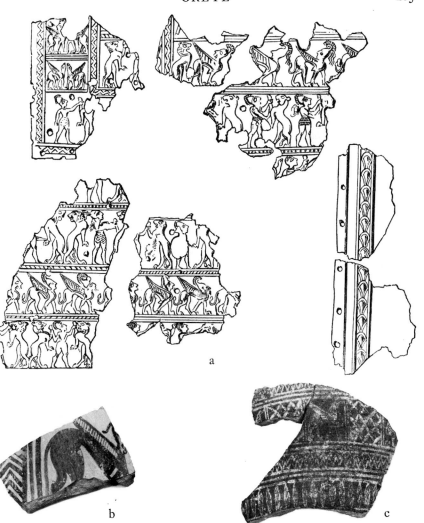

FIG. 92 BRONZE RELIEF FROM KAVOUSI, WITH COMPARANDA
(a) the Kavousi relief (*AJA* 5, 148 fig. 11); (b) Knossos,
BSA 67 pl. 24, 14, H. 5.4; (c) Knossos, Unexplored Mansion,
H. 11.8

its LG stage, is represented by some pieces of plating from Kavousi (fig. 92a), found in a plundered tholos tomb with pottery and other metalwork[51] of *c.* 750–680 B.C. Parts of at least eight figured friezes are preserved, with smaller panels at the side, and a zigzag border. Here are files of helmeted sphinxes, passant or regardant; heraldic griffins; and warriors grappling with one or two lions. The themes (except for the griffins) we have already seen on the Teke

a

b

diadem and the Fortetsa quiver (pp. 99–100); the style, though influenced by these earlier works, has become dry, neat, and mechanical through repetition. Comparable sphinxes and griffins have recently been found on a few late eighth-century pieces of pottery from Knossos (fig. 92b–c).

The cave-shrine on the north face of mount Ida is one of several places associated with the birth and childhood of Zeus. According to the legend, the young god's life was threatened by his father Kronos; but he was saved by his attendant priests, the dancing Kouretes, who drowned his infant wails by clashing their armour. Although the cave was already a place of worship in Late Minoan III times,[52] its richest offerings are of the eighth and seventh centuries. This is also the period of the bronze votive shields which, in spite of their strongly oriental character, were designed and offered in commemoration of the local myth; in comparison with their abundance in this cave, such shields rarely occur elsewhere in Crete, and very rarely indeed outside the island.[53] Among the other bronze offerings in the cave, closely related to the shields, are several shallow bowls, a vessel in the shape of a human head,[54] and a gong (*tympanon*) portraying an oriental rendering of the cult in its orgiastic aspect: two winged demons clash their *tympana* on either side of the vigorous young god, who treads upon a bull and waves a lion above his head.[55]

The shields are of two sizes: the larger bear an animal protome (lion or eagle) in the centre, while the smaller have central omphaloi. Both classes are of oriental origin,[56] appearing in contemporary and earlier Assyrian scenes as the equipment of Urartian foes. No less oriental is the range of themes in the embossed decoration. Narrow animal friezes – lions, bulls, stags, goats, or griffins – occupy concentric rings round the outside; the central field of the protome shields may show hunting scenes, men embattled with lions, or heraldic pairs of lions or sphinxes, sometimes attending a nude goddess of wild nature.

In spite of their oriental character, it is unlikely that the *tympanon* or any of the shields are imports. Because of their relevance to the Idaean cult, they are more plausibly attributed to immigrant eastern smiths and their Cretan pupils,[57] and their diversity of style implies more than one Cretan centre of production. Both types of shield were known at Knossos, to judge from the clay lids which imitate them (p. 272); and some of the earlier omphalos shields may be assigned to the Knossian school in its LG stage. The winged lions of fig. 93a, for example, are in the neat, compact, and semi-hellenized style of the Kavousi relief; also characteristic of this school are the thin, straight wings, whereas the grazing stags recall the earlier group of Attic gold diadems (pp. 123–5 fig. 38a). Quite different is the full-blooded oriental manner of an almost complete protome shield, fig. 93b, showing two turbulent scenes of hunting. In the centre a fallen warrior struggles to free himself from the jaws of a vast lion; another such lion sniffs blandly at a lotus flower, without any thought of his approaching doom. No attention is paid to scale; spaces between big animals are merely filled up

FIG. 93 BRONZE VOTIVE SHIELDS FROM THE IDAEAN CAVE
(a) *KB* no. 54, *AM* 10, 66, H. 13.6; (b) the Hunt shield,
KB no. 6, D. 83

with little animals. Here we see a riot of incongruous ideas, brought directly from the Levant, and especially from the Neo-Hittite art of North Syria: thence come the archers' close-fitting caps, the tall conical helmets of the warriors, and the purely decorative stripes on the lions' rumps. The latticing of their manes is an Assyrian notion, also applied to the sprawling creatures on several of the later shields.[58] This particular shield belongs to a large group made in some Cretan centre other than Knossos, and betokening the arrival – perhaps during the late eighth century – of a new guild of oriental smiths, whose style and iconography were never much modified by local taste.

Indeed, the shields are hard to date, since they show so little rapport with other forms of art in Crete and elsewhere in Greek lands. There are, however, a few helpful clues from shape and context. A Knossian MG lid with a lion protome[59] suggests that the Idaean series had begun by 750 B.C. at the latest. Fragments of a shield exported to Delphi,[60] with a frieze of straight-winged sphinxes in the Knossian manner, occur in a deposit dated by Corinthian LG pottery to c. 750–730 B.C. Some details of the *tympanon* scene are derived from Assyrian art during the reign of king Sargon II (722–705 B.C.).[61] Finally, from the context of two shields found in Arkades tomb L,[62] it seems that the series continues far into the seventh century.

Conclusions

We begin with a few survivals from the distant past. Praisos and Dreros, two remote hill-towns, had no doubt been settled by refugees during the disturbances at the end of the Bronze Age. By the late eighth century, when peaceful conditions had returned, many similar strongholds had been deserted. Yet these two settlements retained their inhabitants, and grew into city-states of mixed stock; for they are the chief sources of the Archaic and Classical inscriptions in the Eteocretan language,[63] descended from the ancient Minoan tongue. During our period, then, it is natural that both places should show signs of extreme conservatism, albeit in quite different ways. At Praisos and in the surrounding country, the old Minoan rite of inhumation persisted when cremation had become the rule elsewhere on the island; the local goldsmiths continued to make a Minoan form of finger-ring; and the local potters produced a curious curvilinear style which resisted the influence of central Crete, making very little use of Geometric ornament. At Dreros the burial customs (p. 277) are as heterodox by Minoan as by contemporary Cretan standards, but Minoan tradition persists in the interior furnishing of the temple, and especially in the stepped place of assembly. This is the earliest known agora in the Greek world; it could only have been planned by a settled and self-assured community; and the desire to plan it stems from a respect for law and order, inculcated by a distant memory of Minoan palatial civilization which had survived the turmoil of the early Dark Ages.

Perhaps because of their self-sufficiency at home, the Cretans took little active interest in the outside world. Their LG pottery was exported only to the Cyclades (Thera, Melos, Delos, and Andros), apart from a single vase in Athens.[64] Thera, the nearest neighbour, was the only regular customer, and some bronze pins from the Theran cemeteries may also be Cretan.[65] The other metal exports are all votives: the gold finial found on Ithaca, the bronze openwork fragments at Delphi, and the embossed shields at Delphi, Dodona, and Miletus. The two offerings at Delphi perhaps lend some colour to the local legend[66] that Apollo himself recruited a crew of Knossian sailors to be his first priests. Outside the Greek homelands, nothing Cretan has been found in Cyprus, in the Levant, or in the west before the foundation of Gela in Sicily (689 B.C.) in which Cretans and Rhodians collaborated.[67] Among the earliest finds there, the Cretan element is represented by cremation pithoi locally made in the southern style,[68] indicating whence in Crete the colonists came. It is worth adding that the name of their leader, Entimos, is also recorded at Gortyn among Cretan cities.[69]

In spite of their apparent lack of commercial enterprise, the Cretans were receptive of many artistic and technical notions from overseas. Exports of Corinthian LG and EPC pottery had a limited effect on the Knossian style; but far more remarkable and important are the influences emanating from the Levant. Crete, like the Dodecanese, had never been wholly isolated from the eastern Mediterranean, and in both regions the initiative in keeping up these contacts had been Levantine rather than Greek. Peculiar to Crete, however, is the appearance of oriental figured imagery expressed in bronze relief – a medium almost unparalleled in other contemporary Greek art.[70] This phenomenon is most reasonably explained by assuming the emigration of oriental smiths to Crete: first a jeweller who established his workshop at Knossos not later than 800 B.C., followed in the mid or late eighth century by a guild of bronzeworkers who made their home in some other Cretan town and set the style for the main group of Idaean shields. Then, shortly after 700 B.C., the Cretans acquired yet another technical notion from the Levant, in the use of the mould for terracotta reliefs and figurines. It is likely that this idea, too, was conveyed to them by resident oriental craftsmen, since with the new technique came the Daedalic manner of rendering the human face, which has its origin in North Syria (p. 366). At all events, Crete has a good claim to have been the first Greek land to adopt the mould for terracotta work.

In addition to the technical and artistic ideas passed on to them by these hypothetical immigrants, the Cretans also received a wide variety of oriental imports in the normal course of trade. Cypro-Phoenician Black-on-Red unguent shapes occur here and there in the cemeteries, together with numerous Cretan imitations. The ivories from the Idaean cave are probably all of Phoenician origin,[71] as are certain bronze bowls from Fortetsa and Arkades.[72] Cretan provenances are recorded for six North Syrian seals of the Lyre-player group;[73] and the remotest source of imports is the hill-country of Luristan in northern Persia, whence at least one bronze openwork pendant came to Crete.[74]

With so much oriental commerce coming their way, the Cretans were becoming prosperous without having to seek their own markets overseas. Why were they so privileged, and why was their island so frequently visited by Levantine shipping during the eighth century? A possible answer is provided by the affinities of the most striking orientalizing bronzes from the Idaean cave. The strong North Syrian style of the *tympanon* is matched by the relief scenes on several conical stands for oriental bronze cauldrons, some exported to Olympia,[75] others to Etruria, the finest example being the stand from the Barberini tomb at Praeneste (pp. 362 f., fig. 113). A rich Etruscan tomb at Capodimonte near Visentium supplies a complete counterpart, probably in an eighth-century context, for the wheeled openwork stand,[76] represented in the Greek homeland only by the fragments from Delphi and the Idaean cave. These stands, and also the style of the *tympanon*, are distributed along a trade route which almost bypasses the Aegean altogether: starting from the Levant, it touches Cyprus and Crete, passes up the west Peloponnesian coast, and thence strikes across to Italy. The Cretans were no doubt supplied mainly by immigrant craftsmen, but, in view of their inertia in other forms of commerce, are not likely to have exported these bronzes any further west, or to have played any active part along this route. It is easier to believe that the ports of Crete, Olympia, and Etruria were visited by Phoenician merchants, especially when the western Mediterranean was coming into their commercial orbit, and when there is other evidence of their contact with Etruria (p. 240). For Tyrian traders on their way to their newly established outposts at Carthage, Motya, and Sulcis in Sardinia, this would be their shortest, safest, and most profitable route; the alternative passage, along the North African shore, would have meant a tedious and fruitless detour along a coast where good harbours are rare.

So Crete acquires an important new role in the late eighth century, as a midway station between the Levant and the lucrative markets of the west. That is why her early orientalizing art finds a reflection in distant Etruria, yet had very little to do with the great Orientalizing movement elsewhere in Greece.

NOTES

1 The 'Praisos' type: *GGP* 250, group (c).
2 e.g., *Fortetsa* pl. 85 no. 1501 motif 11aj.
3 ibid. pls. 63–4 no. 1047.
4 Brock, ibid. 150–2.
5 Especially scales, leaves, arcades, and horizontal S's; see *BSA* 49 (1954), pl. 23.
6 ibid. pl. 146.
7 ibid. 122–3 pl. 107.
8 *GGP* 53h (MG), pl. 55h (LG).
9 Above, n. 1.
10 *BSA* 67 (1972), 80; 87, F 27.
11 *GGP* 255 n. 8.
12 *GGP* 260, pl. 57a,c.
13 *Hesperia* 14 (1945), pl. 5.
14 cf. U. Jantzen, *Festscrift E. v. Mercklin* (Waldsassen, 1964), 60–1 pl. 33, 3, a pyxis from Vryses near Khania.
15 Knossos, *BSA* Suppl. 8 (1973), 21–2, A 34, pl. 10; Amnisos, *PAE* 1936, 83 fig. 1.
16 Knossos, Unexplored Mansion, Well 8a, excavated 1973.
17 Boardman, *BSA* 57 (1962), 31–2 fig. 3 pl. 4a.
18 A Late Minoan III clay coffin was found by the entrance to the dromos.
19 The urn, fig. 88 no. 8, is our fig. 86f.

20 e.g., *BCH* 79 (1955), 307–8 fig. 4 (Sykia); cf. Pendlebury, *BSA* 38 (1937–38), 100 ff. pls. 12–13, 25–7.
21 Kurtz and Boardman, *Greek Burial Customs* 173 fig. 29.
22 e.g., *Ann* 10–12 (1927–29), fig. 156.
23 *Vrokastro* pl. 18.
24 *AJA* 5 (1901), 137 ff. fig. 5.
25 Drerup, *Arch Hom* O 42 fig. 35.
26 *Ann* 35–6 (1957–58), 269 ff. figs. 104–8.
27 *Ann* 39–40 (1961–62), 405 ff. figs. 48–52 (room P); 408 ff. figs. 54–9 (room AA).
28 S. Marinatos, *BCH* 60 (1936), 247 ff. pl. 31.
29 *InscrCret* I, 84 ff. no. 1.
30 Plutarch, *Theseus* 21.
31 This and other examples are mustered by L. Banti, *Ann* 17–19 (1941–43), 40–50 fig. 27.
32 G. Rizza, *Gortina* 25 fig. 45.
33 Higgins, *BSA* 64 (1969), 151 fig. 44a.
34 D. Levi, *AJA* 49 (1945), 229–30.
35 Boardman, *BSA* 62 (1967), 58, 61 pl. 9.
36 *BSA* 12 (1905–06), 64 fig. 1.
37 Chamber tomb I: *Vrokastro* 138 fig. 82.
38 Platon, *PAE* 1954, 367.
39 Jacobsthal, *Greek Pins* 17–18.
40 Willemsen, *OlF* III, 175–6.
41 e.g., *BSA* 35 (1934–35), 96 fig. 10a.
42 Boardman, *CCO* 132–4 fig. 49a.
43 H. W. Catling, *Cypriot Bronzework in the Mycenaean World* (Oxford, 1964), 198–9 nos. 18–20.
44 *Vrokastro* 121 fig. 71; *AAA* 6 (1973), 107–8 fig. 6.
45 e.g., *GKG* pl. 150.
46 U. Naumann, *Opus Nobile (Festschrift U. Jantzen)*, Wiesbaden (1969), 114 ff. pl. 17.
47 *GKG* pl. 203.
48 *AD* 25 (1970), B 458 fig. 400d.
49 S. Marinatos, the excavator, thought that the *sphyrelata*, and the horn altar on which they stood, belonged to a slightly later period than the foundation of the temple: *BCH* 60 (1936), 255 f.
50 Heights: Apollo, when complete, *c*. 0·80m.; the goddesses, 0·45m. and 0·40m.
51 Boardman, *KCh* 23 (1971), 5 ff.; cf. above p. 146.
52 *AR* 1957, 23.
53 Provenances: Idaean cave, sixty-two; Palaikastro, five; Phaistos, four; Arkades, two; Delphi, Dodona, and Miletus, one each.
54 Boardman, *CCO* 80–4 no. 378.
55 Kunze, *KB* no. 74 pl. 49.
56 Snodgrass, *EGAW* 51–5.
57 Dunbabin, *GEN* 40–41.
58 e.g., *KB* nos. 2–4, 8.
59 *Fortetsa* no. 1439 pl. 107.
60 *BCH* 68–9 (1944–45), 45 ff. figs 8, 9 pl. 3, 1.
61 F. Canciani, *BOOC* 114–16.
62 *Ann* 10–12 (1927–29), figs. 440, 489; Boardman, *CCO* 83.
63 *InscrCret* III, vi, 1–6; *Revue Philologique* 20 (1946), 131–8.
64 *GGP* 382 nn. 1–4; *Zagora* I, 58.
65 e.g., *Thera* II, fig. 490b; Jacobsthal, *Greek Pins* 17 no. 55a.
66 *Homeric Hymn* iii, 391 ff.
67 Thuc. vi.4,3.
68 *GGP* 257 n. 4; 375 no. 10.
69 *InscrCret* IV, p. 19; cf. Huxley, *ClassPhil* 68 (1973), 125.
70 A few frs. at Olympia, but in a rigid Geometric style: *Olympia* IV pl. 18 nos. 294–6
71 Kunze, *AM* 61 (1936), 218 ff. pls. 84–7.

72 *Fortetsa* no. 1559; *Ann* 10–12 (1927–29), fig. 408.
73 *JdI* 81 (1966), 29–30.
74 *Fortetsa* no. 1570; perhaps also *Gortina* fig. 32.
75 Herrmann, *OlF* VI, 179 ff. pls. 69–73; U3, U5, U6.
76 *NSc* 1928, 440 ff. pl. 8.

III

Life in
Eighth-century Greece

11 The Recovery of Literacy

No aspect of the Greek Dark Ages is more poignant than illiteracy. The syllabic writing of Linear B, which had served the needs of Mycenaean palatial administration, was forgotten in Greece after the destruction of the Mycenaean palaces. Thereafter we know of no inscriptions in the Greek language until the earliest alphabetic graffiti on Geometric pottery, none of which is older than 750 B.C.

In addition to these graffiti, four other kinds of evidence bear on the birth of the Greek alphabet: literary, linguistic, epigraphical, and archaeological. According to Herodotus (v. 58, 1–2), the Greeks first learned to write from Phoenician immigrants to Boeotia led by Cadmus; although Cadmus is a figure from the heroic past, it is clear that by 'Phoenician letters' the historian meant the alphabet, and not the Linear B syllabary which had passed into oblivion during the Dark Ages.[1] The role of the Phoenicians as teachers is confirmed by the names of each individual letter, meaningless in Greek, but based on real words in Phoenician and other western Semitic languages – and, furthermore, these words explain the original form of the sign: thus alpha answers to the Semitic 'alep denoting an ox, and the corresponding Semitic sign in its oldest form (c. 1500 B.C.) is just recognizable as an ox-head. Since the forms of each Phoenician letter underwent many changes, comparison with the earliest Greek inscriptions will help to determine the period when the Greeks first learned to write alphabetically – for here the LG graffiti give us no more than a *terminus ante quem*. And, since the local Greek alphabets adopted in each city differ considerably from each other all through the Archaic period, the first Greeks to learn alphabetical writing should produce the letter forms which are nearest to their Phoenician prototypes. Finally, the archaeological evidence bearing on these matters is indirect, but nevertheless quite important and circumstantial, drawing our attention to the times when, and the places where, Greeks and Phoenicians are known to have been in close contact.

Some oriental ideas – for example, the Tree of Life design or the frieze of grazing animals – could have been copied by Greek artisans directly from oriental imports. Other notions, like the difficult techniques of granulation and filigree in goldwork, could not have been learned without the help of an oriental teacher; and so it must have been with the alphabet, immeasurably the greatest legacy of the Orient to the rising civilization of Greece. Somewhere we must imagine a hitherto illiterate Greek, memorizing by rote the names of the Phoenician letters, repeating them in the order in which he heard them spoken, and learning to associate each name with a sign drawn by his Phoenician instructor. He would quickly grasp the acrophonic principle, whereby each sign represented the initial sound of the name applied to it: thus β for *bet*, γ for *gimel*, δ for *dalet*. On this assumption he would hear *'alep* as the vowel α; but vowels were not rendered in the Phoenician script, and in fact the sign represents ', a consonantal glottal stop peculiar to Semitic tongues. Other Phoenician sounds, alien to Greek ears, are *yōd* (consonantal y) and *'ayin*, another form of glottal stop; their letters were pressed into service for the Greek vowels ι and ο. Of the two Phoenician aspirates, the mild *hē* became ε, while the more violent *ḥēt* did duty for the Greek aspirate.[2] The Phoenician *wāw* gave birth to two Greek letters: the semi-vocalic Ϝ (pronounced as w) and the vowel υ. From the start, then, the Greeks adapted the Phoenician alphabet to the needs of their own language, in a way which may have been quite unconscious; and these early modifications are shared by every local version of the Greek alphabet. ·But where there was room for a more conscious choice, local differences quickly grew up. For example, Phoenician has no less than three sibilants, *samek*, *ṣadē*, and *šin*; most Greek dialects, only one. Chaos ensued, aided perhaps by confusion in Greek ears between *samek* and *šin*, and between *ṣadē* and *zayn*. In most Greek alphabets *samek* (or *šin*?) was converted into ξ, which the Ionians pronounced as š (sh); for the simple sibilant, some Greek cities evolved *san* from *ṣadē* (or *zayn*?), others sigma from *šin* (or *samek*?), while a few incorporated both letters. Eventually, nearly all Greeks felt the need to improvise extra letters at the end of their alphabets, to render consonantal sounds absent in Phoenician – φ, χ, ψ; and it is here that their local scripts show the widest divergences. Finally, ω was first added in Ionia, where its earliest recorded appearance is at Smyrna in the late seventh century.[3]

When did the Greeks first learn to write alphabetically? Clearly at a time when they had become acquainted with the Phoenicians through frequent visits; before 900 B.C. such visits appear to have been extremely rare. More precise is the testimony of Phoenician letter forms (fig. 94); cursive graffiti on pottery are more relevant here than monumental inscriptions on stone, if we bear our Phoenician instructor in mind. The oldest form of Phoenician *kapp* consists of three radiating strokes; but from *c.* 850 B.C. onwards one stroke is prolonged downwards, and this is the version copied by the Greek κ. Conversely the *dalet*, too, develops a downward tail after the late ninth century, whereas it is the older form, a simple triangle, which inspired the Greek δ; nevertheless, a triangular version still occurs on a late eighth-century Phoenician bowl from Cyprus.[4] For three early Greek forms – digamma, crooked iota, and *san*, Phoenician stone inscriptions offer no close parallels; but resemblances have been noted[5] with the *wāw*, *yōd*, and *ṣadē* on incised sherds from Samaria, perhaps datable to the reign of Jeroboam II (*c.* 774–766 B.C.). These graffiti, however, are not Phoenician but Hebrew, and it might now be more appropriate to compare the *wāw* and *yōd* of a Phoenician graffito recently found in the destruction debris (*c.* 800 B.C.) of the first Phoenician temple at Kition. The oldest extant inscription in the Greek alphabet (fig. 95a), datable to *c.* 740 B.C., already includes a χ, one of the supplementary letters added to the original Phoenician repertoire. Before this pot was inscribed, it would be reasonable to envisage an earlier generation of writing, when the Phoenician alphabet was accepted without addition or subtraction, and without any conscious alteration of the sound-values. In our present state of knowledge, then, the birth of the Greek alphabet is most likely to have occurred

PHOENICIAN   GREEK, 8th CENTURY B.C.

	Shipitbaal inscription (c 925–900 B.C.)	Mesha inscription (c. 830 B.C.)	Kition inscription (c. 850–800 B.C.)	Kara Tepe inscriptions (8th cent. B.C.)	Cyprus, bronze bowl (c. 730 B.C.)	CRETAN (Herpetidamos)	ATTIC (Dipylon oinochoe)	EUBOEAN (Pithecusae, Lefkandi)	
'Alep									Alpha
Bēt									Beta
Gimel									Gamma
Dalet									Delta
Hē'									Epsilon
Wāw									Digamma
									Upsilon
Zayn									Zeta
Ḥēt									(H)eta
Tēt									Theta
Yōd									Iota
Kapp									Kappa
Lamed									Lambda
Mēm									Mu
Nūn									Nu
Samek									Xi
'Ayin									Omicron
Pē									Pi
Ṣadē									San
Qop									Qoppa
Resh									Rho
Šin									Sigma
Tau									Tau
									Phi
									Chi

FIG. 94 COMPARATIVE TABLE OF PHOENICIAN AND EARLIEST GREEK ALPHABETICAL SCRIPTS

ALL LETTERS SHOWN IN RETROGRADE FORM

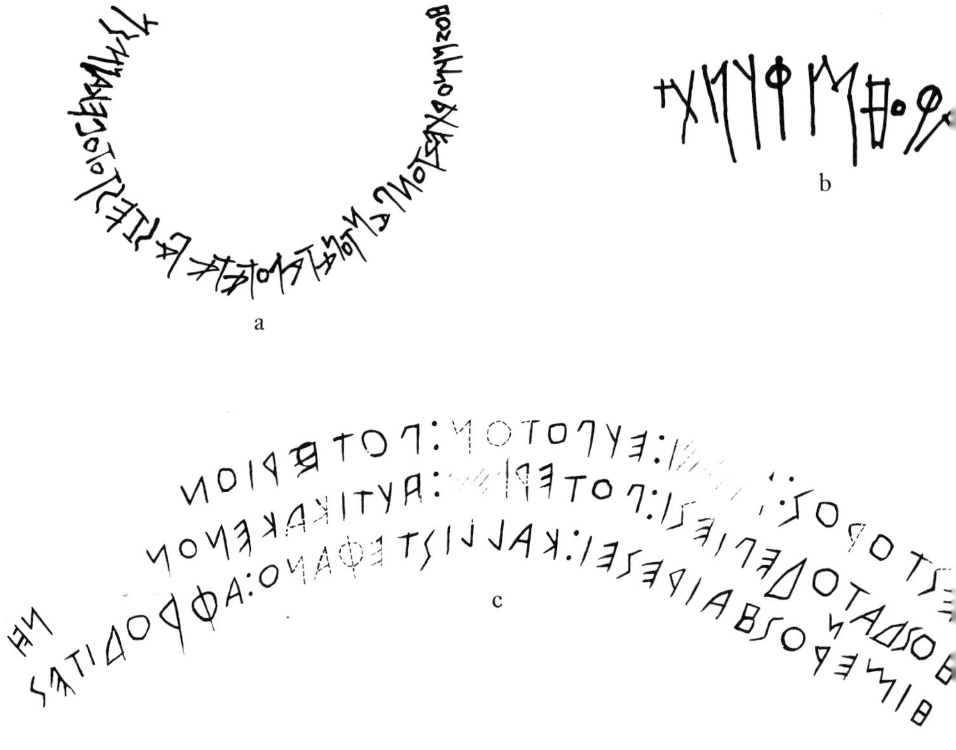

FIG. 95 EIGHTH-CENTURY GREEK GRAFFITI
(a) from the Dipylon oinochoe (Athens):
Ϝος νυν ορχεστον παντον ἀταλοτατα παιζει τοτοδεκλλμιν
(b) from the Rhodian Qoraqos skyphos (Copenhagen):
Ϙοραϙο ημι ϙυλιχς
(c) from the Nestor kotyle (Pithecusae):
Νεστορος: ε[ιμ]ι: ευποτ[ον]: ποτεριο[ν:] Ϝος δ' α<ν> τοδε π[ιε]σι: ποτερι[ο]:
αυτικα κενον Ϝιμερος αιρεσει: καλλιστε[φα]νο: Αφροδιτες
(*Transliterations after L. H. Jeffery, LSAG*)

somewhere within the first half of the eighth century.

To determine the birthplace is much more difficult; but, with this end in view, we shall briefly present the claims of the various places in the Greek world which have produced eighth-century inscriptions.

We start with Athens, source of the earliest datable inscription: a graffito on the shoulder of a LG Ib oinochoe from the Dipylon Workshop (fig. 95a). As in all Phoenician and much early Greek writing, the letters read from right to left. A complete hexameter verse announces a dancing competition: 'He who, of all the dancers, now performs most daintily'; the garbled sequel, in a less skilful hand, seems to award the oinochoe to the winner. Unusually close to their Phoenician prototypes are the sidelong α, the crooked ι, and the curved π; the first is shared only by Pithecusae, the last only by Pithecusae and Crete. The Athenian case is slightly weakened by some negative evidence: after the Dipylon oinochoe, no more Attic inscriptions are known until the graffiti from the Hymettus sanctuary on Subgeometric vessels around and after 700 B.C., and these might appear to inaugurate a fresh start with upright α, straight ι, and rectilinear π; it has even been doubted whether the Dipylon oinochoe was inscribed by a local man.[6] But we must not forget the outward-looking character of Athens during the most likely period for the genesis of the Greek alphabet. Athenians of 800–750 B.C. wishing to learn Phoenician letters would not have lacked opportunities; although their pottery has not been found at Al Mina, Attic MG II exports reached the eastern Mediterranean in some quantity, and the oriental goldsmiths working somewhere in Attica (p. 80) may have been Phoenician-speaking.

The oldest Cretan inscription, perhaps before 700 B.C., comes from the town of Phaistos: a retrograde graffito on a large domestic pithos, claiming it as the property of one Herpetidamos. The main strength of the Cretan case, however, lies in the old-fashioned character of the local alphabet, which suggests first-hand acquaintance with Semitic writing. Unusual near-Phoenician forms include five-stroke μ, crooked ι, and curved π; more striking still is the absence of the non-Phoenician supplementary letters, φ, χ, and ψ. (This 'primitive' alphabet is shared by Melos and Thera, two of the very few places which imported Cretan LG pottery.) Without having to leave their own shores, Cretans would have had many chances of meeting literate orientals; the island was frequently visited by Phoenician traders all through the eighth century, and one thinks also of the Levantine goldsmith and his family who used the tholos tomb at Teke near Knossos.

For Rhodians, too, opportunities for meeting Phoenicians would have been at home rather than in the Levant; East Greek pottery at Al Mina goes back only to c. 720 B.C., too late for the birth of the Greek alphabet. The Dodecanese, on the other hand, had been visited by Phoenician traders since MG times, and from c. 750 B.C. onwards there is some trace of a small Phoenician community residing among Greeks at Ialysos, engaged in marketing unguents locally and farther west. One of the very oldest Greek graffiti is on a glazed skyphos fragment bought in Rhodes, not closely datable, but of mid-eighth-century type.[7] The inscription, which reads 'I am the cup of Qoraqos' (fig. 95b), already includes a χ (compare the Dipylon oinochoe), and there are no unusual near-Phoenician forms; the alternative guttural qoppa, before o and v, is quite usual in early Greek writing.

The claim of Corinth is comparatively weak. Her pottery, though widely exported all through the eighth century, does not occur in the Levant before the last two decades. A closed deposit in the Corinthian Potters' Quarter has produced an extensive graffito incised in a neat and compact style, giving a list of personal names. All the published and datable sherds from this context appear to be of the late eighth century, but it is not clear when the deposit was sealed.

Most epigraphists are reluctant to allow such accomplished writing until the sixth century, when closely comparable forms are known from Corinth.[8]

The Euboeans were among the most energetic Greek traders in the Levant during the period in question, if we accept the exported pendent-semicircle skyphoi as being largely of Euboean origin; at all events, a more exclusively Euboean LG style is present among the Greek pottery at Al Mina. In the home-land, three short graffiti from Lefkandi are unlikely to be later than *c.* 710 B.C., when the town was abandoned; one shows an almost vertical five-stroke μ,[9] recalling a Phoenician *mēm* of the late ninth century at Zinjirli.[10] In the west, the colony of Pithecusae has been prolific of eighth-century inscriptions. The most celebrated is on the 'Nestor' kotyle, including two lines of hexameter verse (fig. 95c): '[?I am] the fair drinking-cup of Nestor; and he who drinks from this cup, straightway shall the desire of fair-crowned Aphrodite seize him'. This vessel, imported from Rhodes, was eventually buried with its owner around 720–710 B.C. [gr. 282], but the carousal for which it was inscribed may have happened a decade or two earlier. The lettering is well-disciplined and compact, in contrast to the spidery writing of the Dipylon and Qoraqos graffiti; the hand was steady, sober, and well-practised. The alphabet includes the near-Phoenician five-stroke μ, which was retained by Euboic scripts for a long time. We cannot assume that the first colonists were already literate on arrival in their new home, since the alphabet could have reached them during subsequent exchanges with their mother-cities. Yet two other Pithecusan graffiti stand closer than the 'Nestor' inscription to the Phoenician prototypes, and may therefore be appreciably earlier, or at any rate imply earlier knowledge of the alphabet. One preserves a sidelong α and a slightly curved π (again, compare the Dipylon oinochoe), as opposed to the upright α and the rectilinear π in fig. 95c; on another, the alter-native sibilants sigma and *san* appear side by side, implying that Euboean experience of the alphabet goes back to a time of uncritical acceptance of the Phoenician repertoire, before any extra letters (e.g., the ϕ of the 'Nestor' inscrip-tion) were added.[11] The colonial script of Pithecusae and Cumae became, in its turn, the parent of the Etruscan alphabet, which made its first appearance shortly before 700 B.C: one of the oldest inscriptions in the Etruscan language is on an imported EPC kotyle found at Tarquinia, bearing the names of its two owners;[12] another graffito claims possession of a local plate, found in the same tomb at Caere as two EPC drinking-vessels, a Rhodian aryballos, and a colonial Greek oinochoe.[13]

A fairly consistent picture emerges: knowledge of the alphabet comes first to those regions of the Greek world which, from archaeological evidence, seem to have had direct dealings with Phoenicians, whether in eastern commerce, or in commerce at home, or in conversation at home with resident oriental craftsmen. Now all early Greek scripts, in spite of their minor differences, diverge con-sistently from their Phoenician parent in the provision of vowels, the creation of *digamma* and v from the same Phoenician letter (*wāw*), and – to some extent – the treatment of sibilants; one might therefore assume that the Greek alphabet was not independently evolved in several places at once, but was first worked out in one particular centre, and thence diffused elsewhere. Yet when we look for this cradle of the Greek alphabet, the evidence does not point decisively in any one direction. On epigraphical grounds, the Euboeans certainly have a strong claim to be regarded as the first Greeks to write alphabetically; and their merchants at Al Mina, living among a Phoenician majority, would have been especially well placed for learning enough Phoenician to master the alphabet at an early stage, and then bringing back their discovery to the Greek homeland.[14] Yet the 'primitive' alphabet of Crete, too, may betray some direct knowledge of Phoenician writing, perhaps acquired from immigrant oriental metalworkers; and it should also be noted that the near-Phoenician form of crooked ι appears both in Crete and on the Athenian Dipylon oinochoe, but not, apparently, in the Euboic script.[15] We cannot, then, exclude the possibility that the Greek alphabet originated somewhere in the Aegean world, from direct contact with Phoenician residents.

A fresh line of argument is opened up by the early alphabetic script of the Phrygian kingdom. At Gordion, the capital city, six graffiti precede the destruction by Cimmerian nomads, dated to 696 B.C. by Eusebius, and to 676 B.C. by Julius Africanus; five were found in the largest royal tumulus burial (MMT), whereas the sixth comes from a settlement deposit earlier than the final pre-Cimmerian buildings. Like early Greek scripts, the Phrygian alphabet contains five vowels and a digamma; and therefore it cannot have been derived independently from the vowelless Phoenician script; somewhere along the line of transmission, Greek and Phrygian scribes must have collaborated. Now the Greeks are most unlikely to have learned their alphabet from Phrygia, since the Gordion graffiti have upright α and straight ι as against the near-Phoenician sidelong α and crooked ι found on – for example – the Dipylon oinochoe. The excavator of Gordion[16] suggested that the vowelled alphabets for both languages were evolved together from Phoenician sources by Greeks and Phrygians residing together somewhere in North Syria (e.g., Al Mina) or Cilicia. Much depends on the chronology of the Gordion graffiti, which is far from certain. In the excavation reports it is argued that the tumulus was closed between 725 and 717 B.C., and that the piece from the settlement may go back into the early eighth century. But a lower dating is also possible, which places the tumulus burial down in the 680s;[17] this would still be consistent with the destruction date given by Africanus, which on other grounds (p. 265) seems the more plausible of the two alternatives. It remains possible, then, that alphabetic writing came to Phrygia from the Greek homeland, without any need for either alphabet to have been first worked out in the Levant; and the existence of late eighth-century graffiti from Old Smyrna indicates an alternative route of transmission, through Ionia and Lydia.[18]

It remains to consider the uses to which the newly recovered art of writing was put. The Mycenaean Linear B script had been largely reserved for palace administration, and only a trained scribe could master its complexities. The very simplicity of the alphabetical system encouraged a much higher proportion of Greeks to become literate. We can watch the process of learning in a number of abecedaria incised on pottery, from the late eighth century onwards;[19] and the rapid spread of literacy is reflected in the casual nature of the earliest graffiti, all of which are concerned with private life. A man incises his name on a drinking-cup, one of his most personal possessions; dancing, drinking, and moments of cheerful relaxation are mentioned in hexameter verse. Two potters of c. 700 B.C., a Pithecusan and an Athenian, each sign one of their figured works in glaze-paint before firing.[20] Inscribed dedications to the gods begin at about this time: the first certain instance is on a Boeotian bronze male figurine offered to Apollo by one Mantiklos (c. 680 B.C.), but a crude and fragmentary stone inscription from the Athenian Acropolis may still be within the eighth century.[21] Considerably later, well down in the seventh century, is part of a legal code from the Cretan city of Dreros, inscribed on stone;[22] this is the earliest known example of Greek alphabetic writing being pressed into the service of the *polis*.

NOTES

1 See, most recently, G. P. and R. B. Edwards, *Kadmos* 13 (1974), 54–5.
2 Later to become η in Ionia, where the aspirate was not sounded.
3 Jeffery, *BSA* 59 (1964), 42 no. 20; on the evolution of the various Greek alphabets, *LSAG* part I. An alternative theory concerning the sibilants, implying even deeper confusion, is offered by B. Einarson, *CP* 62 (1967), 1 ff.
4 *AJA* 37 (1933), 13 fig. 3.
5 *LSAG* 18.
6 Jeffery, *LSAG* 68; *contra*, Guarducci *ArchClass* 16 (1964), 136.
7 *Sukas* I, 174 fig. 64; for the low offset lip cf. two other glazed skyphoi from contexts of c. 750 B.C.: *ClRh* 6–7, 194 no. 3 fig. 232 (Camirus tomb 82, see above p. 247), and *Exochi* fig. 106 (gr. M, 3).
8 See, most recently, A. Boegehold, *GRBS* 15 (1974), 25 ff.
9 *Lefkandi* 33–4 fig. 79.
10 *AJA* 38 (1934), 364 no. 9.
11 E. Peruzzi, *Origini di Roma* II (Bologna, 1973), 24 ff. pl. 4c,a.
12 H. Jucker, *StEtr* 37 (1969), 501 ff. pls. 135–6.
13 G. Colonna, *StEtr* 36 (1968), 265 ff. figs. 1–4.
14 Jeffery, *LSAG* 10–12; cf. Cook and Woodhead, *AJA* 63 (1959), 175–8.
15 M. Guarducci, *Geras A. Keramopoullou* (1953), 342–54, argues the case for a Cretan origin of the alphabet; also *ArchClass* 16 (1964), 124–7, and cf. now Jeffery, *Kadmos* 9 (1970), 153, and *AG* 181.
16 R. S. Young, *Hesperia* 38 (1969), 252 ff.
17 Snodgrass, *DAG* 349–50.
18 Jeffery, *BSA* 59 (1964), 40; graffito no. 2 (c. 700 B.C.) *may* be in Lydian.
19 *LSAG* 69 pl. 1, 3c; 116–17 pl. 18, 2; *Hesperia* 30 (1961), 146 fig. 1 pl. 23.
20 *AR* 1971, 67 fig. 8, Pithecusae; *LSAG* 110 pl. 16, 1, part of a signature by the Early Protoattic Analatos Painter (cf. J. M. Cook, *Gnomon* 34 (1962), 823; id., *Mélanges A. Varagnac* (1971), 175).
21 *LSAG* 90–1 pl. 7, 1, Mantiklos; 69–70 pl. 1, 2, Acropolis.
22 *LSAG* 310–11 pl. 59, 1a.

12 Towns and Villages

Geometric Greece is rich in graves, but traces of the living are comparatively scarce. Whereas eighth-century burials have been excavated at well over a hundred sites throughout the Greek world, fewer than fifty have produced any evidence of settlement. At most of these places the architectural remains are either negligible or missing altogether, the evidence often being confined to a handful of Geometric sherds found in later contexts. The chief reason for this state of affairs is the flimsy nature of most Geometric houses, especially on the Greek mainland where it was the custom to build in mud brick on a rough stone base. This sort of structure had little chance of surviving the hazards of later periods, whenever wide and deep trenches had to be dug for the laying of massive and monumental foundations. Hence we may never gain anything more than a very sketchy knowledge of those major Geometric cities on the mainland which were also destined to enjoy the most distinguished future: Athens, Corinth, and Argos. Thanks to the huge overlay of Archaic, Classical, Hellenistic, Roman, and more recent periods, the remains of Geometric houses in these cities are very scanty indeed; at many points nothing is left except for domestic deposits in wells. However, by taking into consideration the wide scatter of contemporary graves, we can roughly plot the inhabited areas; and in each case it seems that the eighth-century city still consisted of a group of detached and unfortified villages, without any obvious centre of public life.[1] The same appears to be true of Eretria and Knossos, two other major cities of this period which are less heavily overlaid, and which may therefore reveal more of their plan to present and future excavators.

Opportunities for exploration are especially favourable at Old Smyrna, a *polis* cut off in its prime by a Lydian army around 600 B.C. The Geometric town was of moderate size, occupying a promontory about 350m. long and 250m. wide. To judge from the main area so far excavated (*c.* 90 × 40m.), habitation was already quite dense by the late eighth century; but there was a curious contrast between the squalor of the private houses and the magnificent walls which enclosed the whole city. To have any fortifications at all was unusual for a Geometric *polis*; the only other complete circuits of these times are at Melia and Emporio, hastily thrown up in rubble to protect the acropolis only. But there is nothing hasty about the walls of Smyrna (fig. 96a pp. 261 f.), which must have been the pride of the city. They have a monumental appearance, far in advance of their time. Even in their original form (*c.* 850 B.C.), the foundations of one bastion consist of sawn ashlar blocks almost a metre long, laid in regular courses.[2] When the circuit was repaired and thickened in the mid-eighth century, the inner foundations were faced with huge hammer-dressed blocks of approximately polygonal shape; although the crevices contain a few small stones, there is already some attempt to fit the blocks together.[3] By *c.* 700 B.C. this style of walling had been adopted at Miletus (p. 261) and Antissa (p. 263) in a much-improved form; thus the invention of true polygonal masonry, where the joints are dressed to fit exactly, may fairly be ascribed to East Greek builders. They must also take the credit for being pioneers in other forms of monumental construction, if we bear in mind the sheer size and spacious planning of the first Hekatompedon on Samos, and the elegant ashlar work of its third and fourth altars (p. 254). Such precocity can hardly be explained by eastern influence, since Ionia had very little communication with Phrygia or the Levant before the end of the eighth century. It has been suggested[4] that the first Ionian settlers might have brought with them some skill in monumental masonry inherited from Mycenaean tradition, which they would then have adapted and transformed throughout the Dark Ages; alternatively, a native Anatolian tradition of fine masonry, as seen in the final walls of Troy VI, may not have been entirely forgotten. Even so, we have no positive evidence of any such skill among the eastern Greeks before the ninth-century circuit of Old Smyrna.

Altogether more primitive are the eighth-century dwellings just inside the Smyrnaean fortifications. Here we have a chaotic jumble of cottages, some rectangular, some oval, but mainly apsidal, and nearly all detached; also a number of curved walls which enclosed courtyards, one of which contains a circular granary (fig. 96b). The long and open-ended apsidal plan has an unbroken history going back to the arrival of the first Greeks (*c.* 2200 B.C.); it became extremely popular in the Middle Bronze Age, continued sporadically in backward areas of Mycenaean Greece,[5] and eventually re-emerged as the chief architectural form of the later Dark Ages.[6] This kind of building was almost always constructed in mud brick on a stone base, and covered by a thatched roof pitched at a steep angle (e.g., fig. 96c). The rounded end was preferred because it solved the problem of weather-proofing, to the extent that all the mud-brick walls could receive some protection from the thatched eaves. Because of their shape and construction, such buildings must remain isolated and detached; they cannot comfortably become part of a larger ensemble. For temples, which require isolation, the apsidal form remained popular on the Greek mainland until well into the seventh century; but not so in settlements, which had to provide for a rapidly rising population. Already in LG times, apsidal houses could flourish only where space was still plentiful: for example, in the Barbouna suburb of Asine (p. 145), or at Lefkandi (p. 196), a town which by now was a shadow of its former self, probably depleted by a steady emigration to the new city of Eretria. Within the walls of Smyrna, the curvilinear dwellings of this period look distinctly cramped and unhappy; perhaps the central part of the town, as yet undug, was better appointed; at all events, after the destruction of *c.* 700 B.C., the Smyrnaeans replaced these hovels with a more tightly knit rectilinear plan, more solidly constructed, and affording much more living space. By the seventh century, apsidal houses were passing out of fashion.

The most vivid impressions of daily life can be obtained from Zagora on Andros, and Emporio on Chios. Their excellent preservation is due partly to

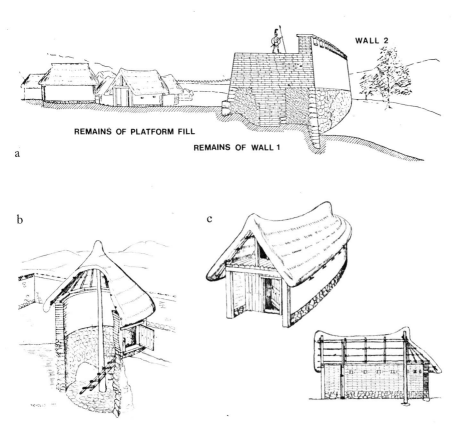

a

b

c

FIG. 96 OLD SMYRNA IN THE EIGHTH CENTURY B.C.
(a) second fortification wall; (b) granary; (c) apsidal house.
Reconstructions by R. V. Nicholls.

their early desertion, and partly to the local tradition of building walls entirely in stone, common to all islands at this time. Despite various similarities, the two settlements differ in size, status, and terrain.

Zagora (fig. 97), founded well before 800 B.C. and abandoned around 700 B.C., may have been a colony of Eretria (p. 199), but was the largest town on the island during its brief existence. The houses are spaciously laid out on a high headland (c. 850 × 550m.), fairly flat on top, but falling away precipitously down to a small harbour on either side. The only easy approach is barred by a massive fortification across the promontory's neck, in places 7m. thick, with the only gate and bastion at its southern extremity. A sanctuary stands in the centre of the town near the summit; the cult persisted long after the desertion of the settlement, the temple assuming its final form during the sixth century.

Emporio (fig. 99) was never more than a straggling village, the sovereign *polis* being on the site of the modern town of Chios. The houses, spread over an area *c*. 300 × 250m., run up a steep terraced hill a little way inland, with a sanctuary of Athena on its saddle; there is another shrine down by the harbour. The layout reminds one of many Aegean island communities today, divided between a hamlet around the harbour (*skala*) and a main village (*chora*) on a hill slope about half an hour's walk inland. The history of the *chora* usually goes back to a time when no coastal settlement was safe from pirates; today, in more tranquil times, many a *chora* is gradually losing its inhabitants, some moving house to the *skala* below. Something similar may have happened at Emporio. The inland village, invisible to any freebooter approaching the harbour, enjoyed the additional protection of a rough circuit 2m. thick round its acropolis. Occupation began in the late eighth century, but the houses on the hill had been abandoned by 600 B.C. The inhabitants evidently moved down to the harbour, perhaps encouraged by the greater safety of the seas, and the consequent opportunities for commerce. Yet the upper sanctuary, like that of Zagora, continued to receive visitors; indeed, nearly all its architecture is later than the desertion of the upper village.

The steep terrain of Emporio allowed very little scope for planning. A main road climbs up from the harbour area to the acropolis; at least two streets diverge from it, following the contours of the hill; along and between them the village grew up in a haphazard manner, each dwelling perched on a narrow terrace, and almost every one a detached building. Zagora, by contrast, occupies a much gentler slope, rising to a broad plateau at the top. Here the houses are grouped together in large clusters, the only fully detached building being the temple. The general alignment of the house walls is so consistent that one might reasonably attribute its original planning to a single master-architect. So far, less than a quarter of the settlement has been excavated, and not much is known about the street plan; but street corners can sometimes be inferred from the rounded corners of buildings (e.g., room D 3), which would have eased the progress of pack animals.[7] The oldest buildings seem to have been in the central area where two phases can often be traced; some of the original rooms were later subdivided (e.g., rooms H 26–7), and one of the outlying districts (J) may not have been settled until the LG period. Here, then, as in other prosperous regions of Greece, one gets the impression of a rapid rise in population during the course of the eighth century.

Following the usual island custom, the houses of both sites are rectangular and stone-built. Rough conglomerate was used at Emporio. At Zagora there was a choice of grey marble and brown schist; the latter was usually preferred, not least because it splits neatly into thin and level slabs, and was especially suitable for thresholds, door-jambs, lintels, and roofing. Flat roofs must have been the general rule; at Emporio most houses have internal column bases, and the tops of pithoi served as chimneys. Some traces of internal supports have been found at Zagora, and the large agglomerations there can only have been flat-roofed; long

FIG. 97 ZAGORA ON ANDROS: PLAN, AFTER 1971 SEASON
By J. J. Coulton (apud Cambitoglou, *PAE* 1972, 260)

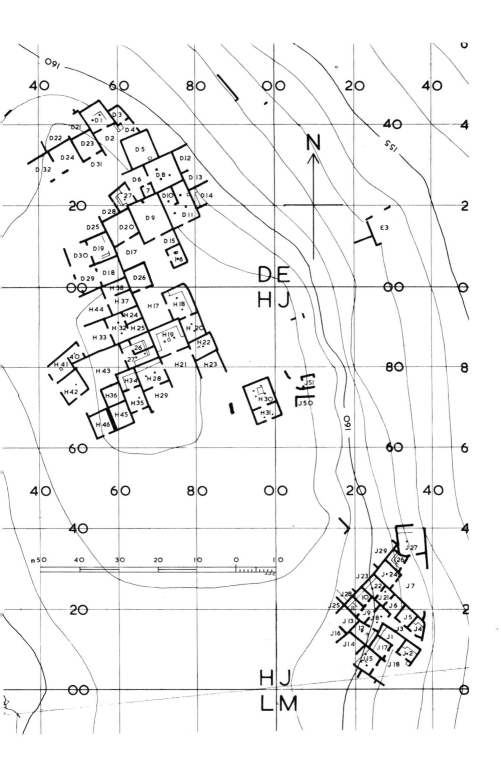

wooden beams probably carried a covering of schist slabs and clay waterproofing in the fashion of many Cycladic houses today.

Two types of house were observed at Emporio, belonging to two different social classes. The simpler kind, for humbler citizens, consists of a single square room, often furnished with a stone bench running along one wall. The more pretentious resembles a Homeric *megaron*: a long hall approached through a porch with two columns *in antis*, and in one case ('The Lower Megaron') a central hearth is preserved. These *megara* housed the aristocracy, and the largest one (18·75 × 6·85m.) was the residence of the local chief; apart from a simple altar in the sanctuary of Athena, this was the only building on the acropolis. The houses of Zagora show more variety, and it is not always easy to define their limits within the large agglomerations. In general, square living rooms are preferred, sometimes standing alone, and sometimes (like *megara*) approached through a porch (e.g., D 1–2, 3–4). There are several open courtyards, one containing a small square enclosure which could have been a pen for animals (D 6, 7: fig. 98). Another courtyard leads to a most impressive hall (H 19, 7·5 × 7·0m.) with a stone bench running round three walls, a large central hearth, a sunken bin both formed of schist slabs, and a paved platform which may have supported stairs to an upper storey; its central position, its nearness to the sanctuary, and its furnishing seem to distinguish it as the home of the leading citizen. Two other rooms leading off the same courtyard may also have belonged to him, but we cannot be sure.

Stone benches, running along one or more walls of a room, are the most characteristic fixtures of Geometric houses. We find them also at Kastro on Siphnos, at Thorikos in Attica, and at Phaistos in Crete, but nowhere are they so abundant as at Emporio and Zagora. They might be used for seating and sleeping – though this is not to deny the domestic use of movable furniture, like the stools, chairs, and beds shown in Attic Geometric funerary scenes,[8] and the chests of which miniatures were made in clay (e.g., p. 55 fig. 13a). A third function of the bench was storage; many at Zagora had rows of pithoi embedded in them, or holes for pithoi (as D 27, fig. 98) – an idea which has a Mycenaean precedent in the palace storerooms at Pylos. Further storage space was provided by the schist-lined bins sunk in the floors, especially suitable for grain or water. The central hearths would have served for cooking as well as for heating.

The supply of drinking-water must often have been a pressing problem. The only apparent source at Emporio is a square stone-lined well halfway between the harbour and the upper village.[9] At Zagora no wells or cisterns have been found within the settlement; there is plenty of water in the neighbouring valleys, but the nearest spring is ten minutes' walk beyond the town wall. To meet an emergency during enemy attack, the Zagoritans could have conserved their rainwater by channelling it down from flat roots into bins and pithoi; there is some positive evidence of this device outside a Geometric house on Siphnos (p. 210), and even today some Aegean islanders find it necessary to lay up a reserve of water in this manner. More fortunate were the Smyrnaeans, who could use a spring just under their fortifications; this they covered with an elegant fountain-house in corbelled masonry some time in the seventh century. A separate bathroom, in the Geometric world, would have been an inconceivable luxury; but Miletus'

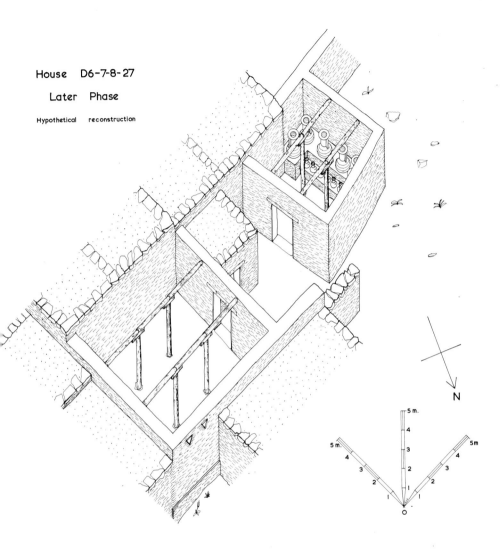

House D6-7-8-27

Later Phase

Hypothetical reconstruction

N

FIG. 98 ZAGORA: ROOMS D8, D7, D6, D27 (L. TO R.)
Isometric reconstruction by J. J. Coulton (*PAE* 1972, 261)

reputation for soft living may perhaps go back to our period, for hence comes the earliest known post-Mycenaean bath – an oval hip-tub from Kalabak Tepe.[10] When seated, the bather would hardly have immersed his ankles.

In one sense the Dark Ages lasted until the early seventh century, for that is the date of the earliest post-Mycenaean lamps.[11] Simple saucers with pinched rims were used for this purpose in the eastern Mediterranean, but these found no

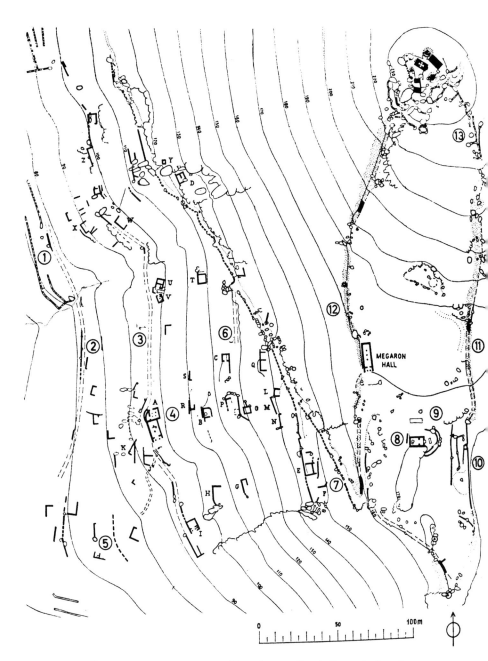

FIG. 99 EMPORIO ON CHIOS: PLAN (Boardman, *Greek Emporio* fig. 4); by M. G. F. Ventris

imitators in Geometric Greece. Perhaps the need for artificial illumination was not acutely felt until the recovery of literacy had become widespread; for feasting, oral recitation, spinning, and weaving, the hearth would have given enough light.[12] Again, Geometric buildings had no basements, in contrast to the Minoan palaces where the basement magazines would have needed lamplight even by day. The houses of Zagora, no doubt, had their dark corners, yet every room was accessible to daylight through at least one exterior wall, and – one presumes – a skylight above the central hearth. By a lucky chance one window was found in 1971 among a mass of upper masonry fallen like a pack of cards; the shape is triangular, like the windows on the Perachora model (fig. 103).

Few Geometric houses afford any clues to their owners' occupation. Spinning and weaving were among the tasks of household women, not of specialist craftsmen; that is the impression given by the wide scatter of loomweights and spindle-whorls at Zagora, where two sets of whorls were found even in the local chief's house (H 19). In some of the large cities, potters certainly had their own quarter by the seventh century, and possibly already by the late eighth; although little or nothing remains of their premises, this inference rests on concentrations of misfired trial pieces in the most westerly district of Corinth, and in the poor area of Athens which later became the Agora.[13] Rather more substantial are the traces of metalworking. A ninth-century establishment at Thorikos (p. 70) was devoted to the extraction of silver by cupellation, and a kiln for the same purpose at Argos dates from Early Protogeometric times.[14] Most striking of all, however, is the metalworking establishment of eighth-century Pithecusae (p. 226), consisting of two blacksmiths' workshops with their forges, and an adjoining dwelling-house. This quarter occupies a ridge on the outskirts of the settlement; there the smiths would have had easy access to their fuel and a breeze to fan their furnaces, without any danger of setting fire to the central part of the town on the acropolis.[15] Iron, bronze, and lead were worked here; commerce with Etruria assured a steady supply of the ores, and a ready market for finished products in metal and clay.

Potters and smiths worked as specialist craftsmen who could reasonably hope to make a living by bartering their handiwork. Master-potters in Corinth were turning out exceptionally fine ware with a view to markets overseas (pp. 186–7), while Peloponnesian bronzesmiths supplied the needs of aristocratic customers wishing to make showy dedications at Olympia and Delphi. The various patterns of commerce, which we have tried to trace in the preceding chapters, imply the existence of shipowning traders who acquired and maintained their wealth as middlemen; one thinks especially of the Euboean merchants who gained a foothold at Al Mina in order to export oriental goods to Greece, to the western colonies, and to Etruria. The Euboean states and Corinth have constantly been mentioned as being the leaders in eighth-century commerce; why was this so? The underlying reason may have been the shortage of arable land – a shortage which eventually forced these cities to found colonies in the west which were more agrarian than commercial. There are also some indications that the ruling aristocracies of Euboea and Corinth not only encouraged trade, but did not disdain to become traders themselves: for Euboea, one observes the knightly imagery on some of the figured vessels from Pithecusae (e.g., fig. 74c); for

FIG. 100 TERRACOTTA FIGURINE OF A DOMESTIC COCK
K gr. 50, no. 1308, L. 15

Corinth, there are the memories concerning the mercantile interests of the Bacchiad oligarchy, and the profitable journeys of the Bacchiad nobleman Demaratus.

The great majority of eighth-century Greeks, however, lived off the land. Farmers and shepherds, as always in Greece, had their permanent homes in towns and villages, not in remote farmhouses and crofts. A day's work might often begin and end with a long walk to and from the ploughed fields or the upland pastures; within the settlement, space had to be found for the penning of flocks and herds, the storage of grain and other fruits of the earth. Thus, to obtain a clear picture of Geometric farming, we need an analysis of organic remains from an excavated settlement, inhabited only during our period. Zagora, when fully studied, may produce some evidence of this kind; meanwhile we must be content with the meagre remains of funeral feasts, chiefly from Athenian graves. The animal bones, where distinguished by the excavator, are usually those of lambs or goats, less often of pigs, and very rarely bovine.[16] The fruit, found in carbonized form, consists of grapes and figs.[17] From the beginning of the Bronze Age the most important Aegean crops have been cereals, olives, and grapes. It would be surprising if the pattern had been any different in the eighth century; that it was similar is indirectly confirmed by pottery shapes, kraters and oinochoai for wine, lekythoi and aryballoi for olive oil, and granary models indicating an interest in grain. In addition, there are the remains of a circular granary at Old Smyrna (fig. 96b), and at Lefkandi the circular foundations of three mysterious structures which could have been granaries, oil-presses, or wine-presses.[18]

Sheep, goats, pigs, and cattle had been raised for several millennia, but the domestic fowl may well have been a newcomer to Greece during our period. Its occurrences in the Aegean Bronze Age are too rare for us to assume any steadfast attempt at domestication;[19] in Mycenaean art it is unknown. The next appearance is around 740 B.C., when a small Athenian boy was buried with a collection of terracotta playthings, including a pair of cocks (one, fig. 100). Thereafter, cocks and hens figure occasionally in the art of the next century,[20] and frequently after that. Aristophanes, referring to this useful creature as the Persian bird,[21] preserves a memory of its original habitat; its arrival in Greek farmyards, no doubt introduced by Levantine middlemen, represents yet another legacy of the Orient to Greece during the second half of the eighth century.

The hard life of a Geometric farmer is vividly described by the poet Hesiod. His father had formerly been a merchant of Aeolian Cyme; later, dogged by failure and poverty, he migrated with his family across the Aegean to become a peasant in Boeotia. He found land at Ascra, a village of the *polis* Thespiae, situated between the fertile plain and the foothills of mount Helicon: 'a miserable hamlet, bad in winter, sultry in summer, good at no time'.[22] If the place has been correctly identified, the poet was being unduly harsh; no doubt this harshness was part of his temperament, but he may also have been drawing an adverse comparison with the even richer plains of Asiatic Aeolis,[23] remembered from his childhood. While tending his lambs on the slopes of Helicon, he heard the call of the Muses.[24] His fame as a poet was secure by the last decade of the eighth century, during the Lelantine War; then it was that he visited Chalcis for the funeral games of the noble Amphidamas, and won a tripod as the prize for song (p. 201). After his father's death he went to law over the inheritance with his ne'er-do-well brother Perses; to no avail, since Perses had the ear of the corrupt noblemen (dōrophagoi basilēes) who dispensed justice and, as their epithet implies, received bribes in food. Hesiod's indignation is distilled in the *Works and Days*, a didactic poem addressed to his brother, exhorting him to eschew dishonesty for fair dealing, and idleness for hard work. The central part of the poem (lines 383–617) offers instruction in husbandry. The cultivation of cereals is the main theme, but there are also brief sections on viticulture. We are taught in detail how to construct a wooden plough; we are then taken briskly through the farmer's calendar, from ploughing and vine-pruning to harvesting, threshing, and the gathering of the vintage.

It has been suggested[25] that Hesiod was composing a tract for the times. According to this view, livestock had formed the staple diet of the Mycenaean and Dark Ages; arable farming, meanwhile, had been haphazard and sporadic. Then, during our period, there was a much more intensive and systematic cultivation of the land, because this was the most effective way of using the land to feed a rapidly rising population. Not that Hesiod praises the arable farmer's life for its intrinsic virtue; but man must needs till the soil, since the angry gods had hidden his livelihood under the surface. This is not the place to pursue the implications of this theory for the Mycenaean age; but in the late eighth century there must surely have been a great increase in food production. Many of Hesiod's audience – perhaps Hesiod's own family, too – may have been farming land which had only recently come under the plough; while their Euboean neighbours, through lack of land, were forced by overpopulation to send out colonial expeditions to Sicily, the Boeotians were able to colonize their own spacious plains and foothills. More open to question is the hypothesis that grain replaced livestock as the chief source of food during the eighth century. After studying the skeletal remains of an Athenian LG family buried within the later Agora, a physical anthropologist[26] thought that meat and milk formed an important part of their diet. Conversely, the clay chest of *c.* 850 B.C. (p. 55 fig. 13a), surmounted by a quintuple granary model, looks like the status symbol of an Athenian aristocratic family who already preferred to advertise their wealth in grain rather than in livestock; and models of clay chests without granaries, which probably had the same connotations, go well back into the tenth and even the eleventh centuries.[27] At Eleusis the worship of Demeter was probably continuous from Mycenaean times onwards (pp. 331–2). It is difficult, then, to believe in any sudden conversion from livestock to agrarian farming during the eighth century.

Thus far we have been dealing almost exclusively with private individuals, their houses, their domestic life, and their occupations. It remains to consider any material evidence of public business. Religion, sanctuaries, and temples will be treated in the next chapter. We have touched briefly on fortifications, which were the exception rather than the rule. The outstanding city walls are those of Old Smyrna, too massive and too careful to have been thrown up to meet a passing danger; their building was a corporate enterprise,[28] indicating a remarkable degree of political cohesion among the people who dwelt inside them. No similar cohesion can be observed on the Greek mainland, where the larger cities still comprised a loose network of unfortified villages.

Literary sources tell us that power was wielded everywhere by an aristocracy of birth, except where monarchy had survived all through the Dark Ages. Political units were based mainly on kinship. The smallest was the *genos*, the aristocratic clan; largest of all was the tribe. Tribal divisions sometimes transcend the limits of the *polis*, and must go back into the disorders of the early Dark Ages before the Ionian Migration; for the same Ionian tribal names recur on both sides of the Aegean, and likewise the same Dorian names are found in the Peloponnese, in Rhodes, and in Crete. At a later stage, but not later than the eighth century, an intermediate unit was evolved: the phratry, or brotherhood. Based originally on a group of *gene*, each phratry was probably swelled by unrelated retainers and followers, who sought the protection of the leading nobleman within the group. Perhaps one or more phratries formed the population of each disjunct village in the larger cities, and of the larger villages in the countryside; such settlements are too large for a *genos*, but too small for a tribe.

In some of the better-preserved towns and villages we can visualize the setting for public affairs. Secular public buildings were as yet unknown; but where the aristocracy is all-powerful, nothing is needed except an open space for assembly (agora in its original sense) where the majority listen and give voice to their opinions, but only a minority are entitled to take the decisions. At Emporio the open space is on the acropolis, between the sanctuary of the patron deity Athena and the *megaron* of the leading nobleman – perhaps the leader of the local phratry. We cannot know what his obligations were to the sovereign *polis* of Chios, 25km. away; but within his village he was a uniquely privileged person. His *megaron* overlooked the only approach to the acropolis, upon which he and his family were the only residents. Over the several hundred people who met outside his house, he may have exercised an almost monarchical sway. Zagora has a similar open space for assembly – again, between the sanctuary and the chief house; there the community must have been considerably larger, well into four figures; and the house, in contrast to the commanding and isolated position of its counterpart at Emporio, looks like the residence of *primus inter pares*. No agora has yet been found at Old Smyrna, where only a small part of the town has been excavated.

Although the known Agora of Athens was not laid out before the time of Solon, there is a dim memory of an older place of assembly on the saddle between the Acropolis and the Areopagus.[29] The site would have been extremely suitable, between the chief sanctuary on the citadel, and the hill where – to judge from the opulent ninth-century burials on its northern slope (pp. 30 f., 55 f.) – one of the leading *gene* may have lived. The existence of this 'ancient agora' has not yet been confirmed by excavation; but the Athenian aristocracy must surely have needed such a place by the eighth century, if we are to credit the accounts of their early constitution. According to Aristotle[30] the Athenian monarchy had been superseded first by a regent (*archon*) elected for life from the Medontid *genos;* later, the *archon*'s tenure was reduced to ten years, and eventually to only one. For the last two reforms Eusebius gives dates of 752 and 683 B.C.

It was in Crete, however, that the agora first became an architectural form, based on the memory of Minoan theatral steps. The agora of Dreros (p. 279) was laid out in the late eighth century, at the same time and on the same alignment as the temple of Apollo Delphinios. A similar concern for civic planning can be seen in the seventh-century *polis* of Lato, where the assembly steps overlook the temple. In neither case is there any sign of a leading aristocratic house near by; instead there is the *prytaneion*, the residence allotted to the elected magistrates. Cretans, like other Greeks, were ruled by aristocracies; but they were also pioneers in drafting constitutional law, defining and restricting the power of those to whom they entrusted their affairs. Given the care which the Drerians lavished on their centre of public life, it is no surprise that they have also left us the earliest known Greek law inscribed on stone, and therefore intended for public view;[31] dating from the mid-seventh century, it enacts that no man shall hold the high office of *kosmos* more than once every ten years.

NOTES

1 cf. Aristotle, *Politics* 1252 b15–26.
2 *BSA* 53–4 (1958–59), 68 ff. pl. 17c.
3 ibid. 98 pl. 10b,c.
4 R. V. Nicholls, *Gnomon* 44 (1972), 699 f.
5 e.g., at Olympia (*AM* 77 (1962), 19 n. 72; 24 nn. 97–8) and at Thermon in Aetolia (*AE* 1900, pl. opposite 191).
6 e.g., at Argos (above p. 36) and Nichoria (*Hesperia* 41 (1972), 251 ff. fig. 9).
7 *Zagora* I, 14.
8 See S. Laser, *ArchHom* C 32 ff., 45 ff., with suggested reconstructions; cf. Snodgrass, *Gnomon* 42 (1970), 159 ff.
9 *Emporio* 40 pl. 10f.
10 *Milet* I.8, 30 fig. 22, apparently from a LG context.
11 *Agora* IV, nos. 1–4; for a possible tenth-century lamp in Argive Pie Ware see Desborough, *BSA* 51 (1956), 129–30 no. 6 pl. 34a.
12 cf. *Odyssey* vi.305, where queen Arete does her handiwork by the light of the fire; cf. Lorimer, *HM* 509 ff.
13 *Corinth* XV.1, 3 ff.; *Agora* VIII, 12, 108, 110–11; XIV, 17, 186.
14 Desborough, *GDA* 162.
15 J. Klein, *Expedition* 14 (1972), 37.
16 Boardman, *JHS* 86 (1966), 2 n. 10; add *ClRh* 3 (Ialysos) 85, 97.
17 e.g., *Hesperia* 18 (1949), 282; 21 (1952), 281.
18 *Lefkandi* 30 figs. 68–70.
19 Two representations on Minoan seal designs (Evans, *Cretan Pictographs*, etc. (London, 1895), fig. 65a and *JHS* 22 (1902), pl. 10 no. 128); the bones of one fowl from a Middle Helladic stratum, *Lerna* I, 47–9.
20 Payne, *Necrocorinthia* 74 n. 9 for Corinthian examples; add *CVA* Providence pl. 8, 1a (Boeotian); *Hesperia* Suppl. II, 133 fig. 96 and *Agora* VIII, nos. 412, 430, 437–8, 445 (Attic); and the bronzes, *Eirene* 6 (1967), 125 ff. (cf. above, pp. 175, 207).
21 *Aves* 483–5.
22 *Erga* 639–40.
23 W. Leake, *Travels in Northern Greece* II (London, 1835), 491 ff.; cf. W. P. Wallace, *GRBS* 14 (1974), 5 ff.
24 *Theogony* 22 ff.
25 T. P. Howe, *TAPA* 89 (1958), 44 ff.; Snodgrass, *DAG* 378 ff.
26 J. Lawrence Angel, *Hesperia* Suppl. II, 246.
27 Smithson, *Hesperia* 30 (1961), 165 pl. 28 no. 42; 37 (1968) 93 ff.; and, from Lefkandi, *Archaeology* 25 (1972), 17.
28 Snodgrass, *DAG* 415 f.
29 Apollodorus, *FGH* 244 F 113; cf. Thompson, *Agora* XIV, 79; J. Travlos, *Pictorial Dictionary of Ancient Athens* (London, 1971), 1–2.
30 *Athenaion Politeia* 3.
31 Jeffery, *LSAG* 310–11 pl. 59, 1a.

13 Sanctuaries, Gods, and Votives

As prosperity gradually returned to the Greek world, the gods received an increasingly generous share of its fruits. During the ninth century, hardly more than a dozen sanctuaries had been receiving votive offerings, and at none of these places can we be sure that the resident deity was honoured with a temple. By 700 B.C. we know of at least seventy places of worship all over the Greek world, of which nearly half already possessed temples (fig. 101).

Our first task is to review the growth of these sanctuaries, paying special attention to the architecture of their temples. Then we shall inquire into the nature of their cults, and the gods who were worshipped. We must also face the difficult problems of origins, assessing the likelihood of any cult going back without break into the Late Bronze Age. The various classes of votives have already been treated in our earlier chapters, where their regional characteristics have received some emphasis; a more general discussion of their purpose will be added here. Especially remarkable are the dedications in bronze, which far surpass in abundance and splendour the analogous finds from graves and settlements. In conclusion we shall try to relate the spectacular development of the sanctuaries to the other manifestations of the Greek Renaissance.

Sanctuaries. Altars and Temples

The Greek temple, as an independent and freestanding structure, is largely a creation of the eighth century. The Minoans and Mycenaeans had had no need of such buildings; their cults were practised in rooms within houses and palaces, around sacred trees and pillars, and in the wild surroundings of caves and mountain peaks. The sanctity of some caves and peaks was still remembered in the eighth century, especially in Crete; there we have observed the Geometric offerings from the peak shrine of Kato Symi, and from the caves of Ida, Dicte, and Amnisos.

After the collapse of Mycenaean civilization, traces of domestic religion disappear. During the Dark Ages it seems that almost all worship took place in the open air,[1] usually round a raised altar for burnt sacrifices. Sometimes the altar was hewn out of the living rock, as at the Delion sanctuary of Paros; but the most widespread form had a stonebuilt exterior and an earth fill, such as we find at the Samian Heraion. There we are unusually well informed about the early structures of the sanctuary. The first two versions of the altar precede the earliest temple, and so cannot be later than the ninth century.[2] Much care was lavished on its subsequent rebuilding; thus Altar III (c. 750 B.C.), which goes with the

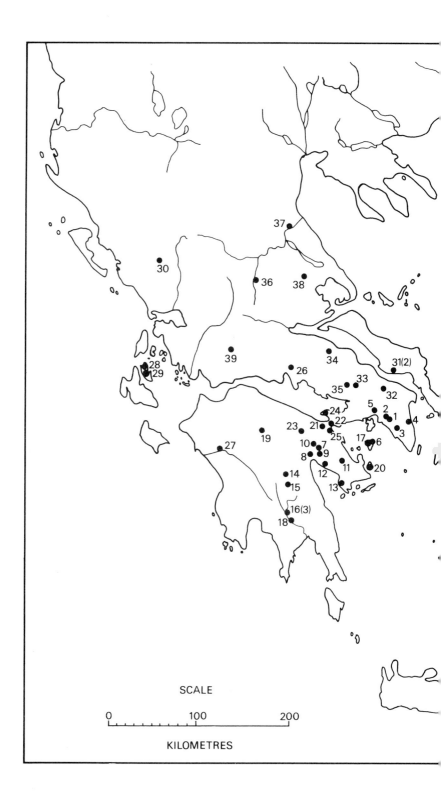

SCALE

0   100   200

KILOMETRES

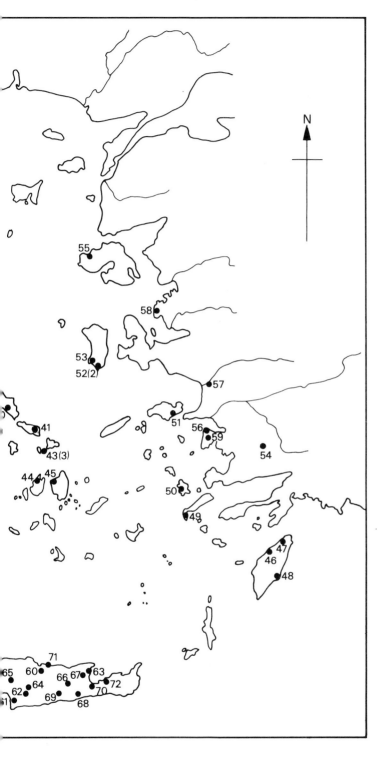

FIG. 101

SANCTUARIES
OF THE
GEOMETRIC
PERIOD
(See Key
overleaf)

Key to Fig. 101

Place names: Alphabetical Index

2 Academy	5 Eleusis	45 Naxos
29 Aetos	52 Emporio (3)	23 Nemea
17 Aigina	57 Ephesus	
71 Amnisos	11 Epidaurus, Maleatas	63 Olous
18 Amyclae	31 Eretria (2)	27 Olympia
55 Antissa	41 Exobourgo	
6 Aphaia		44 Paros, Delion
7 Argive Heraion	37 Gonnos	24 Perachora
8 Argos	62 Gortyn	61 Phaistos
69 Arkades		53 Phanai
12 Asine	13 Halieis	38 Pherae
49 Aspripetra	3 Hymettus	36 Philia
1 Athens		58 Phocaea
42 Ay. Irini	47 Ialysos	28 Polis
	65 Idaean Cave	32 Ptoion
4 Brauron	22 Isthmia	
		51 Samian Heraion
20 Calauria	35 Kabeirion	54 Sinuri
50 Calymnia	34 Kalapodhi	25 Solygeia
46 Camirus	68 Kato Symi	16 Sparta (3)
21 Corinth	72 Kavousi	
	60 Knossos	14 Tegea
43 Delos (3)		33 Thebes
26 Delphi	48 Lindos	39 Thermon
66 Dictaean Cave	19 Lousoi	9 Tiryns
59 Didyma	15 Mavriki	
30 Dodona	56 Miletus	70 Vrokastro
67 Dreros	10 Mycenae	40 Zagora

Place names: Numerical Index

1 Athens	25 Solygeia	49 Aspripetra
2 Academy	26 Delphi	50 Calymna
3 Hymettus	27 Olympia	51 Samian Heraion
4 Brauron	28 Polis	52 Emporio (2)
5 Eleusis	29 Aetos	53 Phanai
6 Aphaia	30 Dodona	54 Sinuri
7 Argive Heraion	31 Eretria (2)	55 Antissa
8 Argos	32 Ptoion	56 Miletus
9 Tiryns	33 Thebes	57 Ephesus
10 Mycenae	34 Kalapodhi	58 Phocaea
11 Epidaurus, Maleatas	35 Kabeirion	59 Didyma
12 Asine	36 Philia	60 Knossos
13 Halieis	37 Gonnos	61 Phaistos
14 Tegea	38 Pherae	62 Gortyn
15 Mavriki	39 Thermon	63 Olous
16 Sparta (3)	40 Zagora	64 Prinias
17 Aigina	41 Exobourgo	65 Idaean cave
18 Amyclae	42 Ay. Irini	66 Dictaean cave
19 Lousoi	43 Delos (3)	67 Dreros
20 Calauria	44 Paros, Delion	68 Kato Symi
21 Corinth	45 Naxos	69 Arkades
22 Isthmia	46 Camirus	70 Vrokastro
23 Nemea	47 Ialysos	71 Amnisos
24 Perachora	48 Lindos	72 Kavousi

first temple, already had a fine casing of ashlar masonry, and a step for the officiating priest (fig. 105). According to the usual custom, the altar stands to the east of the temple, opposite the entrance; but its different alignment is a reminder of its higher antiquity.

Wherever temples were built, altars precede them; this is the general rule throughout the Greek world. At Olympia the ash-altars of the various deities, and the mound of the hero Pelops, were the main, if not the only, sacred structures in the sanctuary during the Geometric period. In Sicily, where no temples are known before 600 B.C., the first Greek settlers at Naxos raised an altar to Apollo Archegetes, and the first colonists of Syracuse were no less prompt in founding an altar to Athena (pp. 233–4).

The first impulse towards the building of temples came at the very beginning of the eighth century, as we know from the excavations at Perachora, Eretria, and Samos. It was felt that the presiding deity needed a house, in which the cult image was to be given the place of honour, and the more important dedications could also be displayed. Apart from the bronze statues from Dreros (fig. 91) the images do not survive; they were almost certainly of wood, and crudely carved; the first Samian image of Hera was remembered as a 'plank' (p. 256), said to have been discovered in the branches of a venerable and sacred willow tree which determined the site of the sanctuary. But the first temples of Samos and Eretria, each a hundred feet long, were far larger than their function demanded. Granted that gods require more space than mortals; even so, there was already an element of local competition, spurring some communities to honour their own gods with an ostentatious piety.

The plans of eighth-century temples were adapted from three current types of domestic dwelling, each of which has precedents in the Bronze Age. The smallest and simplest has a square or broad rectangular shape, furnished with a stone bench along the back wall. A good example is the Heraion of Delos, very similar to the least pretentious houses of the settlements on Andros and Siphnos; many votives were found in the crevice behind the bench, on which they had presumably been displayed. A more sophisticated version of this plan is the Delphinion at Dreros (fig. 102), which probably had a porch; its interior furnishing has already been described (p. 280). Bench houses were known in Geometric Crete, notably at Phaistos; but the ancestry of this temple goes back to the benched shrines of Minoan palaces. Its interior sacrificial hearth, on the other hand, is derived from the Mycenaean *megaron*, a form introduced by Greek settlers during the Late Minoan III period. This feature recurs in the two seventh-century temples at Prinias in central Crete, but is foreign to the usual eighth-century practice elsewhere in Greece. Bench temples are known only in Crete and the Cyclades, the islands where it was the custom to build walls in stone to their full height.

A more widespread type of plan is the long apsidal hall, almost always approached through some sort of porch or anteroom. There is no need here to rehearse its long pedigree, going back on the Greek mainland to the Middle Bronze Age; it is enough to recall that, at the time when the first temples were being built, long apsidal houses were fashionable on both sides of the Aegean (p. 304). Except for Antissa on Lesbos, the sites with apsidal temples are all on the Greek mainland, where they were constructed of mud brick on a stone foundation; the roof was pitched at a steep angle, and covered with thatching. One of the earliest was the temple of Hera Akraia at Perachora, founded around 800 B.C.; to judge from its scanty remains this was a one-roomed building about 8m. long and 5m. wide. Among its votive offerings is a clay temple-model (fig. 103), the best preserved of at least five examples, giving a rough idea of a similar building in elevation. Here we see a shallow porch sustained by two pairs of columns in front of the side-walls (prostyle). The interior is lit by a row of small windows, square above the doorway, triangular elsewhere.[3] The roof is a tall convex vault, giving the temple a height twice its width. The broad eaves, suggestive of thatching, were meant to keep rainwater well clear of the walls, which would have been in vulnerable mud brick.

Apsidal temples have also been found at Eretria, Mycenae, and Galataki (ancient Solygeia) near Corinth; a fragmentary curved wall at Eleusis may belong to yet another. The Solygeia temple is the latest, built well after 700 B.C. when the apsidal form was no longer favoured in settlements (p. 304). Of outstanding interest are the two apsidal buildings in the sanctuary of Apollo Daphnephoros at Eretria: the 'bay hut', shortly followed by the first Hekatompedon.

The 'bay hut' (fig. 104a, H: 11·50 × 7·50m.) is one of the oldest buildings of Eretria. The surviving remains consist of a very low stone foundation, and a large number of clay column bases. There is no trace of the usual mud-brick walls, and the clay bases could only have supported slender wooden columns and an extremely light superstructure. Yet the columns were so disposed that they, and not the walls, would have taken the weight of the pitched roof. Two columns prostyle carried the porch, slots in the façade foundations received rectangular posts to reinforce the front wall, the entire 'horseshoe' wall was encased between pairs of attached columns placed inside and outside, and three columns near the centre formed a long triangular base upon which the king posts and the rafters were supported. An ingenious reconstruction (fig. 104b) produces a building which looks remarkably like the Perachora model.

Enclosed within this singular construction, the walls could have been even less substantial than the framework of wooden columns and beams; their only function was to keep out the rain. The excavators have put forward the intriguing and persuasive suggestion that this building was inspired by the first mythical temple of Apollo at Delphi, a hut built out of bay wood brought by Apollo himself from the vale of Tempe. But what was mythical in Pausanias' day must surely have had some reality in c. 800 B.C., if only because even the boldest architect needs a visible exemplar to guide him. It follows that the prototype at Delphi would have been in existence, and on view to Eretrian visitors, at this time; no such building has yet been found, but its flimsy foundations might prove hard to detect under the substantial buildings of Archaic, Classical, and later monuments. Perhaps the Delphic oracle had already assumed its role of advising the founders of new cities; in which case the Eretrians might well have chosen this way of rendering homage and thanks to the god who had guided them to their new home, the god whom they worshipped as Apollo Daphnephoros, 'bringer of the bay '.

The function of this very fragile building is not at all clear; at all events,

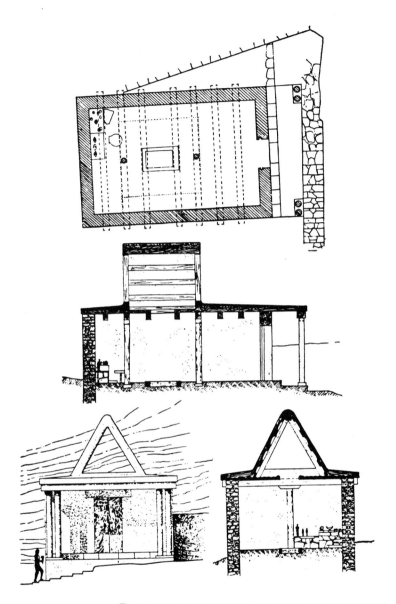

FIG. 102 DREROS, THE DELPHINION: PLAN, ELEVATION, SECTIONS
(BCH 60 pl. 31). The cult statues are shown in fig. 91

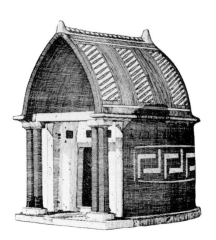

FIG. 103 PERACHORA, TEMPLE MODEL (*Perachora* I pl. 9)
(a) as preserved, (b) with roof restored; L. 35.6

the centre of the cult was a square altar (M) with a sacrificial pit, or *bothros*.
Facing it, but on a slightly different alignment, the front of a temple (K) was
started but not carried very far, soon to be replaced by the first Hekatompedon
(L). This is by far the longest of all apsidal temples and, like the first Heraion
at Samos, five times as long as it is wide; even so, in view of its great size, a
row of internal columns was needed to support the ridge roof. The long sides are
enlivened by a graceful convex curve.

The third type of plan is long and rectangular, the descendant of the Mycenaean *megaron*, and the ancestor of Doric and Ionic temples. The most primitive,
and possibly the earliest, is Megaron B at the sanctuary of Apollo at Thermon in
Aetolia. It has been assigned to the tenth century on the strength of some painted
sherds in a handmade ware of northern character; but these are not easily datable,
and may not be older than the eighth-century bronze figurines which constitute
the earliest evidence of cult. This temple, measuring 21.40 × 7·30m., follows the
alignment of the Mycenaean apsidal building adjoining it (Megaron A), and
has the same threefold division into a deep anteroom, a main room, and a
small room at the back; it may be that the ruins of the Mycenaean house were
still visible when Megaron B was built. All the exterior walls, except the façade,
are slightly convex, and the east side-wall is well enough preserved to show an
inward lean. There were no internal supports, but eighteen stone slabs form a
horseshoe round the side and back walls. These were once thought to be bases for
a primitive peristyle, but it is more likely[4] that they supported wooden posts
leaning against the eaves to buttress the rafters of a ridge roof. A sacrificial
bothros and other burnt deposits were found inside this building; some may go
back to an open-air cult before the temple was built.

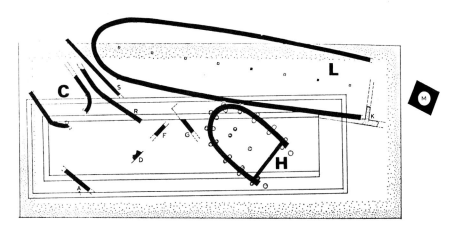

0 1 2 3 4 5   10m

a

b

FIG. 104 ERETRIA, SANCTUARY OF APOLLO DAPHNEPHOROS
(a) plan, *AntK* 17, 70 fig. 1; (b) reconstruction of bay hut by
P. Auberson, *AntK* 17 pl. 14

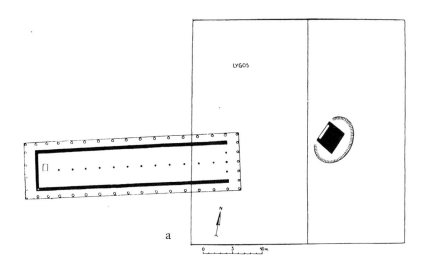

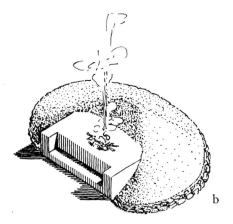

FIG. 105 SAMOS, HERAION
(a) Hekatompedon I, earliest form, with Altar III, *AM* 58,
162 fig. 14; (b) Reconstruction of Altar III, *JdI* 49, 145 fig. 4 top

Some doubt also surrounds the date of a narrow *megaron* on the acropolis of
Tiryns (20·90 × 6·90m.), overlying part of the *megaron* in the Mycenaean
palace. It shares the same floor level, and its central axis coincides with two of the
Mycenaean column bases, which were re-used *in situ*. The excavators saw here the
Geometric temple of Hera, whose offerings were found 22m. away in a *bothros*
deposit of *c.* 750–650 B.C. Other scholars, disturbed by the implication that the
Mycenaean *megaron*'s plan was still known in the eighth century, prefer to assign

the later *megaron* to a twelfth-century rebuilding of the palace. Until the stratified pottery from this area is fully published, this controversy cannot be resolved. A much smaller *megaron* at Asine (9·60 × 4·30m.), on the summit of Barbouna hill, must be the temple of Apollo Pythaeus, the only building spared by the Argives who destroyed the town in *c*. 710 B.C. (p. 154).

The first Heraion of Samos (fig. 105; pp. 97–9, 253–4) is a most adventurous building for its time. Built around 800 B.C., it was the earliest temple to establish the canonical length of a hundred feet, often followed in the Archaic period. A later eighth-century repair surrounded the temple with the earliest known peristyle of wooden columns – in the context, a lavish and spectacular method of protecting the mud-brick walls against the elements. As with the slightly later Hekatompedon of Eretria, a row of columns down the centre supported the ridge roof; at the back, the base of the cult statue was set slightly off centre, so that the internal supports should not obscure it. The open façade, with columns *in antis*, may be an East Greek speciality during our period, found also in the *megaron* houses of Emporio (p. 308). A comparison with the largest *megaron* there is instructive: the Heraion is almost twice as long, but has approximately the same width. The grandest house-plans could be elongated in the service of the gods; but the length of available timbers limited the width of a Geometric building to an absolute maximum of 8m.

Most Geometric sanctuaries, as we have seen, had no temple; where one existed, it was usually the only sacred building on the site. Some cults, however, were already needing additional buildings by the end of our period, to house an overflow of votive gifts. Thus, around 700 B.C., the Samians erected the first of several small treasuries near the temple.[5] On Delos the situation is obscure (pp. 215-16), but the long building under the Oikos of the Naxians may have served a similar function. An emergency arose at Perachora around 730 B.C., when the apsidal temple by the sea appears to have collapsed; while the centre of the cult remained down by the harbour, a rectangular building (9·50 × 5·60m.) was at once constructed 200m. up the valley, to receive dedications old and new.[6]

The Gods: Problems of Continuity

Votaries of our period did not inscribe their offerings; their gods must be deduced from later dedications, and from topographical allusions in written sources. Arguing from hindsight, and from a natural conservatism in religious matters, we assume that no sanctuary changed its deity after the Geometric period. Changes there certainly were, after the Mycenaean collapse; this is only to be expected at a time of destructions, migrations, and other upheavals. But when life had become settled once again, and when the political geography of Greece had become fixed, any further changes would be surprising.

By this reckoning, almost all the divine cults of our period were for members of the Olympian pantheon. To judge from the quantity of their shrines, the gods who received the most worship were Athena and Apollo. Athena was already worshipped as the guardian of the city in Athens, Sparta, Tegea, Ialysos, Camirus, Lindos, Emporio on Chios, Miletus, Phocaea, and Syracuse; her only sanctuaries outside a *polis* are the Marmaria at Delphi, and one at Kierion

(Philia) in Thessaly. For Apollo, conversely, the only urban shrines are at Eretria, Corinth, and Dreros; the others are either far from the nearest *polis*, like Delphi, Thermon, Ptoion in Boeotia, the Maleatas sanctuary on a mountain near Epidaurus, Delos, Phanai on Chios, and Didyma; or just outside the town, as at Thebes, Asine, Argos, Amyclae, Naxos, and Paros; to this list we must add the altar of Apollo at Naxos in Sicily.[7] Apollo shares Delos and Dreros with his mother Leto and his sister Artemis. Like her brother, Artemis has her other shrines in wild places like Lousoi and Mavriki in Arcadia, or just outside a settlement as at Sparta, Ephesus, Aulis, Pherae, and Brauron.

Zeus, king of gods and men, presides over Olympia with his consort Hera. His other cults are at Dodona, Pherae, and near the summit of Hymettus; another of his peak sanctuaries was on mount Ithome, a rallying point during the First Messenian War. In the caves of Ida and Dicte the Cretans worshipped him as a young god. Hera's shrines, apart from the great sanctuary of Samos and a small temple on Delos, are all within Dorian states of the north-east Peloponnese: Argos, Tiryns, Solygeia, and Perachora in the territory of Corinth.

To the other Olympians, less attention is paid. Poseidon receives worship at the Isthmian and Calaurian sanctuaries; an ambiguous graffito from the shrine at Zagora on Andros may refer to him or to Athena Polias.[8] A sanctuary of Aphrodite has been found at Eretria; in Crete she shares the hill-shrine of Kato Symi with Hermes (who also has a cave-shrine at Patsos), and with Ares an early temple near Olous. The cult of Demeter is well established at Eleusis and Knossos; but the paucity of her shrines seems surprising, especially if there had been any conscious effort to convert from livestock to arable farming in order to feed the rising population of the late eighth century (cf. p. 314). Dionysos is worshipped at Ay. Irini on Keos. Finally, on the volcanic island of Lemnos there is a non-Greek cult of the local fire-god, whom the Greeks came to know as Hephaistos.

While none of the twelve Olympians went unrecognized, other gods also received their due. Eighth-century offerings have been found in the cave shrines of Pan at Aspripetra on Cos, and of Eilithyia at Amnisos; both places were already known in Neolithic times. The Aeginetans worshipped Aphaia, a local maiden goddess with Minoan affinities. Apollo shared Amyclae with the youthful god Hyakinthos, and the Mysteries of the Kabeiroi were celebrated at a sanctuary in the Theban countryside; these cults, too, are of Prehellenic origin, although the Theban Kabeirion has produced no finds earlier than the eighth century.

The last paradox brings us to the problems of religious continuity through the Dark Ages, which require only a brief discussion here.[9] Even if many sanctuaries were new in Geometric times, the identity of the god will in many cases imply a continuity of memory inherited from a much earlier period. This principle applies not only to deities like Aphaia, Hyakinthos, and the Kabeiroi, who are clearly Prehellenic; it also applies in large measure to the Olympians themselves. Many of their functions are inherited from Minoan and Mycenaean deities, as we know them from archaeological evidence and from figured art – Athena's from the Household Goddess, Aphrodite's from the Dove Goddess, Artemis' from the Mistress of Animals, and the Cretan Zeus' from the young son and consort of the Minoan Mother-Goddess. And, as is well known, most of their names already figure in Mycenaean palace archives as the recipients of offerings: there are certain references to Zeus, Hera, Poseidon, Athena, Artemis, Ares, and Hermes; there are possible allusions to Dionysos, Demeter, and Apollo by the name Paiawon (Healer), while the personal name Hephaistios betrays knowledge of Hephaistos.[10] But there are also many other Mycenaean divinities who do not survive into later religious practice, perhaps because they never enjoyed more than a local veneration. During the ensuing upheavals, then, some of the old gods passed into oblivion, while others were transformed by local practice, or assimilated with the cults of Dorian newcomers. One of the chief novelties, perhaps, is the concept of a divine family residing on the towering peak of Olympus just beyond the northern limit of the Mycenaean world. There, on the highest mountain in Greece, the Hellenic Zeus has his natural domain as god of the sky and upper air; and, as the autocratic father and monarch of the gods, he has power to draw up his unruly family from their various abodes throughout the Greek world.[11]

So much for the general continuity in Greek religious beliefs; but when we look for a continuity of cult at any one sanctuary, the archaeological evidence is often negative, or at best inconclusive. To begin with, we must consider only those shrines where Mycenaean remains have been found underneath or near by, excluding from our inquiry any places where the first Greek settlers arrived in post-Mycenaean times.[12] Even so, about half the remaining sanctuaries in use during the eighth century have produced no offerings of the Dark Ages. Of the remainder, ninth-century votives have been found on the Athenian Acropolis and Hymettus, at the three sanctuaries of Sparta (Athena, the 'Heroön', Artemis Orthia), at Amyclae, Aetos on Ithaca, the Samian Heraion, and Kato Symi, and in the Dictaean cave; and possibly also at Olympia, Antissa, Miletus, and in the Idaean cave. For the tenth century the list is briefer: Hymettus, Aetos, Delos, Ay. Irini on Keos, Camirus, and the Dictaean cave; possibly also Eleusis, Amyclae, Olympia, and the Samian Heraion. The eleventh century is a blank, except perhaps for the Dictaean cave.

Even when we make allowance for the steep rise in population during the eighth century, the tangible evidence for worship during the intervening centuries still seems extremely slender. In many places, perhaps, it was not the usual practice to offer any artifacts to the local god, owing to the poverty of the Dark Ages; in which case the sanctity of the shrines might have been observed without leaving any trace of a cult, except possibly for a few undatable burnt bones. Such a theory is hard to believe where Dark Age artifacts are lacking altogether, and where the Mycenaean finds below include no votives either;[13] here we must also take into consideration the antiquarian enthusiasms of the late eighth century (pp. 346 ff.) when any chance discovery attributed to the remote and legendary past might be treated with an extraordinary veneration.

A more plausible case for some continuity of memory, at least, can be made out for those places where Mycenaean votives are followed by intermittent offerings during the Dark Ages. We begin with an interesting group of five sanctuaries where there appears to have been a change of deity.

At Ay. Irini on Keos (pp. 209–10) the evidence for such a change comes from the finds themselves. There we have a unique instance of a Bronze Age temple being re-used by later worshippers. The origin of the sanctuary was neither Minoan nor Mycenaean, but native Cycladic; yet from the fifteenth century until the desertion of the town in the twelfth, the deity is a goddess of Minoan character, portrayed in a series of terracotta cult statues with raised arms. The cult languished during the Dark Ages, but was not forgotten. In the innermost room a stratum of tenth-century pottery is followed by a steady accumulation of votives from c. 750 B.C. into the fourth century. A head from one of the Minoan statues was discovered and venerated by eighth-century worshippers; but to their eyes a pointed Minoan chin might easily have passed for a male beard. The only deity mentioned in later graffiti is Dionysos, whom the donor of an Attic LG I kantharos (p. 76) must already have had in mind.

Apollo was the chief deity of Delos in historical times, but during the Late Bronze Age it seems to have been otherwise. As we have seen (p. 215), the richest nucleus of Mycenaean objects lay under the early Archaic temple of Artemis, associated with a narrow one-roomed structure (Ac) on the same alignment. That this building, too, was a temple is suggested by the character of the deposit, which includes gold jewellery, and ivory plaques for the adornment of a throne; also a number of bronze arrowheads, suitable for an archer goddess. As at Ay. Irini, worship here was intermittent during the Dark Ages, which are represented by only a small amount of tenth-century pottery. Yet when the temple of Artemis was erected shortly before 700 B.C., the fact that it was deliberately built over and aligned with the Mycenaean building leads us to believe that the cult had never been entirely forgotten. By then, Apollo had become established as the lord of Delos; yet the memory of his sister's seniority is preserved in descriptions of his birth on the sacred island.[14]

The original deities of Delphi were remembered as Ge or Gaia the earth-goddess, and her two daughters Themis and Phoebe the Titaness;[15] then Apollo came from Mt Olympus, vanquished monstrous Python, and took over the sanctuary. His reign had clearly begun by our period, when his oracular advice was sought by leaders of colonial expeditions. Yet his votive offerings will hardly take us back before 800 B.C. (p. 178); the Dark Age material, sparse as it is, comes only from houses and burials. The settlement lay under the northern part of what became Apollo's Hieron, and overlying a small Mycenaean village without any obvious sign of a cult. But under the Marmaria sanctuary of Athena Pronaia there seems to have been a late Mycenaean shrine which amassed nearly two hundred terracotta figurines of the Psi type, portraying a goddess with raised arms. Although these figurines are also found in Mycenaean settlements and tombs, such a large accumulation would be unthinkable in any but a religious context. It is conceivable that the earth-goddess had her original sanctuary here, before the Mycenaean village was finally overwhelmed by an avalanche.

Olympia is rich in local lore about its earliest cults, as recounted by Pausanias in his fifth and sixth books. Before the ascendancy of Zeus, the chief deities there were Ge, Kronos, the Mother of the Gods (possibly equivalent to Rhea, the consort of Kronos), and Eilithyia. Other objects of veneration were the mound of the hero Pelops, the pillar of king Oinomaos, and the olive tree planted by Heracles. With so many possible allusions to worship in the Bronze Age – the tree and the pillar are particularly suggestive – it is disappointing that no Mycenaean votives have been found, apart from two female figurines from an outlying area.[16] Among the early landmarks which have been securely identified, the 'mound of Pelops' certainly goes back to the second millennium, since one of several Mycenaean apsidal houses was allowed to encroach upon it. This very fact, combined with the absence of votives, makes it difficult on present evidence to accept a theory that the mound was already a cult centre in Mycenaean times.[17] No less problematical is the dating of votives ascribed to the Dark Ages. A large quantity of primitive figurines, human and animal, in terracotta and in bronze, has been arranged by the excavators in a plausible stylistic sequence, thought to be continuous at least from the tenth century onwards; but this chronology must remain conjectural since there is no stratigraphical evidence to support it, almost no comparable material from elsewhere, and no painted pottery from Olympia to confirm the existence of the sanctuary during the early Dark Age. Almost all the human figurines are male, and one type is considered to represent Zeus himself: both arms are raised in a commanding gesture, thought to indicate the god's epiphany.[18] The date of the earliest figure, if we could but know it, would give us a *terminus ante quem* for the introduction of the worship of Zeus at Olympia.

At each of the four places so far considered, an Olympian god takes over the sanctuary from one or more goddesses; but at Amyclae it is a youthful vegetation god, Hyakinthos, who is supplanted by Apollo. In local legend he is presented as Apollo's young favourite, accidentally killed by his master; his death was still lamented in Classical times at the Hyakinthia festival. A late Mycenaean cult is proved by a deposit containing pottery and figurines, ending in the twelfth century; then there is a considerable gap during the early Dark Ages, followed by a steady flow of votives (mainly pottery) beginning around 900 B.C. or shortly before.

The pattern is by now familiar. In each case a break in continuity comes during the early Dark Ages, when the old cults languish. This was the time when settled life was disrupted, when there was much reshuffling among the population of the Greek homeland: Ionians move to Keos and Delos, North-West Greeks to Elis, Dorians to Laconia and probably infiltrating Delphi. After taking possession of their new homes, the newcomers establish their own gods in the local sanctuaries when peaceful conditions have returned. Yet the old gods were still remembered, and still worshipped at subsidiary shrines within the sanctuaries;[19] and local legend interwove the old with the new. Henceforth there are no more changes of deity; but the offerings are sparse until the eighth century when the habit of mass-dedication begins. This sudden increase was occasioned not only by the rapid rise in population, but also by the return of prosperity, and the growing fame of the great sanctuaries, Olympia, Delphi, and Delos.

We now pass to those places where continuity must be assumed, however thin the archaeological evidence may appear. Good examples are the sanctuaries of Aphaia on Aegina, and of the young Zeus in the Dictaean cave. Both afford evidence of a cult in the Late Bronze Age, in the form of figurines and other votives. For the Dark Ages, the Dictaean cave has a sparse but fairly continuous series of offerings; Aphaia has nothing at all. Yet both places preserved the worship of a Prehellenic deity, escaping the imposition of any new god.

Finally, the sanctuary of Demeter at Eleusis, where the oldest recorded votives are of the eighth century; yet the most recent excavator has made out a persuasive case for complete continuity, partly based on architecture, and partly on written sources. A Mycenaean *megaron*, enclosed in a precinct but isolated outside the town wall, is hard to intrepret as anything other than a sacred building, however unusual such a building may have been for the religion of the Late Bronze age. It may have survived into the early Dark Age, but was eventually succeeded by a Geometric apsidal (or oval) temple of which only a small part remains. From then onwards the sanctuary steadily grew, and great trouble was taken to expand the sacred area by terracing the slope; and the spot occupied by the *megaron* remained the nucleus of every successive temple until the suppression of the Mysteries in early Christian times. For the Dark Ages there is nothing to show, except for a mention of 'latest Mycenaean and Protogeometric sherds' in the fill of the Geometric terrace; yet Herodotus records (ix. 97) that the worship of Eleusinian Demeter was carried across the Aegean by the first Ionian settlers at Miletus. The cult must therefore be at least as old as the eleventh century; it almost certainly has a higher antiquity, since Attica was not overwhelmed by any newcomers during the period of upheavals.

Votive Offerings

Pottery forms the largest class of finds at almost all Geometric sanctuaries. Most vessels served to contain libations; after the liquid had been poured out, the pot would be left behind by the worshipper. Large trays, such as have been found at the Samian Heraion (fig. 82b), would have conveyed some solid offering, such as fruit. The condition of the pottery is often sadly fragmentary; it may be that the vessels were deliberately smashed, whether by the votary or by the resident priest, to prevent re-use by mortal hands.

In general, the shapes are the same as those found in burials and settlements, but two rare forms were made exclusively for votive purposes. The Corinthians, in their handmade fabric, produced imitations of ring-shaped votive cakes recalling the modern Greek 'koulouri', and especially intended for the cult of Hera Akraia (p. 173). The other shape is an ornate rectangular plaque with one handle, designed to be hung on a wall; local schools are represented in the LG fragments from the Athenian Acropolis and the Argive Heraion, while Apollo's sanctuary on Aegina received both the Attic and the Argive varieties.[20] Miniature pots at Tegea, painted in a Geometric manner,[21] might seem to initiate a fashion which became widespread among the dedications at Archaic sanctuaries; yet the local style is so backward that even the earliest may be Subgeometric, well into the seventh century.

More specifically votive are the figurines in terracotta and bronze; those in bronze, at any rate, are seldom found in any secular context. At Olympia, where Geometric pottery is extremely rare, figurines form by far the most numerous class of offering; the same is true of Dodona, the Theban Kabeirion, and Lousoi in Arcadia. Human figurines, male and female, sometimes represent the deity, perhaps more often the votaries; horses may allude to the status of the wealthier votaries; bulls, goats, stags, and other animals serve as substitutes for real sacrifices; bronze beetles, somewhat incongruously, remind the deity to protect the

FIG. 106 OLYMPIA B 1240: TRIPOD CAULDRON, FIRST GROUP H. 65

crops against a familiar pest. The terracottas are either handmade or wheelmade, the use of the mould being unknown before 700 B.C. The wheelmade technique, first practised in Late Mycenaean times, had never been wholly forgotten during the Dark Ages;[22] all through the Geometric period there is a continuous sequence of wheelmade animals at the Samian Heraion. Surprisingly, there are no such terracottas at Olympia, where complete continuity has been claimed; the figurines there are all handmade, apart from the wheels for chariot groups.[23]

Another large category of votives is formed by articles of personal adornment – long pins, fibulae, and jewellery. Although they were not infrequently offered to male deities, the largest concentrations have been found at sanctuaries of Hera (Argos, Perachora), Athena (Lindos, Camirus, Emporio, Tegea, Philia in Thessaly), Artemis (Sparta, Pherae), and Aphaia. In earlier phases of the Geometric period, such objects are known to us mainly from cemeteries; but by LG times we rarely find them deposited in graves, the gods now being the chief recipients. Many of the bronze dress pins offered at Perachora and the Argive

FIG. 107 OLYMPIA Br 5471 : CAULDRON HANDLE, SECOND GROUP
D. 15.4 (detail, fig. 48a)

Heraion must have been specially made for Hera; such is their length (up to
0·82m.) and elaboration (up to nine globes) that they could hardly have been
worn with any ease by mortal women.[24]

Another homely object to be enlarged to an enormous size is the bronze tripod
cauldron. Such vessels were already well established in the domestic repertoire of
the Late Bronze Age, *in corpore* and in Mycenaean archives. It is not clear
whether they were made in metal all through the Dark Ages; small clay versions
from graves of the tenth and ninth centuries may imitate contemporary bronze, or
they may be miniatures of larger clay cauldrons when bronze was lacking.[25]
For the bronze cauldrons of the Geometric period Olympia offers by far the
fullest series. In the most recent general study[26] they are classified in five groups
according to shape and technique; handles and legs are cast in the first four
groups, hammered in the fifth.

An almost complete cauldron (fig. 106) is a fine example of the first group,
which are still small enough to have been used as kitchen utensils. The legs are

solid cast, and polygonal in section. As with all subsequent groups, each leg is attached to the cauldron by a large plate which is riveted to the bowl and follows the curve of its profile, while small struts give further support; also riveted to the bowl are the plate and vertical strap which hold each ring-handle in position. The handles of this first group, roughly triangular in section, are ribbed and carry a rope pattern, which is repeated on the upper parts of the legs; perhaps the handles of the most primitive cauldrons had been of rope, so that the vessel could be lifted off the fire without burning the hands.[27] As with everything Geometric from Olympia, the date of this cauldron is hard to determine; but it cannot be much, if at all, later than 800 B.C., in view of the many later technical and artistic developments which must fall within the eighth century.

Cauldrons of the second group already have a more monumental and decorative appearance. As the size increases, small vertical bars are needed to prop the handles; yet bronze is saved by hollowing out the sections of the legs, and eventually the handles have become flat except for one or two concentric ridges. Figured appendages now begin to crown the handles; at first bulls' heads, then horses, are soldered on. Relief decoration, when applied to handles, straps (fig. 107), and legs, often consists of false spirals. It has been conjectured[28] that this motif may have been copied from the characteristic ornament of the rod tripod stand, a Cypriot form invented in the twelfth century and found sporadically in the Greek world during the next four hundred years;[29] the tenth-century moulds from Lefkandi, which carry this design, may have been intended for the legs of these tripods. Yet, even if we grant their influence on tripod cauldrons, their contexts cover such a wide chronological range that it would be unsafe to base on them any deductions concerning the dating of our second group.[30] A less hazardous approach is to compare the short-legged horse of fig. 107 with the terracotta on an Attic MG II pyxis lid (p. 76, fig. 24a), a comparison which confirms the generally accepted dating of this group to the early eighth century.

From now on, the tripod cauldrons dedicated at Olympia are objects of prestige rather than utility; only fragments survive, but many of the complete vessels would have stood over 1m. high. They were probably the thank-offerings of victorious athletes (p. 181), and the enlargement of the form coincides approximately with the traditional foundation-date of the Games, 776 B.C. As their ornament grows more elaborate, so it becomes possible to distinguish local styles; the last three groups overlap considerably in time, but their occurrences at other sanctuaries give us reason to believe that each group represents a different centre.[31]

In the third group, the legs are no longer cast solid; the sections are at first full of re-entrants, but eventually they resemble three sides of a hollow rectangle, or a double T. The outer faces are richly decorated with linear motifs in relief: zigzag, M pattern, false spirals, and arcs. Near the top there is sometimes a square panel containing a Maltese cross or a six-leaved rosette within a circular frame; the figured scene on fig. 108a is an unusual alternative. The handles are now further lightened by openwork zigzags, and often crowned by horses which are soldered on to them, sometimes accompanied by their masters.[32] The style of the figurine attachments, and the prevalence of similar legs and handles at the Argive Heraion, make it seem likely that these tripods were the work of Argive

FIG. 108 OLYMPIA, TRIPOD LEGS
(a) B 1665, third group, H. 18.5; (b) B 1730, fourth group, H. 46.7

smiths. The figured panel of fig. 108a should be roughly contemporary with the first phase of figured work in Argive LG pottery, as represented by the giant pyxis Argos C 209 (fig. 45a). The commanding figure who raises his arms and flourishes a long spear might be Poseidon Hippios; the idea of showing a god standing on horseback was probably derived from Neo-Hittite art,[33] but the addition of a manger, and of a small linear panel above the horse's croup, are authentically Argive notions.

A fourth group, not very numerous, is distinguished by the fanned grooves which rise in shallow steps across the legs (fig. 108b) and handles alike. In section the handles are flattened, the legs resemble double Ts. Although no handle preserves its figured attachment, every one has rivet holes for a horse

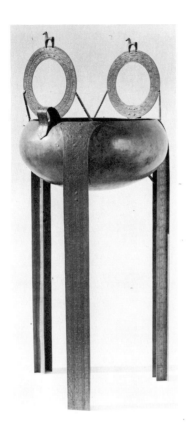

FIG. 109 OLYMPIA, RECONSTRUCTION OF HAMMERED TRIPOD,
FIFTH GROUP Reconstruction: M. Maass, *OlF* X pl. 50

alone, or a horse with its master; a possible forerunner is the wheeled tripod
Ithaca no. 3, where the leg is cast solid and massive, but the handle is flattened,
with three concentric ridges and two rivet holes for a horse. The distribution of
this group suggests a Corinthian origin, the only non-Olympian provenances
being Ithaca (nos. 10,12) and Delphi.[34] A leg from Olympia (fig. 108b) is
exceptional in having figured scenes – two rampant lions in combat, and two
helmeted athletes (often interpreted as Apollo and Heracles) claiming a tripod
as their prize; their lithe bodies recall the bronze figurines of the later eighth
century, especially those of the Corinthian school (pp. 176–7. fig. 58e,f).
   For the fifth and final group of Geometric tripod cauldrons, the casting
technique is abandoned, the legs and handles being hammered out over a
wooden core. The handles are now entirely flat, whereas three plates are soldered

together to make the usual double-T section of each leg. Outside surfaces are profusely engraved with false spirals, zigzags, and broken cable. The new technique permitted a further increase in size; a composite reconstruction, fig. 109, has a total height of 1.55m., and other hammered tripods from Olympia are reckoned to have exceeded 2m. More care was now needed in securing the enormous handles, which in our illustration are 0.31m. in diameter. In this case, long diagonal rods bind the vessel's rim to the outer edge of the handles, at 90° from where they join the cauldron; some rods are even supplied with human hands.[35] Eventually the handles are held by tall and slender human figurines standing on the rim of the cauldron, their hands riveted to the handle plates; at the same time, elegant horses continued to crown the handles. Outside Olympia, fragments of the hammered group are very rare at Delphi; there are a few pieces at Dodona, but the largest accumulations come from Delos and the Athenian Acropolis, and the last site has produced a group of fine figurines which must have served as handle-holders.[36] It seems, then, that Athens was the leading centre for hammered tripod cauldrons, though probably not the only centre.[37] The style of the latest Athenian holders shows that such cauldrons were still being made in the early seventh century, concurrently with the new Orientalizing protome cauldrons. The earlier holders (e.g., fig. 41a) go back into the last quarter of the eighth century; cauldrons like fig. 109, which should precede the introduction of such figures, perhaps begin in the third quarter.

Throughout the eighth century, tripod cauldrons are by·far the most impressive offerings at the major sanctuaries; but shortly before 700 B.C. the variety becomes much richer. It was then that the practice of dedicating armour and weapons first became common, notably at Olympia; perhaps this is a reflection of the hostilities in which much of the Greek world was then involved. Then, too, exotic *orientalia* began to arrive in abundance, especially at Olympia, Delphi, and the Samian Heraion: ivories, figured bronze bowls, and the imported exemplars of those protome cauldrons which were to fire the imagination of so many Greek craftsmen during the next century (pp. 362ff.).

Conclusions

During the course of the eighth century, the enormous increase in votive offerings cannot wholly be explained by the rise in population. Take, for example, the distribution of Geometric metal objects: before 800 B.C. they come almost entirely from burials, but in LG times the vast majority are dedicated at sanctuaries. Since metal is a reliable index of riches and prosperity, we infer that in the late eighth century the gods were receiving an increasingly high proportion of the wealth then available. In trying to account for this phenomenon we should give separate consideration to local sanctuaries belonging to one particular *polis*, and to those larger sanctuaries which were already on the way to becoming Panhellenic. Of the local sanctuaries, those of Samos and Eretria are especially remarkable for their temple architecture. Their *hekatompeda* are among the earliest of Greek public buildings, whose erection implies careful planning by the *polis* in the service of the patron deity. They must have been a great source of pride among the local inhabitants. Likewise, even where no temple yet existed, local pride also required the embellishment of sanctuaries with votive offerings, given by each citizen according to his means. The sharp rise in the volume of these offerings is another symptom of the growth of corporate feeling in each *polis*.

At a time when the Greek world was already being riven with hostilities between neighbouring states (pp. 163–4, 200–1), the greater sanctuaries were becoming an important unifying influence. The Delphic oracle gave advice to visitors from far and wide, especially to leaders of colonial expeditions; according to one view,[38] Apollo reserved his favours for Corinth, Chalcis, and their allies, but there is also a hint of an earlier association with Eretria (p. 322). Delos, during our period, was a meeting-place chiefly for islanders and Athenians. The quadrennial festival of Olympia was attended mainly by Peloponnesians; yet, if the hammered tripods have been correctly assigned, the Athenians will have been making showy dedications there at least a generation before their first recorded athletic victory (696 B.C.). While all Greeks could meet there in peace, there was nevertheless a lively competition in the magnificence of votive offerings; hence the steady increase in the size of monumental tripods, designed in at least three different states. The subsequent history of Greek bronzework is closely connected with the expanding prestige of the great sanctuaries, and the intense rivalry which they inspired was always a powerful stimulant to the vitality of Greek art.

NOTES

1 Desborough, *GDA* 281
2 The excavators thought that Altar I was built as early as *c.* 1000 B.C. (*AM* 58 (1933), 150), but this date has not yet been confirmed by the published finds.
3 cf. the window from area J at Zagora, p. 311.
4 Drerup, *ArchHom* O 14 ff.
5 *AM* 58 (1933), 167, building III.
6 This is the excavators' 'temple of Hera Limenia'. J. Salmon (*BSA* 67 (1972), 174 ff.) has shown that it was not a temple at the time of its construction; the central hearth was added much later, and there is no place for a cult image. I follow Salmon's view that only one cult of Hera flourished at Perachora: Hera Akraia 'who has her temple by the harbour' (Limenia).
7 Thuc. vi.3.1 'outside the present town'.
8 *PAE* 1972, 266 ff.
9 cf. Snodgrass, *DAG* 394–401; Desborough, *GDA* 280–7.
10 M. Ventris and J. Chadwick, *Documents in Mycenaean Greek* (Cambridge, 1973, 2nd edn.), 125–9, 410–11.
11 *Iliad* viii.17–27.
12 e.g., the cities of western Anatolia (except Miletus), Syracuse, and new sites in the homeland such as Eretria and Zagora.
13 e.g., the Argive Heraion, Solygeia, Perachora, the Isthmian and Calaurian sanctuaries.
14 (Apollodorus) *Bibliotheke* i.14.1; Servius, *Comm. Vergil Aen.* iii.73.
15 Aeschylus, *Eumenides* 1 ff.; cf. D. S. Robertson, *CR* 55 (1941), 69 f.
16 *OlF* VII, 8 pl. 2, 1.
17 cf. Herrmann, *AM* 77 (1962), 18 ff.

18 *OlF* VII, pls. 28–33; *GKG* 117–21.
19 Except possibly at Ay. Irini, where the cult is not mentioned in any literary source.
20 Attic: Boardman, *BSA* 49 (1954), 195 ff.; Argive, *GGP* 143 pl. 31h.
21 *BCH* 45 (1921), nos. 232–42.
22 Desborough, *GDA* 282–3.
23 *OlF* VII, 2–3.
24 Jacobsthal, *Greek Pins* 13–15.
25 Snodgrass, *DAG* 284. Ninth-century clay examples: Cos Seraglio gr. 28, Rolley, *Études déliennes* 502 f.; Acarnania, *AD* 24 (1969) A 84 f. pl. 50a,b.
26 Schweitzer, *GKG* ch. 7.
27 Benton, *AJA* 63 (1959), 95.
28 Benton, *BSA* 35 (1934–35), 112–13; Amandry, *Gnomon* 32 (1960), 462.
29 Catling, op. cit. (p. 291 n. 43) 192 ff., nos. 6, 10, 16, 18–20; add *Ergon* 1974, 98 fig. 91, from a Theran tomb of *c.* 720–650 B.C.
30 e.g., Schweitzer, *GKG* 192–3.
31 M. Weber, *AM* 86 (1971), 17–20.
32 *GKG* pls. 191–2.
33 Carter, *BSA* 67 (1972), 50; cf. above fig. 51b.
34 *FD* V, figs. 191–2; BCH 97 (1973), 512 no. 3.
35 *OlF* III, pl. 84, top right.
36 e.g., *GKG* pls. 153–61, 164–8; above p. 128.
37 cf. Rolley, *Études déliennes* (1973), 504 f.
38 Forrest, *Historia* 6 (1957), 160–75.

14 Recollection of a Heroic Past

During the second half of the eighth century, the Greeks became increasingly aware of a vanished heroic age – an age which, on archaeological grounds, we have learned to equate with the Mycenaean world shortly before its collapse. The princes of that remote age had become the heroes of epic poetry; a new respect for them, and a new interest in establishing links with them, appear in three kinds of material evidence. First, there is the rapid growth of hero-cults in several regions, as shown by the new practice of leaving votive offerings in Mycenaean tombs. Secondly, some rich burials of our period seem to have been influenced in various ways by accounts of heroic funerals in epic poetry. Thirdly, in some LG figured scenes there are reminiscences of the heroic age, whether through reference to a specific story, or in details added to lend heroic colouring to a generic theme. With these visible manifestations of interest in the heroic world, this chapter will be largely concerned; but first we should briefly consider their chief cause, the great flowering of epic poetry which culminated in the work of Homer.

The Circulation of Epic Poetry

Memories of Mycenaean times could reach later Greeks only through oral tradition, and mainly through oral poetry. No other mode of transmission was possible during the Dark Ages; the sagas were passed on from master to pupil, embroidered by poetic imagination and coloured by the occasional anachronism. From *c.* 750 B.C. onwards the newly recovered art of writing might have helped oral bards to compose and elaborate their poetry, and their works could have been recorded before death in a more or less permanent form. How soon this actually happened has for long been a matter for discussion and conjecture; suffice it to say that only a small proportion of oral poetry was recorded in writing, and only a small proportion of what was written down is preserved for us. To survive complete, an oral poem must have won enough acclaim from its first hearers to be thought worth writing down, and must then have retained the respect and admiration of all subsequent generations in antiquity. The only works which have passed this double test of time are the *Iliad* and *Odyssey* of Homer, and the two major poems of Hesiod. Other oral poets are shadowy figures, known to us only from brief quotations by later writers.

Homer was a native of Ionia. Various traditions make Smyrna his birthplace, and in Archaic times a clan of Chiot bards were known as the Homeridai. His ancestors, who joined in the Ionian migration, had brought with them the memory of Mycenaean exploits and achievements; these sagas – and especially the saga of Troy – were elaborated in hexameter verse by many generations of Ionian bards, until Homer himself gave them monumental expression. We cannot be certain whether any other region could boast such an unbroken tradition of oral poetry, lasting all through the Dark Ages. All we know is that an awareness of Ionian epic had spread to the mainland of Greece by the second half of the eighth century. It may be that the hexameter at this time was a characteristically Ionian metre;[1] if so, the hexameter graffiti from Athens and Pithecusae (fig. 95a,b) will illustrate the progress of this eastern Ionian influence across the Greek world, among people who knew that they, too, were descended from Mycenaean heroes. More conclusively, the poets of the Greek mainland – even in lands which had been overrun by non-Mycenaean newcomers – were making considerable use of the same artificial dialect and diction that we find in Homer.

Embedded in Homer's language are a few words and forms inherited from Mycenaean Greek, which in historical times survived only in the ultra-conservative dialects of Arcadia and Cyprus. There is also a small Aeolic ingredient, perhaps assimilated by Ionian bards through contact with their Aeolian neighbours in the eastern Aegean, or possibly deriving from the Aeolian parts of the Greek mainland before the migrations. But by far the largest component is the Ionic of the eastern Aegean, a dialect which did not find its definitive form until well into the Dark Ages – possibly not before the ninth century.[2] Thus, when Ionic aspects of the Homeric dialect appear in the eighth-century poetry of the Greek mainland – not only in the works of Boeotian Hesiod[3] but even in in the epic fragments of Eumelus, a poet of Dorian Corinth[4] – the primacy of Ionian epic seems assured; if there had been any independent schools of epic recitation on the Greek mainland, they must have been thoroughly submerged by Ionian influence during the course of the eighth century.

How, then, can we explain this great flowering of Ionian epic, which broke down the barriers of local tradition, established a *lingua franca* for hexameter verse, and made such a powerful impression throughout the Greek world? If one has any belief in the power of individual genius, then it is needless to look any further than the *Iliad* of Homer for the poem which first carried Ionian prestige so far and wide. Conversely, if any pre-Homeric Ionian poetry had had such an impact, it would be difficult to explain why none of it has been preserved by later generations.

If we pursue this hypothesis further, knowledge of the *Iliad* will already have spread across the Aegean before Hesiod[5] and Eumelus had begun to compose in Ionic hexameters. Hesiod's career can be traced back at least as far as *c.* 710–700 B.C. when he attended the wake of a Chalcidian nobleman who fell in the Lelantine War (pp. 201, 313). Eumelus, a Corinthian aristocrat of the ruling Bacchiad clan, composed a hymn for a choir of Messenians performing at Delos; this poem must surely go back to their days of freedom, before the outbreak of the First Messenian War in *c.* 730 B.C. (pp. 163–4). Since the two surviving lines are in the Doric dialect, one might argue that their author had not yet succumbed to Ionic influence; but he was also remembered as a senior contemporary of Archias the founder of Syracuse, and it would be straining the available evidence to place his *floruit* any later than the third quarter of the century.[6] Another consequence of our hypothesis is that Homer's dialect, and his description of Nestor's cup (*Iliad* xi. 632–7), were known to a literate Euboean colonist of Pithecusae (p. 300) who died soon after 720 B.C.; the East Greek kotyle which he inscribed could perhaps go back into the 730s, but not earlier. From these various clues it would appear that the *Iliad* had already begun to enjoy a wide circulation in the middle years of the century.

Only a small proportion of the Trojan saga is treated in the two Homeric epics. The *Iliad* presents a brief episode towards the end of the war, but well before the sack of Troy. In the *Odyssey*, generally agreed to be the later work, we follow the adventures and homecoming of one Greek hero during the ten years after the war. Perhaps as a tribute to Homer himself, his successors felt the need to fill the gaps in the narrative; hence arose a cycle of eight epics covering the whole of the Trojan matter, in which the *Iliad* and the *Odyssey* occupy the second and seventh places respectively. Of the other six poems a few extracts survive in quotation, but their contents are fully summarized for us by Proclus, a scholar of later antiquity. The cycle opened with the *Cypria*, dealing with the judgement of Paris, the rape of Helen, and the earlier stages of the Trojan war; this poem was usually attributed to Stasinus of Cyprus, who, according to one account, married Homer's daughter. The immediate sequel to the *Iliad* was the *Aethiopis*, composed by Arctinus of Miletus who was said to be a pupil of Homer; here the narrative of the war was carried down to the death of Achilles. Then followed the *Little Iliad* by Lesches, a Lesbian poet; this was an episodic work describing the final stages of the war, and overlapping considerably with another work by Arctinus, the *Sack of Troy*. Thus far, all the poets of the Trojan cycle were eastern Greeks who, if we accept local memories, lived not later than the early seventh century: Stasinus and Arctinus would belong to the generation after Homer, and Lesches was thought to have been older than Terpander, the Lesbian lyric poet who was active around 675 B.C. (p. 262). After a long interval, the last two epics were added to the cycle by poets from other parts of the Greek world. In the *Returns*, Agias of Troezen (*floruit c.* 628 B.C.) related the homecomings of Greek heroes other than Odysseus; and the *Telegoneia*, by Eugammon of Cyrene (*floruit c.* 566 B.C.), told of the later adventures and death of Odysseus himself.

The Trojan cycle enjoyed a special prestige owing to the fame of Homer, but other sagas were not neglected. A shorter cycle dealt with the legends of Thebes; Eumelus is credited with an early *Argonautica*. Hesiod, in his *Theogony*, compresses various stories concerning the birth of the gods, their conflicts with the Titans, and some of the labours of Heracles; these themes were elsewhere expanded into epic poems, of which very few traces survive. There was no major poem about Theseus until the late sixth century, when he had become the national hero of Athens; yet, as we shall see, shorter lays about him may well go back to our period.

Once the barriers of local tradition had been broken down, enthusiasm for the heroic age spread rapidly. Recitations of epic poetry were encouraged by aristocratic rulers, especially by those who claimed descent from the heroes themselves.[7] Talented bards who made their name at local festivals could soon win a wider acclaim by performing at the great Panhellenic sanctuaries. In their

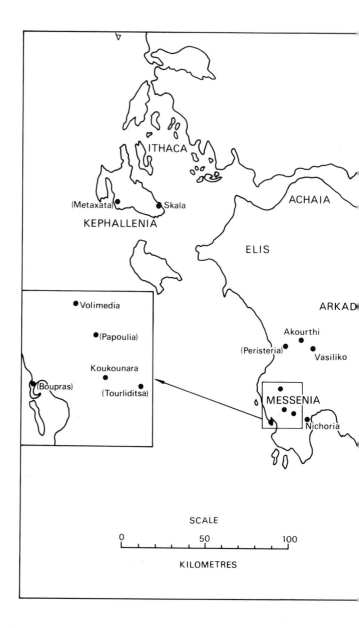

FIG. 110 SITES WHERE LATER VOTIVES HAVE BEEN FOUND IN MYCENAEAN
TOMBS. At unbracketed sites the offerings begin *c.* 750–650 B.C.;
at bracketed sites, not before 650 B.C.

audiences they might quickly inspire a particular interest in a local hero, or a general reverence for all things heroic. Of this interest and reverence there are many symptoms in the material record, which we shall now review.

Hero-Cults

Excavators of Mycenaean tombs have often found small clusters of later material, either in the chamber, or in the dromos. These deposits, consisting mainly of pottery, are not associated with any burial, or any contemporary settlement; it is reasonable to see the objects as votives, offered to the Mycenaean incumbents. The offerings begin soon after 750 B.C. and indicate a new respect for the Mycenaean dead at about the time when knowledge of the *Iliad* was beginning to spread across to the Greek mainland. Copious deposits, going back to LG times, have come to light in the tholos and chamber tombs of Mycenae, the tholos tomb at Menidi in Attica, and in the chamber tombs at Argos, at Prosymna near the Argive Heraion, and at Volimedia in Messenia; other LG deposits, less well documented, are reported from a chamber tomb at Thebes, and a tholos tomb at Analipsis in south-east Arcadia; seventh-century deposits from Kephallenian chamber tombs have also been mentioned. Some of these tomb-cults persisted for many generations; in several Messenian tombs the offerings continued down to Hellenistic and even Roman times, and include whole sacrificed animals. By contrast, no such votive deposits have ever been found in the Mycenaean tombs of Thessaly, Achaea, Laconia, Crete, and Rhodes; and we should hardly expect to find them in Ionia, which – apart from Miletus – had hardly been touched by Mycenaean settlement.

How can we best account for the geographical distribution (fig. 110) of these cults? Since well over a thousand Mycenaean tombs have been excavated, the blank spaces, too, deserve an explanation. Let us forget the relative importance of each region in Mycenaean times; it is more profitable to view the question through the eyes of eighth-century Greeks, hearing – in many cases for the first time – of heroic splendours belonging to their remote past. The sheer size and elaboration of Mycenaean collective tombs would have seemed impressive, to their eyes: not only the princely tholoi with their sophisticated corbelling, but even the rock-cut chamber tombs of ordinary Mycenaean families, each one approached by a long and carefully hewn dromos. We should, however, make an exception here of those lands where collective tombs were still used in the eighth century – as is almost always the case in Crete, frequently in Thessaly, and sometimes (though rarely) in Achaea and Rhodes;[8] the accidental discovery of a Late Bronze Age tomb in any of those regions might have excited comparatively little interest, and this would explain the absence of later votives.

By contrast, the other districts of the mainland – certainly Attica, Boeotia, the Argolid, and Messenia – were no longer accustomed to large family tombs; the Argives sometimes allowed double or triple burials, but individual graves or pithoi were the general rule. Very occasionally, later burials had been lodged in Mycenaean tombs;[9] but all these belong to the Dark Ages, and only serve to show how little respect was paid to the old tombs before the diffusion of Homeric epic. Then, soon after 750 B.C., begins the flow of votives, the gifts of ordinary people whose imagination had now been fired by tales of a heroic past. In regions where the contemporary forms of burial were so much simpler, any large Mycenaean tomb would at once be acclaimed as 'heroic': *omne ignotum pro magnifico est*. These offerings express the homage felt for the men of a more glorious age; as Hesiod would put it, the miserable race of iron (among whom he himself was numbered) was doing honour to the godlike race of heroes who had won their glory in grim battle and dread war – the wars round Thebes and Troy[10] which were on the lips of bards throughout the Greek world.

The desire to pay this form of homage was by no means confined to the actual descendants of the Mycenaeans; indeed, the deposits are especially common in the Dorian lands of Messenia and the Argolid, where the ruling class could claim descent from Heracles, but no other ties of kinship with the departed heroes. Just as Dorian epic poets, like Eumelus of Corinth, adopted the composite Ionic dialect of Homer, so Dorian audiences listening to the Trojan saga were filled with a general reverence and enthusiasm for anything remotely heroic. Thanks to the surpassing genius of Homer, the heroic past became the common property of all who called themselves Greeks.

Before leaving these tomb-cults, it is worth remarking that they were essentially impersonal. Most votive deposits continue into periods when one might expect to find the recipient mentioned in graffiti. In fact, the only known inscription was discovered by Schliemann in the earth above the Grave Circle at Mycenae; it is on a late Archaic sherd, bearing a dedication to an anonymous hero: τοῦ ἥρωος ἐμί.[11]

So much for the symptoms of general reverence. We now pass on to the sanctuaries founded in honour of particular, named heroes, always in the lands where they lived, but never in tombs: Academus near Athens, Odysseus on Ithaca, Agamemnon at Mycenae, Menelaus and Helen at Therapne near Sparta. Academus was remembered as a founder hero of Athens; in LG times he received a many-roomed temple where sacrifices were burnt in his honour;[12] but his cult may go back much earlier than this, if a copious deposit of EG I kantharoi, 150m. away, was also intended for him.[13] Odysseus, as we learn from a Hellenistic graffito, had his shrine in the Polis cave;[14] to judge from the fine series of bronze tripods offered there, his cult must have been established by 800 B.C. at the latest. Thus both heroes were probably worshipped long before the circulation of Homeric epic; indeed, their worship may well embody a continuous memory about them through the Dark Ages, as neither Attica nor Ithaca suffered any major change of population during those troublous times. Academus and Odysseus could have been venerated as ancestral figures in their own lands quite independently of epic influence.

An altogether different origin is probable for the cults of Agamemnon, and of Menelaus and Helen. Neither seems to have begun much before 700 B.C., by which time Mycenae and Therapne would have been settled by Dorians for three centuries. Thus, as with the Argive and Messenian tomb-cults, the votaries had little or no kinship with the heroes; once again, the impulse to set up these sanctuaries must have been supplied by the diffusion of the Trojan saga. Here we may observe a more political aspect of early hero-worship; in singling out Agamemnon, Menelaus, and Helen for special veneration, the Dorian rulers

FIG. 111 CHARIOT B FROM TOMB 79, SALAMIS, CYPRUS: RECONSTRUCTION
Karageorghis, *Excavations ... Salamis* III, 70 fig. 11

may have been making a deliberate attempt to enhance their control over a subject population by annexing the central figures of Mycenaean saga as their own local heroes.

Finally, mention should be made of what one might call an anti-hero cult, of which our only knowledge comes from scattered literary references; the sources diverge over details, but the general burden is as follows.[15] Each year the people of Ozolian Locris sent two noble maidens as suppliants to Athena at Troy. On their way to the sanctuary any Trojan could kill them with impunity; if they arrived safely, they served the goddess as menials for the rest of their days. This was the atonement prescribed at Delphi for the sacrilege of their fellow-countryman Ajax son of Ileus, who had impiously seized Cassandra in Athena's temple during the sack of Troy, and dragged away the goddess' wooden image to which she was clinging. When was this strange custom inaugurated? Certainly not before Troy (VIII) was resettled in LG times after three centuries of desolation; but probably before 673 B.C. when the first colonists of Locri Epizephyrii in southern Italy (p. 238) included women from the same Hundred Houses who had been chosen to supply the unfortunate maidens for Troy.[16] Thus it may well have been the story of Ajax' sin, as told by Arctinus in the *Sack of Troy*, which stirred the conscience of the Locrians in the first place.

'Heroic' Burials

The circulation of epic not only prompted the worship of heroes; in several places there were frequent attempts to emulate the magnificence of heroic funerals. Nowhere is this more apparent than at Salamis in Cyprus, a wholly Greek city which had been founded by Mycenaean refugees at the beginning of the Iron Age. Here we are concerned with the royal tombs of their descendants, who were cremated in finely built chamber tombs. Thanks to careful excavation, the burial customs are known in considerable detail, and may be closely compared with the funeral of Patroclus as described in *Iliad* xxiii, lines 108–261.

The body of Patroclus was conveyed on his chariot to the place of burial. Sheep and cattle were slaughtered in his honour. Achilles larded his friend's corpse with their fat, so that it should burn on the pyre more briskly; he also offered gifts of amphorae, containing honey and oil. A large cattle bone was found in the dromos of Salamis tomb 2, and another Greek-Cypriot royal tomb at Old Paphos (Kouklia) produced the skull and forelegs of a sheep.[17] Most of the Salamis tombs have plenty of large amphorae stacked in the dromos, and one from the enormous tomb 3 is inscribed e-la-i-wo in the Cypriot syllabic script: i.e., ἔλαιον (olive oil).

To return to Homer: Achilles, with loud laments, slaughtered the four chariot horses and placed them upon the pyre. The princes of Salamis were content with two-horse vehicles and their horses were not burnt with them; yet every royal burial there has at least two horse skeletons in the dromos, and at least the impressions of the chariot poles to which they had been attached. Tomb 79 showed traces of four chariot teams belonging to two successive burials; all the metal parts survive from one of the later chariots, and the impressions of wood were so clear that a reasonably certain reconstruction of the chariot could be achieved (fig. 111).

Achilles then proceeded to butcher twelve young Trojan prisoners; this savage act of vengeance is recalled by an inhumed male skeleton from the tomb 2, whose hands had been bound together.

When the body had been consumed, Patroclus' pyre was quenched with wine. In the dromos of Salamis tomb 1 the pyre deposit was covered with a thin layer of brown mud, and above that were six unburnt and unbroken pots (jugs, oinochoai, bowls) which had evidently been used for putting out the flames.[18]

Then the hero's ashes were gathered into a golden urn (*phiale*) and wrapped in a soft linen cloth. Large vessels of gold are the preserve of epic poetry; but the earliest of the Salaminian cremations (tomb 1) was housed in a cauldron of bronze, and traces of cloth were noted on its inner face.[19]

The main ceremony was now over, and Achilles could turn his thoughts to the funeral games. Eventually, after his death, his friend's ashes were to be mingled with his own, and a great mound of earth was heaped over their final resting-place.[20] Tomb 3 at Salamis was covered with a vast tumulus some 10m. high.

For most of these practices, if taken singly, the hardened sceptic could adduce parallels from pre-Homeric Cyprus, or from other lands not too far distant from the Greeks; thus the Phrygians often heaped up large tumuli over their royal burials (p. 266) and occasionally sacrificed horses in them, chariot teams were sometimes offered in Etruscan tombs, and one human sacrifice is recorded from a Cypriot tomb of the Middle Bronze Age. It is the *combination* of so many features in the Salaminian tombs which should incline us to take the Homeric comparisons seriously. And, apart from a single eleventh-century cremation from Kourion,[21] these practices were new to the island;[22] during the Greek Dark Ages the Cypriots normally inhumed (as throughout the Bronze Age), and chariot burials and large mounds were quite unknown. Let us suppose, then, that the princely burials of Salamis were influenced in large measure by the circulation of epic poetry, and especially of the *Iliad*. As the earliest chariot burial occurred not later than 750 B.C.,[23] this influence would have reached the island well before the career of the local poet Stasinus, author of the *Cypria*. Yet his use of the Ionic dialect, his participation in the Trojan cycle, and his alleged family ties with Homer himself, give us the impression that Greek Cypriots were already aware of Ionic epic before he began to compose.

At the other extremity of the Greek world, we find the Euboean colonists of Pithecusae quenching their pyres with wine, and covering their cremations with tumuli. Here the mounds are of rubble rather than earth, but the evidence of quenching is more positive than at Salamis; in many burials the *only* unburnt vessel is an oinochoe, carefully placed above the cremated remains and the charred fragments of the other offerings. Among people who knew of Nestor's cup and composed Homeric hexameters for a drinking party, these reflections of Homeric funerals are hardly surprising. Their enthusiasm for things heroic was certainly shared in each of their two mother-cities. In Chalcis we hear of the funeral games held in honour of Amphidamas, at which Hesiod says that he won the prize for song; perhaps because the city was already an important centre for epic recitation, it was thought natural that a brave war-leader should be given full heroic honours at his funeral. Concerning his Eretrian peers and foes we now have plenty of complementary evidence from the archaeological record. In the four warrior cremations by the West Gate (pp. 196–7: grs. 5, 6, 8, 9) Homeric rites are recalled at several points: the offensive weapons were burnt on the pyre with the bodies;[24] the cremated remains were wrapped in cloth, and then deposited in bronze cauldrons. A horse's tooth from gr. 9 seems a tenuous indication of animal sacrifice, but a whole horse skeleton has also been reported from the other Eretrian cemetery, by the sea.[25] Traces of a seventh-century cult above the West Gate graves show that the warriors were accorded heroic status after their deaths, and were worshipped as the guardians of their city. It would not be extraordinary if Amphidamas received similar honours in Chalcis.

Attica is the only other region where there is any sign of epic influence on the current burial customs, varied as they are. We have already noted a few rich Athenian cremations in cauldrons (pp. 120, 126), some with warlike gear, and all dating from the LG period when inhumation – for the moment – was the prevailing rite. When there was a general movement back to cremation around 700 B.C., the aristocracy set a new fashion for grandiose tumuli, each crowned by a marker (or stele),[26] and covering a single grave. The earliest are in the Kerameikos cemetery,[27] but the idea soon spread to the landed nobility in the Attic countryside.

It is here that we should face the central contradiction in all Homeric accounts of funerals: almost all Mycenaeans were inhumed, but the poems speak only of cremation. This is not the place to guess how this inconsistency may have arisen; but, viewing the matter through the eyes of eighth-century Greeks, one cannot help wondering whether the pursuit of 'heroic' practices may not sometimes have involved them in a puzzling dilemma: were they never struck by the incongruity between Homeric cremations, and the inhumed remains which worshippers at Mycenaean tombs must often have encountered? Perhaps the problem only arises in Attica, for that is the only region known to have combined tomb-cults with 'heroic' burials. Could the coexistence of these two practices explain the double change in the prevailing rite, from cremation to inhumation in *c.* 770–750 B.C., and back again to cremation at the turn of the century? If the return to cremation was prompted by epic funerals, could the experience of coming upon venerable Bronze Age skeletons have caused the earlier conversion to inhumation? One thinks especially of Eleusis, where many Geometric burials overlie an extensive Middle Helladic and Mycenaean cemetery of cist graves; one cist was actually re-used in MG I (though for a cremation), another received a fine LG I oinochoe as an apology for the accidental disturbance of its occupant by a gravedigger; and an impressive group of cists, which may have been the monument shown to Pausanias as the *heroön* of the Seven against Thebes, was piously enclosed by a wall during the LG period.[28] Since the Eleusinians were so well acquainted with the graves of their predecessors, it may be no accident that the same cemetery has also produced two of the oldest adult inhumations of the Geometric period, dating from the years around 800 B.C.; these are the rich graves Alpha and Isis (pp. 78–80). Whatever the cause may have been, the Attic movement towards inhuming can hardly be connected with epic descriptions, and in any case the change began too early, and the first inhumations are female; if our suspicions are correct, inhumation was revived because it was known to be the ancestral custom, and certainly not because it was thought to be in any way 'heroic'.

Returning to epic funerals and their impact on real life, we may make three final observations. First, they had no immediate effect on the current burial practices except among the descendants of the Mycenaeans – i.e., the Cypriot Greeks, the Ionians of Euboea and Pithecusae, and the people of Attica; the Dorians, meanwhile, continued stolidly with their customs unchanged.[29] Secondly, the Homeric practices do not themselves reflect the burials of any one age, but were accumulated over several centuries within the oral tradition of epic poetry; horse-burials, animal sacrifices, mounds, and markers were all known in Mycenaean times, but cremations and funerary cauldrons must be post-Mycenaean. Finally, different innovations were adopted in different places often far removed from one another, but within the same period: thus tumuli came into fashion in Cyprus, Attica, and (in stone) Pithecusae; cremations with unburnt pouring vessels occur in Cyprus and Pithecusae; and cremations in bronze cauldrons are common to Cyprus, Athens, and Eretria. All these features recall Homeric funerals, but all except the first are post-Mycenaean; thus any common derivation from previously existing practices is out of the question. It is hard to escape the conclusion that these new features in the burial customs of our period were directly inspired by the circulation of epic poetry.

Heroic Scenes

In reviewing the rise of hero-cults under epic influence, we noted how a general reverence for 'heroic' tombs was eventually followed by the foundation of shrines to specific heroes. The renascent art of figured drawing was affected in much the same way. At first, pictures of general warfare might be given a 'heroic' colouring, without alluding to any particular story. Later, and mainly from *c.* 730 B.C. onwards, there are a few daring experiments in portraying specific themes known from myth and legend.

Let us first consider Paris A 519 (pp. 111–13, fig. 33b), the least fragmentary battle scene from the Attic Dipylon Workshop. This, like many smaller *disiecta membra*, comes from the back of a vast krater which marked the grave of an Athenian nobleman, and showed his funeral on the front. The picture may have some reference to his own exploits in an age which was probably far from peaceful, yet the resemblances to Homeric fighting are unmistakable: there is the same emphasis on personal valour, on single combat, on the taking of booty, and on the moment of violent death. Some scholars have even seen a deliberate archaism in the so-called Dipylon shield, here seen on the extreme right and in the lower zone; this curious contraption, they hold, never existed *in corpore*, but was freely copied by Geometric painters from representations of the Mycenaean figure-of-eight shield, in order to give their scenes an authentically heroic colouring. This view has aroused scepticism for many good reasons; the weightiest objection lies in the fundamental difference in structure between the Dipylon shield and its supposed Mycenaean model, when terracotta miniatures are considered.[30] A more likely instance of archaism is the chariot platform seen at the extreme right, off which the dead warrior is dragged to the ground by his foeman. Chariots had been used as engines of war in Mycenaean times, but thereafter became obsolete in Aegean fighting; in the *Iliad* their chief function is to carry warriors into and out of the fray, but any occurrence of a chariot in a Geometric battle scene might reasonably be attributed to epic influence.

Alongside this generic scene of warfare, we see the earliest overt allusion to a specific story – indeed, the only such story ever attempted within the Dipylon Workshop. A warrior is in combat with a pair of Siamese twins; they have been identified with the Actorione or Molione, the young Elean brothers who fought against Nestor in his youth.[31] Their physical handicap is implied by Homer (see below), and mentioned by Hesiod.[32] This otherwise obscure theme would have had a special interest for the Neleid *genos* of eighth-century Athens, who claimed descent from the kings of heroic Pylos; it might therefore have served their grave-monuments as a distinctive family crest.[33]

After their introduction by the Dipylon Workshop, the twins figure nine more times in Geometric art before disappearing from the repertoire in the early seventh century;[34] we see them on three more Attic vases, on sherds from Corinth, Sparta, and the Argive Heraion, on the intaglio under a Laconian bronze horse, and on the square catchplates of two Boeotian fibulae. The non-Attic versions sometimes show the twins by themselves, as on the intaglio, and never

a

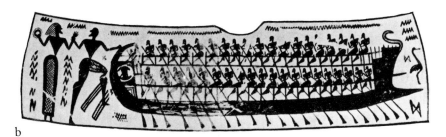

b

c

FIG. 112 MYTHICAL SCENES, ATTIC LG

(a) Oinochoe, Agora P 4885: the Molione twins escaping from
Nestor (*Hesperia*, suppl. II 70 fig. 44); (b) Krater, London
1899.2–19.1: embarkation of Theseus and Ariadne (*JHS* 19 pl. 8);
(c) Oinochoe, Munich 8696: shipwreck, perhaps of Odysseus
(Hampe, *Gleichnisse*, pl. 11)

progress beyond a simple duel; as for their meaning, the twins' fatal encounter
with Heracles[35] would have been better known among non-Athenians than
Nestor's exploit. By contrast, all three Attic scenes place the twins in a wider
context. The latest, on a stand in Munich, shows them embattled beside another
conflict which is clearly mythical, though hard to interpret.[36] On the well-known
oinochoe Agora P 4885 (fig. 112a) the twins are making their inglorious escape

from the fray; one brother steps on to a chariot, while the other fights off a warrior attacking them from behind. As in Homer, the chariots play no part in the fighting; and the action recalls the climax of the battle between the young Nestor and the Epeians, when Nestor would have slain the Actorione-Molione had not their father Poseidon rescued them under a thick mist.[37] Finally on New York 14.130.15, one of the later grave-kraters,[38] we see them in more peaceful circumstances; they appear once among the mourners, twice (in successive vehicles) in a frieze of chariots, and once beside a tripod, the prize for some contest. There may be an allusion to the funeral games of king Amarynkeus, in which Nestor lost the chariot-race to the Actorione;[39] here Homer surely implies that the twins were physically inseparable, if they were allowed to compete together in what was strictly a solo event. If this is another Neleid grave-marker, its painter displays a wayward turn of mind; he has chosen a theme unflattering to his patron, and garbled it by repetition.

Even within the limitations of Geometric figure technique, stories about such freaks of nature are easily rendered and understood. So, too, the combats between a man and a fabulous monster. Centaurs, by the late eighth century, were firmly established in the repertoire of gold diadems, bronzes, seals, and vase-painting. Processions of them in friezes (e.g., fig. 36b) may be purely decorative; but a single centaur, confronting a human figure with hostile intent,[40] must express a myth. Some scholars[41] have supposed that early centaur representations may indicate other monsters such as Typhoeus, whose struggle with Zeus for the mastery of the world is described by Hesiod in the *Theogony*. Geometric portrayals, however, are quite consistent with the centaurs of legend; they usually carry fir branches, the centaur's traditional weapon; one, on an Attic ovoid krater,[42] returns from hunting, like later representations of Cheiron; another, on a square seal in Munich,[43] tries to abduct a woman, recalling Nessos and Deianeira; and Nessos again, attacked by the archer Heracles, surely appears on an earlier seal from the same school (fig. 50b).

Among other exploits of Heracles, his slaying of the Lernaean hydra and the Nemean lion are mentioned in Hesiod's *Theogony* (313–17, 326–31). Both stories have Boeotian illustrations contemporary with the poet on bow fibulae,[44] and the hydra recurs on a Chiot bronze seal;[45] both hydra scenes include a second human figure who should be Heracles' companion Iolaus, as well as the crab sent by Hera to torment him. The lion combat also appears thrice on an Attic LG stand;[46] this rendering has been adapted from an oriental man-versus-lion composition which Greek metalworkers had been borrowing all through the eighth century (cf. figs. 32c, 92a).

We pass now to the stories in which all the agents are normal human beings. For the Geometric artist, their expression posed much greater difficulties. Painted inscriptions, naming specific heroes, do not figure on pottery until well into the seventh century; thus, for the hardened modern sceptic, any Geometric picture of purely human activity can be explained away as a genre scene, drawn from everyday life. For example, a ship scene on a krater in London (fig. 112b) shows what might appear to be a perfectly ordinary occurrence. A man steps towards a departing ship, gripping a woman's wrist. Perhaps he is bidding her farewell; more probably he is haling her on board, to judge from his energetic forward gestures. If the painter intended anything more specific, the story must be deduced from the circular object which she is flourishing so obtrusively in her right hand. Several heroines have been proposed, of whom the most likely is Ariadne, escaping from Crete with Theseus after the slaying of the Minotaur; here she would be displaying the crown of light with which she had illumined the Labyrinth.[47] If the crown provides the only key to recognition, it is fruitless to object that its function in the legend is irrelevant to a scene of embarkation; on the contrary, our painter would be anticipating a common expedient of Archaic narrative artists, who supply personal attributes to identify people, and not to lend circumstantial colour to the action in which they are seen to be involved. Visual attributes are thus comparable to personal epithets in epic poetry; Achilles is always swift-footed, even when seated in his tent.

The painter of our scene was a bold innovator in several other respects (p. 117); if he also invented the personal attribute to assist the recognition of mythical scenes, we should not be surprised. But would his intention be immediately understood by his contemporaries and imitators? On several slightly later amphorae and hydriae, similar crowns are sometimes held by the leaders of female dances. The earliest amphora of this group,[48] showing seven girls on one side and seven youths on the other, might well refer to the Crane dance on Delos, with which Theseus' party celebrated their deliverance from Crete. In the later scenes, where youths and crown are often omitted, the theme easily degenerated into a conventional formula; but the mythical connotations were remembered in a Subgeometric scene by a Euboean settler in Italy, combining a mixed dance, a crown, a crane, and oars to signify arrival by sea.[49] Another likely allusion to the Theseus saga may be seen in the Minotaur figurines (e.g., fig. 41b) which supported the hammered handles of Athenian bronze tripods.

In conclusion, we return to the Trojan cycle. An Attic oinochoe in Munich shows a shipwreck (fig. 112c), with eleven warriors in distress. Eleven fish await their prey. Our attention is directed towards the only upright figure, securely perched upon the keel in the exact centre of the picture. His companions are still alive in the water, but he alone is likely to save himself. The painter may have been thinking of a shipwreck in the *Odyssey* (xii.403 ff.), from which Odysseus was the sole survivor. A generation later, a Pithecusan colonist painted a less precise version: five men, eighteen greedy fish, no survivor, and no obvious relation to epic.

Around and soon after 700 B.C., themes from the cyclic epics begin to appear. On a votive clay shield from Tiryns,[50] an extremely tall warrior is about to slay a skirted Amazon; perhaps the scene is from the *Aethiopis*, Achilles slaying the queen Penthesilea. The same epic included the death of Achilles; on the sealing, fig. 75d, we see his huge body being carried out of battle by Ajax (cf. p. 189 n. 41) in a composition repeated many times in Archaic art. Lastly the insidious Wooden Horse on wheels, described both in the *Little Iliad* and in the *Sack of Troy*, appears on the same Boeotian fibula which bears Heracles' combat with the Lernaean hydra.

The overwhelming majority of Geometric figured scenes are generic, timeless, and universal; allusions to specific myths are extremely rare, and their interpretation can never be entirely certain. But it would be unreasonable to deny the

artists of our period any wish to experiment in this direction, on the grounds
that their supposed attempts to portray any one theme are inconsistent with each
other, or with literary accounts. The first authors of these attempts were in
advance of their time; if their notions were misunderstood, simplified, or garbled
by their imitators, we should not on that account impugn their own efforts to
portray a particular story. By the second quarter of the seventh century, many
mythical scenes can be recognized without difficulty, occasionally with the help
of inscriptions, but much more often through the concentration on circumstantial
details, and the consistent use of personal attributes. These narrative techniques
were not learned in a day, but much was owed to the imaginative pioneers of LG
times.

Conclusions

Veneration of heroic forebears, imitation of heroic burial practices, enthusiasm
for depicting heroic deeds: when we view the archaeological record, these are the
most obvious manifestations of influence from Ionian epic poetry upon the
everyday life of the eighth century. In large measure, the heroic and contemporary worlds had become intermingled. A Euboean war-leader was buried with
heroic honours, including funeral games; when games are represented on Attic
funerary vessels, who can say whether they belong to the heroic past, or to
contemporary life? During these years – much more so than in the Dark Age –
the matter of epic poetry would have seemed real and immediate. Travellers and
colonists in western waters were following in the wake of Odysseus; at home,
amid the increasing bitterness of wars between neighbouring states, warriors
were reliving the glory and the tragedy of the *Iliad*. The recovery of their heroic
past gave the Greeks a new pride and confidence in themselves; and when the
deeds of a bygone age become such a fertile source of inspiration, one may justly
speak of a Greek Renaissance on the analogy of a later epoch.

NOTES

1 M. L. West, *CQ* 87 (1973), 181 ff., 189; *contra*, J. A. Notopoulos, *Hesperia* 29 (1960),
   177 ff.
2 E. Risch, *MusHelv* 12 (1955), 65; cf. J. Chadwick, *Greece and Rome* N.S.3 (1956), 42.
3 G. P. Edwards, *The Language of Hesiod in its traditional context* (Oxford, 1971), 131,
   201–3.
4 Huxley, *Greek Epic Poetry* (London, 1969), 60 ff.
5 For a different view cf. M. L. West, *Hesiod. Theogony* (Oxford, 1966), 46 n. 2; *CR* 87
   (1973), 20.
6 cf. Dunbabin, *JHS* 68 (1948), 67 nn. 70–3.
7 e.g., Agamemnon of Aeolian Kyme; the Neleids of Miletus, Naxos, and Athens.
8 pp. 180, 95–6. Of Laconian Geometric burials we know nothing.
9 e.g., *Hesperia* 24 (1955), 218–19, Athens; *AD* 3 (1917), 203–4, Thebes; A. W. Persson,
   The Royal Tombs at Dendra near Midea (Lund, 1951), 11, 42; *AE* 1914, 101 f., 106 f.,
   Tragana near Pylos; *AE* 1973, 47, Nichoria.

10 cf. *Erga* 156–65, 176–9.
11 Jeffery, *LSAG* 174 no. 6 pl. 31.
12 Drerup, *ArchHom* O 31, with refs.
13 *PAE* 1958, 8 f. pl. 6.
14 *BSA* 35 (1934–35), 54 fig. 7.
15 See Huxley in E. Badian (ed.), *Ancient Society and Institutions, Studies presented to V. Ehrenberg* (Oxford, 1966), 147 ff.
16 Polybius xii.5; cf. Lorimer, *HM* 450–1.
17 *BCH* 87 (1963), 286.
18 P. Dikaios, *AA* 1963, 154–5.
19 ibid. 144–7.
20 *Odyssey* xxiv.76 ff.
21 *AJA* 58 (1954), 131 ff.
22 The Lapithos tombs (*SCE* I, 265, eleventh-ninth century) offer other precedents for human sacrifice, but one hopes that this was never a normal practice at any time.
23 The cauldron cremation in tomb 1 (*AA* 1963, 145 fig. 13) is associated with an Attic MG II skyphos.
24 cf. *Iliad* vi.418, *Odyssey* xi.74; for pre-Homeric occurrences in Athens, however, see pp. 30–3.
25 Kourouniotis, *AE* 1903, 8–9 n. 1.
26 cf. *Iliad* xvi.457, xvii.434 f.
27 Kübler, *Kerameikos* VI.1, 89 f.
28 For these various graves see Mylonas, *PAE* 1953, 81 ff. fig. 10 (cf. Pausanias. i.39.2); *PAE* 1955, 72 ff. pls. 21b, 22a1, and 76 pls. 24b, 25a (cf. *GGP* 32 no. 41).
29 In the seventh century, however, one of the Theran cremations is in a bronze cauldron: *Thera II*, tomb 17.
30 Lorimer, *HM* 165–7.
31 *Iliad* xi.709–10.
32 fr. 17b, ed. Merkelbach-West.
33 For part of a similar 'crest' cf. the left-hand extremity of Paris A 517; *GGP* 30 n. 1, 351.
34 Full list, Ahlberg, *PE* 246.
35 Pausanias v, 1.10–2.1.
36 Fittschen n. 936a; cf. E. Walter-Karydi, *Gymnasium* 81 (1974), 177 f. fig. 2 pl. 1b.
37 *Iliad* xi.750–2.
38 Ahlberg, *PE* 240 ff. fig. 22a–g.
39 *Iliad* xxiii.630–42.
40 e.g., the New York bronze group, *GKG* 185.
41 e.g., E. Buschor, *AJA* 38 (1934), 128 ff.
42 Beazley, *The Development of Attic Black Figure* (1951), pl. 2.
43 Schefold, *FGS* pl. 6c.
44 *GKG* figs. 125–6.
45 *BSA* 35 (1934–35), pl. 31, 39.
46 *K* pl. 69 no. 407.
47 C. Robert, *Archäologische Hermeneutik* (1919), 38; the crown was Ariadne's attribute on the sixth-century chest of Cypselus at Olympia (Paus. v.19.1). For other possibilities see Fittschen, 53 ff.
48 Fittschen n. 277 figs. 1–3.
49 *BICS* 15 (1968), 86 ff. fig. 2.
50 Schefold, *FGS* pl. 7b.

15 Oriental Influences

Ever since the awakening of the mid-ninth century, the arts of Geometric Greece had been subject to sporadic influences from the Near East. Gold, an oriental luxury, is the earliest medium of these influences. The difficult techniques of granulation, filigree, and inlaying had been forgotten in Greece since Mycenaean times; they were first recovered in Attica and Crete, under the instruction of immigrant oriental craftsmen. These masters also passed on to their pupils a wealth of oriental imagery. Sphinxes, griffins, roaring lions, lions fighting men and sometimes overcoming them, rows of grazing animals – each of these subjects makes its debut on orientalizing gold diadems made in Athens or Knossos, or on Knossian bronze reliefs made under the influence of a resident oriental jeweller.[1] The Idaean bronze shields, which reflect the work of a later immigrant guild, introduce the Tree of Life, and a nude fertility goddess flanked by wild animals. All these themes had been foreshadowed in Minoan or Mycenaean art; but it is in oriental guise that they reappear, and after a long absence.

For the time being, oriental influence was virtually confined to technique and imagery. Here the Cretan metalwork is exceptional, in that it maintains an oriental style for a long time, without much concession to local taste; yet it had no effect on the rest of the Greek world. Everywhere else, oriental notions were quickly hellenized, in accordance with the local Geometric tradition. Thus the later Attic diadems are Geometric in style, and sometimes also in theme (fig. 38d); the first post-Mycenaean seal-engravers often adopt oriental shapes, but the engraving is crudely Geometric (fig. 50); Syrian figurines, with their tilted heads and deep-set eyes, had only a passing influence on Geometric bronzes (figs. 41a, 58c,d); the ivory girl from Athens (fig. 42b–d) shows how a fleshy Syrian prototype could be translated into a graceful Geometric idiom. Vase-painting, the art in which the Geometric tradition was most firmly rooted, was especially resistant to the freer style of oriental prototypes: thus the varied animal processions on the earlier Attic diadems were rigidly standardized and geo-metricized by the Dipylon Master (fig. 33c); and much the same can be said of the Euboean Cesnola Painter's Tree of Life (fig. 61c), and of the Attic adaptations of a North Syrian cult scene (pp. 122–3 nn. 37–8) to suit local funerary ritual.

Towards the end of the eighth century, however, the Geometric tradition was becoming exhausted, even in the conservative medium of vase-painting. All forms of figured art now begin to lose their former rigidity, under oriental in-fluence; and Geometric linear ornament is gradually superseded by plant motifs of oriental origin. Such are the chief symptoms of the great Orientalizing move-ment which was eventually to transform the style and character of Greek art;

but this movement did not come to fruition until well into the seventh century, and in this brief chapter we are concerned only with its tentative beginnings. Before descending to further details, we should review the state of the eastern Mediterranean world during the period in question, in so far as the Greeks are concerned.

The Greek merchants who had settled at Al Mina (pp. 93–5) would have found a world not unlike their own. As at home, the political units around them were small. Their emporium was one of several along the North Syrian coast, well placed for exchanges with the Aramaean principalities inland; the nearest of these were Unqi and Hama. During the early eighth century there was relative peace; Assyria was in temporary decline, while the principalities and emporia enjoyed the benevolent protection of Urartu, the powerful kingdom in the Armenian highlands. Assyrian fortunes revived, however, with the accession of the energetic king Tiglath-Pileser III; the conquest of the Levant was achieved during his reign (745–727 B.C.), and consolidated by king Sargon II (722–706 B.C.). Unqi was annexed in 739 B.C.; Hama, after a pitched battle, was razed to the ground in 720 B.C. The merchants of Al Mina now found themselves within the Assyrian empire, and cannot have been untouched by these commotions; some havoc, contemporary with the fall of Hama, is indicated by the repair of warehouses at the beginning of level VII. Thereafter, Greek pottery is no longer found inland; yet the Greek merchants were allowed to remain in the emporium. To judge from the various pottery fabrics in level VII, the Greek element even increased at the expense of the Levantine; and the long-established merchants from the Cyclades and Euboea were now joined by Rhodians and Corinthians.

The Rhodian colony of Soloi in Cilicia (p. 95 n. 52) must have been another centre of Greek commerce, whence a small amount of LG pottery – mainly East Greek – travelled to the native Cilician settlements of Tarsus and Mersin. In default of any deep sounding on the site, we can only guess that its foundation should have preceded the Assyrian annexation of Cilicia in 709 B.C. In these parts we hear of the only recorded clash between Greeks and Assyrians, when Greek mercenaries are said to have supported a local rising against king Sennacherib.[2] The date, 696 B.C., roughly coincides with a major remodelling of Al Mina at the beginning of level VI; the Greek merchants there may well have suffered for the temerity of their fellow-countrymen in Cilicia.

Yet the proportion of Greek traders at Al Mina still continued to grow; not because the Assyrians had any reason to favour them, but rather because of a steady exodus of Phoenicians. Where was their destination? One clue is offered by the resemblances between Levantine wares at Al Mina, and the earliest pottery from the Phoenician colony of Motya in western Sicily.[3] Harassed by Assyrian pressure on their homeland, and lured by commercial prospects in their new colonies, many Phoenicians must have sought out more tranquil markets in the western Mediterranean. As we have seen (p. 290), their most convenient and profitable route would have taken them through south Greek waters. Perhaps we can catch an anachronistic glimpse of them in the deep-sea yarns of the *Odyssey*, in which their ships appear off Crete and the western Peloponnese;[4] that is, in the central part of their long voyage to Carthage, or perhaps to the rich markets of Etruria.

Thus, in spite of the Assyrian conquests, exchanges between the Aegean and the Near East continued in ever-increasing volume; and the initiative was neither wholly Greek, nor wholly oriental. As before, the most important route was by sea, starting from the Levantine emporia, passing Cyprus, and entering the Aegean by way of Rhodes or Crete. Phoenician traders, some on their way further west, would have found Greek customers for their figured bronze bowls, ivories, paste scarabs, and other ornamental luxuries. More oriental craftsmen, too, may have fled in this direction, leaving the ruins of the Aramaean and Neo-Hittite cities; some of the immigrant smiths who produced the Idaean shields may have been among their number, although the series had probably begun before the Assyrian conquests (p. 288). Lastly Greek merchants, returning home from the Levant, brought with them a wide variety of oriental artifacts, and raw materials too: ivory from the Syrian interior,[5] gold from the Melas valley near Al Mina,[6] copper from Cyprus, and perhaps tin from the distant Zagros mountains in Iran. Furthermore, because they spent much of their time living among orientals, these merchants are also the most likely carriers of oriental tales concerning the origin of the world, the birth of the gods, and the early conflicts between them. Such stories, if brought home by Euboean travellers, would quickly have reached the ears of Hesiod in Boeotia; and it is generally agreed that his *Theogony* owes much to eastern epic, although the precise sources of inspiration are still debated.[7]

Such then, were the relations between Greece and the eastern Mediterranean at the close of the eighth century. While the Geometric style was becoming exhausted, Greek vase-painters and other craftsmen could turn for fresh inspiration to a wide variety of *orientalia*: not oriental pottery (which was perfunctorily decorated if at all, and rarely exported), but chiefly ivories, bronzes, metal reliefs, and other articles which were both precious and portable. Most of the models, in so far as we can detect them, belong to the schools of North Syria and Phoenicia, the regions with which the Greeks had the closest dealings.

The debt to Phoenician art was comparatively slight. Many of the new ideas from that quarter were probably communicated through imported ivories and bronze bowls. The ivories are a likely source of the palmette, lotus (e.g., 56a), and cable motifs which invade the decoration of Greek Orientalizing pottery; but their figured style, a suave mixture of Egyptian and Assyrian ingredients, had little appeal for the Greek imitator. The shallow bronze bowls are distinguished by concentric zones of decoration inside,[8] embossed and sometimes incised; from *c.* 735 B.C. onwards they gave rise to a class of similarly decorated Attic skyphoi (p. 117 fig. 35b, c), in which the figured themes are geometricized and adapted to local taste. The centre of these bowls is often filled with rays or tongues, motifs of floral origin; hence they pass to Protocorinthian and other Orientalizing schools of pottery, appearing on the shoulder of a pot (fig. 56a) or just above the foot.

'North Syrian' is a vague but conventional geographical term. It embraces the art of the Neo-Hittite principalities, modified at this time by the taste of their Aramaean princes. All these states lay inland, some in North Syria, others in south-eastern Anatolia; the western limit lies somewhere near Ivriz in Cappadocia, where a vast rock relief depicts the local dynast, Urpalla. Each of these

FIG. 113 ORIENTAL BRONZE CAULDRON AND STAND FROM THE
BARBERINI TOMB, PRAENESTE Rome, Villa Giulia, H. 130

rulers, living under the menace of Assyrian aggression, aped the luxury of the
Assyrian court on a smaller scale. Their art found monumental expression in the
stone reliefs which adorned their palaces, and in the stone lions which guarded
their gateways and temples. More than any Phoenician artifacts, the style of these
sculptures had a profound influence on Greek Orientalizing art; but the influence
was indirect, since they may have been seen by Greek merchants and travellers,
but hardly by Greek craftsmen working in their homeland. Among the more
portable forms of art, North Syria possessed a versatile school of ivory work, for

which the chief centre was the ill-fated city of Hama. The style of this school differs from Phoenician work in its stronger rendering of human features, especially the staring eyes; hence came the inspiration for an Athenian Geometric masterpiece (p. 130 fig. 42b–d) well before the Orientalizing movement had begun to gather momentum. When the movement was already under way, the Daedalic art of seventh-century Greece owed much to the style of North Syrian terracottas, of which we shall speak presently. But during the last years of the eighth century, when the general ferment was just beginning, no other class of *orientalia* made a stronger impact in Greece than the bronze cauldrons with protome attachments. First, a brief description is required; we shall then consider the case for attributing them to North Syria, and the many ways in which they influenced the Orientalizing art of Greece.

From the Geometric tripod cauldrons which they eventually superseded, these vessels differ in the following respects. Whereas the Geometric tripod legs are riveted on to their cauldrons, the oriental bowls are detachable. Their stands are of two types: either a rod tripod resting on animal feet, or a tall hollow cone topped with a schematic palm flower and embossed with figured decoration. The cauldrons have a lower centre of gravity than their Geometric counterparts, and are decorated with protomes riveted to the rim. These may be of sirens, bulls, lions, or griffins, and their number varies from two to twelve. The human head and arms of each siren emerge from a flat plate representing wings and tail; behind, a small ring-handle is attached through a loop. The bulls sometimes bear similar handles, but the lions and griffins never; they are modelled on a larger scale and are purely ornamental – apart from the apotropaic function of scaring away evil spirits.

In the east, these cauldrons and their stray attachments have been found only at various sites in Urartu, and in rich tombs at Gordion (p. 266) and Salamis in Cyprus. All other examples[9] come from Greece and Italy, mainly from Greek sanctuaries and Italian tombs; fig. 113 shows the most complete cauldron with a conical stand, from the Barberini tomb at Praeneste in Latium. The protomes from Greece include sirens and bulls which are certainly oriental originals, and many local imitations of all four types.

Although the eastern finds constitute only a small proportion of the total, the oriental origin of these vessels is beyond doubt. The siren protomes, which include bearded male heads as well as female, have been called 'Assurattaschen' on the assumption that they were derived from earlier Assyrian representations of the god Ashur where the god's bust is surrounded by a winged disc; yet the creatures on a recently found cauldron from Salamis are true sirens, equipped with birds' bodies and claws which stand out in relief from the plate.[10] More conclusively, cauldrons with conical stands (though without protomes) are portrayed in Assyrian stone reliefs from the ninth century onwards, either as furniture in cult scenes, or – more often – as booty carried off by Assyrian soldiers from neighbouring lands;[11] and for the bearded siren attachments there is a ninth-century prototype on a bronze jug from Luristan.[12] We cannot tell exactly where the type originated, and during our period there may well have been more than one oriental centre of production. Arguing from provenances, many scholars have supposed that Urartu was the chief source of cauldrons and

FIG. 114 EARLY PROTOCORINTHIAN LEKYTHOS-OINOCHOE, PORTRAYING
ORIENTAL CAULDRON New York 23.160.18 H. 9.2

protomes; yet the search for parallels in other figured art has usually led to the
stone sculpture of the North Syrian region. Thus the sphinxes on the Barberini
stand are comparable in style to the rock monument at Ivriz,[13] and other good
parallels among the North Syrian reliefs had been adduced for the imported siren
protomes in Greece.[14] North Syria, then, is the most likely source of the oriental
protomes imported by the Greeks; the thorough pillaging of Aramaean and Neo-
Hittite cities, remorselessly described in Assyrian records, may explain why no
similar finds have been made in those parts.

Oriental cauldrons, with their curious attachments, quickly seized the imagination of Greek craftsmen, potters as well as smiths. Reproduced in clay, the bowl
became the dinos of Orientalizing vase-painting (e.g., p. 262); an early rendering
of the conical stand, by a Euboean living in Etruria, is still decorated in the LG
manner (p. 233 fig. 76b). Athenian potters, serving the needs of aristocratic
funerals, evolved a large hybrid form combining the new stand with the old

FIG. 115 SIREN ATTACHMENTS TO BRONZE CAULDRONS FROM OLYMPIA
(a–b) Oriental original, Olympia B 4260, H. 14; (c–d) Greek
imitation, Athens 6123, H. 13.2

ring-handled cauldron. The oriental version soon appears in figured scenes: fancifully on the earliest Attic cauldron (p. 119 fig. 37b), more convincingly on an EPC lekythos-oinochoe of *c.* 700 B.C. (fig. 114).

To return to bronze: the griffin and lion heads on the Barberini cauldron (fig. 113) conform closely to North Syrian types as seen on monumental sculpture and in other media, but comparable bronze protomes in the east are very rare: one griffin from Gordion, eight griffins on the cauldron from Salamis already mentioned, and one lion from the Urartian site of Karmir Blur.[15] These are hollow-cast, whereas almost all the early examples from further west are hammered, in accordance with a prevailing fashion in Greece (figs. 47b, 91). Thus it may be that all the griffin and lion attachments from Greece[16] and Italy – including those on the Barberini cauldron – are Greek adaptations of oriental types, added to oriental cauldrons; and it has even been suggested that the griffin protome may have been a Greek invention.[17] At all events, the griffin protome had a special appeal for Aegean metalworkers, in whose hands it underwent a local development all through the seventh century, eventually outlasting all other types of attachment. The most striking features of the North Syrian griffin – horse's ears, topknot, and gaping mouth – are all exaggerated in the later Greek versions in which the technique changes from hammering to casting. The lions soon disappear from the Greek repertoire of cauldron protomes; but the North Syrian type, well represented on the Barberini cauldron, supplies the model for the elegant creatures on the finest Protocorinthian vases up till the middle of the seventh century. These are the so-called 'Hittite' lions, remarkable for their compact, almost cubical heads, and their flat, pug-like features.

Finally we must consider how eastern influence affected Greek renderings of the human face. In Geometric vase-painting the silhouette figures had been virtually faceless, and even the most accomplished Geometric bronzes and ivories (e.g., figs. 41a, 42b–d, 49a–b) reveal more concern with the anatomy of the body than the facial details. Much more sensitive in this respect are the faces of the original siren attachments (e.g., fig. 115a–b), with their huge almond eyes, their generously proportioned noses, and the comfortable roundness of their contours. In an early imitation of *c.* 700 B.C. (fig. 115c–d) this facial type has been translated into a Hellenic idiom. The oriental model has stimulated a new interest in facial features, but the general effect is livelier and more alert. The hard Syrian stare is replaced by an inquisitive expression of wide-eyed wonder. Each feature is exaggerated and more sharply defined; thus the smoothly receding 'Armenoid' profile of the original is now broken up by a huge aquiline nose; and the long, soft locks of oriental hair are replaced by shorter and broader tresses, punctuated with horizontal incised zones. In contemporary vase-painting, where faces are now rendered in outline, human features are over-emphasized in much the same way; this is especially true of work by the Analatos painter, the leading personality of the Early Protoattic style.[18]

Our Greek siren is still boldly three-dimensional, like most Geometric figurines; but not long afterwards there arose a much shallower style of modelling, derived from North Syrian work in another medium. Shrines of Astarte, the Levantine goddess of fertility, abound in mould-made terracottas showing the goddess touching her breasts. Shortly after 700 B.C. the type was introduced into

Crete, perhaps to meet the religious needs of immigrant oriental craftsmen; and with it came the habit of making figurines in a terracotta mould, unknown in Geometric Greece. In Crete, Rhodes, and the Peloponnese, local imitators applied the new technique to male and female types alike, and quickly improved on the rough style of the Syrian originals. Yet, like the originals, their figurines were made in a single mould, and roughly finished on the back; the profile is inevitably shallow, and the only satisfactory view is frontal. In the earliest Hellenic versions the typical face is almost triangular, with pointed chin, large features, a straight fringe across the brow, and layered tresses of hair not unlike those of fig. 115b. This sober and austere style was to prevail and develop itself through most of the seventh century, and in most branches of Greek plastic work – especially in relief work, for which it was most suitable. It has been named Daedalic, after the legendary pioneer of the sculptor's art; the name is apposite, since the canons of this style were followed by the first Greek lifesize statues in stone,[19] made shortly before 650 B.C.

NOTES

1 See pp. 100–1 fig. 32c; pp. 123–4 fig 38a–c; p. 285 fig. 92a.
2 Berossos *apud* Euseb. Vers. Arm., *FGH* 680 F7c(31). cf. D. Luckenbill, *Ancient Records of Assyria and Babylonia* II (Chicago, 1926). paras. 286–8.
3 cf. *GGP* 388 n. 2.
4 *Odyssey* xiii.271 ff., xiv.301 ff.; cf. J. D. Muhly, *Berytus* 19 (1970), 19 ff.
5 A complete tusk was found at Al Mina: *JHS* 85 (1965), 13 n. 28.
6 R. Maxwell-Hyslop, *Western Asiatic Jewellery* (London, 1971), 230.
7 M. L. West, *Hesiod. Theogony* (Oxford, 1966), 18 ff.; P. Walcot, *Hesiod and the Near East* (Cardiff, 1966), especially 122 ff.; G. S. Kirk, *Greek Myths* (Harmondsworth, 1974), 113 ff.
8 See pp. 58–60 fig. 15 for an early example.
9 If we ignore sixth-century cauldrons and protomes from France, which are late Greek imitations.
10 *Salamis* III, 97 ff. figs. 18–23.
11 K. R. Maxwell-Hyslop, *Iraq* 18 (1956), 152 f. figs. 1–5.
12 B. B. Piotrovskii, *Urartu* (London, 1967), 42 fig. 28; cf. O. Muscarella, *Hesperia* 31 (1962), 328 f.
13 Barnett, *JHS* 68 (1948), 10 fig. 6.
14 Herrmann, *OlF* VI, 65 f. pl. 28; id., *JdI* 81 (1966), 119 figs. 31–6.
15 Piotrovskii, op. cit. 43 fig. 29.
16 Except for a few small griffin-birds, which are cast and evidently imported: *OlF* VI, 133 ff. pls. 55–6.
17 Benson, *AntK* 2 (1960), 58 ff.
18 cf. *BSA* 35 (1934–35), pls. 39–41.
19 R. M. Cook, *JHS* 87 (1967), 28–31.

16 Epilogue

The final emergence from the Dark Ages, the dawning of a Renaissance, the consolidation of the city-state: these are the main historical developments in eighth-century Greece. We have surveyed many of their symptoms in various parts of the Greek world, and in various aspects of daily life. It remains to consider the chief causes, and their interaction with one another.

We begin with the external cause: the revival of frequent exchanges with the eastern Mediterranean, after a long period of comparative isolation. Seen from a Near Eastern point of view, the Greeks were doubly fortunate in that they dwelt far enough away to escape the menace of Assyrian armies, but well within the range of maritime trade with the Levant coast. They could thus evolve their own political and social institutions without fear of foreign interference – even their nearer neighbours in the Anatolian hinterland gave them no trouble before the seventh century. At the same time, their eastward exchanges enabled them to learn from civilizations older than their own, and less seriously disrupted by the commotions at the end of the Bronze Age. Their creative powers were stimulated by the imagery of imported oriental artifacts, and by the recital of oriental myths; skilled techniques, especially in metalwork, were taught by oriental craftsmen who settled in Attica and Crete; and the mastery of the Phoenician alphabet put an end to over four centuries of Greek illiteracy.

Progress out of the Dark Ages was not uniform, but came by fits and starts. Thanks to the resumption of oriental traffic on a small scale, there was an early glimmer of light in the middle of the ninth century; it is visible in the exotic finds from the richer graves at Lefkandi and Athens, and in the traces of Phoenician visitors to Crete and the Dodecanese. But this proved to be a false dawn; the awakening was temporary, and confined to the paths of eastward trade.

The real dawn came in the middle of the eighth century, and gradually illuminated the whole of the Greek world. Five of its most striking manifestations are roughly simultaneous: the first outburst of figured art on the Dipylon grave monuments, the beginning of the colonial movement to the west, the rise of the great Panhellenic sanctuaries, the flowering of Ionic epic and its Panhellenic circulation, and the recovery of literacy. Except for the last, these are all local developments arising from within the Greek homeland.

These symptoms of progress were accompanied by a rapid rise in population which must have been a major cause of recovery, just as the Dark Ages were inaugurated by a disastrous fall in numbers; whereas between the thirteenth and eleventh centuries it has been reckoned that Greece was depopulated by three-quarters,[1] during the course of the eighth century the number of inhabitants was *doing possibly?*

at least doubled and probably trebled.[2] Such a rapid growth enabled a greater part of the population to turn away from agriculture towards specialized crafts, and this may partly account for notable advances in the sophistication of pottery, bronzework, jewellery, ivory carving, and seal engraving. But there was also a more urgent demand for raw materials rare or lacking in Greece, especially metal ores which were most easily supplied from Etruria and the eastern Mediterranean; hence a steady increase in the activity of Greek merchants outside the Aegean. Especially energetic were the merchants of Corinth and the Euboean cities, whose rising populations were the hardest hit by the shortage of arable land. It was natural that these cities should also take the lead in western colonization, especially in the great exodus of the late eighth century; even so, land hunger still threatened those who stayed behind, and provoked a disastrous war between Chalcis and Eretria for the possession of the small plain which fed them. Conflicts of this nature must have enhanced the internal cohesion of each *polis* at home; and the citizens of each new *polis* in the west, as they warded off hostile natives, must have enjoyed a similar feeling of belonging together.

Such, then, were the mixed blessings arising from the population explosion: craftsmen and merchants became increasingly important, while land hunger led to colonial expansion and wars between neighbouring cities. For those who remained on the land, Hesiod underlines the urgent need for efficient husbandry. A farmer is still expected to feed his household off his own acres; it may be difficult to make ends meet, yet Hesiod himself has to contend not only with poor land, but also with a rapacious landed gentry. In default of any helpful archaeological evidence, we cannot yet know how far Hesiod was a typical farmer of his time. One wonders, for example, how soon the hard-pressed Euboeans and Corinthians found it necessary to import grain from overseas, as became the general custom in later times. In return, later Greeks produced a superfluity of wine and olive oil for export; and olive oil (about which Hesiod is silent) may have been the base for the unguents which the Corinthians began to export in EPC globular aryballoi.

From these materialistic topics we turn to the real matter of the Greek Renaissance. An Ionian school of bards had preserved lays of heroic ancestors who had fought at Troy; these lays were worked into two monumental epics by an oral poet of surpassing genius, remembered by the name of Homer. Knowledge of his poetry spread quickly across the Greek world, not least through public recitation at the great Panhellenic sanctuaries. With the invention of the Greek alphabet it was open to his followers to ensure that his work should be preserved without embroidery or distortion by lesser hands. His poems inspired a rebirth of interest in anyone or anything belonging to the period which we know as Mycenaean. The aristocrats of the day were quick to claim heroic ancestors, and Athenian vase-painters were commissioned to show heroic deeds on aristocratic grave monuments. Epic recitals induced a feeling of pride, confidence, and euphoria which finds its reflection in a temporary elephantiasis in the visual arts: witness the largest kraters and amphorae among the Dipylon grave-markers, the huge bronze tripod cauldrons celebrating victories at the Olympic games, the vast pins offered to Argive Hera, and the correspondingly enormous Boeotian fibulae engraved with heroic scenes. All Greeks felt themselves to be the heirs of a heroic tradition, transcending local barriers; the diffusion of epic helped to bind the Greek world into a closer unity, just as the great sanctuaries became meeting-places for worshippers from every Greek land.

At the same time, local divisions were hardening. The *polis* was becoming established as a permanent feature of Greek society, as each community progressed from loose tribal organization to government by central authority. To judge from the vague memories preserved in literary sources, this change occurred in different places at different times and in different ways; and even when much more evidence than we now possess is recovered from Greek settlements, the material record may never be able to shed much light on this topic. But at least we can observe the strong force of diverse local traditions in pottery, bronzes, and other artifacts, surely reflecting a deep awareness of the *polis* as a self-conscious and self-sufficient unit. In an atmosphere of lively competition, each city excelled in different fields, and took pride in its own way of doing things. For those who study Geometric Greece, this regional variety is one of the greatest attractions of the period.

If viewed from the standpoint of later Greek achievements, Geometric art may appear 'small, bleak, and thrifty'.[3] But if our approach is from the bleakness of the Dark Ages, the eighth century is seen to be one of the most creative periods in Greek art and history, imbued with the vigour of a rising civilization.

NOTES

1 Snodgrass, *DAG* 364–7; cf., however, O. Dickinson, *Antiquaries' Journal* 53 (1973) 100–1.

2 In 1971 Snodgrass (loc. cit). gave the following statistics for the number of sites occupied in successive centuries, exclusive of Crete: *c.* 320 in the thirteenth century, *c.* 130 in the twelfth century, *c.* 40 in the eleventh century. For subsequent centuries, if we include Crete, the corresponding numbers on my reckoning are *c.* 120 in the tenth century, *c.* 140 in the ninth century, and *c.* 260 (also including the western colonies) in the eighth century. (Among these, the Cretan sites number *c.* 20, *c.* 28, and *c.* 40 respectively.) These figures are based partly on surface surveys, and may therefore do less than justice to Geometric sites; for Mycenaean sherds are easily found in the many places deserted at the end of the Bronze Age, whereas Geometric occupation is almost always followed by later phases. In guessing the rise in population we must also allow for the increasing size of major cities in LG times, and the greater density of habitation implied by a count of wells used during successive periods in the area of the Athenian Agora: cf. p. 109, and *GGP* 360 n. 1.

3 Beazley and Ashmole, *Greek Sculpture and Painting* (Cambridge, 1966) 4.

Glossary

Abecedaria: Series of alphabetic letters, written for practice or instruction.
Agora: Place of assembly.
Amphora: A large jar with two handles, placed horizontally or vertically.
Amphoriskos: A small amphora.
Anta: Forward end of a side-wall projected to form a porch.
Apsidal: With one end curved; used of buildings or tombs.
Aristoi: 'The best people'; aristocrats, upper classes.
Aryballos: Small unguent flask with short neck.
Ashlar: Style of masonry, squared and dressed in rectangular blocks.
Bothros: Pit in a sanctuary, for sacrifices or votives.
Bucchero: Grey-black pottery, fired in a kiln from which oxygen has been excluded.
Chamber tomb: A tomb designed for multiple burial, cut into rock; the burial chamber is approached by a narrower passage (*dromos*).
Cist (grave): A grave lined and covered with stone slabs, usually intended for single burial.
Dromos: See Chamber tomb.
Ekphora: A funeral procession, carrying the deceased to the place of burial.
Fibula: A brooch, for fastening drapery.
Filigree: Decoration of gold jewellery, consisting of thin wires soldered on a background.
Genos: Aristocratic clan.
Glaze: A term used (erroneously) for a dark coating on Greek Iron Age pottery, consisting of a solution of the clay.
Granulation: Decoration of gold jewellery, consisting of minute grains of gold soldered to a background.
Hekatompedon: A temple, one hundred feet long.
Heroön: A sanctuary founded in honour of a hero.
Hoplite: A heavy-armed Greek soldier, equipped with bronze armour.
Hydria: A water jar with one vertical handle from mouth to belly, and two horizontal handles on the belly.
Impasto: Used of Italic pottery with a dark monochrome coating.
Intaglio: A design cut into a seal.
Kados: A two-handled jar for cooking.
Kalathos: A shallow bowl with wide and flaring mouth.
Kantharos: A drinking-vessel with two vertical handles.
Kegelhelm: An early class of Greek helmet, tall and conical.

Koinē: A common style diffused over a wide area.

Kotyle: A hemispherical drinking-vessel, with two horizontal handles.

'Koulouri': A clay votive offering, imitating a ring-shaped cake.

Krater: A larger mixing-bowl, usually with two handles.

Kriophoros: A figure of a man carrying a ram.

Kyathos: A mug with two vertical handles.

Lakaina: A drinking-vessel popular in Laconia, with two horizontal handles and a very tall rim.

Lekythos: An oil flask with narrow neck, round mouth, and one vertical handle.

Lekythos-oinochoe: A slowing-pouring vessel with trefoil lip.

Megaron: A long hall, preceded by a porch or anteroom.

Metope: A square panel; the term is applied to the decoration of Geometric pottery on the analogy of the Doric frieze in architecture.

Oikistes: Official leader of an expedition to found a colony.

Oinochoe: A wine jug, with trefoil lip.

Phiale mesomphalos: Shallow bowl, with central boss (*omphalos*) inside.

Pie Ware: Handmade pottery of the Argolid, with decoration suitable for a pie-crust.

Pilgrim flask: A two-handled flask with lentoid body, of Near Eastern character.

Pithos: A large storage vessel, of coarse ware.

Pit (grave): A grave cut into earth or rock, not lined with any masonry.

Polos: A cylindrical hat, flat on top.

Prothesis: The ceremony of laying out the deceased on the bier; lying in state.

Protome: The forepart of an animal, or the bust of a human figure.

Pyxis: A circular clay box with lid.

Repoussé: Decoration on sheet metal, produced with a hammer and punches.

Skyphos: A drinking-vessel with articulated lip and two horizontal handles.

Spectacle fibula: A brooch consisting of two wire spirals mounted on a safety-pin.

Sphyrelaton: The process of hammering bronze over a wooden core.

Stele: Upright stone slab, marking a grave.

Stirrup-jar: A closed jar with a false spout on the top supporting the handles (the stirrup), and a real spout on the shoulder.

Subgeometric: Used of artifacts made in Geometric manner after an Orientalizing style had come into general use.

Sub-Protogeometric: Used of artifacts made in Protogeometric manner after a Geometric style had come into general use.

Synoikismos: Amalgamation of scattered villages into a united state with a capital city.

Tholos (tomb): A tomb with a chamber constructed of corbelled masonry, resembling a beehive, and approached by a dromos.

'Triglyph': In the decoration of Geometric pottery, a narrow vertical motif separating the metopes (q.v.), analogous to the triglyphs of a Doric frieze in architecture.

Tumulus: A mound.

Tympanon: A bronze gong.

Bibliography

and Site Index

GENERAL WORKS

B. Schweitzer, *Die geometrische Kunst Griechenlands* (Köln, 1969); English translation, *Greek Geometric Art* (London, 1971).

J. Bouzek, *Homerisches Griechenland* (Praha, 1969), chs. 5–7.

C. G. Starr, *The Origins of Greek Civilization* (New York, 1961), chs. 4–11.

A. M. Snodgrass, *The Dark Age of Greece* (Edinburgh, 1971).

V. R. d'A. Desborough, *The Greek Dark Ages* (London, 1972).

STUDIES OF SPECIAL TOPICS

R. M. Cook, *Greek Painted Pottery* (2nd edn., London, 1972), ch. 3.

J. N. Coldstream, *Greek Geometric Pottery* (London, 1968).

R. A. Higgins, *Greek Terracottas* (London, 1967), ch. 5.

H.-V. Herrmann, *JdI* 79 (1964), 17 ff., on bronze figurines.

M. Weber, *AM* 86 (1971), 13 ff., on bronze tripods and figurines.

S. Benton, *BSA* 35 (1934–35), 74 ff., on bronze tripods.

A. M. Snodgrass, *Early Greek Armour and Weapons* (Edinburgh, 1964).

C. Blinkenberg, *Fibules grecques et orientales* (Copenhagen, 1926).

R. A. Higgins, *Greek and Roman Jewellery* (London, 1961), chs. 10, 11.

J. Boardman, *Island Gems* (London, 1963), part 2.

J. Boardman, *Greek Gems and Finger Rings* (London, 1970), ch. 3.

M. Andronikos, *Archaeologia Homerica vol. W: Totenkult* (Göttingen, 1968).

D. Kurtz and J. Boardman, *Greek Burial Customs* (London, 1971).

H. Drerup, *Archaeologia Homerica vol. O: Griechische Baukunst in geometrischer Zeit* (Göttingen, 1969).

T. J. Dunbabin, *The Greeks and their Eastern Neighbours* (London, 1957).

J. Boardman, *The Greeks Overseas* (Harmondsworth, 1964).

Note. The detailed bibliographies which follow do not pretend to be exhaustive. Site publications with Geometric pottery are more fully listed in *GGP* 399 ff. In the following pages special attention will be given to site reports which have appeared more recently than *GGP*, and to articles dealing with Geometric material other than pottery. References are to graves, unless otherwise stated; chance finds are not mentioned, unless they are of unusual interest.

CHAPTER 1

ATTICA. Athens: Kerameikos: *K* grs. 1–4, 7, 14, 18, 19, 38, 39, 74, 75a; Areopagus: *Hesperia* 2, 552 ff.; 18, 275 ff. (gr. with clay boots); 21, 279 ff. (warrior gr.); Acropolis, west slope: *Hesperia* 43, 372 ff.; other plots: *AAA* 1, 20 ff. (Kriezi gr. 10); *AD* 19, B 54 f. (Ay. Dimitriou 20, Ay. Markou 6–12); 20, B 56 (Aischylou 31); 22, B 110 ff. (Poulopoulou 20). **Eleusis**: *AE* 1912, 38 f. gr. 41 (cf. *AJA* 44, 481). **Marathon**: *PAE* 1939, 29 ff. gr. 2.

Handmade pottery: J. Bouzek, *Sbornik* 28 (1974), 1 ff., 'The Attic Dark Age Incised Ware'.

THE ARGOLID. Argos: *TGA* I, grs. 14/1, 16, 106/1; *AD* 24, B 106 f.; *AAA* 3, 180 ff.; *CGA* 162 n. 1 (apsidal house). **Tiryns**: *AM* 78, 48 ff. (grs. III/1, XXIII/1); *Tiryns* I grs. 2, 19. **Mycenae**: *BSA* 50, 241 ff. (grs. G 603–4); 68, 87 ff. (gr. G 607). **Nauplia**: *PAE* 1955, 234 (gr. 34).

On the burials: R. Hägg, *Boreas* 7.1 (1974), 'Die Gräber der Argolis'.

THE CORINTHIA. Corinth: *Hesperia* 17, 204; 33, 89 ff.; 39, 16 ff.; *Corinth* VII 1, 10 ff. nos. 22–53 (from modern well shaft). **Zygouries**: Blegen, *Zygouries* 174 ff.

BOEOTIA. Vranesi: *AM* 30, 132 f.; *PAE* 1904, 39 f.; 1907, 109; *GGP* 196 ff. pl. 42.

PHOCIS. Medeon: *AD* 19, B 224; C. Vatin, *Médéon en Phocide* 59 ff.

EUBOEA. Lefkandi: *AR* 1970, 9 f.; 1971, 7 f.; Themelis, *AAA* 2, 98 ff.; *GDA* 195 ff.; *Lefkandi* 28 f. (bronze foundry rubbish).

THESSALY. Marmariani: *BSA* 31, 1 ff. **Homolion**: *AD* 17, B 175. **Larisa** (Platykambos): *Thessalika* 5, 37 ff. **Pherae**: Bequignon, *Récherches archéologiques à Phères* 50 ff. **Sesklo**: *PAE* 1965, 7 ff. **Halos**: *BSA* 18, 1 ff. (grs. 4, 7, 8). **Theotokou**: *PGP* 148 (gr. B). **Iolcos**: *AD* 18, B 140 f.; *Thessalika* 5, 47 ff. (grs. 4, 5). **Kapakli**: *PGRT* 3 ff., with full study of Thessalian Sub-PG pottery. **Other sites**: *DAG* 205 f.

SKYROS. *BCH* 61, 473; *AJA* 55, 149; *PGP* 165 ff.

TENOS. Kardiani: *Ann* 8–9, 203 ff.

RHODES. Ialysos: *ClRh* 3, 146 f. (gr. 141); 8, 161 ff. (Marmaro gr. 43); *AD* 23, A 82 f. (Cremasti gr. 98).

COS. *PGP* 222 ff.; *GDA* 172 ff.

CRETE. Knossos: *Fortetsa* (tombs III–V, L); Ay. Ioannis, *BSA* 55, 128 ff. (tomb I). **Gortyn**: *PAE* 1966, 189 ff. **Modi**: *KCh* 7, 485 ff.; **Vrokastro** tombs 1, 3.

CHAPTER 2

ATTICA. Athens: Kerameikos: *K* grs. 13, 36, 41–3. Areopagus: *Hesperia* 16, 196 f.; 37, 77 ff. (the rich lady). Other plots: *AAA* 1, 20 ff. (Kriezi grs. 5, 7); *AD* 20, B 78 (Kavalotti, grs. δ, ε); 22, B 102 f. (Mitsaion/Zetrou); 23 B 55 f. (Erechtheiou 20, gr. 6). Alleged grave groups, with gold jewellery, in Berlin/ Munich (*AM* 43, 51; *CVA* Munich 3, 28) and Toronto (*JHS* 51, 164 ff.). **Thorikos**: *Hesperia* 30, 299 ff.; *Thorikos* I, 81 ff.; II, 25 ff.; III, 31 ff. (settlement, with silver processing).

EUBOEA. Lefkandi: *Archaeology* 25, 16 ff.; see also under ch. 1.

CYPRUS. Kition: Phoenician colony: *BCH* 92, 307 ff.; 95, 377 ff.; 99, 831 f. Karageorghis, *ProcBritAcad* 1973, 20 ff.

COS. *GGP* 267 ff. (grs. 1, 8, 27), 346 f.; *BICS* 16, 2.

CRETE. Fortetsa tomb OD: tombs II, X, P, TFT (earliest burials). *AM* 60–1, 218 ff. (ivories from **Idaean cave**).

CHAPTER 3

ATTICA. Athens: Kerameikos: *K* grs. 11, 12, 20, 22, 23, 37, 69, 76, 82, 86; *AM* 91, 15 ff.; Areopagus: *Hesperia* 43, 325 ff.; other plots: *AAA* 1, 20 ff. (Kriezi grs. 2, 3, 14); *AD* 18, B 41 ff. (Garibaldi, Zambeliou); 20, B 78 Kavalotti gr. β); 22, B 95 (Kriezi gr. 40); *BSA* 2, 25 (Kynosarges). **Eleusis**: *EA* 1898, 82 f. (gr. 19); 96, 110 (gr. 11); 103 ff. (gr. α, Isis gr.; cf. *CVA* Athens 1, pls. 3–6); *PAE* 1954, 59 (gr. Γ 11); 1955, 72 ff. (grs. Γπ 14, Γ 16, Γ 18); 1956, 60 (gr. θ 52). **Marathon**: *PAE* 1939, 29 ff. (grs. 1, 5). **Piraeus**, Palaia Kokkinia: *PAE* 1951, 119 ff. (grs. ε, λ). **Anavysos**: *AD* 21, B 97 ff. (grs. 2, 11, 29, 51).

Jewellery: Higgins, *BSA* 64, 145 ff. MG figured pottery: Benson, *Horse, Bird and Man* (1970).

THE ARGOLID. Argos: *TGA* I, grs. 6/1, 14/2, 32, 89, 90, 129, 176/1, 191; *AD* 16, B 93 (Phlessas gr. 3); 17, B 55 f. (Alexopoulos grs. α, δ); 18, B 57 ff. (Makris grs. 1, 4). **Tiryns**: *AM* 78, 30 ff. (grs. X, XVI); *Tiryns* I, grs. 16, 24, 30. **Mycenae**: *BSA* 49, 260 ff. (gr. G II/1). **Berbati**: *Stockholm Stud.Class. Arch.* 4, 81 ff. **Nauplia**: *PAE* 1954, 234 (gr. 21). **Lerna**: *Hesperia* 23, 7.

THE CORINTHIA. Corinth: *AJA* 9, 411 ff. (cf. *Corinth* VII 1 nos. 54–66); *AJA* 41, 544 f.; 45, 31 (cf. *Corinth* VII 1 nos. 73–7); North Cemetery, *Corinth* XIII grs. 14–24; Potters' Quarter, *Corinth* XV 1, 8 (gr. 5). **Clenia**: *AJA* 59, 125 ff. **Ay. Theodoroi**: *AD* 17, B 53 (grs. 2, 4). **Perachora**: Salmon, *BSA* 67, 161 ff. (earliest finds from sanctuary).

BOEOTIA: *GGP* 198 f.

THESSALY. Halos, pyres: *BSA* 18, 8 ff.

EUBOEA. Lefkandi: *Lefkandi* 26 ff. (settlement, levelling fill). **Eretria**: *AE* 1903, 1 ff. (cemetery by sea); *AD* 20, B 285 pl. 336a (sanctuary of Apollo, earliest pottery).

THE CYCLADES. Naxos: Naxia: *PAE* 1937–38, 117; Tsikalario: *AD* 18, 279 ff.; 20, 515 ff. **Donousa**: *AD* 24, B 390 ff.; 25, B 426 ff.; 26, 465 ff.; *AAA* 4, 210 ff.; 6, 256 ff. **Thera, Kimolos, Rheneia, Delos**: see under ch. 7.

THE LEVANT. Riis, *Sukas* I ch. 7, with historical reconstruction. **Al Mina**: *JHS* 60, 2 ff.; for dating, *Iraq* 21, 91.

RHODES. Camirus: *ClRh* 6–7, 189 ff. (gr. 80; tombs 82, 83). **Exochi**: *Exochi* grs. V, Y. **Vati**: *AAA* 8, 223 ff.

COS: *BdA* 35, 320 (gr. 68).

CARIA. Asarlik: *JHS* 8, 69 ff. (tomb C). **Iasos**: *Ann* 43–4, 498 ff.; 47–8, 464 ff.

IONIA. Colophon: *HM* 105 ff.; 348 (fibulae). **Samos, Miletus, Melia**: see under ch 9.

CRETE, Knossos: *Fortetsa* tombs LST, X, TFT, F, earlier burials; also VIII/5, VII/13, P/65; Teke: *KCh* 1, 633 (cf. *GGP* pl. 52a,d); *BSA* 49, 215 ff. (tholos with jewellery, earlier burials); Atsalenio: *BSA* 63, 133 ff. (earlier burials); Mastamba: *PAE* 1970, 270 ff. (earlier burials). **Vrokastro**: *Vrokastro* 163 ff. (bone enclosures 6, 12); 170 ff. (rectangular shrine). **Piskokephalo, Rhotasi**: see under ch. 10. **Kavousi Kisamou**: *AD* 24, B 432 ff.

Teke jewellery: Boardman, *BSA* 62, 57 ff.; Higgins, *BSA* 64, 150 f. Fortetsa bronze quiver and belt: *CCO* 134 ff.; *BOOC* 31, nos. 97, 98.

CHAPTER 4

GRAVES. Athens: Kerameikos: *K* grs. 5, 6, 8–10, 15–17, 21, 24–35, 45–68, 70–3, 78–83, 85, 88, 90–100; *AD* 18, B 29 f.; *AA* 1964, 467 ff.; *AM* 89, 1 ff.; Odos Peiraios ('Dipylon'): *Annali* 1872, 131 ff., (cf. *CVA* Louvre 11, 3 ff.); Rayet and Collignon, *Histoire de la Céramique grecque* (1884) 23 f.; *AM* 18, 73 ff.; *AD* 17, B 22 f.; 23, B 82 (gr. 15). Kriezi 24: *AAA* 1, 20 ff. (grs. 12, 16); *AD* 22, B 92 ff. (grs. 26, 45, 72, 106); Agora area: *Hesperia* Suppl. 2, 6 ff. (family plot); Areopagus: *Hesperia* 21, 69 ff.; 29, 402 ff.; Kynosarges: *BSA* 12, 80 ff.; *AAA* 5, 165 ff.; *AD* 27, B 93 ff.; Kallithea: *BCH* 87, 404 ff.; *AD* 19, B 65 ff.; other plots: *AM* 18, 414 (Pnyx); *PAE* 1956, 47 ff.; 1958, 5 ff.; 1959, 8 ff. (Academy); 1959, 6 (Nymphaeum); *AD* 11, B 2 (Kalisperi/Karyatidon); 17, A 86 ff. and 22, B 106 ff. (Parthenonos) 18, B 37 f. (Diakou/Anapafseos); 19, B 60 (Meidani 12–14); 22, B 79 ff. (Erysichthonos/Neleos); 112 (Robertou Galli 9); 23, B 55 f. (Erechtheiou 20 gr. 4); 88 ff. (Promachou 5, Sapphous 12); 24, B 39 (Demophontos 5); 25, B 56 (Demetrakopoulou 110 gr. 8). 27, B 62 (Theophilopoulou gr. 4).

Eleusis: *EA* 1898, 29 ff. and 1912, 1 ff. (numerous grs.); *PAE* 1955, 76 (gr. Γ 10). **Piraeus**: Palaia Kokkinia: *PAE* 1951, 117 ff. (gr. η); Nea Kokkinia: *AD* 17, B 43. **Aigaleos**: *AJA* 64, 71; *AD* 19, B 70. **Phaleron**: *AD* 2, 13 ff; *AJA* 46, 25 ff. (grs. 47, 83). **Trachones**: *AM* 88, 1 ff. **Vari**: *BCH* 82, 672; *AD* 20, B 112 ff. **Anavysos**: *PAE* 1911, 110 ff.; *AD* 21, B 97 ff.; **Thorikos**: *Thorikos* I, 47 ff.; III, 42 ff.; IV, 71 ff. **Merenda**: *BCH* 85, 626 ff.; *AAA* 1, 31 ff.; *AD* 25, B 127 ff. **Markopoulo**: *AD* 26, 38 ff. **Spata**: *AD* 6, B 131 ff. **Draphi**: *BCH* 82, 681. **Marathon**: *PAE* 1934, 35 ff.

Burial customs: Kraiker, *Bonner Jahrb.* 161, 108 ff. (gr. markers); Andronikos, *ArchHom* W ch. 2; Kurtz and Boardman, *Greek Burial Customs* ch. 4; Bouzek, *Homerisches Griechenland* 180 ff. (social standing of the deceased).

POTTERY. Figured vase-painting, workshops and hands: Nottbohm, *JdI* 58, 1 ff.; J. M. Cook, *BSA* 42, 139 ff.; Villard, *Monuments Piot* 49, 17 ff.; Davison, *AGW*; Brann, *Agora* VIII, 4 ff.; *GGP* 29 ff. Iconography: Ahlberg, *FLS* and *PE*.

WELL DEPOSITS: *Hesperia* 30, 93 ff.

JEWELLERY: Ohly 9 ff. (diadems); Higgins, *BSA* 64, 147 ff., 152 f.

BRONZES: Karouzou, *AE* 1952, 137 ff.; Weber, *AM* 86, 21 ff.; Touloupa, *AM* 87, 57 ff. (tripods from Acropolis).

IVORIES: Kunze, *AM* 55, 147 ff.; Riis, *Sukas* I, 169 ff. (the Hama school).

CHAPTER 5

ARGOLID. Argos: *TGA* I grs. 1 (spits etc.), 6/2, 13, 14/3, 23, 43, 45 (panoply), 66, 80, 84 *bis*, 106/2, 124, 128, 152, 163, 175, 176/2, 190; *BCH* 85, 675 f. (Raptis); 91, 834 ff. (grs. 297–8); 844 ff.; 95, 740 (grs. 316–17); *AD* 23, B 127 f. (Kymbouropoulos); 26, B 81 f. (Stavropoulou); 27, B 134 ff. (Papanicolaou/ Georga).

Tiryns: *AM* 78, 47 ff. (grs. II, III/2, IV, VIII, XXIII/2); *Tiryns* I grs. 22, 26, 38, 39, 41. **Mycenae**: *BSA* 49, 260 ff. (gr. G II/2); 51, 128 f. (gr. G 605); *AE* 1912, 127 ff. **Nauplia**: *PAE* 1953, 201; 1954, 232 ff.; 1955, 233 ff. **Lerna**: *Hesperia* 43, 80 ff. **Asine**: *OpAth* 6, 134 ff.; *Boreas* 4.1, 31 ff. (house, and grs.); *AD* 27, B 231 ff.; *Asine* 192 ff. (grs.); 39 f., 81 f. (houses); 312 ff. (house deposit). **Argive Heraion**: *AH* I and II; *AJA* 43, 410 ff.; *Hesperia* 21, 173 ff.

Pottery: Courbin, *CGA*.

Burial customs: Hagg, *Boreas* 7.1; Courbin, *TGA* I, 99 ff.

Spits and firedogs: Courbin, *BCH* 81, 368 ff.; id., *Annales* 14, 209 ff. (analysis of spits); *AAA* 2, 436 ff.

Panoply armour: *BCH* 81, 340 ff.; Snodgrass, *EGAW* 13 ff. (Kegelhelm); 72 ff. (corslet); Catling, *Antiquity* 39, 150 ff.; Snodgrass, *Studies in Honour of C. F. C. Hawkes, The European Community in Later Prehistory* 33 ff.

Bronze figurines: *AH* II pls. 72–3; Herrmann, *JdI* 79, 24 ff., 45 ff.; Weber, *AM* 86, 18 f. (tripods).

Seals: *AH* II pl. 139; Boardman, *IGems* 112 ff.

ARCADIA. Tegea: *BCH* 45, 335 ff. (sanctuary, pottery, bronzes). **Lousoi**: *JOAI* 4, 1 ff. (sanctuary, bronzes). **Mavriki**: *AE* 1952, 1 ff. (sanctuary, bronzes).

Bronzes: Schweitzer, *GKG* 163 ff. (figurines); Jacobsthal, *Greek Pins* 7 ff. (pins and fibulae).

LACONIA. Sparta: *AO* (sanctuary of Artemis Orthia, pottery, bronzes); *BSA* 13, 142 ff. (sanctuary of Athena Chalkioikos); *AD* 27, B 244 ff. **Amyclae**: *EA* 1892, 12 ff. *AM* 52, 12 ff. (sanctuary of Apollo, pottery, bronzes).

Pottery: Lane, *BSA* 34, 101 ff.

Bronzes: Herrmann, *JdI* 79, 20 ff., 42 ff.

Chronology: Boardman, *BSA* 58, 1 ff.

MESSENIA. Nichoria: *Hesperia* 41, 251 ff.; 44, 85 ff; *AD* 26, B 135 ff.; (settlement, apsidal houses); *BCH* 84, 700; 85, 697; *AAA* 1, 205 ff; *AE* 1973, 25 ff. (earlier burials); *AD* 25, B 186 (LG warrior pithos burial). **Volimedia**: *GGP* 223 ff. **Other sites**: *AD* 20, B 207 ff. (grs., chance finds).

CHAPTER 6

THE CORINTHIA. Corinth: central area: *AJA* 41, 543 ff. (pins and jewellery republished in *Corinth* XIII); *AJA* 37, 567; *Hesperia* 42, 2 ff.; *Corinth* VII 1, nos. 103–15; temple of Apollo: *Hesperia* 45, 203 ff.; North Cemetery: *Corinth* XIII, grs. 25–62; Potters' Quarter: *AJA* 37, 605 ff. (settlement deposit with graffiti). Well deposits: *Corinth* VII 1, nos. 116–34; *Hesperia* 17, 208 ff.; 18,

153 f.; 20, 293 f.; 45, 99 ff. **Ay. Theodoroi** gr. 3 (see under ch. 3). **Perachora**:
Perachora I ch. 2, Akraia votive deposit.

Pottery: LG-EPC: Neeft, *Bull. Ant. Beschaving* 50, 97 ff.; EPC Orientalizing: Payne, *Protokorinthische Vasenmalerei* 1 ff.; Dunbabin and Robertson,
BSA 48, 172 ff.

Bronzes: Herrmann, *JdI* 79, 28 ff., 47 ff.

Growth of Corinthian state: Roebuck, *Hesperia* 41, 96 ff.

PHOCIS. Medeon: Vatin, op. cit. (ch. 1) 68 ff. **Amphissa**: *AD* 18, B 130.
Corycian cave: *BCH* 96, 907 f. (bronze horse). **Delphi**; settlement: *RA* 12
(1938) 207 ff; *BCH* 74, 321 ff.; 85, 357 ff.; burials: *BCH* 59, 276 ff.; 61, 44 ff.
(museum area); 68-9. 52 ff. (near Marmaria); *FD* V, 153 ff. (Pylaea);
sanctuary: *RA* 12, 209; *BCH* 68-9, 36 ff. (votives under Sacred Way); *BCH*
62, 305 ff. (bronze votives under museum).

Bronzes: *FD* V (figurines and tripods); *FD* V. 2 (republication of figurines
by Rolley).

ACHAEA. Pharae: *PAE* 1930, 83 ff.; 1952, 400 ff.; 1956, 196 ff.; *BCH* 85, 682.
Drepanon: *AE* 1973, B 15 ff. **Other sites**: *DAG* 211.

ELIS. Kyllene: *BCH* 81, 568. **Ancient Elis**: *PAE* 1973, 113 (complete LG
krater). **Agrapidochori** (Elean Pylos); *AD* 20, B 214 ff.; *AAA* 1, 285 ff.
(mainly post-Geometric, wells etc.). **Olympia**: well: *AD* 18, B 103; sanctuary:
OlF V, 158 n. 3 (pottery); Herrmann, *Olympia: Heiligtum und Wettkampfstätte*
(1973) 66 ff.

ITHACA. Aetos: *BSA* 33, 27 ff. (cairns); 43, 1 ff. and 48, 255 ff. (sanctuary,
pottery, and other finds). **Polis cave**, sanctuary: *BSA* 35, 45 ff. (site and
tripods); 39, 8 ff. and 44, 307 ff. (pottery).

Bronze tripods: Benton, *BSA* 35, 74 ff. (general study).

AETOLIA. *AD* 17, B 183 **(Calydon)**; 22, B 320 **(Calydon** and **Pylene)**.

ACARNANIA. Palaiomanina: *AD* 17, B 184 (pithos gr., LG pottery); 22,
B 323 (gr., metal objects); 24, A 74 ff. (PG pottery).

CORCYRA: *AD* 18, B 180 ff. and 20, B 391 ff. (disturbed cemetery); 21, B 320 f.
(sanctuary, bronzes).

EPIRUS. Dodona, sanctuary and bronzes: *PAE* 1929, 117; 1931, 86 f.; 1932,
50; 1958, 105; 1967, 45 ff.; *AD* 18, B 149 f.; Carapanos, *Dodone et ses ruines*
III pl. 49; Blinkenberg, 106 ff.; Dakaris, *AntK* Beiheft I, 47 f.

Vitsa: *AD* 21, B 289 ff.; 22, B 346 ff.; 23, B 287 ff. (B 290, settlement); 24,
B 249 ff.; Hammond, *Epirus* (Oxford, 1967), 414 f.

CHAPTER 7

EUBOEA. Lefkandi, settlement: *Lefkandi* 29 ff. **Chalcis**, settlement: *BSA* 52,
1 ff.; *AD* 16, B 151 (wells); 26, B 252; *BCH* 98, 687 f. **Eretria**: cemeteries:
AE 1903, 1 ff. (by the sea); *Eretria* III (by west gate); settlement: *AE* 1969,
143 ff.; sanctuary of Apollo: *BCH* 96, 752 ff.; 98, 687; *AntK* 14, 59 ff.; 17, 60 f.
General survey: Auberson and Schefold, *Führer durch Eretria* (1972) 16 ff.

Pottery: *BSA* 47, 1 ff.; 52, 1 ff.; *AntK* 10, 134 f. (with Cypriot imports);
11, 99 ff.; *AD* 20, B 285 ff.; *BICS* 18, 1 ff. (Cesnola painter); *AAA* 3, 318 f;
BCH 96, 269 ff. (crab aryballoi).

Gold diadems: *AM* 38, 289 ff.; Ohly, 46 ff.; *AntK* 12, 73; *Eretria* III, 36 ff. Bronze cauldrons: *Eretria* III, 22 ff.

BOEOTIA. Thebes, Pyri: *EA* 1892, 213 ff.; *AD* 21, B 197 f.; 26, B 212 f. **Rhitsona**: *JHS* 30, 341 f. (grs. 1, 6, 75). **Paralimni**, Kamilovrysi: *AD* 21, B 201; 26, B 215 ff.; *BCH* 96, 704 ff.; 98, 163 ff. **Kabeirion**, sanctuary: Wolters and Bruns, *Das Kabirenheiligtum bei Theben*. **Ptoion**, Sanctuary: Ducat, *Les Kouroi du Ptoion* (1971) 49 ff.

Pottery: Hampe, *FGS* 20ff.; Canciani, *JdI* 80, 18 ff.; Ruckert, *Frühe Keramik Böotiens, AntK* Beiheft 10 (1976).

Terracotta dolls: Grace, *Archaic Sculpture in Boeotia*, 10 ff.; Dörig, *AntK* 1, 50 f.

Bronze fibulae: Hampe, *FGS*; De Vries, *Forsch. u. Berichten* 14, 111 ff.

THESSALY. Halos, pyres: see under ch. 3. **Pherae,** sanctuary: see under ch. 1. **Philia,** sanctuary: *AD* 18, B 135 ff.; 19, B 244 ff.; 20, B 311 ff.; 22, B 295 f.

Bronze figurines: Biesantz, *Die thessalische Grabreliefs* 158 ff.; S. Karouzou, *AM* 91, 23 ff.

Fibulae: De Vries, *Teiresias* 1, 10; Bouzek, *Graeco-Macedonian Bronzes* 130 ff.; Kilian, *Fibeln in Thessalien* (*Präh. Bronzefunde* 14.2, 1975).

THE WESTERN CYCLADES. Keos, Ay. Irini, sanctuary: *Hesperia* 31, 281 ff.; 33, 332 ff. **Siphnos,** Kastro, settlement: *BSA* 44, 6 ff.; *ArchHom* O 50 f. **Kimolos,** Hellenika: *BCH* 78, 146; *AM* 69–70, 153 ff. (pottery). **Melos**: *BSA* 2, 70 f.

Melian seals: Boardman, *IGems* 115 (A 5), 135 f. (L 1).

THE NORTHERN CYCLADES. Andros, Zagora, settlement: *Zagora* I; *PAE* 1972, 251 ff.; 1974, 163 ff.; **Tenos,** Xombourgo, sanctuary: *ArchHom* O 10, 55.

Tenian relief pithoi: Schäfer, *Studien zu der griechischen Reliefpithoi* ... 67 ff.; Kondoleon, *AE* 1969, 215 ff.; Ervin, *AD* 18, A 40 ff. and *AJA* 80, 19 ff.

THE CENTRAL CYCLADES. Naxos: Kaminia, *PAE* 1939, 119 f.; Aplomata, *PAE* 1960, 258 ff.; 1961, 195 ff.; 1963, 153 ff.; Palati, settlement and sanctuary: *AM* 54, 152 ff.; *AA* 1972, 354 ff., 386 ff. **Paros,** acropolis: *AM* 42, 73 ff.; Delion sanctuary: Rubensohn, *Das Delion von Paros*. **Delos,** sanctuary: G. de Santerre, *Délos primitive et archaique* 201 ff., *ArchHom* O 5 (building Γ), 19 (building under Oikos of the Naxians), 23 (Heraion), 24 (Artemision); *BCH* 71–2, 148 ff. (the Artemision deposit).

Pottery: *Délos* XV (Geometric from Delos and Rheneia); Buschor, *AM* 54, 142 ff. (recognition of 'Parian' and Naxian); Kondoleon, *AE* 1945–47, 1 ff. (on Naxian).

Bronzes from Delos: Rolley, *Etudes déliennes* (*BCH* Suppl. I) 491 ff.

THERA: *AM* 28, 1 ff. (Mesavouno); *Thera* II and *PAE* 1974, 194 ff. (Sellada). Burial customs: Kurtz and Boardman, *Greek Burial Customs* 177 ff.

CHAPTER 8

PRECOLONIAL EXCHANGES. Veii, Quattro Fontanili: *NSc* 1963, 77 ff. figs. 4, 47, 64; 1965, 49 ff. figs. 27, 36, 40; 1967, 87 ff. fig. 81; 1970, 178 ff. fig. 65; 1972, 195 ff. fig. 36; *BSA* 68, 191 f. **Cumae,** Osta: *MA* 22, fig. 52, pl 18.

Capua: *DdA* 1, 159 ff. fig. 8b. **Pontecagnano**: *DdA* 3, fig. 14a. Chevron skyphoi: Ridgway, *StEtr* 35, 311 ff. The sequence at Veii: Close-Brooks, *StEtr* 35, 323 ff.; *NSc* 1965, 53 ff.

PITHECUSAE. Cemetery: Buchner, *Atti e Memorie* 1954, 3 ff.; *RM* 60–1, 37 ff.; *Metropoli e Colonie* . . . (Taranto Congress, 1963) 263 ff. Cemetery and settlement: Buchner, *Expedition* 8, 4 ff.; *AR* 1971, 63 ff. Metalworking quarter: Klein, *Expedition* 14, 34 ff. Lyre-player seals: Buchner and Boardman, *JdI* 81, 1 ff. General: Ridgway, in *Greeks, Celts, and Romans* (ed. C. F. Hawkes, 1973) ch. 2.

CUMAE. Cemetery: *MA* 13, 225 ff.; 22, 213 ff.; acropolis: *RM* 60–1, 51 ff.

NAXOS, settlement: *BdA* 49, 149 ff.; 57, 211 ff.

SYRACUSE. Native settlement: *MA* 25, 427 ff., 500 ff.; sanctuary of Athena: ibid. 523 ff.; colonial settlement: *NSc* 1925, 315 ff.; *DdA* 3, 141 ff.; Fusco cemetery: *NSc* 1895, 109 ff.; *AJA* 62, 259 ff.

LEONTINI. Native cemetery, S. Aloe: *RM* 15, 62 ff.; colonial settlement: *NSc* 1955, 362 ff.; *Cronache d'Arte* 1, 1 ff.

MEGARA HYBLAEA, settlement: *BdA* 45, 263 ff.; *Megara Hyblaea* II (pottery). **Thapsos,** re-use of Bronze Age tomb: *MA* 6, 103 f.

THE STRAITS. Vallet, *Rhégion et Zancle* (1958). **Mylae**: Bernabo Brea, *Mylai*. **Canale**: *MA* 31, 211 ff.

SYBARIS: *NSc* Suppl. (1970). Native settlements near by: La Genière, *MEFR* 82, 621 ff. **Amendolara**: *MEFR* 85, 7 ff.; **Francavilla**: *Atti e Memorie* 6–7 (1965–66) 1 ff.

TARAS: *Ann* 37–38, 8 ff.; Scoglio del Tonno: *Ann* 33–34, 8 ff.; *Dragma M. P. Nilsson*, 460 ff.; **Leporano** (Satyrion): *BdA* 49, 67 ff.; *NSc* 1964, 220 ff.

WESTERN PHOENICIANS: **Carthage**: Cintas, *Céramique punique* 456 ff., 490 ff. **Motya**: *Ann. of Leeds Oriental Soc.* 4, 118 ff.; *GGP* 388 n. 2; *NSc* 1941, 284 ff. fig. 25 (faience situla). **Sulcis**: Pesce, *Sardegna punica* 70 fig. 116. **Spain**: Niemeyer, *MDOG* 104, 5 ff.

CHAPTER 9

RHODES. Ialysos: *ClRh* 3, 37 ff. (grs. 8, 39, 51, 56–8, 61–3); 8, 172 (Marmaro gr. 51). **Camirus**: *ClRh* 4, 342 ff. (grs. 200, 201, 203, 204); 6, 32 ff. (grs. 7, 8, 22, 23, 25, 26, 85). **Exochi**: *Exochi* grs. A–D, L, M, X. **Lindos**, sanctuary: *Lindos* I (small finds and pottery).

Pottery: Johansen, *Exochi* 84 ff. (general survey of Rhodian LG artifacts); *BICS* 16, 1 ff. (imitations of Cypro-Levantine).

Terracottas: Higgins, *BMCat Terracottas* I, 32 ff.; *Greek TCs* 19 f.

Bronze fibulae: Blinkenberg types IV, XII.

Jewellery: Higgins, *GRJ* 104 ff.

COS. *GGP* 287 f.; *Ann* 8–9, 267 ff. (**Aspripetra cave**).

SAMOS. Heraion: architecture: *AM* 58, 150 ff.; *ArchHom* O 13 f. Pottery: *Samos* V; *AM* 54, 9 ff.; 58, 47 ff.; 72, 35 ff.; 74, 12 ff. Terracottas: *AM* 65, 57 ff.; 66, 1 ff.; *AA* 1964, 493 ff. Wood: *AM* 68, 89 ff. Bronzes: Gehrig, *Bronzen aus dem Heraion von Samos* (1964). Ivories: Barnett, *JHS* 68, 3 f.; Freyer-Schauenburg, *Elfenbeine aus dem samischen Heraion* (1966).

CHIOS. Kato Phana (Phanai): *AD* 1, 72 ff.; *BSA* 35, 138 ff. **Emporio**: Boardman, *Greek Emporio*.

CARIA. Halicarnassos and Lelegian sites: *BSA* 50, 85 ff.; **Iasos**: settlement: *Ann* 39–40, 533 ff.; 43–4, 417 ff.; 45–6, 554 ff.; 47–8, 461 ff.; cemetery: see under ch. 3. **Beçin** (old Mylasa?): *Belleten* 1971, 1 ff. **Sinuri**, sanctuary: Robert and Haspels, *Sanctuaire de Sinuri* II, 9 ff.
Pottery: *Belleten* 40, 3 ff.; *AA* 1977, 8 ff.

IONIA. Miletus: *IM* 7, 114 ff.; 9–10, 36 ff.; 18, 87 ff., 144 ff.; 19–20, 113 ff.; 25, 259 ff.; *AR* 1960, 48; 1965, 50; 1971, 44; Kleiner, *Alt-Milet* (1966); Kalabaktepe: *Milet* I.8, 5 ff. **Didyma**: *AA* 1964, 333 ff.; *ArchHom* O 59 f. **Melia**: Kleiner, *Panionion u. Melie* (*JdI* Erganz. 23). **Ephesus**: *JOAI* 23, Beibl. 247 ff. **Smyrna**: *JOAI* 27, Beibl. 159 ff.; Akurgal, *Bayraklı* (1950) 58 ff.; id., *Die Kunst Anatoliens* 8 ff.; *BSA* 53–4, 1 ff.; *ArchHom* O 44 ff.

NORTH-EAST AEGEAN. Burunjuk (?Larisa): Schefold, *Larisa-am-Hermos* III. **Antissa**: *BSA* 31, 166 ff.; 32, 41 ff. **Troy**: *Troy* IV, 247 ff.

ANATOLIAN HINTERLAND. Xanthos: Metzger, *Xanthos* IV, 21 ff., 188 ff. **Sardis**: *BASOR* 162, 9 ff.; 186, 17 ff. **Gordion**: *AJA* 59, 1 ff.; 60, 249 ff.; 61, 319 ff.; 62, 139 ff.; 64, 227 ff.; 66, 153 ff.; 68, 279 ff.; 70, 267 ff.; 72, 231 ff.; Phrygian bronzes: *AS* 11, 185 ff.; Phrygian textiles: *AA* 1973, 149 ff.; Phrygian pottery: *AS* 24, 169 ff.; Phrygian furniture: *Expedition* 16, 2 ff.; Phrygian chronology: Young, *8 Cong. Int. Arch. Class.* (Paris, 1963) 481 ff.; Akurgal, *Die Kunst Anatoliens*, 117 ff.; Snodgrass, *DAG* 348 ff.

CHAPTER 10

POTTERY. Knossos: *Fortetsa* tombs I, II, VII, VIII, X, F, P, P2, TFT; *BSA* 55, 163 ff.; 67, 77 ff. (settlement). **Afrati** (Arkades), southern style: *Ann* 10–12, 78 ff. **Kavousi**, eastern style: *Ann* 10–12, 562 ff.; cf. *Vrokastro*, 51 ff. Relief pithoi: Schäfer, op. cit. (ch. 7) 9 ff.; *BSA* 57, 31 ff.

BURIAL CUSTOMS. Tholoi: **Ay. Paraskies**: *AE* 1945–47, 47 ff.; **Rhotasi** (Rhytion): *KCh* 12, 468; **Kavousi**: *AJA* 5, 143 f.; **Sykia-Adhromyloi**: *PAE* 1954, 365 ff. Single burials: **Dreros**: *Et. Cret.* 8, 18 ff.; **Episkopi Pediados**: *PAE* 1952, 628 ff. Caves with inhumations: **Piskokephalo**: *PAE* 1953, 292 ff.; **Zou**: *PAE* 1954, 363 f.; **Praisos** (Vavelloi): *BSA* 12, 36 f. Rectangular shafts: **Praisos**: *BSA* 8, 248 ff. (tomb C).

SETTLEMENTS. Vrokastro: Hall, *Vrokastro*, 86 ff.; **Kavousi**: *AJA* 5, 137 ff.; **Phaistos**: *Ann* 35–6, 265 ff.; 39–40, 377 ff.; **Dreros**, agora: *BCH* 61, 10 ff. General study: Renard, *AntClass* 36, 570 ff.; Drerup, *ArchHom* O.

SANCTUARIES. Dreros: *BCH* 60, 219 ff.; **Gortyn**: Rizza, *Gortina*; **Afrati** (Arkades): *AD* 24, B 415 ff.; 25, B 455 ff.; **Kato Symi**: *PAE* 1973, 188 ff.; 1974, 228 ff.; *Ergon* 1976, 171 ff.

JEWELLERY: *BSA* 62, 60 f.; 64, 150 ff.; 70, 169 ff. Idaean Cave: *AJA* 49, 313 ff.

BRONZES. Tripods: *BSA* 40, 51 ff. Openwork stands: *CCO* 132 f.; *BCH* 68–9, 56 ff. (Delphi). Figurines: U. Naumann, *Opus Nobile* (*Festschrift U. Jantzen*) 114 ff. *Sphyrelata* statues: *CCO* 137; *BSA* 62, 61 (revised dating). Idaean shields and other reliefs: Kunze, *KB*; Boardman, *CCO* 138 ff.; Canciani, *BOOC*.

CHAPTER 11

PHOENICIAN ALPHABET. Driver, *Semitic Writing* . . . (1944); add Dupont-Sommer, *Memoires de l'Academie* 44, 9 ff. (graffito from Kition).
INVENTION OF THE GREEK ALPHABET, various views: Rhys Carpenter, *AJA* 37, 8 ff.; Cook and Woodhead, *AJA* 63, 175 ff.; Jeffery, *LSAG* 1 ff.; Guarducci, *ArchClass* 16, 124 ff.; Naveh, *AJA* 77, 1 ff.
EARLIEST GREEK INSCRIPTIONS. *LSAG* 76, 1 (Athens); 239, 1 (Pithecusae); 356, 1 (Rhodes). Add *Lefkandi* 33 f.; Peruzzi, *Origini di Roma* II (1973) 24 ff. (Pithecusae); *KCh* 21, 153 ff. (Phaistos).

CHAPTER 12

THE LARGEST SETTLEMENTS. Athens: Travlos, Πολεοδομική 'Εξέλιξις Τῶν 'Αθηνῶν (1960) 23 fig. 7. **Corinth**: *Hesperia* 42, 3 fig. 1 and Roebuck, art. cit. (ch. 6); **Argos**: Hägg, *Boreas* 7, 1 fig. 6; **Eretria**: Themelis, *AE* 1969, 150 f. figs. 3, 4; **Knossos**: Hood and de Jong, *Archaeological Survey of the Knossos Area* (1957) 6 ff. fig. 2.
SMALLER SETTLEMENTS. Smyrna: *BSA* 53–4, 1 ff. **Andros**, Zagora: *Zagora* I; *PAE* 1972, 251 ff.; 1974, 163 ff. **Chios**, Emporio: Boardman, *Greek Emporio* (*BSA* Suppl. 6). **Dreros**, agora: *BCH* 61, 10 ff.

CHAPTER 13

SANCTUARIES. Altars: Yavis, *Greek Altars* (1949) ch. 3. Bench temples: see under chs. 7 (**Delos**, Heraion) and 10 (**Dreros**). Apsidal temples: **Perachora**: *Perachora* I, 27 ff. (temple models, 34 ff.); **Eretria**: *AntK* 17, 60 ff. (reconstruction of bay hut), and see also under ch. 7. **Mycenae**: *PAE* 1962, 85 ff.; 1963, 110 ff. **Solygeia**: *PAE* 1958, 135 ff. Long rectangular temples: **Thermon**: *AD* 1, 242 ff.; *ArchHom* O, 14 ff.; **Tiryns**: *Tiryns* III, 213 ff.; Blegen, *Korakou* 130 ff.; **Samos**: *AM* 58, 150 ff.
THE GODS, and problems of continuity. Dietrich, *Origins of Greek Religion* (1973); Desborough, *GDA* 278 ff. **Eleusis**: Mylonas, *Eleusis and the Eleusinian Mysteries* (1961) 31 ff.; Travlos, *Temples and Sanctuaries of Ancient Greece* (1973, ed. Melas) 77 ff.
VOTIVES. Higgins, *Greek TCs* ch. 5; Jacobsthal, *Greek Pins*; Willemsen, *OlF* III (Olympia tripods); Schweitzer, *GKG* ch. 7 (classification and dating of tripods); Weber, *AM* 86, 13 ff. (geographical allocation of tripods).

CHAPTER 14

HERO-CULTS. Geometric votives in Mycenaean tombs: Blegen, *AE* 1937, 377 ff. (Prosymna); *BSA* 25, 312 f., 366 and 48, 80 f. (Mycenae, tholoi); *PAE* 1952, 470 and *Archaeologia* 72, 23 (Mycenae, chamber tombs); Deshayes, *Fouilles de la Deiras* 215 ff. (Argos); *PAE* 1953, 242 ff. (Volimedia, cf. *GGP* 98, 223); *AD* 3, 86 n. 1 (Thebes); *PAE* 1954, 273 (Analipsis); *JdI* 14, 103 ff. (Menidi); *PAE* 1955, 96 (Aliki).

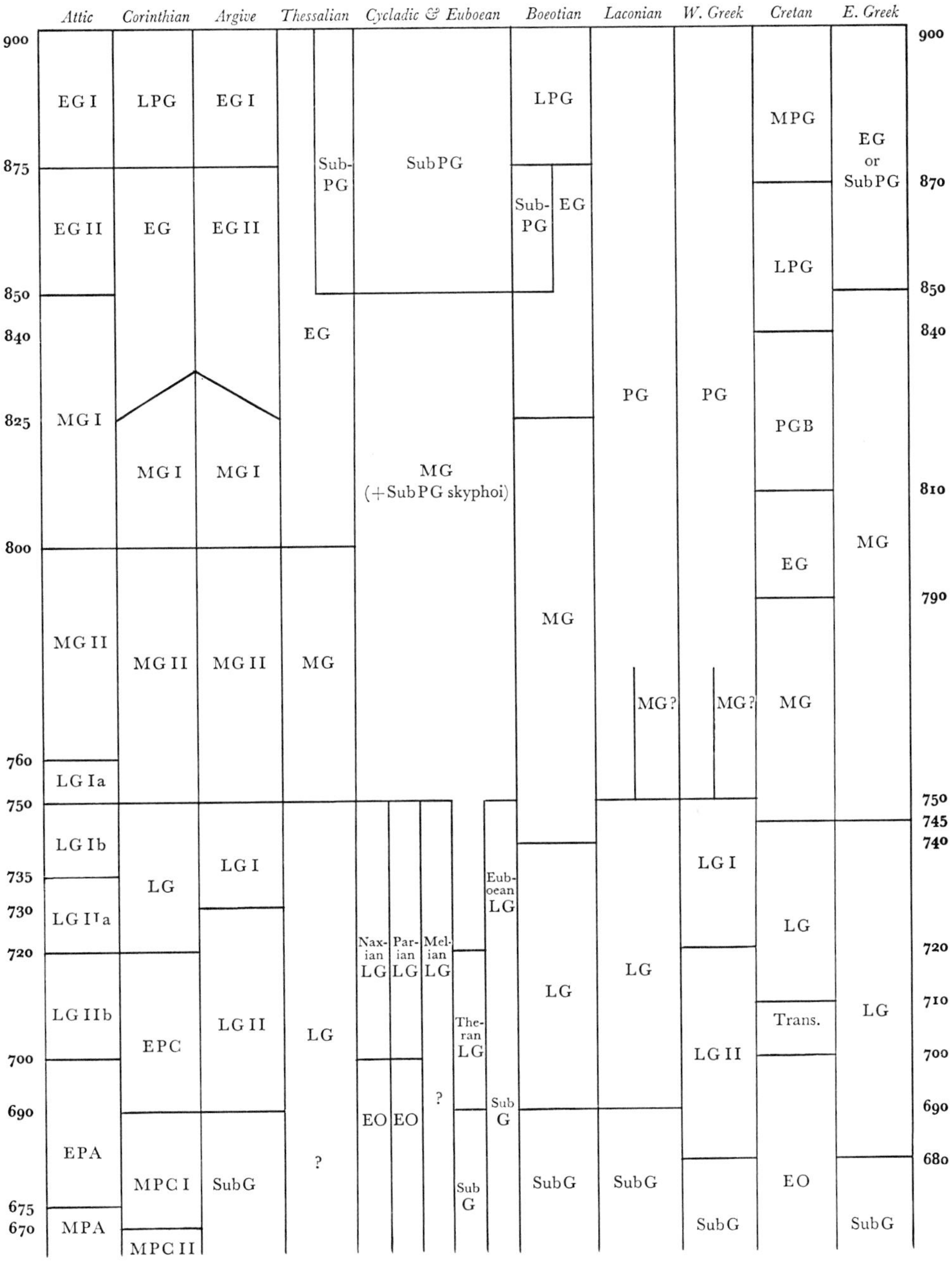

Attic	Corinthian	Argive	Thessalian	Cycladic & Euboean	Boeotian	Laconian	W. Greek	Cretan	E. Greek
EG I	LPG	EG I			LPG			MPG	EG or SubPG
EG II	EG	EG II	Sub-PG	SubPG	Sub-PG / EG			LPG	
			EG			PG	PG	PGB	
MG I	MG I	MG I		MG (+SubPG skyphoi)				EG	MG
MG II	MG II	MG II	MG		MG	MG?	MG?	MG	
LG Ia									
LG Ib	LG	LG I			Euboean LG		LG I	LG I	
LG IIa				Naxian LG / Parian LG / Melian LG		LG	LG	LG	LG
LG IIb	EPC	LG II	LG	Theran LG	LG		LG II	Trans.	
EPA			?	EO / EO / ?	Sub G			EO	EO
	MPC I	SubG		Sub G	SubG	SubG	SubG		SubG
MPA	MPC II							SubG	

FIG. 116 TIME CHART FOR THE GEOMETRIC PERIOD (*GGP* 330)

385

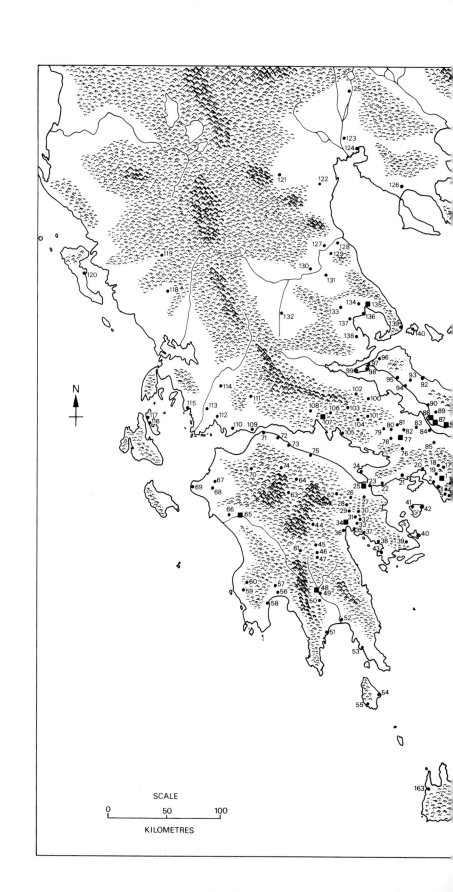

N

SCALE

0   50   100

KILOMETRES

FIG. 117
GREECE
AND THE
AEGEAN:
GEOMETRIC
SITES

Key to Fig. 117

Place names: Alphabetical Index

Key to Fig. 117

Place names: Numerical Index

1 ATHENS	53 Daimonia	105 Medeon
2 Palaia Kokkinia	54 Kastri (Kythera)	106 Corycian cave
3 Phaleron	55 Kato Leivadi	107 DELPHI
4 Trachones	56 Pharai (Messenia)	108 Amphissa
5 Aliki	57 Antheia	109 Kryoneri
6 Vari	58 Nichoria	110 Calydon
7 Anavysos	59 Ano Englianos	111 Thermon
8 Lavrion	60 Volimedia	112 Pylene
9 Thorikos	61 Asea	113 Palaiomanina
10 Brauron	62 Nemea	114 Agrinion
11 Merenda	63 Lousoi	115 Astakos
12 Markopoulo	64 Priolithos	116 Aëtos
13 Hymettus	65 OLYMPIA	117 Polis bay
14 Spata	66 Salmone	118 Dodona
15 Draphi	67 Elean Pylos	119 Vitsa
16 Marathon	68 Elis	120 Corcyra
17 Menidi	69 Kyllene	121 Pateli
18 Liossia	70 Pharae (Achaea)	122 Vergina
19 Aigaleos	71 Drepanon	123 Vardaroftsa
20 Eleusis	72 Neos Erineos	124 Nea Anchialos
21 Megara	73 Aigion	125 Chauchitsa
22 Ay. Theodoroi	74 Asani	126 Olynthos
23 Isthmia	75 Derveni	127 Gonnos
24 Perachora	76 Erythrae	128 Homolion
25 CORINTH	77 THEBES	129 Marmariani
26 Clenia	78 Kabeirion	130 Argissa
27 Athikia	79 Haliartos	131 Nea Lefki
28 Zygouries	80 Akraiphnion	132 Philia
29 Mycenae	81 Ptoion	133 Pherae
30 Berbati	82 Paralimni	134 Sesklo
31 Argive Heraion	83 Rhitsona	135 IOLCOS
32 Dendra	84 Aulis	136 Demetrias
33 Tiryns	85 Tanagra	137 Phthiotic Thebes
34 ARGOS	86 ERETRIA	138 Halos
35 Nauplia	87 LEFKANDI	139 Theotokou
36 Lerna	88 CHALCIS	140 Skiathos
37 Asine	89 Theologos	141 Skyros
38 Kandia	90 Psachna	142 Thasos
39 Troizen	91 Avlonari	143 Lemnos
40 Kalauria	92 Kerinthos	144 Zagora
41 Aigina	93 Daphni	145 Amonakliou
42 Aphaia	94 Limni	146 Kardiani
43 Halieis	95 Rovies	147 Ktikados
44 Mantinea	96 Oreoi	148 Exoburgo
45 Tegea	97 Chironisi	149 Ay. Irini
46 Mavriki	98 Yialtra	150 Rheneia
47 Analipsis	99 Lichas	151 DELOS
48 SPARTA	100 Kalapodhi	152 Kastro (Siphnos)
49 Therapne	101 Orchomenos	153 Antiparos
50 Amyclae	102 Elatea	154 Paros
51 Mavrovouni	103 Mavroneri	155 Delion
52 Helos	104 Vranesi	156 Naxia

Index

Index

Printed in Great Britain by
The Garden City Press Limited
Letchworth, Hertfordshire SG6 1JS